MODERN AGRICULTURE AND RURAL PLANNING

By the same author

FARM BUILDINGS

JOHN WELLER DIP ARCH, ARIBA

MODERN AGRICULTURE

AND RURAL PLANNING

THE ARCHITECTURAL PRESS, LONDON

85139 394 2
Printed in Great Britain by Willmer Bros Ltd, Birkenhead, Cheshire

ACKNOWLEDGMENTS

Acknowledgments are due to the following for maps and illustrations: Walton Adams, 373 (3); Aerofilms, 50 (1), 235, 257; the editor of the *Architects' Journal*, 55, 56, 121–25, 127, 178–80, 182 (1), 369; the editor of the *Architectural Review*, 52, 233; Lionel Brett, 181, 258 (2), 259; British Visqueen Ltd, 402 (1); Richard Burn, 128; Sylvia Crowe, 126; Esso Petroleum Co Ltd, 177; the editor of *Farmbuildings*, 51; the editor of the *Farmers Weekly*, 53 (3), 54, 183, 184, 234, 238, 264, 313, 315–17, 319, 320, 376, 402 (2); Fisons Pest Control Ltd, 401; Donald C. Good, 373 (4); Graphotos Studios Ltd, 372 (2); the editor of the *International Asbestos Cement Review*, 260–63, 375; the Manchester Corporation, 318; Nicholas Horne Ltd, 239; Andrew Paton, 236; Geoffrey C. Phillips, 182 (2); Photographic Services (Berks) Ltd, 374; the editor of *Practical Power Farming*, 404; the *Radio Times* Hulton Picture Library, 50 (2), 314; Turners Asbestos Cement Co Ltd, 53 (2); Peter M. Warren, 240 (1), 370; Donovan C. Wilson, 372 (1).

CONTENTS

6

ILLUSTRATIONS

INTRODUCTION

A crisis in the stewardship of rural land faces urban Britain. An affluent, industrial society has neglected its basic responsibilities towards land-use, has forgotten the nature of its stewardship and the day of reckoning is at hand. During the last decade pressures on the countryside have become complex and intense. Though critical for the future of the nation they are confused by ignorance and muddled thinking. With a crisis looming there is little time in which to establish priorities from first principles. It seems impossible to resolve the deep social conflicts between communal needs and private ownership, public direction and personal liberty and the demands of an expanding industrial population and those of increasing food production. In these circumstances, with responsibilities for a balanced use of land confused by a multitude of conflicting social pressures, it is difficult not to be a prophet of doom. Tomorrow, perhaps ten years from now, will be too late to resolve priorities for rural land. Salvation will be found only if the nation accepts its responsibility and undertakes its duty as steward. If not an inheritance of centuries will be squandered. Yet even at this late hour rural planning remains an unknown, unloved and unpractised art.

Apart from national apathy, the reasons for the impending crisis are clear. Pressures on rural land-use are being generated by internal and external changes. The cumulative effects from these pressures comprise a major social and visual revolution. In farming change is an agrico-industrial revolution of unprecedented scale. In the urban population rising numbers and affluence are creating a new social order based on mobility and leisure. In industry new sources for power and automation are leading to a period of rapid and complete redeployment of manufacturing location and organisation. In international events the hub of world power, military and economic, is

11

rapidly shifting, leaving Britain without her traditional resources for importing food from wealth gained from exports and the Empire.

The roots of these changes are set deep in history, nourished by geographic, climatic and geological considerations. The real manifestations of change have taken place within the last decade, their dramatic qualities being seldom apparent before 1950. The nature and significance of the crisis did not become clear until the present decade of the 1960s. By 1980 changes now apparent, but barely out of their infancy, will have made an impact on the nation and countryside that can only be termed a revolution, with profound social and economic consequences possessing visual and moral implications. The change between now and the end of the century will be as radical and dramatic as the difference between Mediaeval Britain and today. It is just possible, by forewarning and forethought, that the consequences of the revolution may be directed for the benefit of the nation. By observation and analysis of the changes governing the present use and future needs of the countryside there is a remote chance that land resources will be planned and not dissipated by the conflicting need and greed of individual sectors of the community. By the nation acting diligently as a responsible steward the countryside, though different in scale and texture from that of 1950, may still be a pleasant place in the next century. Responsible stewardship giving a moral lead to the nation will only succeed if based on a new definition of the purpose and scope of rural planning. But it is more probable however that vested interest, power politics and individual greed will squander our one basic resource, our real currency, the land of Britain.

It is essential for Britain to develop a sane and balanced approach to land ownership and land-use as a communal responsibility, critical to the future of every person in the land. At the centre of the problem is the thorny issue of land nationalisation. It may be, in the last resort, that the only solution will be for the nation to own the land collectively. The situation is desperate enough to cause a reaction against the magnitude of present problems into the fantasy of a better ordered landscape directed by skilled planners, delicately manipulating resources for the common good. Whatever the merits of nationalisation, for another generation at least, and probably for much longer, collective ownership is a fantasy which in practice would prove an illusion. It is useless to believe that we possess the knowledge to nationalise land for the common good. Such thought stems from vanity, for we are too ignorant to act as a responsible steward to that extent. Until such time as we understand, quantitatively and qualitatively, the nature of our land resources and priorities for their use total stewardship must be foregone, even if considered desirable. To analyse the situation and train planners skilled in rural land problems would take at least a generation even if a crash programme were to be

12

started immediately. There is at present no indication that the nation is willing to devote herself to the necessary studies and training. In these circumstances it is vitally necessary to create a creditable philosophy of rural planning to direct and control as far as possible rural land-use.

In the final analysis it is not possible to separate or differentiate between town and country planning. They are both facets of the same national problem. But in practice there are two distinctions. Firstly urban problems quickly impinge on the countryside, due to mobility and growth in the urban population and the location of industry. Moreover urban populations draw on the rural resources for food, timber, water and leisure in a more pertinent and demanding fashion than countrymen require urban artefacts. The complexity of the first, as a planning problem, is more intractable than the second. Secondly since the 1947 Town and Country Planning Act was formed, urban planning and legislation has become relatively successful and sophisticated, while in comparison rural planning is non-existent. Changes in use in the countryside are the least understood or co-ordinated facet of national planning. This is the node from which the gathering crisis branches.

Within this gathering crisis a number of deeply held, traditional and, in the past, reasonable beliefs and attitudes must be jettisoned. This requires an intellectual and physical transformation which will strain the moral character of the nation to breaking point. For this reason failure to transform the situation in a balanced and co-ordinated manner is probable. Old concepts die hard.

The most important change of attitude required is to overcome the belief, born of generations of practical experience, that Britain is a major food importing country, and to see her as potentially a food exporting nation. This needs an act of faith, transforming inherent fears with much heart-searching towards our responsibilities. In the process our attitudes to most other national problems and priorities must be changed. We must rethink our trading agreements with other countries. We have to make far-reaching economic readjustments. We have to husband our agricultural land. We have to promote factory farming and, as a corollary, restrict traditional or extensive farming systems. We have to establish long-term faith with our progressive farmers. We have to encourage a vertically integrated, monolithic food industry with the farmers as members of a team, losing in the process the image of John Bull, independent and individual, working his own land. In spite of many political difficulties agriculture is already remarkably near the point where Britain could be largely self-supporting for most foods and in some spheres is poised for an expansion of food exports. An act of faith by the nation, within the space of a few years, could transform the balance of payment difficulties by a progressive policy towards intensive

13

land-use and food production. To be successful such a policy must be backed by a new rural planning act regulating city and urban regions with food production zones, governing the interaction of population and food supply within an integrated food industry and planning the use of rural land in a co-ordinated policy for food requirements—all being directed and controlled by a ministry responsible for rural planning and agriculture but working in partnership with a ministry for town planning, including housing, transport and industry.

The background to the crisis and changing attitudes, actual and potential, is the population explosion in a hungry world. Only international effort and co-operation could turn the tide against history and feed the rising millions. Apart from the hungry poor of the world other nations outside Europe and America have entered an industrial revolution and are becoming affluent enough to raise their standards of living and diet. Within this decade food available on international markets has declined dramatically in relation to demand. In consequence prices are rising throughout the world. Meat exports from the Argentine and wheat surpluses in the United States are fading from the world scene. Even traditional food sources from the Commonwealth, such as butter from New Zealand, are diminishing as other outlets are expanding in Asia, South America and even India and Africa. The situation will become more critical and competition for buying food intense. Fifty years ago four-fifths of all international food trade was absorbed by Britain. With our declining position in the league for industrial exports, and therefore for affording food imports, the position will become progressively difficult, if not grave, unless we become agriculturally self-reliant. The food import bill, as an internal problem, strains our economy. The £1,700m spent on foreign food is a heavy burden unnecessarily borne. We could reduce our total import bill for all goods by a fifth (that is by £1,000m) by an expanded home agriculture, restricting food imports to £700m for those products we cannot grow ourselves.

Old concepts die hard indeed. It is sad, and may soon be tragic, that we do not help ourselves in the one sector where we could resolve our economic difficulties. We are in error when we treat agriculture as industry's sleeping partner. Agriculture could be, and to some extent is already, a vital part of the national economy. This does not mean that we should immediately break all trading agreements with other countries where these are designed to restrict home agriculture in order to buy foreign food. But we should have a policy aimed to rationalise these agreements over the next decade. Since international food markets are expanding there will be less onus for us in the future to absorb foreign food surpluses. Purely to cater for our own internal population expansion and improved diet we shall have to increase our agricultural production by almost a half before

14

the end of the century, even if we kept food imports at the present level and made no attempt to decrease them.

The possibility that Britain could become an agricultural or even food exporting nation in a world with urgent new markets for such products should be considered as a serious objective for the next decade. Since agricultural machinery is already a major export the food and allied industries could without too much effort expand to export £500ms worth of goods by 1970, equal to an eighth of all our present exports. This makes home agriculture doubly important because it could substantially cut imports and also raise exports. With new processing techniques developed during the last two years for dehydrating food and making unrefrigerated milk safe for months temperate countries could do much to improve tropical diets. Britain could soon find herself exporting milk, milk products and eggs to the Mediterranean, Africa and Asia Minor. In addition breeding stock and even fatstock are developing into a worthwhile export as meat becomes a more important element in diets throughout the world. It is possible that long before 1980 British farmers will have lost their traditional fear of being ruined by cheap food imports. Many of the opportunities now opening for British agriculture will be lost unless a firm lead is given to the farmers both in food production and rural land economy.

A rational use of the countryside is threatened by the needs of urban Britain. Agriculture is suffering from the external pressures generated by changes in the social and industrial fabric of the nation. These are aggravated by the outdated belief that farmland is expendable and good land taken from agriculture can be replaced by improvements to medium quality land elsewhere. This situation is made more difficult by the reaction of many farmers to this predicament. Their attitude is that the loss of any farmland is to be resisted. A deep social conflict, based on fear and misunderstanding, between the urban and agricultural communities is becoming serious and making rural planning an impossible task.

The conflict between urban and agricultural needs cannot be resolved by emotion, prejudice or ignorance. It is essential that priorities for rural land-use should be established. The need for reappraisal of the situation is urgent and must be based on detailed current knowledge of the resources available. Many statistics are collated, but the overall information concerning the land, especially rural land, is a national disgrace which prevents the formation of a policy for land-use.

The last detailed survey of the ownership and distribution of the land was the Domesday record of 1086. The last reconnaissance of agricultural land by soil classification was three decades ago, prior to the mechanical and chemical revolution in farming which has changed the scope of soil fertility. Changes in land-use and loss of farmland to other needs are undetailed. Although maps are revised by rotation, cartography of the land bears little relation to the physique of the countryside since building, roadworks, hedge removal, afforestation and other changes are too rapid. Ecological and microclimatic changes, brought about by the urban and farming revolutions, are largely unrecorded. The growth of intensive farming, the location of factory farms and their relation to extensive farming are unknown. The character and form of modern agriculture is therefore unrelated to the physique of the land and its potential for improved fertility.

As a base for rural planning it is essential to organise a crash programme classifying the land by soil and terrain, ecology and climate, ownership and organisation and to establish from this classification the actual and potential output from each acre. It is known that too many hedges restrict mechanisation and reduce the cultivated acres. It is also known that half our farmland is inadequately drained, that half is grassland with yields far below their potential, that half our dairy herds have less than thirty cows and that much corn is grown in under ten-acre fields, being wasteful of labour and other resources. Though overall agricultural output has risen by almost forty per cent during the last decade alone, and by 100 per cent since 1939, this represents only the tip of the iceberg. The potential for increasing food production may well be nine-tenths hidden. Without an investigation of resources this potential must remain unknown. No sensible policy for urban growth can therefore be formed, yet pressures to absorb farmland for urban needs are intense. It is probably that we should reduce the area of present farmland by as much as a quarter by the end of the century to allow for urban needs. We cannot afford a mistake and permit fertile or potentially fertile land to be taken from agriculture on this scale.

Two million more acres of land are the minimum which will be required for direct urban expansion by the year 2000, when about a sixth of Britain will be urban in character. Industrial redeployment, concentrating urban growth around new sources for power, could easily accelerate this expansion beyond present expectations. Changes in social concepts towards patterns of living are generating more extravagant demands on land. Pressures for better living conditions from the present 54m population in Britain will be inflated by the additional 20m predicted for the growth in numbers during the rest of this century. Not only will new and rebuilt cities and towns change the physical structure of the country, concentrating people in many areas still rural in character, but new motorways connecting urban regions will unleash intense pressures on all parts of the countryside. During this decade the twin power of mobility and leisure has become a major force in social patterns, making it essential to reformulate many planning concepts. The desire to live in the villages and country and

16

commute to work, or more frequently to own a weekend house away from urban areas has almost become a basic principle of modern life. The countryside has somehow to be planned to absorb this influx. To suit the need for recreation we must be prepared not only to use the uplands and marginal terrain on the fringe of agriculture, but release millions of acres near urban concentrations. Much of the uplands and marginal areas must be devoted to forestry. The need to extend commercial woodlands far beyond the modest growth permitted by the Forestry Commission is a matter of urgent priority.

A new rural code is required to cope with the pressures on the countryside from the urban community. Farmers will have to accept that land will shrink substantially in area. Their remaining land must be farmed intensively, being treated as a factory floor. There will be no room in these areas for either extensive agricultural systems or multi-purpose land-use combining recreation with food production. Two popular concepts will have to disappear, one sacred to farmers and the other to planners and the public. We cannot afford to under-employ fertile land by permitting low yields, which can at present be profitable in some farming policies, or think that small fields or permanent grassland can provide reasons for public access. Intensively farmed land suitable for modern machinery will be in large blocks for the most part hedgeless. Interspersed within these agricultural zones, following bands of poor terrain caused by geological faults, intractable subsoil or difficult gradients, will be linear recreational areas and shelter belts of trees giving ground cover for wild life and water retention. These bands will replace many of the existing hedgerows and footpaths across the countryside. If there are no natural faults farmers will in some cases have to accept the formation of recreational areas and shelter belts on fertile land, but leaving farmland in productive and economic blocks. The contrast of these linear belts, suitable for recreation and shelter, with large arable blocks of cultivated crops including grass, or in other parts with vast forestry zones sweeping across the contours, could be as visually exciting and satisfying as the present landscape created for different social functions and agricultural methods.

A balanced division between recreational, agricultural and silvicultural needs can only be attained if the suitable land available for each purpose is recorded and analysed. Failure to undertake this research and study will perpetuate social tension and land-misuse, since every acre is potentially valuable and should be used to its best advantage. Only by this approach to a planned use of rural land will it be possible to obtain the level of food production essential for economic survival and be able to designate building and roads for the vast areas needed for urban expansion. At the same time a rational policy towards water conservation and supply has to be evolved within this complex problem. In spite of reasonable rainfall and humidity, Britain is threatened by a serious water shortage. Urban needs for domestic and industrial use, coupled with the needs for agricultural irrigation severely strain present supplies, which are in any case completely inadequate for future requirements. Traditional storage methods by reservoir, expecially sited near urban areas in the South-east, are extremely wasteful of farmland.

Many possibilities for new conservation methods are becoming practical. Both river barrage and underground sub-strata storage schemes are rousing interest, and desalination of seawater might soon be economic. It is certain that with water requirements becoming increasingly important for modern industry and society that bold new techniques for conservation must be developed. Irrigation alone can transform the fertility of much farmland. Water supply and conservation, at last being tackled on a national scale by the recently created Water Resources Board, is matter that must be integrated within a national plan for land-use.

Although urban Britain is creating enormous pressures on rural land, agriculture is also in an acute state of flux. Changes in food production during the last decade are in all spheres of agriculture revolutionary, both technically and organisationally, and they are gathering momentum. This revolution will in its own terms alter the character of rural Britain. Unless forethought is taken the nature of the changes will be in conflict with those desired by the urban community and, during the next decades, there will be a long series of arguments, inquiries, appeals and enforcement orders. Social tension on the scale which will be generated by the magnitude of the revolution will be harmful to the well-being and progress of the nation. A sound policy for planning rural requirements, taking into account all sectional needs, is the only hope for channelling the changes into the right pattern for a balanced use of land.

The rate of technical progress in agriculture is remarkable. Labour productivity during the last decade, with overall numbers of workers falling by almost a third, has risen by five to six per cent a year. This is considerably above the national average. Output of meat and dairy foods in the same decade rose by about a third, with the broiler industry developing from scratch to provide 200m birds a year. Due to better strains, cultivation and fertilisation, grain output per acre has steadily risen. Mechanisation has almost ousted all manual labour except on poorer farms. Giant machines make it possible for one man to cultivate 200–300 acres, tend hundreds or even thousands of fattening stock, manage and milk over 100 cows or handle twenty to sixty tons of produce in an hour by pushing a button. Within the quarter century since 1940 the agricultural transformation has been as great as the previous quarter millenium. Pre-war British agriculture supported less than 16m people. Today it feeds 28m, half the population. In this period grain output rose by nearly 150 per cent, fruit by 100 per cent, sugar beet by fifty per cent and vegetables, including potatoes, by twenty-five per cent. This rise in production was in spite of well over 1m acres passing into urban use, much of it in the fertile South and East, and a reduction in the full-time labour force, including a post-war influx, of over a third of those working the land in 1940.

This technical revolution has been remarkable in itself. Other industries have made dramatic technical improvements. More peculiar to farming, especially within the last few years, has been the rapid change in organisation. In agriculture the Mediaeval social structure lasted to some extent until after 1950. Since 1960 the new agrico-industrial revolution has gathered momentum and will soon have swept away the last vestiges of an independent and fragmented farming system. Food production, processing and distribution are rapidly being integrated within a single organisation, often with international ramifications. These changes are being generated by farmers themselves and by new trading patterns making their impact on agriculture.

The organisation and distribution of farms are changing as rapidly as the value of land spirals. Since 1958 the value of farmland has trebled and in places quadrupled. Farm systems have to be intensive to justify land prices of £250–£300 an acre, and sometimes of up to £400. Old-fashioned concepts of having two acres to each cow have to be reversed so that now two cows have to be fed from each acre. Labour has to be organised to work a five-day week, each hour productively used. Management units balancing labour and machines with planned output have to be large. Farms are being rapidly amalgamated to allow for larger and more economic units. More than 4,000 farms disappear by amalgamation each year. Small intensive farms can still prove economic, especially if several work in a co-operative. It is the rapid disappearance of 150–300 acre farms, with a dramatic rise in farms of over 300 acres, that is helping to change the landscape. At present rates of change, by the end of the century, half the farmland would be managed in units of more than 300 acres and the rate is likely to increase. In contrast, the average farm size is still at present not much over seventy acres, though half the total farm output comes from only a tenth of all holdings.

The management of modern intensive farms is a skilled business requiring techniques as advanced as any industry. Planning farm work is becoming a task for computers. Farmers have to be top-grade managers and labourers skilled specialists. Training men for the new industry is as arduous as in any sphere, though much educational reform is still required in agriculture. Similarly financing agriculture is becoming industrial in scale, with many economists advocating that joint-stock companies, already appearing, must be the base for the agricultural expansion vital for the nation. Farmers are becoming big businessmen and *vice versa*. The distinction between a modern farmer and an industrialist is often a quibble of terms. Agriculture has barely tapped its potential value for raising capital for its own expansion and as farming becomes industrial it must promote its own expansion rather than rely on government finance.

Co-operation between farmers is proving a significant change of this decade. Age-old self reliance is giving way beneath the threat of food processors and retailers integrating their industries in food production. To retain some power against the pressure of the external industrial giants, farmers are at last in desperation beginning to pool their resources and to share their overheads. Some go further and co-operate at management level. This is a significant social revolution, breaking down the tradition of centuries. Beyond the farm gate the revolution is equally dramatic as old trading patterns by barter and auction give way to forward planning with firm contracts. It is probable that the open market in country towns as well as the giant city and London markets will have disappeared before the end of the century. It is impossible to supply the supermarkets, which are sweeping much of the retail trade into a stream-lined, pre-packed food organisation, with produce of standard quality and required at regular times, unless agriculture is pre-planned. Contracts have to be planned a season, a year or several years ahead. Fluctuating production levels, planned at the last moment, are anathema to the modern food industry.

Integration among farmers, or between farmers and the processors and retailers is changing the nature and tempo of agriculture. The result of these internal and external pressures is that factory farming is inevitable. Conserving land resources in order to raise food production to the levels required will mean that with few exceptions livestock will be kept in intensive buildings. Large fields and chemical farming will banish much wildlife from the production zones. Nature reserves and linear recreational areas must help to balance this loss. Farm animals will not be seen in the landscape. The spring may indeed be as silent as Rachael Carson lamented. It is however pointless and in the last resort suicidal, to lament the changing landscape. Since the ecological and visual change will be vast and revolutionary in scale, it is more important to develop a constructive attitude to rural land-use. At its root factory farming is not based on intensive housing of animals. It is essentially an arable revolution in the mechanisation of grain, grass and vegetable husbandry, supported by chemical control over the crops. Animal fodder is increased in output from each acre when it is taken to the livestock rather than grazed. At the same time its conversion into flesh is more productive when all external factors, including environment, are controlled. Meat production can be justified only when fodder production and conversion are controlled. Similarly eggs and milk are also held by the same economic laws.

The change in the landscape will prove so drastic that we cannot risk it occurring by chance at the whim of individual business organisations, whether controlled by farmers or an integrated food industry. Not only must the ecological and climatic balance of the landscape be controlled so that the changes do not destroy the fertility of the land, but also the visual appearance of our environment, though changed in scale, must be enhanced by public areas supporting trees and natural wild life. As the farming businesses become bigger and more powerful so will changes be more rapid and drastic. Within the short space of a few years whole regions could lose their natural balance unless change is watched and directed in regional plans. Perhaps of equal importance is the need to plan the future factory farms to suit urban as well as rural needs. The flow line from field to customers poses many problems for locating the various associated industries. In the case of livestock held in multi-hundred units there are the additional problems, which are becoming acute, of handling fodder to the animals and effluent back to the land. Livestock units should be planned radially round the factory abattoirs serving the conurbations. Agricultural road or rail transporters could become an important element in the transport patterns of Britain.

As food production becomes a matter of precision and the ownership or control of land passes into industrial or business concerns, (with agricultural buildings becoming located in regional agrico-industrial centres) so do planning problems become intense. One feedlot for 10,000 cattle built in the wrong place can disrupt the entire transport densities in a large region. One cotel, or milklot, built out of context of an over-all rural plan related to consumer zones, could disrupt a large area of countryside. Since feedlots, cotels, provender mills, packing stations and machinery centres will be required to serve the new agricultural industry, with most existing farmsteads becoming redundant, the future landscape and road patterns may be dismal and chaotic. Recent experience suggests that the visual quality of the countryside and the efficiency of road networks are unlikely to be improved unless regional development plans are formed.

We must consider the problems concerning land-use as urgent. Rural planning must become the responsibility of a new ministry, embracing food production and distribution, including its processing and by-products, as well as urban expansion into the countryside, including land changes for building and transport, recreational requirements, water conservation and timber supplies. Above all the ministry must be concerned with the nature of food requirements for the future population of the United Kingdom*. It must be concerned

* In this book 'Great Britain' refers to England, Scotland and Wales, while 'United Kingdom' includes Northern Ireland.

with the future of farming in regional development areas, and be responsible for the collation and analysis of the data concerning present and potential land uses. It must also be responsible for the forward planning necessary to expand food production for Britain's survival and for the resources needed for that expansion. It will therefore become responsible for the distribution and location of factory farms to serve the mainly urban population. There is also urgent need to form a new national land policy, concerned with town and country land distribution, regional agriculture and farm centres. But all will prove to be vain unless a new type of agrico-rural land planner is trained to cope with the intricate problems facing those concerned with rural land-use. The nation must take heed and undertake the stewardship of rural land-use, being prepared to devote time, energy and finance to channel future development for the benefit of the community. Time is short before present changes will have done irreversible damage.

1 RURAL PLANNING

Introduction

The land of Britain, particularly the countryside, is a matter of deep and personal significance to many people. The subject of rural land-use is political dynamite. It is difficult to examine with detachment present trends and potential changes in the landscape. It is impossible to form opinions, synthesise the many interrelated land uses and project a coordinated plan for the land, as it may be by the year 2000, without evoking the wrath of most sectors of the community. There are few prepared to make a cool, dispassionate appraisal of the situation without letting personal feeling or vested interest cast a bias on their analysis.

The roots of the problem are geographic and historic. The island situation, with its varied mixture of highland North and West and lowland South and East, has cast the mould for racial characteristics which are believed to differentiate the Briton from the Continental. Asian and Mediterranean migrations before Mediaeval times were ended in many cases by a final coalescence of tribal physique and customs forming the British race of mixed ancestry. Warring, basically tribal, factions gave way to a united kingdom, served by manorial lords, sometimes dominating, sometimes protecting, their serfs. The temperate climate and fertile land, underlain with rich mineral and coal deposits, helped to create a wealthy, adventurous and technically skilled population, who developed a fine balance between independance and inter-dependance, tenacity and detachment, pugnaciousness and tolerance. Centuries of tension generated a concept of individial ownership and liberty, producing the freemen and yeomen who became the backbone of the race from Elizabethan to Victorian times, and who, by ruthless conquest, created the largest and most far-flung Empire of history. Within this historic development, which produced the concept of freedom, lie the roots of a problem concerning rural land-use and planning, critical to the future of the country, yet almost—if not entirely—insoluble because of intricate and passionate social forces beneath the surface. These forces are held in delicate balance after a long history of bloodshed and compromise. Yet if new concepts of land-use are not evolved in the near future other social forces, now becoming more powerful but unco-ordinated, will wreck this balance during the next decades.

The largely urban population generated by the industrial revolution, but now entering a second revolution of automation and industrial redeployment, has new needs for the land of Britain. In the earlier part of this century, following the free trade movement of Victorian business principle, the countryside became a neglected and decaying waste, impoverished and depopulated. Ownership of rural land became a matter of social and political, rather than financial, consequence. For the rich, food was abundant and relatively cheap being imported from all quarters of the world in exchange for industrial goods manufactured by the poor, who worked for low wages and remained undernourished in their slums. Compassion slowly prevailed and the first steps were taken towards a planned Britain.

Recognition that disease embedded in the community was no respecter of persons and that national health depended on sanitary housing conditions for all led to the first Planning Acts. In spite of the Depression at the centre point between the wars, national and individual wealth began to prosper and spawn a rash of low-density housing in ribbon developments across rural Britain. Agricultural land was cheap, food production and farmers were unprotected and of little political concern. Many people, however, living in the tradition of Shakespeare's 'demi-paradise', loved the pastoral landscape, and in the 1930s created the first of the Town and Country Planning Acts to protect it. But these and other pre-war acts did little, in fact, to prevent urban expansion into the countryside.

The Depression had one beneficial effect. Areas of unemployment and declining industry caused the Government to set up an inquiry to examine this new social phenomen. Moreover, the new national consciousness concerning social and land problems caused the Government to form another committee to investigate the utilisation of land in rural areas, setting out their wish to maintain a prosperous agriculture and also the well-being of rural communities. The threat, and later the realisation, of a second world war changed the narrow attitude of the urban population to rural land-use. By the end of the war a wave of new ideas, gestated during the hostilities, were legislated. Nevertheless, all post-war planning—for both town and country—has been weakened by several inherent faults. With regard to rural land in particular, these are basically fourfold.

No Government has been prepared to place all land-use and

24

planning, including food production, under one ministry. Diversified authority has led to unco-ordinated planning. Secondly, and of great importance, qualified planners have been too few to cope with the complexity of the problem and data has been scanty or non-existent regarding many aspects of land-use and soil classification. Thirdly, since it has been unprepared to nationalise all land the community has not resolved the basic problem of controlling land-use, yet permitting private ownership within a system of compensation when land values are changed by such control. This problem still confuses attempts to plan land development and change of use. Finally, deeply embedded in post-war rural planning concepts, has been the belief that the only yardstick for agricultural prosperity is land area. But as first suggested by Professor Dennison in 1942, it has become increasingly evident that economic food production depends on the trinity of acreage, labour and output. Output has, due to increased yields, expanded until it is about double the 1942 level, though acreage and labour have rapidly declined.

Increased output has proved possible, due partly to government financial aid, but also to mechanisation, factory farming techniques and vertical integration, whereby farm management, food processing and retail outlets are closely linked.

Food production must be expanded, possibly to double present levels, before the end of this century, but from considerably reduced acreages. More land is required for urban expansion and, equally important, urban relaxation. Land is also required for services, forestry and water conservation. Due to wastage of the potential in existing resources, without planning there would not be enough land available for all urgent needs. This would lead to serious social stress. With rural planning, however, it is possible that the nation could enter the next century not only with a balanced community, but also with an efficient and attractive landscape. Nevertheless, existing planning machinery is completely inadequate for present problems, still less future changes. Unless new concepts are rapidly evolved, there is no hope for either the landscape or the nation.

1b History of agricultural development

In 1962 McCrone began his study of the position held by agriculture in the British economy by showing it to be unique compared with other countries[1]:

> One of the chief characteristics which distinguishes British agriculture from that of other nations is the small part it plays in the national economy. There is no other country in the world which produces so small a proportion of its own food supply, employs so

small a part of its working population in agriculture or earns from the production of food so small a part of its national income.

A few pages later he explains the reason for this:

> There are various reasons for the exceptional part that agriculture plays in the British economy. Undoubtedly one of these is the particular form which the industry took in Britain when it emerged from the revolution caused by the Acts of Enclosure and the abolition of the manor system. Many of the characteristics which British agriculture then acquired have had a profound effect on the industry ever since and distinguish it from its Continental counterparts. Agricultural revolutions of various types took place all over Europe during the last two centuries but the important characteristics of the British one was that the bulk of the power was vested in the landlord rather than the peasant proprietor. For the most part the landlords arranged the enclosures and let out the land to tenants who remained under their overriding control. This meant that many of the poorer people, in particular the yeoman cottar class, found themselves deprived of a livelihood and were gradually compelled to seek work in the new industrial towns.

This statement summarises the essential difference between British and continental agriculture. The history of agricultural development reflects, in fact, the social history of the country, from the breakdown of the feudal system to the emergence of a leading industrial nation.

The feudal manorial system, which has left its mark on the appearance of the country and the social balance of rural communities, began to break up during the lifetime of Chaucer. The open field was the basis of cultivation almost throughout the country but especially in the Midlands—though some systems having enclosed fields were known in Mediaeval times, particularly in the North and West. Each village would normally have two, three or four huge unenclosed fields, subdivided into strips, owned and farmed by members of the village. Each 'farmer' would own several strips scattered in the fields, acquired by inheritance or marriage. One field would lie fallow while others were cropped and, after the hay or corn had been cut, these would become common pasture until the following season. The fields were regulated by the villagers as a community asset on a democratic basis. On this democracy was superimposed the feudal power of the lord of the manor, by which he could command the service of the peasant serfs (that is the villagers) on certain days to work his land, could prevent them leaving the village and could demand that their corn be ground at his mill. As Trevelyan pointed out[2]:

> This system of cultivation, originated by the first Anglo-Saxon settlers, lasted down to the time of the modern enclosures. It was

economically sound as long as the object of each farmer was to raise food for his family rather than for the market. It combined the advantages of individual labour and public control; it saved the expense of fencing; it gave each farmer a fair share in the better and worse land; it bound the villagers together as a community, and gave to the humblest his own land and his voice in the agricultural policy to be followed for the year by the whole village.

Though many strip-fields continued until Stuart times and, in some cases, even into the nineteenth century, the manorial system of cultivation based on serf labour was largely replaced by farm leases, hired labour and wages during the fourteenth and fifteenth centuries. This process of change was in fact accelerated by the Black Death in 1349, when nearly one half of the population died. Serfdom, as a social institution, could not survive this calamity and labour became a valuable commodity commanding high wages. Field services, due from the serfs to their lord, became commuted for money payments. At the same time, the lord of the manor, if he did not hire labour to work his land, would lease his demesne for money or kind. This, in turn, gave rise to a new class of yeoman farmer. Moreover, many of the strips made derelict by the Black Death were amalgamated and became controlled by yeoman farmers, also employing labour like the lord of the manor. Much of this change had come about by Chaucer's death in 1400, setting the pattern of agriculture until the time of the enclosures.

By the Elizabethan era, the yeoman class was established, numerous and wealthy. Many yeomen cultivated their own land, some of which might be enclosed and some in open fields. Other yeoman were tenants, sometimes leasing considerable acreage from the powerful landowners. A peasant class of small farmers working holdings continued to exist, but many became landless labourers working for the yeoman farmer or the lord of the manor. At this time, however, with inflation and other national economic problems causing unrest, there were already agricultural pressures. Some leases were renewed annually, others were copyhold tenures. The economic structure of agriculture was not therefore uniform and by the seventeenth century a surfeit of labour caused agricultural wages to rise far more slowly than their counterpart elsewhere. Marketing for the urban population developed. It became harder for the peasant smallholders to survive amid rising prices and social pressures and during the seventeenth century, under financial compulsion, the practice of landowners enclosing the open fields became more apparent. Land began to pass into the hands of fewer landowners and the peasant class began to diminish. It also suited the land-owners to lease their land to a few efficient yeoman farmers rather than numerous peasants. This in turn helped to accelerate the change towards improved farming methods in the hands of less men who desired enclosed fields rather than open, strip cultivation. Many farmers at this time became famous for the spectacular success of their new methods. In Norfolk, for example, Coke revolutionised farming techniques and land tenure on the Holkham estates, increasing their rental value in the forty years from 1776 from £2,200 to £20,000 a year. Holkham became renowned throughout Europe; and the tenants, secure with long leases based on a strict cultivation policy, prospered.

By the time Victoria came to the throne in 1837, agriculture had more or less taken the form known until the mid-twentieth century. The enclosure movement was nearly complete, the location and size of farms and their buildings, with the basis of land tenure, were established and the principles of scientific farming acknowledged. The transformation from the feudal agricultural society was complete. Tracy summarised the position of agriculture by the middle of the nineteenth century and shows the important distinction between Britain and other European countries because of the absence of a revolution against the aristocracy[3]:

> In Britain, the enclosure and consolidation of agricultural holdings over a long period led to the creation of comparatively large, unified farms. The landed aristocracy had never been overthrown and indeed played an important role in this process, which they guided to their best advantage: when their feudal power had gone, they still formed an important class of landlords, letting out most of their land to tenant farmers. The process created another class, that of the landless labourers, many of whom were forced off the land and into the growing towns. This move from the land was stimulated by the Industrial Revolution, in which Britain had a long lead over all other countries, and, as a result the population living from agriculture formed a smaller proportion of the whole in Britain than in any other country. Further, overall economic progress was reflected in agriculture: the structure of agriculture, with large farms and a class of wealthy landowners ready to invest in their estates, made British farming particularly receptive to technological progress, and in the middle of the nineteenth century it was the most advanced in the world.

The pattern for future agricultural troubles, however, was already being set during the nineteenth century. Although (unlike continental practice) farms were inherited, for the most part, by the eldest son, so that estates remained large rather than split among many descendants, there was no coherence in agricultural policy at a national level. There were divisions of interest and opinion between landlords and tenants, landlords and yeomen, arable and livestock farmers and hill and lowland farmers. Thus in a period of growing political strife, agriculturalists and farmers could present no coherent pressure group to protect their interests. Since the urban population rapidly expanded with the Industrial Revolution, it was unfortunate that the rural community failed to counteract its diminishing numerical and political superiority by having a united policy. From 1801 to 1901, the population of Great Britain rose by nearly 250 per cent, that is from 11 to 37m. In the same century (though at the time of Trafalgar about a third to a half of the working population was directly or indirectly engaged on the land) by 1901 the proportion declined to a twelfth, with less than 1½m people working the land from over 16m workers. During the last forty years of the century, which included both the zenith and the nadir of agricultural prosperity, the number of farmers and farm workers fell at a fairly steady rate of about 14,000 a year, irrespective of the financial state of agriculture. This was indicative of the growth of industrial towns and cities during the nineteenth century and the decline of rural communities. This change was dramatic and had considerable social repercussions, though the social and political state of the country, with the sweeping changes occurring in industry, were more important. Nevertheless, the Victorian era had a profound effect on agriculture which has dominated the first half of the twentieth century.

The Napoleonic War disrupted trade and created a period of serious food shortages. In the decades that followed, as the population began to expand, food continued in short supply until, in the 1840s, a hungry and socially disturbed population was on the edge of revolution. Conditions were aggravated by the survival of Mediaeval Corn Laws which placed a duty on imported corn when home corn prices fell below a recognised minimum. The price of bread, therefore, became unstable and tended to be high, being upheld by artificial means. Pressure to repeal the various Corn Laws developed into a political storm, confused and intensified by the terrible potato disease which blighted crops and brought Ireland to starvation by 1845 and 1846. Fear of starvation and revolution, following the many years of the campaign demanding cheap bread for the growing industrial population, led to the repeal of duties on corn in 1846. At the same time, duties on meat, cattle, potatoes and vegetables were also abolished. The abolition of duties was a catharsis for public and political opinion. It created a new age of free trade which suited the expanding industrial population with its upsurge of trade. It appeared that Britain was at the hub of the world and prosperity was her birthright. Industry and the industrial population were the new power in Britain, benefitting from free trade with the Empire, America and Europe. Moreover agriculture, which also benefitted from industrial prosperity, did not suffer from competition with imported foods. For three decades after the repeal of the Corn Laws, agriculture prospered. It was an age of consolidation and expansion and many model farms were created. Farmers still look back at their grandfathers, who lived in the golden age of British Farming during the early 1870s, as the last of those possessing stability and security.

By about 1875 the foundations of agricultural prosperity were undermined. Wet summers produced bad harvests, that of 1879 being one of the worst recorded. There were several animal epidemics between 1875 and 1885 which ruined many farmers, disease striking swiftly and without mercy. At the same time America had recovered from the Civil War and had completed her transcontinental railway in 1869. Cheap internal transport, a series of good summers and a revolution in shipping methods made it economic to sell American corn in Britain for the first time, imports almost doubling between 1870 and 1880. As a result, home production fell by more than a half. During the 1880s, imports continued to rise and prices fall. New techniques in refrigeration made it possible to import frozen meat. Beef imports more than trebled between 1875 and 1890. Free trade made it not only possible to feed the growing population, some of whom were considerably improving their standards of living, but to reduce food prices. It was an attractive policy for an industrial population to accept. That a large sector of British agriculture was ruined, and confidence in farming was not restored until the second war following this depression, was of little consequence compared with the benefits of free trade. It was in any case, an age for private enterprise and it was accepted socially and politically that it was right for those who were economically weak to go to the wall. Success alone merited consideration; failure was an unfortunate necessity for progress to thrive.

During the last quarter of the nineteenth century, when agriculture became a depressed industry, the British government refused to protect farmers against the consequences of free trade, still less adopt measures to alleviate their distress. The period of high farming, with landowners providing capital to develop new scientific techniques in agriculture, was rapidly replaced by an era of economy in farming methods and production. In turn economy became neglected when buildings were unrepaired, hedges uncut, ditches blocked and the land allowed to revert to nature. The agricultural population continued to decline. However the depression was not uniform in its effect throughout the country. Arable areas suffered more severely than livestock farms. Not only did cheap imported meats become prevalent ten to fifteen years after the influx of American corn, but the second also made it possible for stock to be fed more cheaply than before the repeal of the Corn Laws.

As Victoria's reign came to its close, agriculture started the twentieth century in Britain as a neglected, under-capitalised, depressed industry. The industrial population, with cheap imported foods easily available, had no desire to protect the British farmer. Moreover, the political power of the landed classes had declined for three quarters of a century since the Reform Act of 1832. Without a united agricultural policy and against overwhelming odds, the British farmer and tenant-farmer, descendants of the yeoman class learnt to be independant, cynical or distrustful of governments and townsmen. During the last years of the nineteenth century food prices began to stabilise in spite of production from restricted acreage. Perhaps because of the growing world population, home production and numbers engaged in British agriculture increased slightly by the outbreak of the Great War. Nevertheless in the same period, though few people began to realise the national dangers of dependance on food imports, the Government gave support for developing Empire trade (including food) rather than protecting British agriculture. The war, with the frequent sinking of trade ships due to new forms of warfare, quickly showed the weakness of dependance on food imports and the state of British agriculture. The Government was forced to promote a national policy for home food production, even though this was neither swift in its formation nor fully effective in execution until the last stages of the war. Nevertheless wheat production rose by over fifty per cent and potato production by about thirty-five per cent. The arable acreage was increased by $1\frac{1}{2}$m acres to 15,852m acres. Even overall livestock numbers remained comparatively stable: though there were nearly $\frac{1}{2}$m more cattle, there were about $\frac{1}{2}$m fewer sheep and almost a similar reduction in the number of pigs.

The lessons of the First War were not learned. At the end of the war farmers formed a pressure group and in 1920 received some financial protection; the following year protection was abandoned and direct competition with imported food was accepted and free trade encouraged. During the 1920s prices fell. Farmers were not only discouraged but suffered hardship; land was taken out of production; land, buildings and equipment were neglected; and labour moved from agriculture into the towns. Depression returned until it was overtaken by the more serious national consequences of the great financial crisis of 1931. The Government at last gave some support to agriculture among its many attempts to save industry and re-establish economic prosperity. Between 1931 and 1933 various marketing boards, including those still extant for milk, hops and potatoes, were established, some import duties on food were imposed and certain crops, such as wheat, were subsidised. In later years further Acts extended the area and effect of the support. During the 1930s, partly due to government intervention and the general economic recovery throughout the country, agriculture became more stable and prices rose. However the reversal of the policy for complete freedom in trade was not undertaken without considerable argument and opposition. But in spite of opposition there was a change in the political climate towards agriculture and, as the European political climate also changed, it was possible for the Government to set up a Food (Defence Plan) Department in 1936. When war came in 1939 there was an established national policy for controlling food, encouraging production and rationing. But old fears persisted and, though the situation was grave, there was reluctance in the early years of the war to encourage maximum food production, on the basis that the postwar period might be embarrassed by a vastly expanded agricultural industry.

Before the start of the Second World War in 1939, the present agricultural revolution based on mechanisation had begun. In 1938 there were 50,000 tractors, fifty combine harvesters and the first prototypes for sugar beet harvesters. The impact of this mechanisation was not dramatic, being restricted for the most part, to the more efficient and leading farms. The manner in which mechanisation was due to change agriculture and the countryside was not then clear. Most of the farmers, being traditional in their outlook and unused to capital investment in the land, were sceptical of the new forms of machinery, distrustful of their effects and hostile to their widespread adoption. Nevertheless there were those who prophesied the eclipse of the horse as the mainstay of power on the farm and saw machines replacing men in many farm activities. In common with all industry, war pressures gave the incentive and provided the resources for the development of new machinery. By 1946, the number of farm machines estimated and given in the annual agricultural machinery census included 179,850 tractors, 40,360 milking machines, 3,250 combine-harvesters, 1,000 grain driers and 57,850 lorries and vans. Food production increased, land was reclaimed for agriculture which had been neglected for half a century; but more important the attitude of the nation towards agriculture changed during the Second War so that farmers were not left unprotected when it ended. In 1944 the Government agreed to give farmers a guarantee that prices for milk, cattle and sheep would be upheld until 1948. Soon afterwards, the 1947 Agriculture Act was conceived by which the National Policy was formed for:

> ... promoting and maintaining, by the provision of guaranteed markets and assured prices ... such part of the nation's food and other agricultural produce as in the national interest it is desirable to produce in the United Kingdom and of producing it at minimum prices consistent with proper remuneration and living conditions for farmers and workers in agriculture and an adequate return on a capital invested in the industry.

Thus it became possible for the second great agricultural revolution to become established and change the conception of food production, which will have far-reaching social, economic and visual repercussions.

REFERENCES

1 McCrone, G. *The economics of subsidising agriculture*, pp23,28. 1962, George Allen & Unwin.

2 Trevelyan, G. M. *English Social History*, p6. 1944, Longmans, Green.
3 Tracy, M. *Agriculture in Western Europe*, p19. 1964, Jonathan Cape.

1c Development of legislation

Rural planning is as Cinderella to her sisters town planning and economic planning; these are the trinity on which the conservation and development of our natural resources must be based in any national plan. If Britain is to survive this century as a civilised and civilising community in a world racked by the terrible forces of hunger—for food in undernourished lands and material advancement in emergent nations—then this trinity must be finely balanced. Each must be guided by the nation to release its full potential for the enrichment of all in the last decades of this century, an enrichment of mind as well as body. Each must be co-ordinated in a national plan— a plan for the advancement and harmony of the 75m people estimated to dwell in the United Kingdom by the year 2000.

Town planning in Britain, with all its faults, limitations and terrible heritage of mistakes, is more sophisticated and relevant to the social problems of this century than that in any other industrial nation. Specific examples of urban design have gained international recognition for their social implications and architectural character. Before the 1939 war, the Bournville housing and factory layouts near Birmingham and the garden city movement at Welwyn and elsewhere were important contributions to urban design. The new town complex in post-war years, with such extremes in town plan layout as Harlow and Cumbernauld, have also gained international acclaim. The development of pedestrian precincts for shopping, pioneered at Coventry, of high density housing at Roehampton and elsewhere, as well as examples of urban renewal, such as the Barbican scheme, coupled to the Buchanan principles for controlling traffic in towns; have all kept Britain in the forefront of town planning as an international skill of fundamental importance for the future of the world. But, even more important than examples of urban design, is the fine balance between individual liberty and the social needs of the community held by the various planning acts. These create a compromise of freedom with control, which, though often inadequate, are nevertheless a sophisticated and complex system preventing the worst excesses of individual greed, and sometimes permitting urban growth of distinction.

Economic planning, by a system of annual budgets, supported by numerous advisory councils and commissions, blunders into the future, since the real economic forces in and between nations are poorly understood. Nevertheless, though in its infancy such planning is becoming part of the national consciousness, recognised as both desirable and essential in one form or another except to a small,

33

B

right-wing element believing an unplanned nation has economic and social freedom. The National Plan outlined in 1965, though not without its critics both in its analysis and recommendations, was recognised by many as being a major step towards harnessing the economic forces of the nation to planned objectives of growth. The social pressures in an expanding population in a crowded island are too great to permit indiscriminate growth in all directions. An objective appraisal of economic trends, leading to tentative aims for the future, planned but flexible, and permitting change as new requirements develop, is an essential for the well-being of the nation. Such plans are slowly emerging as one aspect or other of national life is studied in depth, whether it is railways, docks, South-east or North-east regions, mines or any other function which is subjected to a period of systematic analysis and appraisal.

Rural planning, in contrast to her two sister planning groups, has never had their glamour nor been accepted, in the same way, as an essential ingredient of national daily life except, perhaps, during the period of enclosure of common land. In spite of several Town and Country Planning Acts and the Barlow and Scott reports of a quarter century ago, little has been done to generate a national appreciation of the conflicting problems in land-use in the countryside. It was not until the creation of the former Ministry of Land and Natural Resources at the end of 1964 that responsibility became a matter of government direction for relating the availability of land with all the various (and conflicting) requirements of the nation, as well as for co-ordinating demands on other natural resources in addition to land. Without a co-ordinated policy for land-use, it is not surprising that the lament made thirty years ago, in 1937, by the late Sir Patrick Abercrombie is basically consistent with the problem today[1]:

> To fit the English countryside to a statutory pattern appears to be a wilful attempt at procrustean bed-making; how can its infinite variety be registered in a legal scheme and the delicate adjustments required by changes to meet modern needs be covered by a set of clauses which must conform to the *intra vires* of an Act of Parliament? One would like to see the country, suitably divided into regions, under the autocratic control of a man who was at once a landscapist, a farmer, and a sympathiser with the needs of those unfortunate people who have to work and live in towns and suburbs. In the meantime, however, we are attempting to construct and to control by means of a general Town and Country Planning Act, a detailed Ribbon Prevention Act, and several chartered corporations with quasi-independent powers (the Electricity Commissioners, the Forestry Commission etc). The synthesis which would be improbable under those diverse planning agencies is further dispersed by the incursion of demands by Government departments which are above the normal law and whose requirements do not form part of a National Plan, but are dictated by an international emergency.

There is today a more detailed Town and Country Planning Act, with planning controlled by County Authorities directed from Whitehall, but still bedevilled by corporations and government departments with quasi-independent powers. In any case such planning that exists is mainly concerned with the location and character of building and works as proposed by individual concerns, rather than producing a positive policy for land-use. For example, the method of using agricultural land for food production is not controlled, the co-ordination of road and rail networks is in its infancy, and the selection of land for development has limited relationship to food production and transport networks. Though some planners may argue that this is not strictly true, some attempt at co-ordination being made, nevertheless such attempts must always be partially obscured by the basic lack of knowledge concerning the structure of land and soil. This had led, rightly, to the call by the National Farmers' Union for soil surveys to be made to supplement the Town and Country Planning Act and protect good agricultural land from uncontrolled development[2]:

> Soil surveys to establish the actual or potential productive capacity of farmland should be made on a nation-wide basis to establish which areas of farm or market garden land should receive priority treatment when development proposals are under consideration.

As discussed later, little is known about the physical structure of the land (p156). Thus, in the last resort, any form of control in land-use must be based on inadequate and, perhaps, misleading information.

As Cullingworth has recognised, not only does 'Town and Country Planning embrace a large part of the activities of Government' but, 'as a task of Government it has developed from public health and housing policies'[3]. In particular, though early examples may be quoted, such as the partial rebuilding of London to Wren's layout after the fire of 1666, town planning was historically the outcome of the industrial squalor of Victorian England. By degrees public awareness of the intolerable slum conditions prevalent by the mid-nineteenth century created a spate of legislation mainly concerned with sanitary control, street widths and basic principles of building layout and structure. Statutory control, though raising health standards, not only produced monotonous districts of terraces and tenements in most industrial towns, but for generations to come made housing and town planning the responsibility of the Ministry of Health. Due to this historic background, planning was straight-jacketed by principles of bodily, rather than spiritual, health. Planning was essentially to prevent disease, fire or other hazards to the body. It was not the intention, in early planning development during the sixty years or so from the Artizans and Labourers Dwellings Act of 1868, to consider questions of land-use, population and industrial location or amenity. There was generally no conception of providing an environment

35

which would stimulate the social, still less spiritual, development of men. A few individuals and charities created occasional pools of enlightened development in the great mass of healthy, but moribund, bye-law housing. In the fifteen years from 1893, half a million acres of farmland were absorbed by the new industrial society without any attempt to regulate or channel this conversion of country to town. A year later, in 1909, the Housing, Town Planning, Etc Act, for the first time introduced the term 'town planning' into English legislation. Moreover it aimed to secure 'in broad outline, the home healthy, the house beautiful, the town pleasant, the city dignified and the suburb salubrious'.

Few schemes were completed under the first Town Planning Act, though this made it possible for local authorities to prepare schemes for any land which was being or appeared likely to be developed, principally in order to raise standards of sanitary conditions and general amenity rather than make a positive contribution to urban location, the distribution of zones of land used for different purposes, or communications. Nevertheless a tentative step had been taken which, at the end of the Great War a decade later, was extended by the Housing and Town Planning Act so that all Boroughs and Urban Districts of over 20,000 in population were required to prepare development schemes. At the same time, on a basis of state subsidies, council housing came into being. All development had to be to specific standards, with three-bedroomed houses with gardens at a maximum density of twelve an acre. This Act did not solve the problems of planning and amenity, but it created the impetus which was to thrust suburban estates across the face of rural England during the next two decades. Planning, as such, was limited to trivia, except in the context of the garden city and a few enlightened planners, such as Ebenezer Howard at the turn of the century and the disciples who followed him. But by degrees an appreciation that planning was more than a medical matter began to be recognised in the 1930s, when the image of the suburban semi-detached house and commuting to London on the electric railways began to reach a peak in the national consciousness of the full life. Country planning was for the first time coupled to town planning in the Act of 1932 and the concept in official, and even in colloquial, language of a town and country planning policy for the country as a whole was born, even though this has remained, for the most part, an illusion.

The Town and Country Planning Act of 1932 brought almost all types of land, whether developed or undeveloped, under planning control, though schemes which required Parliamentary sanction to become law took about three years to prepare and pass the period of appeal and amendment. Once approved they could not be varied except by the same procedure and time lag. Schemes did not prevent development during the period of incubation; but developers, who did not apply for permission during the period of 'interim' control, might become responsible for the removal or alteration of their works to conform to the scheme once approved. Nevertheless, as today, few cases of enforcement were known when there was a breach in a planner's scheme, provided lip-service was paid to general principles. The 1932 schemes were mainly for zoning land-use for residential and industrial development. There was no control of development once a scheme was approved except in the general terms of zone, density and so on. In fact, as Cullingworth points out, by 1937 half the country was covered by draft schemes, but in such general terms that 'sufficient land was zoned for housing to accommodate 350 million people' and [4]:

> . . . the pre-war machinery of planning was defective in several ways. It was optional on local authorities; planning powers were essentially regulatory and restrictive; such planning as was achieved was purely local in character; the Central Government had no effective powers of initiative, or of co-ordinating local plans; and the 'compensation bogey'—with which local authorities had to cope without any Exchequer assistance—bedevilled the efforts of all who attempted to make the cumbersome planning machinery work. By 1942, 73 per cent of the land in England and 36 per cent of the land in Wales had become subject to 'interim development control', but only 5 per cent of England and 1 per cent of Wales was actually subject to operative schemes; and there were several important towns and cities as well as some large country districts for which not even the preliminary stages of a planning scheme had been taken. Administration was highly fragmented and was essentially a matter for the lower tier authorities; in 1944 there were over 1,400 planning authorities.

Planning during the 1930s followed of course in the wake of the depression at the start of the decade, and unemployment, both actual and as a potential national disaster, created a difficult climate. Depressed areas with little industry and high unemployment presented more critical planning problems for the community than providing urban areas of balanced development, or integrating all community needs, or rural districts with agriculture and amenity harmonised. Regions of industrial depression caused the Government to appoint Sir Montague Barlow in 1938 to investigate the causes and trends of the geographical distribution of the industrial population and see if remedial action should be taken. From his report flowed a new era of planning concepts, profoundly affecting urban and rural life and eventually land-use.

As already discussed, rural planning was almost unknown before the 1939 war, the term 'country' having little relevance in any of the Planning Acts. The problems of using the countryside and rural amenity were not completely neglected either by the nation or the Government. There is a long tradition of interest in rural life, and

37

government sympathy and support to the main voluntary organisations concerning themselves with the countryside, many of which received royal direction or, at least, an Act to widen their scope with legal powers. Chart 1 indicates some of the organisations and legislation which developed between mid-Victorian times and the second world war influencing the social structure and outlook of rural Britain, though the principal Acts of Parliament have been of more recent origin.

CHART 1: GROWTH OF ORGANISATIONS AND LEGISLATION
CONCERNED WITH RURAL AMENITY UP TO 1939

1750–1850	Enclosure Acts of Parliament
1828–1960	Game Acts
1865	Commons, Open Spaces and Footpaths Preservation Society
1877	Society for the Protection of Ancient Buildings
1882	Royal Forestry Society of England
1889	Royal Society for the Protection of Birds
1895	National Trust for Places of Historic Interest or Natural Beauty
1907–1953	National Trust Acts
1912	Society for Promotion of Nature Reserves
1914	Town Planning Institute
1919	Forestry Commission
1921	Rural Industries Bureau
1923	Men of Trees
1925	Roads Improvement Act
1926	Norfolk Naturalists' Trust (first of several county trusts)
1928	Roads Beautifying Association
1929	Institute of Landscape Architects
1931	Census (showing conurbation growth)
1932	Town and Country Planning Act
1933	Local Government Act (protection of wild plants)
1935	Restriction of Ribbon Development Act
1937	Trunk Roads Act
1938	Royal Commission on Geographical Distribution of the Industrial Population (Sir Montague Barlow)

The impact on the countryside of these various societies and acts has proved more important than formal planning, at least until recent years. The National Trust has become the largest landowner in Britain apart from the Crown and the Forestry Commission (p.194), and by the Act of 1907 has the purpose of 'promoting the permanent preservation, for the benefit of the nation, of lands and tenements (including buildings), of beauty or historic interest and, as regards lands, for the preservation (so far as practicable) of their natural

38

aspect features and animal and plant life'. The National Trust has over the years made a major contribution to the preservation of several important tracts of landscape, as well as notable buildings, for the most part without retarding agricultural progress and providing at the same time public access to much of their property. The countryside would be poorer without their benevolent interest in rural problems. Similarly the promotion of nature reserves by the National Trust and the society formed for that purpose in 1912, reinforced later by the Nature Conservancy set up in 1949, and now part of the Natural Environment Research Council, have done much to protect wild life in areas of particular importance. There are now over 100 special reserves as well as nearly 2,000 classified sites of scientific interest. The Council for the Preservation of Rural England, though sometimes tending to be opposed to change, even progressive change regarding agricultural and social development, has nevertheless done much to highlight the need for care in rural planning. In these circumstances, with the undercurrents generated by such societies and councils, it is impossible to say that within the first decades of this century there was no national consciousness of the needs of the countryside—even though the 'pre-war machinery of planning was defective'. Such consciousness was not however co-ordinated, so that the conflicting pressures and demands on land-use in the countryside had no base for a national policy.

The Barlow Commission made their report in 1940, recording the lack of any national authority to control or plan urban growth. In particular they recognised the disadvantages of the conurbations, as they were later called, especially emphasising the inherent dangers in having a quarter or more of the population concentrated in twenty to thirty miles of London as serious threats to the social and economic well being of the nation. They recommended that a new central authority was essential, though they differed in their attitude to the powers to be vested in a national planning network, placing different emphasis on research, advice and execution. An authority planning dispersal from congested urban areas, studying the location of industry, vetting town planning proposals and, when necessary, modifying them and being responsible for deciding between development as garden city or suburb, as satellite town or expansion of existing towns, was the basis for many of the post-war planning concepts arising from the ideas of the Commission. A minority urged immediate action to be undertaken by a powerful executive under a new Ministry, embracing the planning interests of the Ministries of Health and Transport as well as those of the Commissioners for Special Areas. The war absorbed the depressed areas into its own urgent needs, thus removing the basis for the Commission's report. Nevertheless it proved a land-mark in national thinking towards a centralised policy for planning and it helped to create a favourable climate in the wartime Government, many members of which looked forward to the possibility of creating a new Britain once hostilities ceased. Various committees were set up in 1941 to report on the national services which would be required as a basis for improving the social life and standards of the country once peace returned. The most important historical event for rural planning was the committee appointed under the chairmanship of Lord Justice Scott to report on land utilisation in rural areas. The terms of reference for the Scott Committee were[5]:

> To consider the conditions which should govern building and other constructional development in country areas consistently with the maintenance of agriculture, and in particular the factors affecting the location of industry, having regard to economic operation, part-time and seasonable employment, the well-being of rural communities and the preservation of rural amenities.

These terms, recognising that changes were inevitable in rural Britain and also pertinent to the nation, proved a new and important development in government attitudes towards planning. The committee showed their sensibility to the issues involved by stating[5]:

> We regard the countryside as the heritage of the whole nation and, furthermore, we consider that the citizens of this country are the custodians of a heritage they share . . . it is a duty incumbent upon the nation to take proper care of that which it thus holds in trust . . . We consider that the land of Britain should be both useful and beautiful and that the two aims are in no sense incompatible.

However, interpretation of the terms of reference was not easy, since they can be construed in several ways, and the committee felt it was necessary to make five basic assumptions for their report in that their aims were towards the[5]:

a Establishment of a central planning authority,
b encouragement of industry and commerce,
c maintenance of a prosperous agriculture,
d resuscitation of village and country life,
e preservation of amenities.

The third aim has proved to be a contentious issue in the last quarter century since, as was natural in 1941, the committee considered that 'the maintenance of a healthy and well balanced agriculture' was synonymous with the continuance and revival of the traditional mixed character of British farming. It came about that there was a tacit assumption that the general structure of agriculture would and should remain basically the same—few could forsee the real nature of the second agricultural revolution at that time only just beginning.

40

Of more significance was the assumption that agriculture generally should retain a prescriptive right over existing farmland (as necessary for the maintenance of a prosperous agriculture) and urban development of land should be allowed only on the basis that it could be shown to be more essential than the need for food production. It was assumed that absorption of farm land for other purposes was, in principle, wrong. This thinking conditioned the concepts on which the Agriculture Act and Town and Country Planning Act of 1947 were based and tended to place farmers in a semi-privileged position in relation to the rest of the community.

It was only Professor S. R. Dennison who, in his twenty-four page minority appendix to the report, dissented from this attitude. He realised that there were three aspects of size which determined the prosperity of agriculture—acreage, employment and output—whereas the rest of the committee concentrated their approach to the problem only on acreage. Dennison's attitude has always attracted the interest of some agricultural economists and planners, and today, due to the rapid agricultural industrial changes of recent years, it has become generally accepted. In the appendix, Professor Dennison enumerated four basic principles for rural planning[6]:

1 All land in the countryside should be included in planning schemes and no interests of national importance should be excluded from the aims of planning.

2 While particular planning schemes will certainly involve preservation of much land in agricultural use, it should not be accepted as a 'necessary principle' that construction in the countryside must be prevented in order to maintain agriculture, to preserve rural communities or to preserve amenities.

3 The introduction of industry into the countryside, under effective planning control, could be of considerable benefit to rural communities.

4 The needs of agriculture (including the protection of good quality land) should be met through the normal machinery of planning schemes and should not be given any prior rights.

These comments are relevant today and should still form part of the basis towards a new plan for rural land. Agriculture, though of vital importance, is only one of the community needs which have essential rights to land-use in the countryside. Not all the comments however of the main part of the Scott Report were of doubtful value, only the emphasis placed on the need to keep farm land almost sacrosanct. Indeed the report believed that national parks were long overdue, though their creation did not come until the National Parks and Access to the Countryside Act of 1949. Moreover the committee touched another issue, still largely unimplemented, in their criticism of agricultural buildings in the planning controls[7]:

> The present exemption granted to agricultural buildings is unsatisfactory. All buildings should come under review, but special criteria will need to be adopted in considering the suitability or otherwise of agricultural buildings from the amenity point of view. There need seldom be, if ever, any incompatibility between good appearance and utilitarian economy on the farm.

The main difficulty in implementing Professor Dennison's recommendations is that the basis of knowledge of the types and distribution of agricultural land is still the analysis made by Professor Dudley Stamp for the Land Utilisation Survey of Great Britain between 1931 and 1939 (p.419). Though agriculture has changed completely in character, with methods for making land fertile, and though nearly $1\frac{1}{4}$ acres of farmland has been lost since 1939, a pre-war survey is the only national assessment of farmland, and there is no analysis of the potential of the land still available for food production, though a new land classification has at last been started by the Ministry of Agriculture with the first map published in 1967.

The basis for modern planning, derived from the Barlow and Scott reports, with their relationship to such studies as the Uthwatt Committee on Compensation and Betterment and the Beveridge Committee on Social Insurance and Allied Services, both set up in 1941, and the Consultative Panel of the Ministry of Works and Building under Lord Reith, also of 1941, which inaugerated the National Planning Series of maps, lay in the creation of a Ministry of Town and Country Planning in 1943. This new ministry, which included some of the powers previously invested in the Ministeries of Health and Works and Building, was created in an atmosphere of personal and political tensions. It became limited in its authority and never fulfilled the pre-war dream of Abercrombie for a synthesis of planning under one man's jurisdiction. Planning in Scotland remained the responsibility of the Department of Health for Scotland. Even in England and Wales, housing remained the province of the Ministry of Health and industrial location of the Board of Trade.

Britain entered its post-war period seeking a new era of urban and rural development, with the Socialist Government returned with a planner's mandate and national enthusiasm for planned reconstruction. This development was intended to be for the good of all, preserving the best of the old but recharging the sources of prosperity by collective action to produce a balanced community. Many had spent the war years thinking deeply about the years of reconstruction lying ahead and a spate of legislation in the early post-war period developed out of the various reports of committees and panels held before hostilities ceased.

REFERENCES

1 Abercrombie, Sir Patrick, 'Country planning'. *Britain and the Beast*, edited by Clough Williams-Ellis, p133. 1933, J. M. Dent
2 *British agriculture looks ahead*, p48. 1964, National Farmers' Union
3 Cullingworth, J. B. *Town and Country Planning in England and Wales*. 1964, George Allen & Unwin
4 Ibid pp20, 31
5 *Report of the Committee on Land Utilisation in Rural Areas*, pp45–47. Chairman Rt Hon Lord Justice Scott PC HMSO, 1942
6 Ibid p123
7 Ibid p50

1d Post-war concepts and failures

Two Acts of 1947 set the pattern of post-war rural planning. The Agricultural Act of that year created the economic conditions, not only for stability but progressive development, for agriculture to become a major industry in the years ahead (p.95). It tended also to give a special bias in rural planning decisions towards farmers, since the nation was pledged by the Act to maintain 'a stable and efficient agricultural industry'. As discussed in the previous section, this pledge generally was interpreted to include the basic attitudes towards land-use which had been defined by the Scott report—the freezing of the countryside into the existing pattern of ownership and food production. The Town and Country Planning Act of 1947 created new machinery for controlling development under the direction of local planning authorities at county and county borough levels. This decision reduced the number of planning authorities from 1,441 to 145, leading to better co-ordination in larger areas. However though it was the intention of the Act to promote regional planning boards above county level, regional planning never began to be even remotely effective until its resuscitation some fifteen years later. In the middle 1960s national thinking has begun at last to be based on economic development areas rather than on the county network derived from history.

The county planners in 1947 were made responsible for producing development plans for all areas. This work still continues, with schemes being completed or detailed and, for the most part, reviewed every five years. Power for the administration of planning and for 'securing consistency and continuity in the framing of a national policy with respect to the use and development of land throughout England and Wales' was granted to the Ministry of Housing and Local Government. Ministerial authority had a wide base, though detailed planning remained at local level. However, by designation, housing and local government, whatever the terms of reference, cannot be considered the same as town and country planning, which was the

43

previous ministry with planning responsibilities. The ministerial change of name was significant, with important undertones in the national consciousness. Rural planning was moreover further fragmented by the independent powers granted to other authorities, particularly those exemptions from planning control made in 1950.

Cullingworth recognised that though *amenity* is one of the key concepts in British town and country planning . . . it appears only four times in the 1947 Act (and the consolidated 1962 Act) and nowhere in the legislation is it defined'[1]. The Acton Society Trust became concerned that industrial growth in the countryside was proving detrimental to amenity and Dr Bracey examined the position for them, reporting in 1963 on the visual, material and social changes in rural Britain[2]. This study was significant since it was the first appraisal of the impact of industry on rural amenities and was therefore one measure for judging the success of post-war rural planning. Due however to the resources available for the study, the research was largely limited to an appraisal of the impact of electrical, atomic and oil processing and distribution, with special attention paid to their effect in southern Hampshire and Dorset. Nevertheless, though limited, the implications for the nation as a whole are clear, particularly in the recognition that the greatest danger for a healthy countryside is 'the rate at which change can be effected by economic decisions taken in the national interest'.

An amenable countryside can only be one which is used with responsibility: the criteria for amenity lie in a social recognition of values, balancing utility with appearance. To the farmer, productive land well managed is amenable. There is conflict when the townsman judges amenity by eighteenth or nineteenth century values, desiring small fields and picturesque buildings. There is also conflict when the farmer sees all land devoid of urban development as agricultural land, irrespective of its potential fertility or social value for other uses. To the planner, amenity can be judged only in a balanced use of all land, an apportionment of the countryside to serve to the fullest advantage all needs of the population, taking into consideration the location, topography and physical structure of the land itself. But the value of the landscape, even in the planner's terms of reference, has an intrinsic quality, derived from a counterpoise gained over the centuries between the natural forces of selection and man's control of his environment. Geographically and historically, in Britain this has evolved a landscape which is, as Dower said[3] 'a national, indeed an international, asset. It is a contribution to the world's heritage as distinctive as Abu Simbel or Venice, as important as the wild life of Africa'. Bracey reported that industrial change in the countryside was sometimes beneficial, sometimes questionable and sometimes downright bad, but that never in its history had changes of the dimensions of modern industry been effected over such short periods as the

44

Fawley refinery extension, built in two years, the Severnside ICI works near Bristol, operable within four years, and the Bradwell nuclear reactor within five years[4]. Bracey found in the industries examined everyday relations between local authority officials and industrial executives were generally excellent, though the genuine interest of industrialists towards amenity problems tended to increase with the size of the industry and the authority of the executive.

Local planning authorities are empowered by the 1947 Act to protect amenity against detrimental acts. Planning, however, which should co-ordinate all parts of national life within a framework for the whole, is fragmented. Statutory authorities, such as for the Services, forestry, roads, railways, gas, water and electricity, largely lie outside the jurisdiction of local planners. In post-war planning, though powers for co-ordination were created, responsibilities were often divided. Main roads were made the responsibility of the Minister of Transport, who designated lines for trunk roads and motorways and formed a scale of priorities for construction by issuing grants. At the same time, in development plans, the Minister of Housing generated traffic requirements which fundamentally affect the road network. Classified roads, as opposed to trunk roads became the responsibility of local highway authorities. As has become evident in recent years, the interplay of motor and rail traffic has national and local implications yet, under the sensible reduction of uneconomic rail lines, public uproar was generated since the effect of rail closures on the road network and bus services were inadequately considered due to the terms of reference laid down for investigation in the Beeching plan for British Rail. Thus even with co-ordination officially required between the Ministeries of Housing and Transport, planning must fail unless all ingredients of good planning are integrated under one ministry, qualified in all aspects of planning. The situation was made worse in 1947 since problems connected with employment, which largely concerns population distribution, were placed under the Board of Trade. Planning control was even further diversified. This situation of fragmented authority has bedevilled all post-war planning.

Government departments and, generally, the Crown do not have to be granted planning permission by a local authority, though they have to submit a notice of proposed development, with the exception of secret developments, minor operations, and repetitive buildings similar to those already existing on a site unless they abut a highway or affect amenity. With these exceptions, consultation can be enforced at ministerial level by the local authorities if they do not like the proposed development. Nevertheless final judgement is vested in the government department concerned. Thus though a farmer can be forced to paint a relatively small barn with dung, large aircraft sheds within yards of the barn, but under the responsibility of a government department, are exempt from planning control (p.275). This ludicrous

45

situation can only lead to social friction. Since statutory undertakings, freed from planning control, include 'persons authorised by any enactment to carry on any railway, light railway, tramway, road transport, water transport, canal, inland navigation, dock, harbour, pier or lighthouse undertaking, or any undertaking for the supply of electricity, gas, hydraulic power or water', it is evident that much can occur in the countryside without any real attempt at co-ordination or planning. This fragmentation of planning has never seemed to worry official attitudes, except, perhaps, that special 'amenity' clauses have been written into some of the acts defining the powers of statutory departments.

The first amenity clause was written into the Hydro-Electric Development (Scotland) Act of 1943 when the responsible board was obliged to have due regard in preserving landscape and objects of architectural or historic interest in the exercise of its functions. Since that time amenity clauses have been created for the North Wales Hydro-Electric Scheme (1955) Milford Haven development (1956) and Electricity Authorities (1957). Trees and buildings are also protected in principle from destruction by various schedules and preservation orders, but in practice the machinery of protection is often strained. Both the Government and the public have developed a conscious and practical attitude towards preservation, with perhaps more success than failure to their credit, and problems of amenity receive better consideration today, reinforced by particular statutes, than in the immediate post-war years. The National Trust is a powerful force towards keeping a balanced countryside, especially in such schemes as operation Neptune, aimed to save the remaining short stretches of natural coastline from urban destruction, which is increasing at the rate of seven miles a year (p.151). The recommendations of the Scott Committee for the creation of national parks came to fruition in 1949 with the National Parks and Access to the Countryside Act. These parks now cover nearly a tenth of England and Wales in ten areas, with almost a score of other areas designated as being of outstanding beauty, and almost 1,500 miles of long-distance paths recommended and approved, including the Pennine Way. The work of the National Parks Commission is extended by that of the Nature Conservancy, set up in the same year (now part of the Natural Environment Research Council), which is now responsible for over 100 reserves in Britain covering more than 350 square miles, including the Cairngorms, one of the largest nature reserves in Europe. Many other official authorities have also been created in recent years in the interests of managing the countryside to better advantage. The Civic Trust (1957), the Geological Conservation Council (1957), and the Council for Nature (1958), for example, have all aided the cause for a better understanding and development of our most valuable basic resource, the land.

46

Recent years have made a positive contribution towards a better policy for rural planning, even though the rate of change is so rapid and the true understanding of the natural resources and needs so slight that there is no ground for complacency. The work of the various committees and councils has been aided by other legislation. The Protection of Birds Act (1954), The Rivers (Prevention of Pollution) Acts (1951 and 1961), the Pipe Line Act (1962), the Caravan Sites Act (1962) and the Water Resources Act (1963), have extended legislation into many areas which profoundly affect the use of land. Many official or voluntary organisations have also important interests in the countryside, often aided by legislation in the promotion of their interests, such as the Central Council for Physical Recreation, the Ramblers Association, the British Trust for Ornithology, the Country Landowners' Association, the Game Research Association and the British Field Sports Society, as well as the Anti-Field Sports League. When in fact the conference on the 'Countryside in 1970' met in 1963, no less than eighty-nine different organisations participated, all of which had interests in the use of the countryside. Moreover the conference produced a chart showing the human impacts on the countryside in which twenty-three main human activities were sub-divided into well over 150 different operations. When responsibility for forming policy relating the availability of land with national requirements was vested in the Ministry of Land and Natural Resources, set up in 1964, there was more hope for a co-ordinated and balanced use of land than at any other time in history. Nevertheless the background to the physical situation existing in 1967, as opposed to theoretical planning attitudes, does not give much confidence for the future, especially with that Ministry now defunct.

It might be thought that with the amount of legislation, the number of organisations and the (for the most part) favourable report by Dr Bracey on the relation of the major industries to rural planning, the countryside was reasonably protected from despoliation and all that was now needed was a period of consolidation, co-operation and co-ordination. This is not so. Lionel Brett has made clear that, as far as the landscape is concerned, rural planning since the war has failed, there being little mitigation in the thought that, had there been no planning, the situation would have been worse. In his valuable study of the actual physical appearance of 250 square miles forming the southern part of Oxfordshire, he has recorded the vanishing, almost to oblivion, of an area of former beauty which many believed to be one of the most delightful counties in England[5]. As one of his survey team recorded 'there wasn't anything exciting in our area that hadn't been there for centuries'. The survey did show that there was still in part a factual distinction between areas of residential countryside and functional farmland or woodland, though other areas were confused by mixed use, and thereby lost their character. Nevertheless he

47

records that only by a hair's breadth does any of the landscape in south Oxfordshire retain an atmosphere of space, and that little which is still rural in character is irreplaceable. He complains moreover that the list of unspoilt villages is now lamentably short and the list of those near the edge of final disaster disastrously long[6]. On the existing situation, as recorded in 1964, he appreciates that the flood of planning permission already in the pipeline has to be superimposed. The population of the area is destined to rise by fifty per cent to over 107,000 by 1981, from that existing two decades earlier. In spite of the Planning Acts decreeing the preparation of county plans, Brett found that the framework of policy laid down by the County Development Plan for Oxfordshire was 'sketchy in the extreme'[7]. The plan 'conveys virtually no information, and is supplemented, as far as our area is concerned, by Town Maps for Henley and Thame which are still under confidential discussion and by red lines drawn round a dozen of the larger villages to indicate the present "urban fences" or limits of development. Apart from this, some fairly crude work has been done on population trends; gravel and lime workings have been tied down to an agreed long-term extraction plan; caravan operators have been steadfastly refused permanent planning permission, and the county map is evidence of an energetic campaign of woodland conservation'.

The failure of planning, as a matter of national concern appreciated at all levels of authority, cannot but be recognised as Brett has stressed, by the publication of the Government's South-east Study (1964), which realised that another 2m people would live in the 10,000 square miles covered by the Report by 1981, yet believed that:

A large part of the population growth in the South-east will not require the deliberate development of growth centres. For the greater part of the population growth, the ordinary planning machinery for allocating land to meet forseeable needs can function satisfactorily, as long as the planning authorities are given warning in time of the size of the population increases to be dealt with in their land budget. Allocations of housing land can then be made by them, for the most part in the form of the normal growth of towns and villages, and, as will be seen, this is the manner in which the greater part of the growth expected in the South-east is likely to be dealt with.

The record of South Oxfordshire since 1947 gives no confidence that this approach to planning, both urban and rural, will be anything but disastrous. Yet though this area is typical of most growth counties, the failure is not basically one of spirit in the planning offices since, as Brett records, the staff under the Oxfordshire County Planning Adviser averages three and excludes an architect or a landscapist. Thus the failure for implementing detailed plans, and sometimes even for preparing outline plans for the development of

48

Model of an Agribusiness Centre near Salisbury by A. J. Sanger ARIBA that won fifth prize at the seventh biennial architectural student competition, Brazil 1963. The design is for a co-operative to serve an area within fifteen miles of the centre, including buildings rented by farmers in a vertically integrated administration. The centre might employ 1,000 people, Britain having sixty co-operatives serving different agricultural zones with outlets to neighbouring conurbations.

At the centre is an administrative and research tower set in a market, with an abattoir, by-product factories and dairy adjoining. At far right is the connection to the road/rail network, near to which are a group of grain and feed silos, car park, and a field equipment centre. There are also social and medical facilities.

The large radial layout includes beef and veal with, in the foreground, a pig fattening unit in vertical blocks. In the background are the smaller blocks for poultry, an egg packing station and a manure collection and methane gas conversion plant.

1

2

3

1 Home Farm, Clophill, Beds.
The zenith of agricultural
prosperity in 1875 left a legacy of
model farm layouts with buildings
grouped round large stockyards
and the farm house left discreetly
on the perimeter.

2 Harvesting in the Chilterns
1936. A horse team reaping with
a cutter only thirty years ago,
but virtually in another age in
contrast to modern farming
methods.

3 Manor Farm, Upper Heyford,
Oxford 1964. Two towers for grass
and one for barley for automatically feeding seventy cows
and about as many bullocks.
Vertical storage is an essential
part of modern farming. Since
many farmsteads are in villages
care should be taken, siting
towers for storage in relation to
church towers. Tower silos are
structurally a welcome feature,
relieving horizontal asbestos
buildings.

51

1

1 Large areas of Britain are still neglected pasture—how many million acres that can be substantially improved is still unknown. By the year 2000 we must turn every acre to good use, either for intensive farming, forestry, water conservation, or urban use as conurbations, village satellites and recreation. Waste land will be a luxury that cannot be afforded.

2 New grain store, Fincham Hall Farm, Norfolk. Designed by W. A. J. Spear ARIBA to dry and store 600 tons of grain adjacent to the existing scheduled farm buildings and hall. The layout was awarded a Civic Trust medal in 1966, the first award for a farm building in seven years.

3 Plastic covered cubicle house for forty cows at Tunstall, Richmond, Yorks. Many farmers are keen innovators and ideas in farm management and building change constantly. Any form of planning control must not stultify experiment. This is the kernel of the problem: how to safeguard the best rural environment from unsightly change yet maintain the speed of progress attained in recent years.

2

3

1

2

1 Cattle exports from Yarmouth.
During recent years, agricultural
exports from Britain, including
cattle, have increased remarkably.
In 1963 15,000 head left Yarmouth
for Holland, but in the next year
57,000 were transported mainly
in small cargo ships which
returned to Britain with fruit and
vegetables.

2 Model of Skelmersdale New
Town, Lancs 1965. Old town at
left centre and new town centre
separated from it by Tawd valley
with industrial estate in foreground
and M6 at right. The new town
for 90,000 people is designed on
maximum segregation of
pedestrians and vehicles, car
ownership at 1·5 cars per family
and Parker-Morris standards for
most of the housing. A new town
of this size is needed every three
months to cater for the growth of
population in Britain.

Cumbernauld new town, Scotland, overlooking Glasgow-Stirling road. Three twelve-storey blocks of flats erected in 1965 (with five further blocks now completed) using industrialised building components. The division between new towns and agricultural land must be clear-cut. Tall flats and houses can be mixed on the periphery of the towns, segregated from the inter-city motorways. Chief architect to Cumbernauld Development Corporation, D. R. Leaker.

villages and rural areas, lies basically in the national lack of qualified sociologists, economists, planners and landscapists, capable of handling work of this complexity. The situation is grave and the bland assumption of the Government that all will be well in the framework of existing planning machinery is short-sighted and disastrous for the future well-being of this crowded country.

Turton has examined the pressures which are developing on the planning machinery in truly rural areas, that is, those not on the fringe of urban areas, nor in coastal districts nor green belt areas, but where development is restricted for different reasons[8]. The rural areas can be those with static or even declining populations. Even rural districts with populations of around 20,000 can generate 300–400 planning applications a year and the rate of applications is increasing[8]:

CHART 2 GROWTH IN RURAL PLANNING APPLICATIONS

	W Suffolk	Shrop-shire	Norfolk
No of planning applications 1960	1980	3232	6892
,, ,, ,, 1962	2589	3856	7684
% increase no applications determined 1960–2	23·9	18·9	11·1
% increase in population 1960–2	2·6	1·3	0·1

For example Shropshire, with a population increase of only 1·3 per cent in two years generated an increase of nearly nineteen per cent in the number of planning applications determined in that period. In contrast the more urbanised pressure area of Hampshire, with a population increase of under four per cent in the same period, had only 0·7 per cent increase in applications determined, and even Hertfordshire, with a 6·3 per cent increase in population, had only 13·8 per cent increase in applications. Similarly the older industrial area of Lancashire, which had about the same percentage increase in population as West Suffolk, nevertheless had an increase in applications of only 8·5 (that is only rather more than a third in percentage terms) of the increase in West Suffolk. As Turton stresses, the rate of planning applications in rural areas seems to be increasing at a faster rate than the more established areas. In fact West Suffolk's population rose by over ten per cent in the six years from 1960. In the same period planning applications (which numbered 3,267 in 1965) showed an increase of over sixty per cent. Obviously this has profound significance for rural planning at a time when the policy for rural districts may be limited to a County development plan showing no more than the existing settlement pattern (which may be intended to remain unchanged) backed occasionally by some village development

57

studies, which often are no more than rings showing areas in which building may be permitted round a village. This defence against the spoliation of the countryside in functional and aesthetic terms, intended by the Planning Acts, is slender indeed—against the pressure for change—so slender that it is not surprising that the basic policy, such as it is, is too often torn to shreds at a time when, as Best and Coppock have stressed[9]:

> Nowhere is the imprint of social and technological change to be seen more clearly than upon the use of land itself. The landscape of Britain in the 1960s is, indeed, in the process of rapid and radical transformation, the widespread extent and rate of which has seldom, if ever, been equalled in the history of this country.

With inadequate planning staff and lack of research data on which to base decisions, with control often vested in different ministries, it is not surprising that rural planning may prove defective. In 1956 Ian Nairn recognised that this was the crux of the problem—and the situation has not changed except that the pressure has increased almost beyond reason[10]:

> As things are going at present, the very best we can hope for is that a rural county (with a good planning officer and a lot of luck in being out of the way of urban sprawl or interference by government departments) will get no worse than at the moment. That is to say, the best we can do is what ought to have been guaranteed automatically by the planning system. More than that—ie positive planning—is almost unknown in Britain, not because of lack of enthusiasm or ability, but simply because the planners have no time left over from trying to plug the leaks in a system which is as full of holes as a sieve.

Eleven years after the comment is still true. The issues at that time were seen 'less of a warning than a prophecy of doom'. None of the recommendations made by Ian Nairn for better planning policies and procedures have been fulfilled. Green belts have not been extended to protect all agricultural land. The planning system still has a vacuum at its centre in that much development is outside its mechanism. Planning is still at county and not regional level—although economic planning is beginning to have regional direction, it has not yet truly changed the character of town and country planning in theory or practice. Development plans for the countryside are still basically a 'vast accumulation of statistics' but are not three dimensional plans, backed by regional studies of terrain, soil and resources. Nairn's prophecy of doom in 1956 is being fulfilled.

Post-war planning dreams have been shattered in many directions and not only in the failure to create positive county plans. The green belt policy of restraining urban growth and providing multi-use land for recreation, forestry and agriculture round urban centres still remains a shadow of its intention (p.152). In recent years the pressure for building in the South-east has cracked the belt in several places, and not all government officials are sympathetic to the ideals of those wishing to check urban growth. The future of the green belts is far from certain. The problem of land values, with some land frozen from urban development by the planners and other land designated for change from agriculture to other uses, has been the thorniest political, moral and economic planning problem of the post-war years. The cumbersome machinery of the 1947 Act, which nationalised development rights over land and created a system of development charges, with certain rights of compensation, was unstable and brought the idea of planned use of land into general disrepute. Unfortunately, with a change in government in 1951 and a new Town and Country Planning Act in 1954, not only was the idea of development charges for land annulled but ideas for generating a balanced and co-ordinated use of land remained outside the scope of official thinking. The situation was not improved by a further Town and Country Planning Act in 1959, which retained the national ownership of rights of development but based compulsory acquisition of land on compensation according to an assessment of a fair market price. Planning principles had become so confused that measures made since 1947 had to be consolidated in another Act in 1962. The concept of a capital gains tax introduced in 1965 has not resolved the difficult economic problems of land held in private ownership but controlled in development by the community. Such control changes the value of land, but the economic rights of ownership in such situations are far from clear as a moral problem, being unresolved both in theory and practice by the community. This leaves planning of land in a difficult and unbalanced situation, neither satisfactory for the community nor reasonable for the private owner.

In 1967 the Land Commission Act set in motion new principles for land ownership and development, the full implications of which for the future are far from clear. It is a powerful tool for the future of rural Britain, since it is believed that its trading functions will prove to be more important than the collection of betterment. There is an incentive for all buyers and sellers of land to trade through the Commission since the transaction is speeded, the right price is ensured, the process costs nothing and the levy goes to the Commission rather than the Treasury. However, the process does not ensure that the transaction will improve the environment and the Commission has no planning staff. Nevertheless, the Commission can buy or compulsorily purchase land to make sure 'the right land is available at the right time for the implementation of national, regional and local plans' and it has 'wide powers to acquire, manage and dispose of land for development and redevelopment'. The direction these acquisitions may take, designed to assist local authorities, is vague and, without a national scale of priorities for land-use, perhaps dangerous—especially since the Commission seems to be an urban organisation with urban standards. Erection of agricultural buildings are exempted from a betterment levy, as are agricultural dwellings until they pass into other hands. The collection of a betterment levy of forty per cent on the increased value of land to be used for building rather than agriculture is an attempt to see that society benefits from development and from land values inflated when planning permission is granted.

The Scott Report in 1942 called for control of the design of agricultural buildings. The spate of investment in new or converted farm buildings continues today at the rate of some £50m a year in England and Wales, with perhaps £80m–£100m spent on buildings and allied equipment in the United Kingdom. The difficult problem of controlling farm building design is considered in a later section (p.274). The 1947 Act exempted farm buildings from planning control unless within eighty feet of a trunk road or over ten feet high within two miles of an aerodrome. Three years later control was extended for buildings in areas of outstanding beauty. Public pressure grew during the following years against the indiscriminate spread of ugly agricultural buildings. In 1960, control was further extended to include all agricultural buildings with a total area of 5,000 square feet erected or extended in two years and which are within 100 yards of each other. Many consider—and in some cases even leading farmers—that this control is inadequate. Wilfred Cave, for example, with a large Wiltshire farm, stated that he sees no reason why farmers should be exempt from planning control when the ordinary suburban dweller has to get permission for even a small garage[11]. In the summer of 1964, the Rural District Councils' Association meeting at Folkestone, called for control of all farm buildings. Earlier that year, the County Council for the Isle of Ely, like other County Councils, called for greater control, since large farm units, more intensive methods of stock keeping and the need for larger buildings have led to industrialised farm structures. By using tower silos, which are vertical storage buildings requiring small ground areas, and discretion in the erection of units, both in space and time, planning control can be evaded*. The erection moreover of large areas of building without planning permission may be granted retrospective authority. This was the case for the beeflot started in 1965 by British Beef Ltd, discussed in the next section. The present situation cannot be considered with equanimity, especially considering that much farm building is made of prefabricated components without much, if any, co-ordination between the different components used.

Attractive countryside in particular is always subject to erosion from urban pressure. Even areas designated as having outstanding

* Towers over 40ft high now require planning permission.

beauty, even the national parks themselves, are not completely safe from outrage. The Electrical Board's pylons across the Sussex landscape from Bolney to Hampshire is a case in point. Similarly, as previously stated, the National Trust has been appalled by the loss of seven miles of natural coastline each year from the 900 which remain—which is already only one third of the total length once available. The thought that $2\frac{1}{2}$m people had holidays in Devon during 1960, numbers which increase each year, but equal at that time to thrice the resident population including Plymouth and Exeter, cannot but generate despair for the natural beauty of that county. Nevertheless the planning authorities in Devon have made a positive attempt to provide guide-lines for development, whether permanent or temporary for the tourist trade, which is a step in the right direction. Industry, for national reasons, may be granted the right to intrude into any landscape. The Esso refinery at Milford Haven, permitted in 1958, was a breach in the cause of scheduling areas for protection from development. Yet the refinery has been sited and landscaped with care. Except to the purist the development is not a landscape failure. The Sizewell atomic station however on a Suffolk coastal promontory gives less grounds for satisfaction. The huge bulk (though detailed with care) is the first of four massive concrete structures to be built, all of which, virtually irremoveable, may be unused monoliths before a century has passed. It is not the reactors alone which present an aesthetic problem—pylons seem to surge out of the landscape for miles around, two great lines converging down the promontory to the reactor, completely distorting the landscape. Adjoining the headland, under the dominant shape of the station and grid, is the peaceful bird sanctuary of Minsmere. A few miles of underground cabling would have done much to improve the station, but this is a failure in industrial and rural planning.

The growth of population alone is enough to cause disquiet when contemplating the future of the countryside. In the last decade the population of the United Kingdom increased by almost $3\frac{1}{2}$m. During the rest of this century the 1964 population of 54m will expand by thirty-five per cent. There are few qualified men to control this expansion and provide an environment for it and the existing confused industrial society. Approximately 20,000 architects, rather more than 3,000 town planners and not much over 200 landscape architects—most of whom are engaged in urban problems. It is not surprising that positive planning has fallen so far short of the ideals hoped for in 1947. With so few planners and other experts in rural needs available, with so little authority crystalized into dynamic centralized units at national or regional level, with authority, in fact, fragmented by quasi-independent powers, it is inevitable that the relationship between the community, rural planning and the future of the landscape is tenuous in the extreme.

REFERENCES

1 Cullingworth, J. B., *Town and Country Planning in England and Wales*, p132. 1964, George Allen & Unwin
2 Bracey, H. E., *Industry and the Countryside*. 1963, Faber
3 Dower, M., 'Industrial Britain: The function of open Country'. *Journal* of the Town Planning Institute. April 1964, p137
4 Bracey, H. E., Ibid, p209
5 Brett, L., *Landscape in Distress*. 1965, Architectural Press
6 Ibid, p151
7 Ibid, p141
8 Turton, R., 'Towards a rural planning policy'. *Journal* of Town Planning Institute. April 1964, p142
9 Best, R. H. and Coppock, J. T., *The changing use of land in Britain*, p17. 1962, Faber & Faber
10 Nairn, I., 'Counter-attack'. *The Architectural Review*, December 1965, p431
11 Cave, W., *The appearance of farm buildings*. Farm Building Association Winter Conference 1965.

1e The need for new concepts

Powerful social forces, struggling for the control and development of the countryside, had by 1965 entered a new phase. Social pressures today are generating new concepts of land-use. Some demands for change or for retaining the present status of ownership, with existing conditions for land development, are partisan, reflecting vested interests of individuals or economic and social groups. Other demands are based on the recognition that the future Britain, already deeply engaged in a second industrial revolution, will not only be over-populated but will have a diminishing capacity to import food.

As previously discussed, though developed and sophisticated by international standards, the machinery for rural planning is devoid of a firm base. Statistics are in many respects inadequate for preparing development plans. Moreover, skilled personnel are too few to be able to cope with the backlog of detailed, and even outline, plans which still remain uncomplete, though it is now twenty years since the 1947 Act set the machinery for putting county plans in motion. With this existing backlog of work there is no hope of coping adequately with the needs of a population expanding in numbers and affluence. Regional planners, capable of co-ordinating the social, economic and geographical entities of the new industrial Britain, which have but little direct relationship with Mediaeval county boundaries, are still largely unknown. The agricultural-industrial revolution is changing the scale and character of farmland, but few recognise the extent of the change to come, nor understand what effect this may have on the use, structure and climate of the land. Unless new concepts prevail, based on a detailed analysis of national resources and needs, the countryside is doomed to be engulfed by urban or industrial development, by factory-farmed food production and the crass misuse of land by an affluent, but ignorant, society—all mixed together in the wrong proportions and places. There is no time to lose if rural planning is to be given a firm base for the future.

At the end of 1962 the *Architects' Journal* recognised that planners, themselves were still not fully alive to the dangers and potential inherent in the present situation. In such circumstances it is not surprising that the community acts as if blind, groping for balance in a landscape where their guidelines are confused by unknown social, economic and political forces[1]:

> The role of the town and country planner has been described as the exercise of judgement: that is to say, resolving conflicting interests and demands over the use of land. This might be described as a negative role, even though the necessity for it is at last being recognised by the more advanced societies of the western world as a minimal requirement for a civilised environment. In a democracy, however, if planning is to succeed, it must be seen to have a more positive role than being merely judicial . . . the idea of creating an ordered environment is still a strange one to most people and the full significance of having control over environment is only slowly being accepted by planners themselves . . . As yet no national effort is being made to discover what kind of environment the architect-planner should be aiming to create. What are the optimum conditions for making a full rich life available—not just to the wealthy minority but to everyone? At present we are trying to solve problems of road, rail, housing, relocation of industry, recreation, central areas, forestry, agricultural water supply and a host of other major and minor items in isolation from each other when in fact many are interacting and interdependent.

The *Architects' Journal* recognised rightly that only on the basis of more research could the different strands be gathered together to weave a pattern of use and development. The situation is largely unchanged today, some five years later. As far as research is concerned—the basis of any sound planning—and as far as the structure and organisation of planning departments is concerned and as far as the co-ordination of all the semi-independent powers having interests in the countryside is concerned, there is still no adequate basis for optimism. This is so in spite of the creation of the Ministry of Land and Natural Resources—now dissolved—the Countryside Commission and the 1965 national conference on 'The Countryside in 1970', all of which are moves in the right direction but have not yielded a radical and satisfactory basis for the future of rural planning.

If there was confidence throughout all sections of the population that the countryside was going to have planned change, in which the needs of urban and rural communities were considered and co-ordinated, it would have been unnecessary for the *Farmers Weekly* to make this impassioned plea at the end of 1965[2]:

> It is right that townspeople should be interested in the preservation of the countryside and want to enjoy it. But it is entirely wrong when proper concern for our 'green and pleasant land' becomes distorted into a desire to shape the countryside as the planner and the townsman want it with a total disregard to the requirements of those who work and live there. Pressures on land, the raw material of the farming business, are constantly mounting. Vast areas are wanted for new towns, roads and airports, mineral workings, and factories. The greatest conflict arises, however, from the need to provide leisure facilities in the open for a growing industrial population. This is a reasonable requirement, but it is quite unreasonable for the countryside to be regarded, as it far too often is, as a vast rustic playground where people may do as they will, where the designs of planners and amenity interests must take precedence, and where time—because time brings unwanted change—must stand still . . . . The very things that help us to grow food more efficiently and abundantly are often anathema to those who set themselves up as the countryside's preservers. Modern farm buildings are 'eyesores'; the creation of larger fields in which modern equipment can function properly and economically is a 'despoliation of nature' . . . The truth is, as every farmer knows, that the most pleasing prospect is that of land well-farmed. The farmer is concerned to farm well and so long as he does, the preservation of the countryside is in safe hands. It is hard to believe this when planning people, in their ignorance and effrontery, deny a man a new house for a son or worker because it would 'spoil the ancient charm' of the village; when a new building is refused because it would be an 'intrusion', or when a building has to be painted green—the worst colour to use in a rural landscape . . . the Minister of Land and Natural Resources outlined the functions of a new body which will take over the national parks and develop other areas for leisure activities. Before this is done, farmers must ensure that their voice is going to be heard. We do not deny the right of the town visitor to enjoy the countryside but we do expect farming needs to be better understood and appreciated. Above all, we insist on the proper preservation of farmers on all bodies concerned with rural amenities. We are prepared to discuss conditions and restraints, but we are not prepared to let them be imposed.

It is worth quoting at length from this farming viewpoint. It is indicative of a complete failure in rural planning since the war that it should be written in 1965. It illustrates the basic fear of agriculturalists that planners are urban people imposing urban standards on rural communities. There is some justification in this. Town planners are not, essentially, food production experts, though they are trained to have some knowledge of agriculture. Similarly, agriculturalists generally have little knowledge of land-use problems, other than

64

farming, and no knowledge of planning principles or aims. It should not be necessary for the *Farmers Weekly* to believe that a planner is, by nature, opposed to agricultural changes and progress with 'a total disregard of the requirements of those who work the land'. A rural planner, above all things, must be able to relate the needs of modern agriculture and rural communities to the urban pressures growing in the countryside. If this has not happened in either image or fact, then planners must change their approach to the problem or their training.

It is argued in later sections that the character and scale of the landscape must change as factory farming revolutionises all aspects of agriculture, though the nature of this change should be studied and channelled for the benefit of the community and not solely for individual farmers, whose methods are unco-ordinated with each other. This change is not against good planning principles, provided the balance of nature is not destroyed, upsetting climate, soil structure and fertility. This is why it is essential that changes, which are rapid and extensive in scale, should be co-ordinated and not be left to individuals. It is too rash to believe that 'the preservation of the countryside is in safe hands' with the farmer, farming well. This is basically true but not only is there a proportion of farmers who farm badly, either through ignorance or lack of capital, but farmers are not trained meteorologists, chemists or physicists. They need guidance in these matters, just as planners do in food production methods, both of which change rapidly in their technique. Since 2,000-acre fields may soon be needed for efficient arable farming (p.244), their effect should be known in advance for one such field owned by one farmer may be unimportant, but a multiple of such fields sweeping across the landscape is another matter. At present farmers individually could bring this about, each farming well within his own perimeter of land, yet creating unprecedented changes when taken together.

It is reasonable, in fact essential, as the *Farmers Weekly* pleads, that farmers should be represented in all matters affecting rural land. It is also reasonable that not only should farmers recognise the need for increased leisure facilities in the countryside but planners should prevent the use of agricultural land as a 'vast rustic playground'. Modern food production is an industry and people do not go to play in factories. There should be no public access on food producing land. At the same time much rural land will have to be taken out of agriculture to provide for recreation—this will need close co-operation between farmers and planners. It is unfortunate that as revealed by the *Farmers Weekly*, farmers have found the principles of planning frustrating. This has generally been the case, perhaps inevitably while planning is basically 'the negative role', as suggested in the above quotation taken from the *Architects' Journal*. A more positive plan, regional in extent, three-dimensional in character, co-ordinating food production with other social needs, might have the understanding and support of the farmer. It is not that most farmers are insensitive to the 'ancient charm' of villages, nor to the beauty of the landscape. Some might subscribe to the principles of 'preservation' rather than controlled change, when the heritage has outstanding characteristics worth conserving in its historical state, provided they believed the overall planning concept was positive and had understanding of their needs. It is sad to see farmers labelling planning people with 'ignorance and effrontery'.

In later sections many samples are quoted of conflict between agriculturalists and other sectors of the community when changes in rural land-use have been proposed. In the autumn of 1965 the Thames Conservancy Board outlined a plan to sink 248 boreholes into the chalk and limestone beds beneath the Cotswolds and the Wiltshire and Berkshire downs, thus providing London and the South-east with an extra 270m gallons a day of water in fifteen to twenty years. The use of underground water resources on this scale would be new to Britain and the scheme has much merit since it might cost only a tenth of more conventional reservoir systems, which would also need ten square miles of farmland. Nevertheless the proposals came as a shock to farmers in the areas concerned; there was an outcry that their interests in the underground supplies had not been considered. Though such proposals would have to receive ministerial sanction before acceptance (in fact the Water Resources Board advised a pilot scheme before granting their approval to the plan) it is clear that its effect on agriculture, especially irrigation, had not in the first instance been fully studied. Farmers naturally became hostile to proposals which might be imposed on them without their having been represented during the period of investigation. Similarly during the public inquiry into the proposals to site a third London airport at Stansted in Essex, held in the autumn of 1965, it became clear that the proposals had been reported without consulting either local planners or local agriculturists. The plea made by the *Farmers Weekly* that farmers should be represented on all bodies concerned with rural amenities makes sense, since in practice food production is often not directly assessed as a factor of relevance or of equal importance to other requirements. Similarly, though the planners for the Ipswich expansion plan consulted the Ministry of Agriculture on general land classifications, the Suffolk agricultural and farming community were not consulted, even though 18,000 acres of good land were to be taken for proposed expansion.

The crux of the problem of planning rural land is, of course, the ignorance of the structure of the land itself. As previously discussed, the National Farmers Union has urged a national study of the country's soil (p.246). The Agricultural Research Council has set up, it is true, a Soil Survey Department for England and Wales, which employs twenty-four specialists and has started boring holes at various intervals and depths in order to prepare soil survey maps of one mile to the inch. Though farmers would like field soil maps, the survey on present resources will not be completed, and then not in detail, until 1990. Scotland has its own Soil Survey Department and has mapped already much of its arable land. As Leonard has suggested[3]:

> Much of this country's farm land would respond to better drainage. Detailed soil mapping, combined with permeability tests, already standard practice in Holland, could help make drainage schemes more effective . . . Though most soil survey activity is at present concentrated on lowland soils, upland hill and marginal areas representing one-third of our total agricultural acreage present an interesting field for study . . . Might the best approach to soil survey work come through a highly integrated attack embracing the surveyor, cartographer, the plant food, drainage, arable, grass and livestock specialist all working in concert?

No realistic plan for rural land is possible without detailed knowledge of the soil available, and therefore of the potential fertility for intensive food production. Similarly, as discussed later, there is scant knowledge of the nature and importance of micro-climates and of how rain is held by the ground, run off, evaporated or transpired (pp.266–67). Moreover knowledge of the distribution and acreage of land of different structure and quality is based on the pre-war surveys of Professor Dudley Stamp (p.160). It seems a pity that the Ordnance Survey map revisions now well under way and due for completion by 1980 could not have been integrated with a survey of land structure. A crash programme of investigation and survey classifying the rural land of Britain and covering all aspects of land structure and use, in particular farmland, is essential if rural planning is to have any meaning or relevance to the community. The Ministry of Agriculture began to reclassify farm land in 1965, using inch-to-a-mile maps, showing how physical characteristics impose long term limitations on its use, affecting the range, yield and cost of crops, within five broad groups[7]:

1 Consistently high yields for most crops, including horticulture,

2 minor limitations for a wide range of all crops,

3 soil, relief or climate restricting crop choice, cultivation or yield to average quality,

4 severe limitations due to soil, relief or terrain, mostly under grass or forage crops,

5 adverse conditions and low agricultural value.

Classification maps should be complete by 1970.

The position is made even more serious since the need for a fifty per cent increase in food production in the United Kingdom before the end of the century seems clearly evident (p212.). If existing imports are to be reduced, then this percentage increase is too low. At the same time, the urban area will cover one-sixth of England and Wales and much other land will be required for recreation. Farm land could in fact have become not much more than 20m acres, used intensively for food production in England and Wales, a reduction perhaps of about a quarter from the existing supply of agricultural land (p.158). These changes have got to come about, due to the pressures generated by the world and this country, whether the nature and potential of the soil and the land is understood or not. However if it is not understood, land will be wasted, food will become more expensive and society will be unbalanced by unnecessary social stresses. It is impossible to decide what land to take out of food production for other purposes if there is no plan for food requirements allied to an assessment of agricultural land requirements. The problem, for example, of absorbing fertile Essex land for a new airport, a new town, reservoirs or recreation for Londoners becomes spurious in any inquiry, analysis being based on emotion, not fact.

Food production is, and has been since the 1947 Act, a delicate balance between national direction, mostly in the form of economic sanctions and grants, and the natural forces of a free market, both tempered by equally delicate trade agreements, principally with Commonwealth countries and (for pigmeat) Denmark. The balance is so delicate that the actual effect has been a seesaw—rapid changes between glut and dearth, cheap and dear prices in the shops, heavy and light Government financial support, a satisfied and an angry farming community. Nevertheless, in spite of the seesaw farming output and efficiency has become a national legend for impressive growth compared with most other industries. What is not clear is whether the same kind of freedom for the farmer, that is freedom from direct national control, will be possible for a further increase in output of at least fifty per cent in a land area reduced by twenty-five per cent, requiring a net increase in land productive efficiency of almost 100 per cent, before the year 2000 (p.212). The problem is complex and the price of failure probably hunger, possibly starvation, and certainly a reduction in the standard of living.

As previously discussed, farmers have been granted a special, almost protected, position in the rural planning machinery since the effect of the Scott Report became seated in the national consciousness (p.40). Today however the rate of change in agricultural techniques and control is so rapid and so large in scale that it becomes even more pertinent to examine the nature of agriculture in the planning complex of controls than even Professor Dennison could have realised in 1942, a quarter century ago. Two fundamental issues became relevant during 1965 for the nature of rural planning, both East Anglian in scope, but significant for the country.

East Anglia has always been a rural community, rather set apart from the rest of the country, due to location and the nature of the population. In fact so remote from the tide of the twentieth century has East Anglia remained that, when a national survey of indigenous surnames was planned in 1965, it was natural to choose these counties, especially Norfolk and Suffolk, as still being Mediaeval in social structure generally and unaffected by industrial migration common to most parts of England. The undertones of Mediaeval agricultural society are only just departing, in spite of recent agricultural changes, as recorded by such people as Ewart Evans[4]. Though agriculturally rich during the Mediaeval wool trade, the eighteenth-century crop rotation experiments, and the late nineteenth century agricultural zenith, the depression of the inter-war years reduced the district to neglect and poverty. Post-war urban expansion largely passed the district by in favour of the South and West until, by the mid 1960s, plans to double the population in East Anglia were accepted.

In 1964, Ipswich was designated a growth city, to be doubled in size in fifteen years as part of the plan for the South-east. Planning consultants were appointed to prepare a development plan accommodating this population expansion, with wide terms of reference, not only being required to study the nature of expansion in Ipswich but relating such expansion to the surrounding countryside within a general radius of twelve to fifteen miles. They were empowered to recommend overspill areas for Ipswich for example, in a small market town such as Hadleigh, ten miles beyond the Ipswich boundary and already due for its own expansion. However, with the exception of studying the potential loss of agricultural land normal in all planning schemes, the Government did not direct the consultants to examine the relationship between food production and supply to the growth in population. In spite of all the new towns and expanded cities built since the war, this aspect of planning has been neglected. The terms of reference for the Ipswich plan were wider than previous schemes. Nevertheless it seems probable that the interaction between food production, supply and population will need more serious study in the future, especially when producing plans for new towns or large urban communities (p.115). A doubled population will require more than double the food of the existing inhabitants, and considerably more than double recreational space in the countryside. Food production, processing, distribution and marketing will have to be reorganised. This has profound significance for local rural communities in relation, in this case, to Ipswich. It would be possible

69

to plan agricultural production and trade in relation to the new city to the benefit of urban and rural communities. Leaving the matter unanalysed and unplanned cannot be to gain maximum efficiency in land-use, a factor critical to East Anglia and the nation.

The second issue concerning rural planning in East Anglia during 1965 was the inauguration of the first British beeflot, based on American techniques of intensive beef production. There are important agricultural as well as planning implications in this venture, now abandoned; only the second is discussed here, the agricultural significance being analysed later (p.388). In 1963 Union International Ltd, a giant American meat company with retail outlets in Britain and a big wholesaling business worth some £80m, began to investigate the possibility of intensive beef production in England, setting up a subsidiary, British Beef Ltd, for this purpose. The aim was to establish a beef fattening unit holding 10,000 head of stock, the unit being possibly the experimental forerunner of some half-dozen beeflots of similar scale in different parts of the country. Previous beef units in Britain had seldom held as many as 500 head, most farmers concentrating on small scale production with a few dozen beef cattle. Moreover traditional fattening still concentrated on keeping cattle till eighteen to twenty-four months, whereas more intensive methods, including the beeflot, were aiming to fatten beef to around the age of twelve months. In addition, and more revolutionary in concept, the beeflot would be a real factory farm with all raw materials bought on contract, including calves, grain and straw, and the end products, finished beef and manure, being sold also on contract with a planned throughput of beasts of around 200 head per week, year-in, year-out. To the traditional farmer this concept of factory production is appalling, since it can be run on smaller profit margins. A group of farmers therefore pressed the National Farmers' Union at their annual meeting in January 1964 to get the Government to stop the 'beeflot barons', threatening traditional production methods, but were defeated by 174 votes to 128—a relatively small margin against intensive husbandry methods.

Undeterred by strong feelings against them, British Beef Ltd bought a sixty-two acre farm at Old Newton, near Stowmarket in Suffolk, in February 1964 and began site clearance for the new unit the following month, with the intention of obtaining the first calves in April. Contracts were made with dozens of farmers for that purpose. The requirements for the beeflot, in planning terms, were threefold. The fulcrum of this kind of beef fattening is the mill-and-mix unit in which the feed is prepared, some 15,000 tons of barley a year being required. The mill-mix building was designed to cover an area of 4,800 square feet, which is 200 square feet less than the statutory area requiring town and country planning approval before erection. The scheme was submitted to the local council and permission was granted for its construction in February 1964, no planning approval being required. The following month, the company released details of their proposed beef housing. Each house was to have a centre passageway taking a self-unloading feed trailer, with mangers on each side of it, being sixteen feet wide overall, and flanked again by cattle pens, liberally strawed, each twelve feet wide. Each building was to be forty feet wide and, as revised in April, were to be 450 feet long, covering an area of some 18,000 square feet. There were to be two rows of eight houses, each row set ten feet apart. The buildings were to be erected very cheaply, using pole barn construction and corrugated iron for the walls and roof cladding, with ventilation gaps at the eaves and ridge and open ends. Liberal bedding would be provided to keep the animals warm. The buildings were expected to cost no more than £3 10s a place and the total layout about £10 a place. By May 1964, three-and-a-half sheds were built and 200 calves a week were arriving at the beeflot for fattening.

By May well over 60,000 square feet of building had been completed and the local Rural District Council at Gipping, responsible for Old Newton, claimed that planning permission had only been granted for one permanent building, the mill-mix unit, and demanded that construction cease. The company stated that they were[5]:

willing to co-operate in any reasonable action decided by the planning authority, but, it would be easy for us to pull out the poles and go somewhere else. East Anglia would then lose our business.

Nevertheless their subsequent application for planning permission was deferred until the June meeting of the county council and the company was condemned for completing the fourth building after being told to cease work. In June the county planning committee rejected the application on three basic grounds:

1 Buildings were out of scale and character with the countryside and construction was below normal standard.
2 There was a danger of effluent entering the watercourses.
3 The road system in the area was inadequate for the heavy traffic required for the beeflot.

During the following months the company negotiated amendments to the scheme with the county planning office and agreed to construct the perimeter buildings with concrete frames and asbestos-cement and to plant trees as well to improve appearance. It was also agreed that drainage would be designed to protect the watercourses and, more particularly, a nearby disused railway would be converted into a road so that the country lanes would be avoided. On this basis, the revised plans were approved for a limited period of five years, but the Minister of Housing and Local Government was to have the last

71

word because of the 'national implications' of being 'on such a scale that the Minister should look at it'.

The company appealed against the rejection of the original plan and the limitations on the amended plan, the appeal being heard locally during two days in January 1965 by an inspector from the Ministry of Housing and Local Government. Several issues were raised by the public inquiry of deep concern in rural planning concepts. However British Beef Ltd outlined its position regarding the lack of an application for planning permission for the complete scheme and the nature of the venture itself[6]. With regard to the former, the company agreed that it was a mistake not to have planning consent, but it had believed that the 'polebarns' were permitted development as 'temporary buildings', therefore it had only applied for the permanent mill-mix building, and it had continued to build after the warning from the county planning officer to stop, since calves were being obtained on contract and housing was needed for them. Moreover, it was claimed, the unit, then holding 4,000 beasts, was uneconomic in numbers in relation to overheads. The company called many experts to testify to the value of this kind of husbandry and outline why this particular form had been selected for the venture. Nevertheless, though this evidence gave support to the agricultural principles involved, it was not clear how these opinions clarified the basic problem of the location in the countryside of an agrico-industrial industry with buildings, when complete, covering over 360,000 square feet, and generating considerable traffic in the neighbourhood. The local council opposed the appeal since they found the mass of buildings required unacceptable in a rural area. The River Board objected because there were no drainage facilities and they considered it impossible to prevent pollution of the watercourses, especially since roads and gangways around the buildings already had become quagmires. The county fire officer was concerned that it would be impossible to control a fire since engines could not pass between the buildings. The county planning officer considered the buildings to be substandard, but the solicitor to the County Council believed the amended plan was worthy of approval though the project needed careful consideration. In June 1965, the Minister granted his approval for the amended scheme, provided all buildings were removed and the land reinstated at the end of ten years.

The factory farm at Old Newton will be the first of many during the coming decades. Some, though not all, will be based on very cheap, 'sub-standard' construction. Great care will be required concerning their siting. If rural planning is to have any meaning, then the selection of suitable sites should be a joint issue between industrialist and planner. In fact in the future a company seeking a farm for this kind of development, as British Beef Ltd did during 1963, should not treat the matter in an insular manner, but should be helped and

72

supported by planners seeking a positive development of the country-side both for intensive food production and urban needs. The situation at Old Newton should never have arisen. Due to the lie of the land, the factory was not a serious threat to the landscape, being far less objectionable than many official constructions in rural parts. Nevertheless the siting was not perfect, local opinion had been upset and the planning machinery broke down. If construction can be carried out without planning consent by companies of international standing, can be continued after being told to stop and can gain retrospective permission for factories covering more than a third of a million square feet without legal prosecution, then any attempt at rural planning will fail. It seems ludicrous that the law can be broken almost with impunity in planning matters. Though tree screening was later agreed in the amended scheme, this seems ludicrous for tem-porary buildings with a ten-year life. Moreover, since the mill-mix unit was granted permanent permission, this building would have been in a peculiar position in 1975 when the land around had to be re-instated as a field. The matter seems to reveal considerable confusion in official concepts of rural planning. Even so, since the planning requirements were not implemented by June 1966, the beeflot was closed by an enforcement order. By 1967 the project was abandoned, perhaps partly due to planning problems, but perhaps also to manage-ment difficulties.

The water supply for the beeflot also caused contention, making the planning of national resources even more ridiculous in practice. Permission was granted to British Beef Ltd at an early stage to draw 5,000 gallons a day from the mains for the livestock, but friction grew between the company and the rural district council and by the end of 1964 another public enquiry was pending concerning a proposed borehole. In February 1965, the rural district council decided not to prevent the company drawing 12,000 gallons a day, even though this was more than double the amount allowed. However they decided not to make a new connection, as requested by the company, increas-ing the supply to 25,000 gallons a day until, as previously agreed, a storage tank for one day's supply had been constructed at the factory. Meanwhile, an application to sink a borehole to extract 100,000 gallons a day, necessary for the complete unit had been refused. The appeal was held before an inspector from the Ministry of Housing in May 1965. The company had not ascertained whether a borehole would be permitted before embarking on the project since it had not been considered there would be any trouble, but a 400 foot borehole drawing water from the Gipping Valley would be required. The appeal was opposed by the local and county councils as well as the Ipswich Corporation. East Anglia is notoriously short of water and a geologist believed no further extraction should be allowed from the Gipping catchment area since the resources were already over-

73

c

strained and were inadequate for the growth in population, therefore jeopardising development. If water levels fell any further there was a risk that sea water could penetrate into the strata, thus ruining supplies. In July 1965, the Minister of Housing over-ruled the local council and ordered a new mains connection giving 25,000 gallons a day to the company. In September 1965, following the appeal, the Minister granted the right to sink a borehole drawing 100,000 gallons a day which is equal to about one per cent of the total already being drawn from the Gipping Chalk for all other purposes in a district where water shortages are not unknown.

It is peculiar that at a time when there was a Ministry of Land and Natural Resources, matters concerning the location of industry in the countryside, potential pollution of watercourses, possible over-crowding of rural lanes due to industrial traffic and the problem of water supplies—and modern intensive agriculture is an industry—were taken to appeal to the Minister of Housing and Local Government. These are national planning matters, basically of land-use, which are surely a matter for a Ministry of Land and Natural Resources. The fragmentation of authority remains in 1967, bedevilling any concept of national rural planning. It is true that the Countryside Commission, incorporating the former National Parks Commission, with 'a new function of encouraging the provision of opportunities for the enjoyment of the countryside generally' is one implementation of a long-standing basic need for improved land-use, provided it includes agriculturalists and planners capable of working on a regional basis. Similarly the creation of small rural parks adjacent to urban areas will facilitate other recreational enjoyment. In 1967 several important, though separate, strides were made towards better rural planning. The Agriculture Act of that year established Rural Development Boards (limited to the uplands) to help farm amalgamation and co-operation, improve communications and public services, and improve facilities offered to tourists by farmers and forestry workers. Regional Boards of this nature are required throughout the country. Secondly, the East Anglia Economic Planning Council began to prepare a comprehensive study of its region, including the collection of factual information (much of which is uncollated) and the outlining of a strategy for development, including population and industrial relationship in expansion, the viability of small towns, and whether villages should absorb com-mutors. Again, all regions need such studies. Thirdly, the Severnside Study started to examine the physical and economic potential of the area so that new cities would be located not where land was easily available, but where they would make a real contribution to both economic growth and the environment. Fourthly, an amateur group, the Chiltern Society, started an £800 survey to establish population trends and their demands on land and services in their district.

74

Fifthly, Norfolk County Council set up a tree nursery costing £1,000 a year to aid the county, and at the same time pressed for legislation to protect hedgerow trees, limit felling and enforce replanting. Nevertheless such proposals, though valuable as contributing to part of the problem of land-use, are as yet only nibbling at the magnitude of the problem in which a completely new concept of land-use and rural planning must be created. Such concepts can only be realistic and creative if they are backed by detailed research, trained specialists, fully co-ordinated plans and centralised authority under one ministry, responsible for all matters concerning land-use and planning. In 1967 in spite of some important strides forward in legislation, in attitudes and practice towards planned land-use, the real basis for a solution, the need for new concepts, is as urgent and distant as in 1947. If a new approach to the problem is not created, and soon, any hope of a satisfactory countryside by 2000, in fact even in the near future, must be abandoned for ever.

REFERENCES

1 'Green and pleasant—and . . . what?' *Architects' Journal*, 12 December 1962, p35
2 'Whose countryside?' *Farmers Weekly*, 19 November 1965, p35
3 Leonard, D., 'The truth about our soil'. *Farmers Weekly*, 19 March 1965, p4
4 Evans, E., *Ask the fellows who cut the hay*. 1965, Faber & Faber
5 Report. *Farmers Weekly*, 1 May 1966
6 Report. *East Anglian Daily Times*, 28,29 January 1965
7 Study Group on Agricultural Land Classification Reports. 1965, 1967, Ministry of Agriculture

2 POPULATION GROWTH AND FOOD CONSUMPTION

Introduction

The purpose of agriculture is to provide food for the world's population. When considering changes occurring in the English landscape, or in the structure of rural planning in Britain, or even in the development of British farming, it is pointless studying them in isolation. The change that is occurring (and visual change is taking place apparent to the most superficial observer) or such change that is about to occur, or that should occur, has validity only in relation to the population of the world and its food requirements. It is deceptively easy to view the landscape as something divorced from the basic need to feed people, or to consider British agriculture as something separate from the needs of foreign races. Considering the rolling downlands, the elm-bordered Midland fields, the black plain of the Fens or the craggy moors and dales of the North and West; considering this scenic and pastoral inheritance granted from the past with its texture of historic events; considering these things in isolation from the reality of the modern world with its interlocking problems is national suicide. Moreover, considering either the landscape or modern farming as something separate from the needs of the urban population, or trying to preserve the countryside in either its present agricultural form or even purely as farmland owned by farmers, is folly. It is essential to consider the planning of rural Britain and the use of agricultural land against the background of the tremendous, even frightening, changes now taking place in the population not only of Britain but the world.

In the second half of this century unprecedented changes are rapidly occurring throughout the world in relation to population, food requirements and the world food trade. These changes have, during the last two or three years, radically altered the relationship between British agriculture and the needs of the nation. The basic premises in fact on which farming has been tolerated by a largely urban population during the first half of this century have crumbled. The implications are profound, both for land-use in Britain and the appearance of the landscape, and they will also have tremendous significance for many social problems. Underlying any consideration of land-use must be cognisance of the world population explosion. Unless there is a dramatic change in man's endeavour and his desire to co-operate, the earth will be unable to support the increase of human life forecast for the end of the century. It is predicted that the hunger of many will turn to famine in another decade. Nevertheless though one third of the world suffers from malnutrition, another third prospers and becomes affluent. The rash of prosperity (albeit often founded on faulty economics) has created demands for protein foods in the world markets which have shaken the foundations of international trade.

The protein shortage, even famine, of the 1960s has changed the basis of British agriculture. The traditional concept, which was the outcome of the first industrial revolution, emphasised that Britain was an industrial giant dependent on imported food from abroad, especially the Commonwealth, so that others could afford to buy her industrial goods. In the wake of this image the countryside of Britain became impoverished and depressed by neglect until the aftermath of the Second World War injected some of the nation's industrial wealth back into the land. The rapid strides to revitalise and reequip British agriculture, made in the two decades since the war, may prove to have been just in time to save the rapidly expanding national population from hunger when food available for importation declines.

Though world food production unfortunately increases slower than population, the growth of British agricultural productivity forming a second era of agricultural prosperity has more than matched the increase of the United Kingdom population. In spite of increased population and consumption of food per person, a smaller percentage of food to overall requirements is imported than before the war. The indication is that productivity can increase still further to feed the additional millions forecast for the British population, perhaps even allowing overall food importation to decline. In recent years exports not only of agricultural goods but food itself have become a sizeable and important part of British industrial wealth. Agriculture in fact, the Cinderella of the inter-war years, has become the largest single British industry. Nevertheless the growing urban population of Britain, with its increased wealth, mobility and recreation, is straining the land resources of the country, so that agriculture seems near to being over-run by the industrial hordes. Land is Britain's most important asset; each acre is precious to her livelihood. The interplay between urban needs and food production must be the crux of all future rural planning.

The various parts of this section examine the facts of present and future population growth and food requirements, not only for Britain but the inter-relation of growth and need between the world and

Britain. The problems of population, diet and land-use cannot be considered for one country in isolation from the rest of the world. It is evident from this section that although many statistics are available much still needs to be known. Changes today are so rapid that appalling consequences can arise before change is apparent.

2b World population and food trends

The present agricultural-industrial revolution must be considered in relation to world food resources. Though increased food production is vital the principal issue governing our survival is the successful control of power-politics concerned with the atomic bomb. The wrongful use of atomic power is terrible to contemplate; almost as frightening is this century's population explosion. The unparalleled growth of population at the present time could lead to a world famine in another decade. It will be difficult, if not impossible, to prevent the use of the atomic bomb as hunger leads to uncontrolled fear and envy.

For mankind (having witnessed the devastation of nuclear explosion and radiation) the writing is indeed on the wall. A hungry world is gripped by an increase in population greater than its apparent capacity to improve food production. In the autumn of 1964 warning was given that if disaster is to be avoided food production must be man's primary aim, based on co-operation between nations and coupled to a campaign for birth control[1]. Contemplation of the existing situation makes optimism a doubtful virtue.

The sudden upsurge in the growth of population is startling. It took perhaps a quarter of a million years for the world population to reach about 1,000m by the end of the last century. From 1900 to 1950 the population expanded by about fifty per cent. By the end of 1964 the population had more than doubled since 1950; it was then estimated that there were 3,283m people in the world. By 1980 it is predicted that there will be well over 4,000m people to feed, and by the end of the century at least 6,000m. According to the United States Population Reference Bureau, with nearly 150m births a year and some 85m deaths, the population was expanding at nearly two per cent, or 65m people, a year. If the trend continues the population could be even 7,000m by the year 2000. Every week increases the world population by well over a million people, most of this increase occurring in areas where the standard of living is the lowest. In the summer of 1964, the Director-General of the United Nations Food and Agricultural Organisation gave this warning[2]:

Whatever measures may be initiated today to control births, the rate of population growth is not likely to show any significant change for several decades. In the developing societies today, children under 15

78

years of age tend to constitute between 37 and 42 per cent of the total population. While that group is passing through the child-producing ages, natural increase will continue to be high even if the family size is falling. Moreover, falling mortality itself will also tend to increase the proportion of young people, since reductions in death rates will occur mainly among infants and children.

Demographic experts believe that under no circumstances will the rate of growth of world population fall below 1·7 per cent a year during the next 30 or 40 years, and the probabilities are that it will be exceeded. At any rate by the end of the century world population would be at least double itself, and we must keep this in view in formulating any realistic programme for international action in the field of economic and social development.

Secondly, 10 to 15 per cent of the world population, that is 300 to 450 million people, actually go hungry at the present time, and from one-third to one-half of mankind suffer from either under-nutrition or malnutrition, or both. If the balance between population and food supply is not rapidly improved in favour of food supply, the number of under-nourished and mal-nourished people will be at least doubled by the end of the century, that is roughly 3,000 million. FAOS *Third World Food Survey*, 1963 has analysed the quantitative and qualitative improvements necessary to provide a minimum adequate diet for the world population, and has estimated that food supplies will have to be doubled by 1980 and trebled by the turn of the century in order to provide a level of nutrition reasonably adequate to the needs of the world's peoples. Whatever may be done to control population, the need to increase food production remains a central issue.

Neither the population increase nor the level of nutrition is evenly balanced on the different continents. Though the overall population may be double by the year 2000, a regional breakdown shows that[3]:

Populations of Europe, North America, Oceania and the River Plate countries of Latin America (Argentina, Uruguay and Paraguay) are expected to increase moderately, reaching 150 per cent over the present number. This group of countries, however, already enjoys adequate levels of nutrition. But in the undernourished countries of the Far East, the Near East, Africa, and the rest of Latin America the population is expected to double in Africa, to treble in Latin America, and to increase by 250 per cent in both the Near East and the Far East. This implies that, even without any improvement in the present level of nutrition, food supplies would have to be increased by 100 per cent for Africa, 200 per cent for Latin America (excluding the River Plate countries) and 150 per cent for the Far East and the Near East by the year 2000.

The United Nations *Statistical Yearbook* for 1964 estimated a world population of 3,160m in mid-1963, with over half this number (excluding the Soviet Union) living in Asia. Only about fourteen per cent lived in Europe and the Americas, and in Oceania no more than just over one-half per cent.

CHART 3: TOP NATIONAL POPULATIONS ESTIMATED IN 1963

Mainland China	:	647m (based on 1957 figures)
India	:	460m
Soviet Union	:	225m
United States	:	189m
Indonesia	:	100m
Pakistan	:	99m
Japan	:	96m

N.B. Another five countries had more than 50m people—Brazil, Nigeria, the Federal Republic of Germany, the United Kingdom and Italy. The average rate of population increase is 1·8 per cent a year. Latin America is expanding its population at 2·6 per cent a year and Africa at 2·3 per cent a year, whereas Europe is expanding at only 0·9 per cent a year. Nevertheless, Europe (with eighty-nine persons per square kilometer—228 per square mile) is the most densely populated, almost four times the world average of twenty-three persons per square kilometre.

In the countries with adequate nutrition—Europe, North America, Oceania and the River Plate—the average person gets 3,050 calories daily, with only fifty-seven per cent in the form of cereals, starchy roots and sugar. In these regions of some 900m people, supplies of calories exceed requirements by about twenty per cent. However in other regions of some 2,300m people, the average person gets only 2,150 calories daily (of which seventy-eight per cent is derived from cereals, starchy roots and sugar) and supplies fall short of requirements by eleven per cent. An appreciable part of the population of the low-calorie regions goes hungry. Without any improvement in nutrition levels—to meet the increase in population—food supplies in these regions must be increased by 150 per cent or by 120 per cent in the world as a whole by 1980.

To achieve a reasonable standard of nutrition, food supplies must be increased as follows above the supplies available today[3]:

	Percentage increase required	
	by AD 1980	by AD 2000
Cereals	45	110
Pulses	95	200
Animal products	85	190

Supplies must therefore be doubled by 1980, and trebled by the end of the century.

Dr Ewell has predicted 'the most colossal catastrophe in history', with a world famine striking hundreds of millions of people in 1980. Famine would reach 'serious proportions in India, Pakistan and

China by the early 1970s, followed by Indonesia, Iran, Turkey, Egypt and several other countries within a few years—and then followed by most of the other countries of Asia, Africa and Latin America by 1980'. Birth control, though essential, cannot take effect in time to prevent famine. Dr Ewell believed that total disaster might be averted by a crash programme in which America and Europe gave some £2,000m of fertilizer or fertilizer plant, increasing food crops in the undernourished areas by fifty to 100 per cent[1]. For example it is expected that Asia will require 27m metric tons of fertilizer by 1980; today about 3m tons are used[9]. World agriculture, using 30m tons of fertilizer in 1965, will use 113m tons by 1980.

Increased population intensifies problems of health. The World Health Organisation was convened to examine environmental health aspects of metropolitan planning[4]. It has been estimated that although population increased by fifty per cent between 1900 and 1950 inhabitants of towns of more than 5,000 people increased by 230 per cent. Statistics indicate that by 1960 a quarter of the world population, then just over 3,000m, lived in urban areas with more than 20,000 inhabitants. Similarly it is predicted that by the year 2000 only a tenth of the world's population of some 600m will be engaged in agriculture. These people must feed the urban populations of over 5,400m. In the growing tropical and sub-tropical cities of the world there is a greater risk of disaster than in the European cities of the nineteenth-century industrial revolution. Over-crowding, with poor sanitation, nutrition and wages is already causing the pattern of disease to change for the worse, particularly when air pollution is an added hazard to health.

The situation in the world today is grim. *The Times* has warned of the approaching 'crisis which everybody knows is coming, like death, and which everybody promptly forgets in the pursuit of life . . . There is nothing mysterious in it. Man is in nature, stretch her as he may. A greenfly outbreak provides a close parallel. Once the greenfly escape from the checks imposed by natural predators the multiplication proceeds in geometrical proportion. If something does not stop it, they would in a relatively few years outweigh the earth. Something always does. So too with man. The question is: will the check be imposed by man on himself, humanely, or by man on himself inhumanely—he can turn the bomb against humanity as he turns insecticide against greenfly—or by Nature most terribly and revengefully ?'[5]

Not all experts foresee disaster as the outcome of the population explosion. Professor Dudley Stamp has claimed that if the world's resources were studied as they should be, then there should be plenty available for all, since the situation was a challenge to man not to let environment be his master[6]. Professor Ritchie Calder, too, has indicated that it should be possible to expand food production catering for the increase in population[7]. Seven-tenths of the world's surface is water and intensive fish farming provides scope for producing considerable quantities of food. Though another fifth is desert, mountain or largely inaccessible forest, a twelfth is arable or pastoral. Nearly half of this cultivable land is, however, subject to erosion. It is probable that soil chemists, plant breeders and agriculturalists will extend the climatic frontiers of cultivation and will redeem deficient soils: but 'water, already in short supply in many areas, may become a more critical factor than the availability of land'. With planning irrigation, coupled with boreholes to the many vast underground lakes or seas, could help redeem much barren land. Calder believes that 'it should be possible to feed our fellow humans, but it demands a new sense of values and a new direction of our scientific resources'.

In spite of the excellent work of the United Nations Food and Agriculture Organisation with its World Food Organisation, the more liberal trade policies of the late President Kennedy, and the National Farmers Union's Farm and Food Plan, which, as one of its aims, desires co-operation to achieve 'a world food policy designed to utilise surplus production for the benefit of the under-developed countries', prospects remain grim. Co-operation has not yet been sufficient to improve the situation. At the end of 1964 the Food and Agriculture Organisation reported[8]:

> There was only a small increase in agricultural production in the 1963–4 season. FAOs preliminary estimates indicate a rise of between 1 and 2 per cent in the world, excluding mainland China. It is probable therefore that the increase in production was slightly less than the growth of population, which is now estimated at about 2 per cent annually. Much more significant, however, than this comparison for a single year is that for five years now there has been no increase in world agricultural production per caput.

Again in 1965, for the third successive year world agricultural production increased by about 1·5 per cent, with a record output in Western Europe, while world population rose by about two per cent. The following year, due to drought, was more serious. In 1966 world population rose by 70m while food output was static. Food production per caput fell by about two per cent[10].

The *Farmers Weekly* has observed that international trade restrictions are detrimental in helping under-developed countries[9]:

> World food production, only just keeping pace with the rapid increase in population, still seems to face too many barriers to higher output and trade. These tariffs and other controls, with rapid changes in demand in some countries, are distorting the pattern of output and requirements of food to an exceptional extent.

It is well known that America has been a major wheat producing country for years with production exceeding consumption (though part of the stockpile of grain is now being released to the hungry world). Moreover, contrary to the wishes of the National Farmer's Union today—as emphasised by the *Farmers Weekly*—'to some extent, the distortions in world trade in foodstuffs are due to go-it-alone farm policies in many countries'. Under existing trade barriers, it is impossible to plan economically and internationally for the maximum rate of food production. In the spring of 1967 Britain gave cautious support to an American food aid plan to release 10m tons of cereals a year. Britain's five per cent share would cost about £10m at current prices.

The pattern of world exports in food bears no relation to the needs of the world. Trade in some protein foods has declined during the last few years, in spite of the urgent need for a more balanced diet by half the population. Egg production, for example, though increasing substantially in North America and Europe, declined as an export from over 539,000 metric tons in 1960 to only 372,000 metric tons in 1963. Butter, cheese and meat exports have increased slowly compared with the need. Grain exports, however, tend to fluctuate with demand. To some extent, the changes in trade reflect changes in the pattern of consumption in the more efficient food producing countries. Though most European countries have increased farm output per caput, a rise in the standard of living has stabilised the demand for starch and cereal foods but allowed a substantial rise in protein consumption. This has helped to restrict protein exports. In fact today there is a serious shortage of protein supplies for all countries (discussed later, p90).

CHART 4: WORLD EXPORTS OF SELECTED FOODSTUFFS[10]:

	000 long tons	2,240 lb		
	1960	1961	1962	1966
Wheat	33,594	40,541	36,695	50,557
Maize	11,844	13,768	18,440	22,098
Barley	5,352	7,331	6,600	5,723
Rice	6,804	6,006	5,164	5,088
Meat (carcass)	2,034	2,106	2,503	2,640
Cheese	470	500	525	—
Butter	591	641	605	—
Eggs	540	533	475	277
Sugar	17,279	20,385	18,930	19,268

In June 1966, seventy-one nations attended a conference on land reform. Once again, many pleas were made that an agricultural

83

revolution with international co-operation was needed to raise food production. To this end a World Food Congress is to be held in 1968, an indicative world plan for agricultural development is now being prepared to cover the period up to 1985. International co-operation is vital to:

1 Create freer trade movements in food, 2 allow surplus production to be used in under-developed countries, 3 increase food production whenever it is economic to do so, 4 help under-developed countries start or expand their agricultural policies, 5 fertilize, irrigate, and cultivate all fertile land in relation to its potential, 6 feed the teeming millions of the hungry and undernourished.

Any consideration of the rural or agricultural policies for Britain must be under the shadow of the population explosion in a hungry world. No food policy can be meaningful except in the context of impendent world famine.

REFERENCES

1 Ewell, Dr R. Chicago Conference of the American Chemical Society, 1 September 1964
2 Sen, B. R. Letter to *The Times*, 7 July 1964
3 Food and Agriculture Organisation of the United Nations. *Six Billions to Feed*. World Food Problems no 4. 1964, the Organisation
4 World Health Organisation. Geneva Conference, 20 July 1964
5 Leader, *The Times*, 2 September 1964
6 Stamp, Professor D. L. Twentieth International Geographical Congress. 21 July 1964
7 Calder, Professor R. Summer Conference of the Agricultural Economics Society. 1964
8 Food and Agriculture Organisation of the United Nations. *State of Food and Agriculture*. 1964, the Organisation
9 'World Food: Too Many Barriers'. *Farmers Weekly*, 11 September 1964
10 Food and Agriculture Organisation of the United Nations, *State of Food and Agriculture*. 1966, the Organisation
11 'Commonwealth Economic Committee and FAO data'. *Farmers Weekly*, 11 September 1964

2c Population of the United Kingdom

The population of Western Europe, particularly in industrial countries, expanded rapidly during the nineteenth century. The population increase today is relatively slow compared with many other parts of the world. It has however become apparent recently that the population of Western Europe is expanding faster than it was believed to be a few years ago. This is particularly true in the United Kingdom.

In England and Wales, the population rose by 250 per cent during the industrial expansion of the nineteenth century. The increase was

84

less rapid in the first decades of the twentieth, and in the mid-1940s it was thought that during the rest of the century the population would decline. It was later assumed however that there would be a moderate expansion and the population would stabilise around 52m, which would give an expansion of sixty per cent during the twentieth century. Much post-war planning was based on this assumption. By 1960 planning estimates had to be revised, since the population increase had risen to about 300,000 a year, indicating that there might be some 58m in England and Wales by the year 2000. But in the early 1960s, the population began to increase rapidly, and in 1962 the Registrar-General warned that the increase would average 400,000 a year, giving an increase of 17m, (or thirty-seven per cent) between 1962 and 2002. The statistical returns showed the following actual and predicted populations[1]:

CHART 5: POPULATION OF ENGLAND AND WALES

Year	1800	1901	1931	1951	1962	1982	2002
Millions	9·2	32·5	40·0	43·7	46·8	54·2	63·8

Live births rose from 0·67m in 1955 to 0·88m in 1966, and are projected to rise to 1·32m in 2000, doubling in forty-five years. There will be 4½m more children born in England and Wales between 1964 and 1980 than were expected in 1955. It now appears probable that the population of England and Wales will increase at a rate of nearly 0·8 per cent a year against the previous estimate of 0·65 per cent. This has profound significance in relation to town and country planning; the Registrar-General said of the new estimate that it 'is clearly of great importance to those concerned with the large number of plans completed or in process over the past few years'. In fact with an estimate of 54m in 1980, and 65m soon after the turn of the century, planners have had to give serious thought to the implications of this increase. For housing the population increase alone a city the size of Reading will have to be built every four months between now and the end of the century (p113). The *Annual Abstract of Statistics* for 1966 showed that the United Kingdom's total population of 54,436,000 should rise to 74,575,000, by the year 2000—that is by more than thirty-five per cent.

At the end of June, 1966, the population of England and Wales was 48,100,000, with about 1¼m more women than men. In the last two years migration from other countries, including the rest of the United Kingdom, decreased in comparison with 1961. Moreover the *Statistical Review* for England and Wales for 1965 recorded the first birth rate fall for a decade—a drop of 13,000 over 1964. A further drop in 1966 with only 17·7 births per 1,000 people against 18·5 in 1964 has given rise to hope that the worst forecasts of population expansion will not be fulfilled. Immigration has been restricted by the Act of 1965, but this will not materially affect the present growth trends. Nevertheless it is estimated that immigration during the last decade has contributed about a million people to the coloured population of Britain. The population of Wales is relatively small, having risen from 0·5m in 1800 to 2·6m in 1931. Today the population is only slightly over 2·6m. The population of England alone is therefore about 45½m. Scotland, which has its own problems of declining densities (except for the conurbations around Glasgow and Edinburgh) had a population in mid-1964 of 5,206,400. This was a small increase of 27,000 above the 1961 census. Northern Ireland had, in 1963, a population of 1,446,000 which, like Scotland, shows a small increase since the war. The total population of the United Kingdom is just over 54½m, and the British Isles, including the Channel Islands, Isle of Man and Eire, about 57m.

The increase is, as already indicated, a problem primarily in England, particularly in the South-east and the Midlands. The population drift, as it has been termed, will be considered later, with its implications as a planning problem for rural England and agriculture. A regional analysis of increases in resident population between 1961 and mid-1964 is given in Chart 6[2].

CHART 6: REGIONAL POPULATION CHANGES 1961–64

Region (*less conurbations)	% Increase 1961–64	Population millions	Con- urbation	% Increase 1961–64	Popula- tion millions
Southern	6·3	2·97			
Eastern	5·8	3·90			
Midlands*	5·2	4·89	w Midlands	2·1	2·39
London & se*	5·1	11·19	London	0·3	8·17
South-western	3·5	3·49			
North-midland	3·4	3·73	Merseyside	0·5	1·39
North-western*	3·3	6·66	se Lancs	1·3	2·45
Northern*	2·4	3·29	Tyneside	0·1	0·86
e & w Riding*	2·3	4·23	West Yorks	1·4	1·72
Wales	1·7	2·66			

Many planners advocate that planning should be based on a regional analysis of problems and requirements rather than traditional county and urban divisions. After the Second World War regional plans for London and the West-midland conurbations were prepared by Abercrombie. Unfortunately politicians failed to recognise that planning should be based on regions with mutual and inter-related development, including industry, transport and population; planning largely

86

continued on what were basically medieval boundaries, rather than ones which grew out of the industrial revolution. It is only recently that there has at last been national recognition of the need for regional planning, and it is still not clear how this will affect the future of Britain.

Accommodating an additional 20m people, which by present trends will be mainly in the South-east, creates planning problems of great complexity. In addition there is the problem created by slum clearance. It has been estimated that there are some 3m houses due for immediate demolition, perhaps at the rate of 200,000 a year for fifteen years, plus others decaying in this period as well as those demolished for other reasons, such as the construction of motorways[3]. In fact a total of 12m new dwellings will be needed before the end of the century to provide for the increased population and to replace all but the best pre-1881 dwellings[6]. Rigby Childs has advocated the preparation of a national plan for housing 20m more people, based on a five-year programme of regional studies, so that population movements may be brought about by government encouragement rather than direction or unco-ordinated planning of urban drift. He has suggested, as shown in chart 7, possible population increases in each region of the United Kingdom[4].

CHART 7: POSSIBLE ALLOCATION OF 20M EXTRA PEOPLE IN UK BY AD 2000

Scotland:	Highlands	0·22m
	Lowlands	3·76m
	Borders	0·10m
England:	North-west	2·30m
	North-east	1·60m
	South-east	3·36m
	South-west	2·04m
	East Anglia	1·44m
	Midlands	1·80m
Wales:	Total	1·44m
Emigration:	Total	2·00m

It is essential that the present concentration of population round London should be to some extent dispersed and the extra population of 20m attracted to new or revitalised industrial regions (p143). Population location is related to problems of economic productivity as well as social attraction, including housing, services and education. Regional planning councils beginning to study the factors governing regional population trends need detailed statistics for analysis. In 1965 the *Abstract of Regional Statistics* showed that Wales had surprisingly the highest productivity, due partly to the concentration of a few large modern factories in South Wales. With only five per cent of the United Kingdom's population Wales has an industrial output of four per cent. This, with its fuel utilisation efficiency, reflects satisfactory results for government industrial promotion in the region. Similar success may await industrial redeployment in the North-east. More significant perhaps for regional population growth will be the North Sea gas field. If a new major city was promoted in the region between the Humber and the Wash it could act as a vital growth centre, giving greater geographic balance to the population (p114). Perhaps however it is Northern Ireland, with the industrial and agricultural revolution dawning in Eire, which offers a major challenge for regional growth. With only 2·7 per cent of the United Kingdom's population, Northern Ireland's industrial output has by far the lowest regional productivity, producing only 1·5 per cent of total output. It has moreover, potentially suitable space for development with many resources as yet untapped.

The forecasted population increases of more than $\frac{1}{3}$m a year will have profound social and visual consequences. Unless there is urgent reappraisal of rural planning and the importance of agriculture in the national economy, there will be serious repercussions leading to bitterness and discontent between different sections of the population. It is impossible to consider the development of modern food production divorced from the vast population pressures on the use of land, especially agricultural land, food requirements and production.

REFERENCES

1 *Registrar-General's Statistical Review of England and Wales for 1961.* HMSO
2 Ibid 1964
3 Anderson, S., *Buildings in the Sixties—Housing.* 1962, Penguin
4 Childs, D. R., *The Times.* 20 October 1964
5 Report. *The Times.* 19 September 1962
6 Stone, Dr P. A. Report. 1966, National Institute of Economic and Social Research

2d Food trends in the United Kingdom

During the rest of this century existing trends in food consumption in the United Kingdom will be subjected to internal and external pressures. The significance of these pressures is becoming rapidly apparent.

Internal pressures will generate a dramatic rise in the overall level of food consumption. This will be in terms of quantity and quality. Increased home consumption has however to be considered against the problem of the growing external pressures on international food resources. As previously discussed, the world population explosion, with its growing demand for improved nutrition, is generating a demand for food greater than the present capacity of increasing production. With the pressure of demand greater than resources, world food prices are rising, and will continue to rise, dramatically during the next decades at a time when Britain's capacity of paying for imports is declining. It is becoming increasingly evident that Britain must restrict her overall level of imports in relation to her shrinking share of international trade. It will become difficult to maintain food imports even at present levels; and impossible, within a sensible national budget, to increase these levels to satisfy either the extra population forecasted for Britain or the natural rise in individual consumption due to improved standards of living. It would be dangerous to believe that the need for more food in Britain before the end of the century can be satisfied by imports drawn from international markets of spiralling competitiveness. It is essential to accept the fact that there must be rapid expansion in home food production.

The pressures on food requirements (and therefore on land-use) in Britain arise from several inter-related factors. Population growth and a reduction of agricultural land areas to urban expansion, albeit mitigated to some extent by increased agricultural productivity obviously create pressures unless imports are raised. In addition, two important trends in food consumption are common to all countries with a rising standard of living. Firstly, consumption of starch declines, while protein substantially increases, and, secondly, expenditure on food per head increases, even though the proportion in total expenditure decreases.

Population growth has been discussed in the previous section. Thus population, at present expanding at nearly 0·8 per cent a year, is expected to increase overall by thirty-seven per cent between 1965 and the end of the century. On this basis alone, food consumption will be expected to increase by thirty-seven per cent above present levels. Consumption rates however vary not only in relation to income but also to age and sex. For reasons discussed below, food requirements will increase at a rate faster than the growth in population.

It seems probable that the age structure of the population by the year 2000 will indicate higher food consumption rates per head than at present. The Registrar-General forecast in 1967 the following population growth:

	1965	2000
Children to 15 years	12·7m	21·1m
Adults	33·7m	43·5
Old people:	8·2m	10·0m
males over 65		
females over 60		

Children up to the age of fourteen have generally an overall consumption rate of about 0·7 of a male adult, though their milk requirements are considerably greater. Consumption rises slightly during the teens, being around 0·8 of the male adult's overall needs. During the teens male children will eat more fats, cereal and potatoes than an adult. The heaviest demands for protein, especially from meat, cheese and eggs, are for males between the ages of fifteen and sixty-four; females of similar age need only 0·75 of the male consumption. Females on average eat as much as males, though proportionally more fruit and vegetables rather than protein and fat. It is only after the age of sixty-five, that consumption begins to wane, generally reduced to 0·8 of adult requirements[1]. It is difficult to relate these factors precisely to national requirements for food by the end of the century. It is nevertheless clear that average food consumption will increase, because there will be larger numbers of adults and adolescents in proportion to the present population.

The birth rate increase during, and immediately after, the Second World War will be reflected in a high age-group of people from fifty to sixty-five, when food requirements are only just beginning to wane. Similarly though people will be living to a greater age than at present the lower birth rate of the 1930s will mean a correspondingly smaller proportion of people over sixty-five. This situation will be exaggerated by the casualties during the war, which eliminated many who would have been in their seventies and eighties by the end of the century. The sharp rise in population between 1950 and 1965 will mean a large group within the thirty-five to fifty age bracket, who in turn should have children well into their teens. The age structure of the population will therefore include a greater proportion of people at their peak for food requirements than in 1965. This factor, coupled with the forecasted thirty-seven per cent increase in population, suggests that overall food requirements by 2000 might be forty-two-to-forty-five per cent more than the present level. Even this increase will be exaggerated by the rise in the standard of living.

It is well known that standards of nutrition have improved substantially since before the war, when in fact about half the population was undernourished[2]. Surprisingly, as the National Food Survey shows, the average energy value of food has only risen by five per cent from pre-war levels to 1963[3]. In fact before the war the average calorie consumption for each person was 3,050 a day. By 1963 it was only 3,200 a day. Of greater significance for national health has been the dramatic improvement in the nutritional, rather than the energy, value of the food consumed. Consumption of animal protein and fat increased by twenty per cent and nine per cent respectively. Moreover the intake of minerals and vitamins A and B has increased by at least twenty per cent. Calcium in particular has been increased by sixty per cent over pre-war consumption. In contrast there have been relatively small increases in the consumption of carbohydrates and vitamin C, and a slight drop in vegetable protein. Meat, liquid milk and eggs therefore all play a larger part in the nation's diet, while bread consumption has become less essential. The changes in food consumption are shown in Chart 8.

CHART 8: FOOD CONSUMPTION IN THE UNITED KINGDOM[4]:
(LB PER HEAD PER ANNUM)

	av pre-war	1946	1963	% over pre-war
flour	194·5	221·2	162·7	− 16
sugar (included in food & brewing)	100·6	79·5	112·6	12
fresh and frozen meat	90·7	70·8	98·5	9
bacon & ham	28·1	15·1	25·2	− 10
poultry	5·1	4·0	14·9	192
fish, fresh, frozen & cured	21·8	26·3	16·8	— 26
liquid milk	217·1	309·4	325·9	50
cheese	8·8	10·0	10·3	17
shell eggs	25·9	18·0	31·1	20
butter	24·7	11·0	19·3	− 21
margarine	0·7	15·1	13·5	55
dried & fresh fruit	86·5	60·0	77·9	− 10
canned & bottled fruit	10·3	2·4	18·4	79
potatoes	190·0	281·2	227·6	20
fresh vegetables & tomatoes	115·3	130·7	99·6	− 14

The most dramatic increase of any single food product has been in the consumption of poultry, now nearly three times its pre-war rate. This has been largely due to the mass produced broiler, which has reduced the cost of poultry so that it is no longer a luxury food. Similarly egg consumption has increased by a fifth, due partly to modern battery and deep litter systems. Liquid milk consumption has increased by a half, and by 1963 had achieved an average of five pints per person per week. Meat consumption, which is discussed in more detail later (p101), has increased by less than a tenth above pre-war levels, with bacon and ham decreasing by a tenth. This is partly due to the substantial rise in poultry consumption, deflecting the choice to the cheaper product. Similarly with increased meat and poultry demand, with a substantial rise in the cost of fishing, fish consumption has fallen by a quarter, in spite of the success of the frozen fish industry in recent years. There has been a marked drop in the fresh fruit and vegetable diet, reflecting perhaps that horticulture, (until recently at least), has spent less on advertising and high-pressure sales than other commodities. Part of this trade has been absorbed by the recent new techniques for preserving fruit and vegetables so that they become what are termed 'convenience' rather than 'seasonal' foods[3]. Potato consumption, which rose dramatically during the war, though falling in recent years, is still a fifth greater than its pre-war level. In contrast, though such products as cakes and biscuits are due to increased wealth more easily available, the overall consumption of flour has declined by about a sixth.

The change of nutritional standards towards protein and away from starch foods reflects the improvement in living conditions created by a rise in personal income. In the decade from 1954 the gross national product rose to about £29,000m, an increase of about eighty per cent, or about six per cent a year[5]. Personal income was nearly doubled in this period. Nevertheless though the proportion of personal expenditure (which amounted nationally in 1964 to over £21,000m, or about three-quarters of the total personal income) increased substantially for such consumer goods as cars, expenditure on food dropped. Once a certain level of affluence was attained personal expenditure was switched from increasing food consumption to other requirements, such as housing, heating and luxuries. In fact during the decade expenditure on food dropped from 6s 1d in 1959 to 5s 2d out of every pound in 1964.

A more detailed survey of food consumption between 1958–63 reveals that the proportion of national expenditure on food dropped from thirty-one to twenty-eight per cent[3], falling again in 1964 to twenty-six per cent. This is partly due to the success of the national policy for cheap food, reflected by an increase in retail food prices during the six years of only eight per cent against an increase in all prices of twelve per cent. Total expenditure on food in this period rose by £370m to nearly £5,000m a year (that is by eight per cent) which, considering the increase in population and food consumed, emphasises the relative cheapness of food in relation to other commodities. Drink, in particular became more popular. Though exaggerated by increases in duty charges the cost of drink consumed rose by nearly twenty-three per cent in this period against the eight per cent increase for food. Expenditure on drink in relation to food is increasing, and is now nearly a quarter of the second against a fifth in 1958.

The National Food Survey made an analysis of expenditure and food consumption in 1963. For this purpose the population was divided into five main income groups, ranging from those with £39 to those with under £9 a week, as shown in Chart 9[6].

The survey indicates that, as is to be expected, higher income groups depend less on starch and more on protein for their diet. The total expenditure on food, which includes an estimated allowance for food obtained free from other sources than shops, for the poorest strata of

92

CHART 9: RELATION OF INCOME TO FOOD CONSUMPTION
PER WEEK IN 1963

HOUSEHOLDS			FOOD CONSUMPTION OF SELECTED ITEMS OZ PER PERSON (MILK IN PINTS: EGGS IN NO)							
Income £ week	% total	value food in shillings	meat	fish	milk	cheese	eggs	fats	bread	potatoes
over £39	2·0	43·3	44·5	7·3	6·2	3·8	4·8	12·8	29·7	41·8
„ £23.10	8·6	37·4	40·1	6·0	6·0	3·6	4·5	12·2	36·6	50·8
„ £14.10	34·3	33·7	38·0	5·7	5·1	3·1	4·3	12·0	41·9	57·5
„ £9	31·8	31·5	37·2	5·5	4·6	2·8	4·0	11·9	47·1	61·4
under £9	20·6	31·1	36·4	6·2	4·4	2·9	3·9	11·2	48·1	57·0

society is about 31s a week including about 10d worth of free food. The richest group, with incomes of more than four times the poorest, spend in fact only a third more on food each week, about 43s, including 2s 3d of free food. Nevertheless in terms of food consumption, the rich get an extra eight ounces of meat, two pints of milk, an extra egg, and an extra ounce of cheese and one-and-a-half ounces of fat a week than the poor. At the same time they eat almost twenty ounces less bread and fifteen ounces less potatoes than those with incomes of under £9 a household. Though a fifth of the households are in the second group, only a fiftieth are in the income bracket averaging more than £39 a week. The bulk of the population, about two-thirds, have household incomes of £10 to £23 a week. Nevertheless in actual and real income terms there is with increased national prosperity a trend for larger proportions of the population to be in the higher income groups. This change will continue, and due to the benefits of automation and increased productivity it is expected to accelerate during the next decades. This will lead to increased consumption per person of protein foods, which tend to be the expensive ones, with a marked decline in starch foods. At the same time though expenditure on food per person will increase, the proportion to total expenditure will continue to decrease, leaving a greater margin of expenditure for other consumer goods and social needs.

The National Food Survey in 1965 showed that about half the national expenditure on food was for basic commodities, such as meat, sugar, eggs and dairy produce. Rather more than a third of expenditure was for manufactured foods and only about an eighth for seasonal foods, such as vegetables and fruit.

It is not easy to predict future trends in food consumption. In the short term, the National Economic Development Council has forecast an overall increase in food consumption until 1970 of two per cent a year. Since the population increase is only 0·8 per cent, this leaves a large margin to cover the benefits of increased affluence and changes in the diet structure. As previously discussed, it may well be that population changes (taking into account the increase in numbers and the proportion of those in the maximum energy consumption group) will increase national food requirements by the end of the century to about forty-two to forty-five per cent above the requirements prevailing in 1965. This estimate must be increased for protein foods, allowing for the increased affluence. Taking into account all the relevant factors, it might not be a rash estimate to predict that protein foods will have to be increased by about fifty per cent between 1965 and 2000. Consumption of starch per person, including flour will decrease. Allowing therefore for the extra population these foods might have to be increased only by forty per cent in the same period. These estimates are at least a working hypothesis for examining the relationship of agriculture to land-use, considered in more detail later (p.212). It is probable that an increase by half for the bulk of the food requirements will not be far short of the estimate needed in planning agricultural expansion. Even grain, becoming less necessary with the decrease in bread consumption, will have to be expanded by at least a half allowing for additional animal fodder.

The prediction that food production must expand by fifty per cent is based on the assumption that imported food remains at the present level and increased food requirements do not mean increased food imports. It may well be in fact that the amount of imported food should be decreased to benefit the overall import to export trade balance. If this factor was desired then agricultural expansion should be in excess of the fifty per cent required to meet the change in demand. At present Britain grows two-thirds of her temperate food requirements. Many believe this should be increased to about four-fifths and some would desire that Britain should be almost self-sufficient in her temperate food requirements. This, coupled with the expansion required to meet increases in population and affluence, would mean a substantial increase in agricultural productivity, intensified by the reduction predicted in the area of farm land. This expansion is not impossible in terms of what is technically practicable. Changes in production techniques to factory farming could absorb the expansion required. It is even possible that this expansion is economically desirable and practicable. The implications of changes of this kind are discussed in later sections.

An important statement by the Agricultural Research Council in 1967 claimed Britain will need twice the present home food output within thirty years—which could be attained at the present twenty-five per cent rate of increase within ten years provided there were 'quite exceptional efforts by farmers, advisory workers and research workers, and many changes in traditional methods of agriculture'[7]. To this end, the ARC during the next decade would encourage research to:

1 Increase the yield of food or feedingstuffs an acre,

2 improve feed conversion rates of stock,

3 reduce waste at all stages from production to distribution,

4 increase labour productivity.

REFERENCES

1 *United Kingdom: Projected level of demand, supply and imports of farm products in 1965 and 1975.* ERS–Foreign—19. 1962, Foreign Agricultural Survey of the Economic Research Service US Department of Agriculture
2 Boyd-Orr, Sir John. *Food, health & income.* 1936, Macmillan
3 *Domestic Food Consumption and Expenditure* 1963, p5. HMSO
4 *Britain: an official handbook.* 1965, HMSO
5 *National Income and Expenditure.* 1964, HMSO
6 'Domestic Food Consumption'. Ibid, p82
7 Report. Agricultural Research Council, April 1967

2e Imported food or home production

The 1947 Agricultural Act guaranteed that the nation would promote and maintain a stable and efficient agricultural industry. Nevertheless it was the intention of the Act that only that part of home food production would be supported which was considered to be in the national interest. The difficulty inherent in this outlook is that the level of home production as a proportion of total consumption, is bedevilled by political, rather than agricultural, considerations. That the situation is difficult is obvious at each annual price review, when the Government, in consultation with the National Farmers Union, determines the support to be given to agriculture for another twelve months. This, in turn, is intended to balance many factors, such as changes in production costs, which create a stable home agriculture, with such problems as 'fluctuations in world food supplies, the national balance of payments, the financial position of the industry, the trend of world price levels and domestic market requirements'[1]. By-and-large at some cost to the taxpayer the Act has worked in its basic intention; but it has led to frequent disagreement and tension between the politicians of successive governments and the farming leaders. The farmers themselves sometimes consider their leaders out of step with their needs.

The traditional, political outlook, created by the industrial revolution and advent of steam shipping, is that Britain is suited to be an industrial, rather than an agricultural, nation. At the turn of the last century, after the collapse of the golden age of agricutural prosperity, there was only about one acre of farmland to each person, which was not enough to support the population. Britain had perforce to import food; the population density has increased throughout the century, thus aggravating the situation. It has been impracticable for Britain to be self-sufficient. It has moreover become the basic tenet of a largely urban population that it is more economic to export industrial goods than it is to grow food, for two main reasons:

1 Money and labour invested in industry give a higher return than agriculture, thereby prospering the nation and supporting higher wages.

2 Exported goods not only cover the cost of imported food, but leave an additional profit, permitting the purchase of other foreign goods and strengthening the value of the pound as an international currency.

Both observations have been true throughout this century, and are indeed basically true today, though not with the same emphasis relevant before the Second World War. They are moreover becoming dubious due to changing world trade.

Two other factors were contingent to the attitude that Britain was an industrial nation capable of importing as much food as required, both detrimental to home agriculture.

1 Purchase of foreign food not only encouraged British exports of industrial goods, but was essential for this purpose in providing an international flow of currency.

2 Agricultural land, even of the best quality, was more valuable when used for industry, since in theory increased national income could be used to buy more food than could be provided from the lost land or, alternatively, could be used to increase productivity from other agricultural land.

The agricultural depression of the 1930s, which was the outcome of the traditional outlook of an urban society, reduced much of the countryside to a desolate state of neglect. Into an impoverished farm condition a handful of pioneers introduced the first steps towards mechanisation. This start, which was received by general scepticism, was given its main impetus by the Second World War, changing the political climate into an acceptance that a stable and efficient agricultural was necessary for national well-being. Since the war agricultural production has been influenced, though not directly controlled, by national planning. Until the early 1950s targets were planned for individual commodities and overall output after which state planning was less specific but grants and deficiency payments helped not only to keep agriculture stable but, in fact, created a rapidly expanding industry. The net result was that, in spite of a rise in population of twelve per cent and in the overall protein consumption per head of perhaps fifteen per cent; and, in spite of a reduction in agricultural land:

1 the volume of agricultural output is almost double pre-war levels,
2 the percentage of food supplies provided by home agriculture has increased,
3 Britain now produces almost two-thirds of her food requirements which can be grown in temperate climates, or half of its overall requirements.

The National Farmers Union calculated that increased home production has enabled some £400m–£450m pounds worth of food imports to be saved each year, based on an assessment of the value of increased production in different commodities, as shown in Chart 10[1].

CHART 10: IMPORT SAVINGS DUE TO HOME PRODUCTION

Commodity	Increase in production Av 1961/2–1963/4 over pre-war	Estimated imports saved (1963 prices): £ million
soft wheat	1·5 million tons	35
barley	5·0 million tons	110
beef	310,000 tons	55
mutton & lamb	60,000 ,,	10
wool	4,000 ,,	2·5
pigmeat	300,000 ,,	75 (as bacon)
liquid milk	715 million gallons	65 (as milk powder)
butter	7,000 tons	2·25
cheese	65,000 ,,	15
eggs	560 million dozen	85
sugar	34,000 tons	15 (raw value)

Had agriculture not expanded, which could have happened to a greater or lesser degree without the 1947 Agricultural Act, and some £400m worth of extra food been imported each year it would have added eight per cent to the overall cost of imports into Britain. This would have seriously widened the balance of payments gap. Moreover, without an expanding agriculture it is unlikely that Britain would be exporting some £300m worth of agricultural goods and food, as discussed in the next section. If agriculture continues to expand, as is the declared policy, then the cost of supporting the population growth should be absorbed by home production. In fact if intensive farming is accepted as the norm, then it should be possible in spite of the population growth to grow between three-quarters and seven-eighths of our temperate food requirements, rather than the present two-thirds (p158).

Agriculture has become so improved in output (reducing the need for food imports) that since 1954 the proportion of imported foodstuffs, including drink and tobacco, has never been above forty per

97

cent of total imports. In 1963 it had shrunk to 34·8 per cent. Nevertheless the cost of food imports in 1963 amounted to £1,678m. But as
prices of food rise in world markets, especially for proteins, the
national food bill will spiral during the next decade unless home
production is rapidly expanded[2].

CHART 11: PER CENTAGE BREAKDOWN OF NATIONAL FOOD
IMPORTS IN 1963

Commodity imported	%	Value £1m
meat & meat preparations	18·6	312·1
fruit and vegetables	16·8	281·9
cereals and feedingstuffs	16·6	278·6
butter and cheese	10·0	167·8
raw sugars	9·2	154·3
tea	6·8	114·1
tobacco	5·9	99·0
other	16·1	270·2
	100·0	1678·0

Thus, post-war agricultural expansion is theoretically saving twenty
per cent of the food bill had no expansion occurred, or some twenty-
five per cent of the present actual cost of food imports. Nevertheless,
with almost £1 in every £3 of imports spent on food, excluding drink
and tobacco, there is no reason for complacency, with a deteriorating
world food situation and a deteriorating national solvency. National
reserves of around £1,000m are so slender that the adverse annual
trade balance is a serious threat to the economy. The total value of
food requirements in Britain from both imports and home production
nears £3,300m, and of this value rather more than £1,000m comes
from foreign countries with climatic conditions comparable with
Britain. If it were possible to restrict food imports only to products
from non-temperate zones, then the national balance of payments
could show a profit.

When the 1947 Agricultural Act was framed, though a stable
agriculture was considered desirable for national well-being, there
was no specific need to seek maximum home food production.
Increased efficiency in agriculture has been welcomed since the early
1950s, but it has never been considered of overwhelming importance.
Over-production has in fact, been considered dangerous at times,
since it has been seen as a threat to food imports from countries which
reciprocate trade by buying British goods. And, since agricultural
support costs roughly about five per cent of total government
expenditure, there are those who consider cheap imported food

98

preferable to subsidised food production. By the mid-1960s the situation had changed; it is now appreciated that home food expansion can contribute substantially to reducing the national trade deficit and that a sudden shift in world food demand has threatened the basis of easy food imports, especially protein. The first signs of the changed situation were apparent by 1963, leading the *Farmers Weekly* to comment in the spring of 1964[2]:

> Who would have thought, two or three years ago, that Argentina would be having meatless days, that Holland would have to import butter to fulfil export commitments, or that most of the world's surplus grain outside the USA would vanish in the space of a few months?... The great changes we have seen in the world's food trade during the last 12 months have not been due entirely to the weather. As incomes and general standards of living have improved, more and more of the world's people have begun to demand a better diet. Where some have lived at subsistence levels on mainly cereal foods, they have asked for meat. In meat-eating countries, they have asked for better meat. Where, as in Europe, they ate mostly veal and pigment, they now want beef and lamb ... what is happening in this rapidly changing pattern of world trade is of importance to all farmers, since at least some of the pressures on the home market are being relieved. New Zealand dairymen have opened up big new markets in Malaysia and the Philippines; her sheep producers have captured 75 per cent of the Japanese market for mutton. Japan has displaced Britain as Australia's best export customer, mostly for wool and foodstuffs, and China has jumped up to fourth place. These trends affect the meat producer most of all. Increasing and more affluent populations will want still more red meat ... imports in the main continental markets leapt nearly 80 per cent in the first two months of this year ... Argentina short of meat for her own people, has reduced her exports to the UK, and there are fears in the Argentine meat industry that the export surplus could disappear altogether by 1970 ... The picture over the broader field shows how delicate the balance now is between world surplus and scarcity. We are much less sure of being able to rely on imports, even for stop-gap supplies, than we were a year or two ago.

This quotation summarises the basic change in world markets. Old allegiances in trade are being swept away; no longer do Commonwealth countries have to export their surplus food to Britain in order to afford British goods. Better markets are arising all round them. In the New Year of 1965, the *Farmers Weekly* returned to the theme[4]:

> It seems only yesterday that the whole of the Western world was worrying over over-growing surpluses. Today, most of these surpluses have disappeared, and supplies of some commodities on world markets are running short. All the signs are that this trend will go

on . . . All over Europe meat is scarce and dear . . . half as much again will be needed in the Common Market area in the next five years; consumption of high protein foods generally will be doubled. Countries like Japan are greatly influencing the new pattern; no longer content with the diet of fish and rice, it has become a major importer of meat, milk and eggs. It is now among the largest customers for the farm products of Australia, New Zealand and the USA . . .

During the last year, the world market for dairy products has moved from surplus to near-scarcity. Britain has had to scour the world for butter; Canada may not be able to supply all the cheese we need; Holland has had difficulty in meeting export commitments, and France, not long ago a notorious dumper of dried milk products on the UK market, is now having to shop around the world for dried skim for stock feeding. And in New Zealand, of all places, it was recently suggested quite seriously that domestic consumption of butter should be reduced so that the export demand could be met . . .

Today, far from being engulfed in a flood of unwanted food, we find ourselves in the position when, within a measurable time, we shall need to produce all the food we can from our own farms. We can no longer rely on an abundance of cheap food from overseas.

These statements are clear and direct. However, another problem complicates the basic need for a rapid expansion in home meat supplies and, to some extent, in cheese and butter, whereby human diet receives protein from animals. In the spring of 1965, the Chairman of Vitamins Ltd, one of Britain's leading suppliers of animal feed-stuffs, warned that Britain could suffer an acute shortage of protein foods for livestock feeding, since much of this was imported from developing countries which will soon need to retain all they can to satisfy their own needs[5]. In 1962, the United Kingdom required 2,340,000 tons of animal feed protein of which only 190,000 tons, or about eight per cent, came from home produced grain. If British livestock is to be increased, then animal feed protein also will have to be increased, but the availability of imported protein will decrease. The basic development required for increased home production of protein is threefold:

1 Increased acreage and increased yield per acre of corn and grass,

2 Synthetic protein diets from resources such as petrol,

3 Increased protein per ton of grain.

In the latter respect, it has been estimated that a rise of only two per cent in the average protein content of British grain, harvesting at some $12\frac{1}{2}$m tons, would provide an additional half million protein tons, which is rather more than one-fifth of present requirements. Since it has been claimed that home meat production may have to expand 500 per cent before the end of the century[6], the need for a crash programme of research and development for animal feedstuffs is evident.

Chart 12 shows, firstly, the percentage of different commodities which Britain produces from home production related to consumption and the extent to which self-sufficiency has improved since before the war and, secondly, the primary sources for imports with percentages related to requirements in 1964 and before the war[7].

CHART 12: % TOTAL UK FOOD SUPPLIES FROM HOME AGRICULTURE

Commodity	Pre-war	1963	1964
Wheat	23	41	47
barley	46	95	96
oats	94	98	98
beef and veal	49	71	70
mutton and lamb	36	41	42
pork	79	98	98
bacon & ham (not canned)	32	38	38
poultry	80	99	98
shell eggs	71	97	98
liquid milk	100	100	100
butter	9	10	6
cheese	24	43	42
potatoes	96	93	95
sugar (refined value)	17	23	27

Commodity	Exported from	% pre-war	% 1964
wheat	Canada	31	29
	Australia	18	8
	France	3	6
beef & veal	Argentine	30	12
mutton & lamb	New Zealand	34	50
bacon & ham	Denmark	33	46
	Eire	4	15
butter	New Zealand	26	36
	Denmark	22	18
	Australia	17	15

The bulk of the £1,000m worth of food imported each year from temperate zones is hard wheat (required for bread), mutton, lamb, bacon, ham, cheese, butter and sugar. In addition seventy per cent home produced beef supplies are upheld somewhat artificially by store cattle brought from Eire for final fattening in Britain. The considerable imports of animal feedstuffs provide artificial support to much home produced milk, eggs, meat (especially poultry, pig-

101

meat, and to some extent beef) as well as cheese and butter. Since Britain is the world's largest food importer, the national diet is particularly vulnerable to changes in world trade. Large food imports from Australia and New Zealand are no longer as vital to their economy, now that their trade has expanded to Japan and the Far East. It is possible that supplies of butter, mutton and lamb from those Commonwealth countries will become difficult to obtain at reasonable (ie relatively cheap compared with United Kingdom production costs) prices. Beef from the Argentine is becoming scarce. It is probable that Canada will wish to sell wheat to Britain for some time, but new markets, especially in Russia, are developing. There is a close agricultural relationship between Britain and Eire, but Eire is now turning attention to European trade in general. Denmark, in particular, has a keen trade relationship with Britain, selling bacon and butter in return for industrial goods. However United Nations accounts in 1964 show British imports from Denmark amounting to £155m (of which food was £132m) and exports to Denmark to £190m; this was against figures for 1955 of £125m (£106m as food) and £107m respectively[8]. Half of Danish exports are food and Britain is the largest customer, but Danish food exports to West Germany between 1955 and 1963 rose from £51m to £65m. Though at present Denmark needs to export food to Britain, but does not fully return the trade by industrial imports, there can be no guarantee that even this source of food will be available for ever, especially since much depends on Common Market developments.

It is evident that Britain cannot increase imports to satisfy the needs of the extra population and the general increase in consumption per head. It seems equally probable that Britain will not be able to continue imports even at the present level for much longer, due to rising world prices. But it is possible for British agriculture to expand, probably in proportion to a fairly rapid decline in food imports. This is discussed in later sections.

REFERENCES

1 National Farmers Union, *British Agriculture Looks Ahead*. 1964, the Union
2 *Britain: an official handbook*. 1965, HMSO
3 'Hungry for meat'. *Farmers Weekly*, 22 May 1964
4 'Brave New Year'. *Farmers Weekly*, 1 January 1965
5 Graves, H. C. H. Annual Conference of Institute of Corn and Agricultural Merchants. April 1965
6 Cadzow, J. B. National Sheep Breeders' Association Conference. May 1965
7 Statistics. Ministry of Agriculture, June 1965
8 Hicks, N. 'The other side of the picture'. *Farmers Weekly*, 11 June 1965

2f Agricultural exports from the United Kingdom

During the last few years the relationship between agriculture and the national economy has changed dramatically. Though subsidised agriculture is no longer the poor relation of other industries. In 1964 the National Farmers Union published their plan for agricultural growth in a pamphlet called *British Agriculture Looks Ahead*. By the following year the Government recognised that increased home food production could help to close the gap in the national balance of payments by reducing imports. Similarly there was a significant change in public opinion. The traditional concept of food imports encouraging foreign purchase of British industrial goods had begun to crumble due to the rapid shift of world trends in the food trade. International shortages of protein foods have made it clear that Britain cannot continue to import food at present levels indefinitely.

This change of attitude in itself must affect the future role of rural planning. Of equal significance however has been a sudden realisation that agriculture, as well as its subsidiary industries, could play an important, if not vital, part in United Kingdom export markets. A decade ago, and even in 1960, the idea that agriculture might become an industry with large export outlets would have been considered ridiculous. Nevertheless food production today could be on the threshold of a new era, not only meeting most home requirements but having a surplus sought after by foreign trade. This new concept could change the basic pattern of land-use requirements, reversing the economic arguments for continued urban expansion at the expense of agriculture.

For several years industries subsidiary to food production have been substantially increasing their export trade. The rapid mechanisation and intensification of British farms, the ferment of new techniques and the pragmatic attitude of farmers to solving technical problems have created an expanding market at home for equipment, stock and artificial aids to husbandry. The industries manufacturing agricultural goods have been able to invest in new factories and production lines until they have become an important national asset, the value of their exports being among the greatest of all national industrial groups.

Exports of agricultural machinery in 1947 were only worth £10m, but by 1965 they had risen dramatically to £168m, With agricultural mechanisation increasing throughout the world, except among the most backward of under-developed areas, the lead Britain gained in agricultural machinery development makes it clear that this export trade has almost no limits. During the Royal Show of 1965, the permanent site at Stoneleigh Abbey proved the value of a national effort in this direction. The showground has now become the permanent shop-window for foreign buyers to see British farm equipment, much of it being demonstrated in practical use. Nevertheless continued success of these markets depends on an expanding efficient agriculture in Britain, giving incentive for new investments by manufacturers.

Fertilizers are a basic requirement for increased world food production, with only three per cent of the dry land in the world still virgin arable land; fertilizer production is expected to more than triple by 1980 (p81). The Netherlands use an average of 370lb of fertilizer an acre a year. Four other countries use more than 90lb an acre, while America averages 40lb. It is not surprising that the chemical industries are making enormous investments in new fertilizer plant. Some of the expansion is taking place in Britain and in a few years the export of fertilizers, which reached 5m tons in 1963, should substantially increase. Similarly exports of pesticides are expanding rapidly, having risen between 1959 and 1964 by seventy-one per cent to nearly 35,000 tons, worth over £11m.

Certain food products have always featured in British export markets, with drink, especially whisky, being a traditional national export. Drink exports of all kinds were worth £97m in 1963. Fishing is a national industry too, and in the same year fish and fish preparations were worth £7·7m in exports. In the small way jams and marmalades are also a traditional product, £2m being exported in 1963. It is not however in these spheres that change has been dramatic in the last few years, but in the export of farm produce. Between 1960 and 1964, farm produce exports rose by sixty-seven per cent from £40m to £72m, including livestock, meat, dairy products, wool, hides, cereals and seeds. Though the average increase is over £6m a year, the sharpest increase of £12m was between 1963 and 1964. In fact the value of all food exports rose by fifty per cent from £100m to £150m.

Britain is a major meat importing country, absorbing fifty-seven per cent of world meat exports in 1960. Nevertheless by 1964 nearly all poultry and pork consumed was home produced and, seventy per cent of beef and veal came from British farms. Only mutton and lamb at forty-two per cent and bacon and ham at thirty-eight per cent home produced, relied substantially on imports for consumpton. Conversely livestock and meat exports, particularly cattle, have substantially increased from £5·4m worth in 1960 to 300,000 beasts in 1964 worth £24·6m. There are two main reasons for this substantial increase in livestock and meat exports. Cattle breeding in Britain has an international reputation and foreign buyers pay high prices for breeding stock. In the five years from 1960, cattle breeding sold for export increased in value from £0·75m to nearly £1·15m. There is no reason why this trade should not expand as demand for cattle increases throughout the world. Live cattle for slaughter in the same period rose from £5·4m to £24·6m. This is a new and profitable development for British agriculture, but the economics governing

104

this trade are confused by artificial factors. Higher European Common Market tariffs and effects of foot and mouth outbreaks caused a setback in livestock exports during 1966.

As previously discussed, meat consumption is increasing throughout the world and traditional sources of supply are strained. Though continental countries are expanding their meat producing capacity, France in particular aiming to supply the beef import needs of the Common Market area by 1970, shortages are unlikely to disappear for a long time. Sales of British cull cows and heavy bullocks to the Continent began to increase in the late 1950s. Sales to the Netherlands, Belgium and West Germany were worth £2m in 1961, but during the first four months of 1965 alone this figure was more than doubled and demand had widened in range for all types of cattle, particularly Charolais crosses. British beef is popular in continental markets since due to a subsidised British agriculture wholesale prices are up to half those in Europe. Meat prices for butchers in Britain are beginning to rise because of foreign competition in livestock markets. Meat exports are largely haphazard, foreign buyers working through dealers in Britain and mostly near the eastern ports. However it seems clear that even if prices are adjusted to some extent to exclude the benefits of the subsidies, Britain could expand her market to the Continent. But, as the *Farmers Weekly* pointed out in April 1964, if these export opportunities are to be grasped, Britain needs to develop:
1 modern hygenic abattoirs, designed to continental standards, which can cut and pack for different markets,
2 facilities for organising the right meat supplies at the right time,
3 a marketing board which can function as an export agency.
Although there is a future for increased meat exports, as well as increased home supplies, unless Britain organises an efficient export trade it is probable that the market will be captured by others. Not only are Australia, New Zealand and America seeking European meat markets for beef, but Eire could deflect the present level of trade in store cattle to Britain into fatstock ready for European consumption. If the latter policy developed, the British meat trade would be seriously upset.

Not only is there the possibility of an increase in the meat export trade, but other farm produce or by-products have foreign outlets, which have increased in value within recent years, for example:

	1960	1964
milk, butter, cheese	£6·8m	£8m
shell eggs	£0·06m	£0·45m
malt from barley	£1·87m	£2·2m
hides and skins	£3·6m	£5·1m
wool	£10·7m	£12·7m

105

D

Only in the case of cereals have exports fallen, from £6·7m to £2·4m during the same period, but this reflects increased home consumption, paricularly for livestock. In the summer of 1966, the British Agricultural Export Council was created to stimulate all sections of the industry and help in market and sales promotion.

With government support and organisation, exports from all sections of agriculture and its associated industries could exceed £500m within a few years. This could represent about twelve-and-a-half per cent of all exports at present levels. Opportunities seem unlimited and the concept of Britain being an agricultural export country is a shattering reversal of traditional thinking in an industrial nation which had little more than a generation ago a bankrupt agriculture.

One other factor is of tremendous significance when considering the export potential for agriculture. The revolution in techniques for processing food has already made dramatic changes in food requirements and markets. Future developments are likely to be equally important for British agriculture. With good prepacking methods, much horticultural produce can be sold abroad, particularly on the Continent, including apples, celery, carrots, lettuce and tomatoes. Frozen foods, which began to develop in the mid-1950s, principally for home consumption, were worth £67m in 1961, representing 56,000 tons of fish and 68,000 tons of vegetables, expanding to £100m in 1964 and estimated to be worth £250m by 1972. At present exports of frozen foods are comparatively low, much of this production being taken by the home market. But frozen food, which has relatively expensive handling and storage costs, is likely to be supplanted, especially for tropical markets, by recent developments in freeze-dried techniques of processing food. Peas have already proved commercially successful in freeze-dried packets. However potentially more important for export markets perhaps the first factory for freeze-dried eggs opened in Buckinghamshire in the spring of 1965. By this method, the weight of pasturised liquid egg is reduced by seventy-five per cent, and powdered eggs can be stored indefinitely without loss of taste, reducing storage and transport costs. This new technique could lead to an important export market and give an improved and cheap diet for undernourished countries.

More important perhaps for British agriculture than any other new food processing technique was the recent experiment for keeping milk fresh for long periods. Milk heated to ultra-high temperatures and packed in aseptic cartons was given a pilot trial in 1963 and was being sold at home and in twenty-five countries by 1966, with an expanding export market in the Middle East. Milk, kept without refrigeration or loss of quality, with full cream or butterfat content, will revolutionise milk production, distribution and diet. It seems

106

certain that this technique will lead to the end of the traditional daily milk delivery to every family, a factor which substantially increases distribution difficulties and costs and is a service without parallel in any other country. It may be that milk will be delivered in bulk only once a week or that supermarkets may begin to sell milk by the gallon at cheap rates. It is also possible that future developments may make dried milk, when reconstituted, indistinguishable from fresh milk and, since milk is eighty-seven-and-a-half per cent water, this would greatly reduce handling costs.

The immediate fear voiced by British farmers of the development of ultra-high temperature milk has been that the milk industry in the United Kingdom would be destroyed by imports from areas where milk is cheaper to produce, such as New Zealand. The liquid milk market in Britain has been protected by regulations on quality which made it almost impossible to import from abroad, though on occasion a little has been brought from Holland. Though milk sales form a substantial part of United Kingdom farm income, being nearly twenty-five per cent in 1963, in a few years production could prove uneconomic against imported milk. The loss of the milk market would undermine several related enterprises, such as animal feed-stuffs and beef production. The fear is based on a real threat. Nevertheless it is more than probable that, rather than milk imports destroying the British milk industry, the demand for milk will outstrip the world capacity for production. As the chairman of Express Dairy, pioneers of the technique, has said: 'We should be in a position to sell in places where it has not previously been possible. I believe that there could be big opportunities for exporting to countries which have not been able to get fresh milk.' Milk consumption throughout much of the Middle East, Africa, India and Asia is abysmally low. The chance of including fresh milk in the diet of tropical countries is an important asset in helping world nutrition standards. It seems likely that more than the excess milk which New Zealand can produce could be absorbed by demand in Asia and India. Britain and other European milk producers should be able to sell their excess milk without difficulty in the Mediterranean countries and Middle East. The opportunity for exporting milk is the biggest challenge facing British agriculture and dairies. If grasped, and Britain leads as pioneers in this field, it could transform the economics of United Kingdom agriculture (p398).

Food production in Britain would change in emphasis should she enter the Common Market (p281). As a major food importing nation, Britain would have to pay more into Community funds by levy than any other member state, probably at least £250m. The more Britain can be self-supporting in food, the stronger her position in the ECC would be. The more efficient farm in Britain, except within some spheres of horticulture, has little to fear from European competition.

107

However, it is far from clear whether joining the ECC would stimulate or restrict Britain's position as a potential food exporting nation.

Though the last three-quarters of a century of cheap imported food and agricultural depression in Britain has left farmers and politicians afraid of future recessions and over-production, there is evidence in the last five years that Britain could become, to some extent, a food exporting country. With increasing world shortages of protein foods, with new food processing techniques, and given the right incentives and organisation by the Government it is possible that the present export of over £85m worth of food and produce from British farms in 1965 could be doubled or trebled in a decade at the same time as food imports are reduced.

3 PRESSURES ON AGRICULTURAL LAND

Introduction

England and Wales are urban countries with urban traditions several generations old. Some city dwellers in fact, though probably a decreasing number, have never seen the countryside. The Industrial Revolution created the modern industrial city which, in turn, created serious planning problems not yet resolved. The second Industrial Revolution, generated by rapid technological advances during recent years, including the birth of automation, will transform the urban and rural shape of Britain during the next few decades. As Davies said, 'the Britain of the 1990s will have been completely redeployed. Whole industrial regions that exist today will disappear to be resited in greater concentration elsewhere' (p137). In this century, though the population is expected to almost double, the urban area is expected to treble, thus covering over sixteen per cent of the total land area. If industrial regions are completely redeployed, which may happen, this estimated growth in urban area may be too low. The urban population will in any case make other demands on land than urban development alone. Recreational needs in particular will be met only by the release of large tracts of land from other uses. At present, four-fifths of the population live in settlements of more than 10,000 people. It is probable that, unless the urban area extends substantially beyond the 6m acres forecast for this century, well over 50m people will live in settlements of over 10,000 people by the end of the century. With so large a proportion of the population being town-dwellers, it is difficult to appreciate that two-thirds of the land area of England and Wales is arable or permanent grass, and another tenth rough grazing. At the present rate of change in land-use, 2m acres will be taken from agriculture by the year 2000. Even if this rate of change was doubled, nearly two-thirds of the land area would still be available for agriculture at the end of the century, representing about

109

24m acres of arable, grass and rough grazing. The country would still therefore be preponderantly agricultural in land-use, though not in population. Farm land is under pressure from many quarters. At least 45,000 acres are taken from agriculture each year for urban needs. Much of this absorption of farm land for other uses is significant for two reasons. It is frequently good farm land which is taken out of production and farmers resent, and sometimes resist, the loss of land, both as individuals and collectively as a union. A loss of 2m acres from agriculture before the end of this century—and probably much more—will have tremendous visual and social effects for the community.

Population mobility, and particularly the drift of population from one region to another, is significant for national land planning and regional development plans. The build-up of population in South-east England has become a matter of national concern, especially since it is recognised that a channel tunnel or an allegiance to the Common Market would create tremendous pressures in Kent and neighbouring areas, acting as a magnet for industry, depots and population which might be impossible to counteract and which would be disastrous for good planning. Regional planning and urban renewal, now taking place in the North-east, might do much to re-establish the balance of population throughout the country. A new city on the Humber and the exploitation of gas from the North Sea could create a new regional area of industrial prosperity. The transference of Government, though improbable, from Whitehall to York, or some other underdeveloped area, could generate a new and better concept of land-use and population distribution. Nevertheless without such dramatic developments the creation of new towns will continue to change the social structure of Britain. It is certain that nearly one in fifty of the population will live in new towns by the end of the century. It is probable that with the creation of more new towns and cities at least one in twenty-five will live in these places. Some existing towns will be so transformed by new building, urban renewal and expansion that they too would appear to be 'new' cities. Not only will new housing and other urban requirements engulf large tracts of land, much of it productive, but these new settlements will have a profound social and economic effect on neighbouring farmland.

It is the new mobility of the population which is more significant for agriculture than the actual rehousing and growth of the urban dweller. Increased wealth, leisure and car ownership are making the population explosively mobile, generating tremendous pressures on the countryside. To cope with the increase in the number of cars, and provide traffic densities no worse than those prevailing in America at the moment, the road network would have to be extended sevenfold before the end of the century. Though this is improbable, many new motorways and roads will have to be built, all of which will increase

110

the mobility of population and flexibility of industrial location. The growth of new industries, based on new sources of fuel, manufacturing processes and integration with other industries, will undoubtedly be phenomena of the next decades. Much of this industry will not be in the traditional manufacturing zones. New zones will become prevalent, many of them in agricultural areas but linked to each other by a new motorway network. Few areas will remain truly rural, or even agricultural, in character. Services, especially wires and pipes, will proliferate across the countryside, linking new industries and urban areas. The industrial regeneration of Britain will transform traditional land-use concepts. It is essential that the evolving pattern is based on a national planning framework.

Within the planned framework for land-use, which is vital if the correct balance is to be gained between agriculture and the pressures ranged against it, allowance will have to be made for the enormous growth in leisure pursuits, much of it in outdoor activities, and in the two-dwelling family, dividing their lives between high-density urban living and weekend country houses. In both cases the car is the vital link, capable of effortlessly covering large distances in a short time along the new motorways. The future will be dominated by the fact that the work period in most people's lives will rapidly decrease from the present two-thirds to one-half of each year. This change, with increased wealth for everybody, must generate radical changes in prevailing concepts of land-use.

The pressures on agricultural land are considerable and increasing dramatically and rapidly. Nevertheless, as discussed elsewhere, increased home food production is essential for the future well-being of the country. Good productive land needs to be husbanded. Poorer land may have to be taken to meet the developing social needs for urban growth, industry and leisure. To attain a new pattern of land-use, farmers will have to be educated and helped financially during the period of transition, otherwise social bitterness and conflict will divide the nation. It is a problem fraught with difficulties.

3b Urban requirements—drift and new towns

The growth in population, wealth and mobility is generating new patterns of urban requirements and national land-use. The proportion of urban land area in England and Wales doubled between 1900 and 1960 and is expected to increase by fifty per cent between 1960 and the end of the century. By 2000 nearly one-sixth of the land will be urban in character. To cater for the population growth a new town the size of Harlow would have to be built every ten weeks from now until the end of the century. However urban renewal may absorb part of the increase in population as well as help to replace existing slums and obsolescent houses. The new industrialised society now taking shape will depend on increased mobility in the working population (p118) and it will become necessary to have a fluid market for dwellings in which they may be exchanged easily and cheaply. This suggests the development of a national house bank, through which property may be held or released according to regional work demand, with empty homes retained to meet future changes. Moreover, as is now perhaps happening, it is essential that regional development plans should help check the continual drift in population into the South-east and, by decentralising office work, reduce the demand for work concentration in the centre of many conurbations, especially London.

Though motorways and car travel make it possible for people to live far from work, or alternatively have a week-end country house in addition to an urban flat (p134), it is probable that the percentage of urban dwellers will continue to increase, perhaps rising from the present eighty per cent of the population to over ninety per cent. During the next decades there will also be a radical change in the location of important industrial centres, many existing concentrations dispersed and resited in new patterns elsewhere[1]. Best has shown that the predicted growth in the urban area will absorb another 2m acres between 1960 and the end of the century, representing four per cent of existing open country, as detailed in Chart 13[2].

CHART 13: GROWTH OF THE URBAN AREA OF ENGLAND AND WALES

Year	Population in millions	Urban area in millions of acres	% total land area
1900/1	32·5	2	5·4
1920/1	37·9	2·2	5·9
1930/1	40·0	2·6	7·0
1939	41·5	3·2	8·6
1950/1	43·8	3·6	9·7
1960/1	46·1	4·0	10·8
1970/1	50·1	4·4	11·9
1980/1	53·8	4·9	13·2
1990/1	58·2	5·4	14·5
2000/1	63·7	6·0	16·2

More than twenty years ago Sir Patrick Abercrombie advocated a series of new towns within thirty miles of London, complete with industry, to relieve the concentration and congestion of work and people in the metropolis (outlined in the Greater London Plan published in 1944). Two years later the New Towns Act promoted a programme for new towns under ministerial designation and a series of development corporations. By mid-1964, sixteen new towns in England were created, with four in Scotland and one in Wales. These towns were centred generally in low density areas, populations existing in the designated areas ranging from only sixty at Aycliffe to 35,000 at Redditch and averaging around 6,000[3]. The ultimate population of these twenty new towns is scheduled to be over 1·3m, with most of them having populations of around 80,000 in England and 70,000 in Scotland. At present rather more than ½m people live in the new town areas. As each town nears completion its management is handed over to the Commission for the New Towns, created in 1962.

London has eight new towns between eighteen and thirty miles from the centre, aimed at decentralising pressure on the metropolis; while the Black Country and the Merseyside each have two decentralisation towns, and Glasgow four of similar function, though originally one of these was intended mainly as a mining growth area. The other three towns are all close to existing industrial concentrations which previously relied on workers travelling from a wide area. Another new town was designated in 1964 at Washington in Co Durham, while several existing towns, such as Ipswich, Peterborough and Northampton were designated as growth towns with the intention that their populations should be doubled. Similarly another new town is planned for north Buckinghamshire—a matter of concern for farmers because of the land required for it and the proposed reservoir to serve it (p176). The land area required for the twenty towns designated by 1964 is 107,485 acres, equal to about thirteen people an acre when their populations reached maximum level. If the projected increase of 20m people by the end of the century was housed in new towns of this density, 1½m acres would be required. This would represent three-quarters of the land expected to be taken from agriculture for urban needs (p171). Earlier new towns were however envisaged as having more open space than existing towns of similar size, whereas plans for recent towns have increased overall densities, though the impression of spaciousness remains, due to compact planning[3]. Stevenage and Harlow, designated in 1946 and 1947 respectively, have planned densities of under thirteen an acre, whereas Cumbernauld in 1955 was designated at seventeen an acre and Skelmersdale in 1961 at nearly twenty an acre. Even if all new towns were planned with densities like Skelmersdale, 1m acres would be needed to house the forecast population increase. Not all new towns reflect the trend towards increased densities. Dawley in Shropshire, for example, though designated in 1963, is planned to have only ten people an acre, due partly to a third of its area being affected by mining, and other land in the Severn gorge geologically unstable.

The proposed new towns will already house nearly two per cent of the total population by the year 2000. This percentage will increase as other towns are designated. New towns have already made their impact on the national consciousness. By the end of the century their image will be an important part of the British pattern of life. New towns are planned generally for populations of about 80,000 people, since it has been thought that housing 6,000 people a year for fifteen years represents the maximum capacity for normal building programmes and the maximum social upheaval that can be tolerated before a community is established[4]. During the last year or two a new concept for building cities rather than towns has begun to prevail. A city of $\frac{1}{4}$m people, about the size of Cardiff, is now considered to be socially and economically ideal. New cities are a product of recent regional development planning and are essential if the population and industrial expansion and relocation are to be properly balanced. At present considerable attention is being paid to city formations. In some cases it is no more than the transformation of such towns as Ipswich into $\frac{1}{4}$m city populations. In the autumn of 1965, at the other extreme, proposals were made to create a city of up to 1m people on the Humber. It has been suggested that this could form a second metropolitan area as a counter-magnet to London, revitalising the 5m population of the Humber region, giving it purpose and form[5]. A more revolutionary proposal was made in 1966 to create a city port for $\frac{3}{4}$m people on the Wash, with a fresh water reservoir capable of supplying 500m gallons daily to the South-east, with the reclamation of 50,000 acres for agriculture and the city acting as another Europort, like that at Rotterdam, and at the same time regenerating East Anglia and Lincolnshire[6]. Housing 20m people (equal to the present population of Canada) needs revolutionary solutions.

Whether new cities or towns are built radical changes in basic planning principles must be included; perhaps (as once suggested possible for a new city in Buckinghamshire) being based on free monorail travel in the urban area. Experiments in housing layouts must become accepted practice. Washington new town is being planned to have flexible social units, each capable of organic growth and contributing to a town also capable of change to suit future needs. In existing cities urban renewal must permit high densities of between 300 and 500 people an acre, living in tall flats among recreated parkland but set close to commercial and industrial areas. Many of these people must have rural week-end houses as well as flats. Dormitory satellite towns, set apart from commerce and industry, could become an alternative type of layout. Whereas at present most dormitories are unsatisfactory since they are superimposed upon existing social patterns, those of the future will be specially designed with their own social centre, but linked together and to the main work and recreation areas by monorail. It may be that some new towns will be for much smaller units than the 80,000

114

considered correct during the previous twenty years, perhaps each having 10,000 to 20,000 people. Although these small towns could include traditional housing they should also include tall flats to give compactness. The latter should make it possible to locate towns on poor terrain in rural settings and amid areas for intensive food production. A dozen such units, several miles apart but linked by efficient free communal travel, might take ¼m people. Four or five units, each of a dozen towns, would themselves be set around and linked to a common centre for regional industry, administration and entertainment, but preferably sited so that no single town was more than thirty-five miles away from it.

New urban patterns must emerge during the next decade. These will profoundly affect rural and agricultural planning. Many planners and sociologists believe the present drift towards large conurbations is wrong economically and socially, especially when choked by inefficient transport systems. Professor Bronoswki said he believed that in the second half of this century great cities would become moribund and sterile, because of a natural desire to live in small communities set apart from each other (social mobility and rural living is discussed in the next section). Lord Holford has expressed the opinion that self-contained towns will disappear by the end of the century due to high population densities and new living patterns. At present four-fifths of the population live in settlements of over 10,000 people. Unless agricultural land is to be lost on an unprecedented scale the population must remain essentially urban in character, though this is contrary to the liberating influences of affluence. The pressures engulfing villages and countryside are immense. Post-war green belt policies are already crumbling with disastrous effects. Allowance must be made for small balanced communities in rural settings, rather than a debased sprawl over the country. There must be overall a network of super-highways linking dispersed or concentrated conurbations of high density flats, low density housing belts, motorised shopping centres, plus those for industry and commerce, with social service centres and park reservations.

In considering new urban forms and the planning of new towns, several important factors have tended to be neglected. In the first place the impact of a new town on the adjoining rural economy and social structure has not been investigated. The introduction of an urban centre, housing tens of thousands of people, into a rural region has several obvious results. No town is ever insular in character. A new town generates commuters in the adjoining villages who work in the designated area but choose to live in the country. Secondly, the new town dwellers seek recreation in the adjoining countryside. Thirdly, the centre of attraction for the local villages gravitates towards the new wealth centre and trade is influenced by its standards. This affects shopping habits, distributory services and overall rural

115

wealth. In the second place, and more revolutionary in concept, no attempt has been made to relate the new towns to their food requirements or the food production capacity of the adjoining agricultural areas (p329). It might be possible and economic to plan a new town, or group of new towns, with an adjoining agricultural region mainly devoted to supporting the urban population. Such a policy might streamline production, processing, distribution and consumption, so that the consumer's prices might be reduced as well as the producer's income increased because of a reduction in overall cost. For example, three new towns might support one modern milk factory capable of supplying a quarter of a million people.

The factory could be sited at any central point, preferably not far from the milk farms. If an average consumption of three-quarters of a pint a head every day was assumed, which is above the national level but new towns tend to have a large child population, and if average yields were assumed to be 900 gallons a cow, which is slightly above national levels but below intensive production levels, then this population would be supported by a little over 9,000 cows. Assuming good production levels, this regional herd might be divided into a series of fifty two-man units, each holding 180 cows, with a further forty men acting as relief milkers ensuring each cowman only worked a five-day week. The regional herd might be supported on 12,500 acres of good grassland, provided 8,000–9,000 tons of concentrate was brought in to supplement the grass each year. The grassland might be managed with sixty to seventy fieldworkers. In addition there might be 5,000 followers to the herd, grazed on approximately another 2,500 acres also supported by additional corn. The youngstock might need another sixty stockmen and fifteen fieldworkers. Thus the total labour force providing milk for the regional factory could be 300 men including managers but excluding additional grain production required for the cows in an area of 15,000 acres. The last might be approximately equal to the total area of the three new towns. Other foods could be planned similarly on a regional basis.

A centralised abattoir could be sited near a rail-road network, linked to the towns and other regions, handling pigs, beef cattle and possibly sheep from livestock units in the region. In some cases, the units might be sited near the abattoir (p328). Egg production and broilers, too, could be produced on a similar basis. If the region was economic for grain production, then a large corn acreage might serve a giant mill, producing concentrate for livestock and flour for the human population. Other products, such as vegetables, might be grown in the region. As all food would be produced by contract there would be no normal market required in the region. By an integrated system of this kind, though the region could still import or export some foods, many economies in the scale of production processing and distribution could be attained. Moreover being

116

largely self-supporting the region would develop a natural social autonomy and a direct relationship between farmer and townsman. The present system of producing milk in Cumberland for processing in London, which may then be distributed in Hertfordshire, seems illogical and wasteful. In planning new towns an opportunity has been lost in integrating the needs of the new population with the agricultural regions in their vicinity.

REFERENCES

1 'The future economic shape of Britain'. *The Times*, 15 September 1965, p16
2 Best, R. *Town and Country Planning Association Journal*, September 1964
3 *The new towns of Britain*, p17. 1964 HMSO
4 Whittle, J. 'Shape of towns to come'. *Architects' Journal*, 24 February 1965, p457
5 Lane, L. 'City of the Humber'. *The Listener*, 2 June 1966
6 Teggin, H. 'City of the Wash'. *The Listener*, 26 May 1966
7 Holford, Lord. Maitland Lecture to Institution of Structural Engineers, 10 November 1966

3c Population mobility

The population of a technically advanced country must be mobile, both in work and residence, so that national resources can be developed without stagnation. As a corollary, recreation for the population must also be mobile.

The second half of this century will be one of social stress, aggravated by the population growth, automation, increased leisure and the desire for mobility. The increase in population has been discussed above (p76). The age of automation is in its infancy and the repercussions will be of profound importance for the structure of society. Sir Leon Bagrit, introducing his Reith lectures in 1964, said[1]:

Science and technology have come to pervade every aspect of our lives and, as a result, society is changing at a speed which is quite unprecedented. There is a great technological explosion around us, generated by science. This explosion is already freeing vast numbers of people from their traditional bondage to nature, and now at last we have it in our power to free mankind once and for all from the fear which is based on want . . .
We have considerably extended our expectation of life. We have enriched our lives by creating physical mobility through the motorcar, the jet aeroplane, and other means of mechanical transport; and we have added to our intellectual mobility by the telephone, radio and television . . . And with the advent of the new phase of science and technology which we call automation, we have the promise both of greater leisure and of even greater material and intellectual riches.

117

But this is not inevitable. It depends on automation being adequately exploited. We shall need to apply our scientific and technological resources to literally every aspect of our society, to our commerce, our industry, our medicine, our agriculture, our transportation.

This description of modern technology, based on automation, is a balanced summary of the present revolution, already creating possibilities of greater leisure. Change in this magnitude, affecting every aspect of society, is unlikely to be painless. In its wake in fact is the fear of redundancy, loss of jobs and insecurity. With planning and co-operation the benefits of automation can be channelled so that the work load is eased for all, rather than suddenly terminated for the few. As Sir Leon emphasised, the benefits may not be immediate in the sense of dramatically reducing working hours but rather the 'increase in our national riches can be for those who need it most—the sick, the infirm, the old, and, of course, the young'. Nevertheless, the general trend towards a working week of thirty-five to forty hours with three, or even four, weeks annual holiday, which will continue to become accepted during the next decade, creates a planning problem for leisure of profound significance for agriculture and the use of land (p144).

It has always been accepted that top-level administrators must be prepared to move their homes according to the demands of their work. With the advent of the vast industrial and commercial firms of the twentieth century, it has become accepted that most executives as well as directors must be domestically mobile. Advancement in many companies depends on movement between different branches of the organisation. Today many executives have to change their homes every three to five years. Similarly technical and professional people advancing their careers will seek new and better jobs every few years, not in their home district as in former times, but wherever opportunity seems best. Many, without ever wishing to emigrate, will spend part of their working lives, particularly when young, abroad. The same principle is becoming accepted, though slowly as a general condition, for the rest of the working population. As industrial patterns change, so must the factory worker be prepared, whether skilled tradesman or unskilled labourer, to move his home to suit the needs of a changing society. Sociologists are well aware of the breakdown of the close-knit social units typical of the earlier part of this century. Social mobility creates many problems, particularly as family groups are dispersed. The elderly and infirm are no longer protected by their family group remaining, as used to be the case, in the same district all their lives. Education of the young, too, is disrupted in a manner which has undesirable consequences.

There is also a rapid growth of mobility in jobs, especially of a technical nature. Trade representatives by the nature of their work have to

118

be mobile. More significant for society, technological development has ceased to be parochial or even national. Most development is international in scope or influence. Nowhere is this more true than in agriculture. Anyone connected with farming development has to be prepared to travel widely to keep abreast of new techniques. Not only have technical personnel become increasingly mobile in recent years, but all forms of raw material and produce are handled over vast distances. It is in fact an axiom of modern society that distance between producer and consumer frequently has no importance in relation to the price of an article. With bulk transport and mechanical handling of materials, the difference in cost for each unit if handled five or 500 miles may be negligible. The transport cost for a journey of 5,000 miles may be insignificant provided the volume of trade is substantial. Much modern commerce is based on this principle. The growth of goods traffic by road, rail and water, and even by air, is a phenomenon of the age. It is nevertheless equally true that centralisation, in production and distribution, can be vital in order to reduce production costs. The correct relationship for economical production between dispersed activities—even if vertically integrated in management—is a difficult problem to analyse and resolve, especially in food production (p329).

Though rail and aeroplane travel are important, car and road transport are more significant for population mobility in town and country planning. In fact, it is the motor age, as it is sometimes known, which soon may paralyse towns and cities and destroy the countryside. The concept of the car as a factor in social living habits has changed the basis of land-use in town and country. It is essential to consider the effect of the car on the social and physical structure of the country before it is possible to resolve the problems of relating modern agriculture and food production to rural planning.

The growth in car ownership, combined with increased wealth and leisure for greater car use, is the crux of the problem. By 1965, there were 9m cars on the roads, with 7m car-owning households—double the numbers a decade previously. It is estimated there will be between 16m to 18m cars by 1980[2]. It is possible that by the end of the century there might be 35m vehicles, 26m being private cars. Buchanan has made a notable study of the relation between traffic and town design[4]. The principles revealed by his report are now being coined under his name, though they are much misunderstood and misapplied. In 1962 he graphically portrayed that the growth of car ownership in this country was a major problem[3]:

At the present time we have ten million vehicles which is three times the number we had before the war. The present number (excluding motor cycles) of vehicles per 1,000 of population is 137. In USA it is 409. Saturation is expected in USA when the figure rises to about 570 per 1,000 population. The same figure applied to Britain for the year 2000

119

produces a total of 35 million vehicles, of which perhaps 26 million would be private cars. This total, which is confirmed by a study of the actual trend in this country, is more than three times the present number of vehicles. One half of this increase may come within ten years. There are people who declare that there is some fundamental difference between this country and USA which will prevent these figures being achieved, but I fail to see what the difference can be. The manufacturers can obviously turn the vehicles out. I can see no reason why by the end of the century there will not be sufficient wealth around for the population to be able to afford this number of vehicles. The only doubt I have is whether there will be enough room for them physically, especially in the crowded conditions of towns, though I very much doubt whether that will be a deterrent to the actual accumulation of vehicles in numbers.

There can be no doubt that the impact of so large a number of vehicles on this small country will be severe. Already in 1962, we have more vehicles per mile of road than any other country in the world. If anyone wants to perform a really alarming exercise I invite him to consider the day when vehicle ownership reaches the proportions now obtaining in USA, and then calculate the miles of road we should have to build here in order to reduce the ratio of vehicles per mile of road to the figure which now obtains in USA. My own attempt to do this leads me to conclude that we would need to increase the present total of about 193,000 miles to no less than 1,600,000 miles. I do not in fact put this forward as a wholly serious exercise because the comparison is spurious in several ways, but it does give some idea of what we are going to be faced with.

Car ownership and the annual mileage for every car is rapidly increasing and, as is well known, the road network of Britain is inadequate to cope with the situation, both in town and country. The motor industry invested £200m in new development schemes between 1960 and 1964. Car output reached a record of 1·6m in 1963, slightly more than 0·6m being exported. In addition, 0·4m commercial vehicles and 0·1m motor cycles were produced, less than half of which were exported. More important, perhaps, is the relation between capital investment in vehicles and roads. Buchanan pointed out that the capital investment in motor vehicles by business and private consumers rose in the decade after 1951 from £240m to over £900m[4]. In contrast, capital investment in roads and public lighting by public authorities in the same period rose only from some £10m to-£20m to £167m. This disproportionate relationship between the two classes of investment is indicative of the growing problem on the roads.

In 1960, the Ministry of Transport introduced a master plan for building 1,000 miles of motorway and the construction and modernisation of 1,700 miles of trunk roads by the early 1970s. By April, 1967, 425 miles of motorway had been completed. It seems probable that by 1970 less than 700 miles will be in operation, while over-loaded

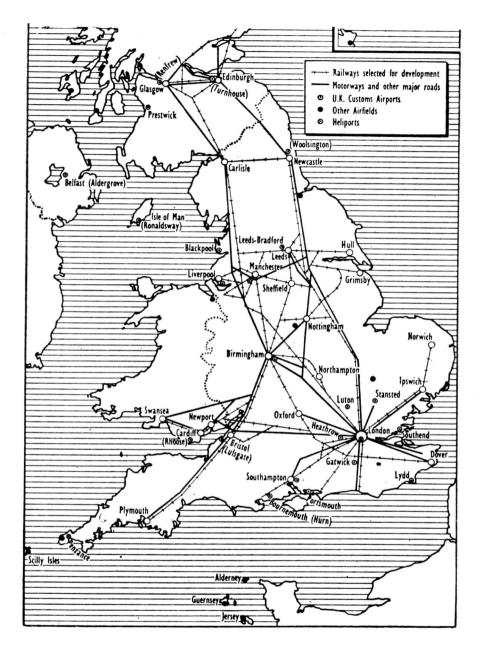

A new metropolitan city needs
first class communications by sea,
air, motorway, rail, river and
canal. Map shows transport routes
as they will be in 1970.

121

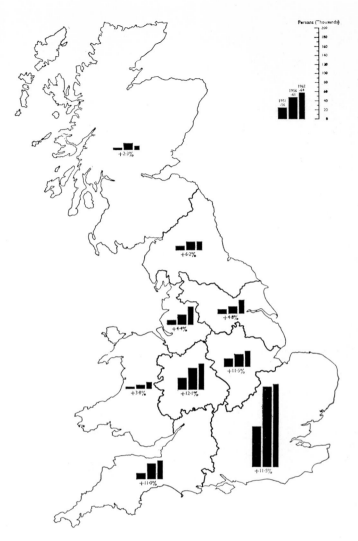

Total population change 1951-64

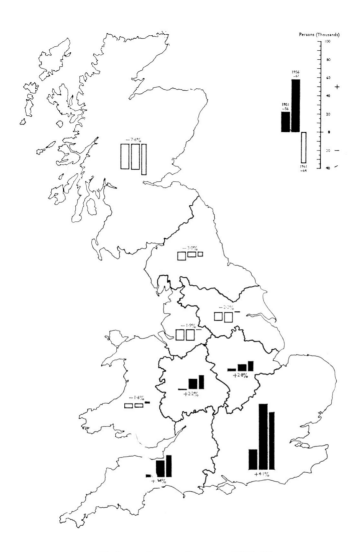

Estimated net migration 1951-64

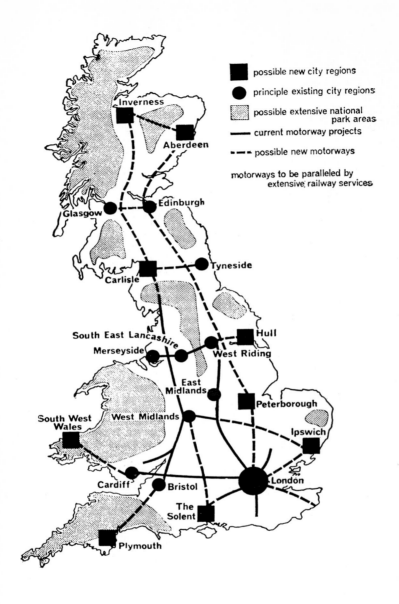

possible new city regions

principle existing city regions

possible extensive national park areas

current motorway projects

possible new motorways

motorways to be paralleled by extensive railway services

Inverness

Aberdeen

Glasgow

Edinburgh

Tyneside

Carlisle

Hull

South East Lancashire

Merseyside

West Riding

East Midlands

Peterborough

South West Wales

West Midlands

Ipswich

Cardiff

Bristol

London

The Solent

Plymouth

'Only' says Professor Ling, 'within the framework of a national plan can the location of new towns be decided sensibly.' Map from 'Towards a national plan' by Professor Ling, printed in *New Society*.

124

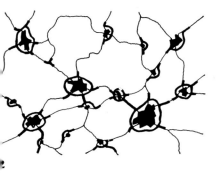

1   The Severn bridge, with 400ft
towers and 3,240ft main span
seen from the Monmouthshire
bank, was opened in 1966.
Already causing new patterns of
mobility from the Midlands into
South Wales. The bridge is a
good addition to a landscape
marred by the service industries.

2   The by-passing of every settlement in every direction would pose
a heavy liability in terms of cost,
land and severance.

1

126

2

1 In contrast to 2, drawing of the Liverpool-Preston Road (A59), showing how new planting can help to merge an unsympathetic road into the landscape.

2 Transport requires land. Earlier rail and canal are joined by new motorways searing across the landscape. Farms are broken into uneconomic units with distorted field patterns within a traditional agricultural landscape.

Church Cottages, Cavendish,
Suffolk 1960. In few cases is
restoration carried out in sympathy
with local traditions, as in this
example. Unfortunately urban
tastes often inflict a fate worse
than death on the indigenous
architecture of rural Britain.

CHART 14: PUBLIC HIGHWAYS IN GB AND N IRELAND IN 1963[5]

Motorways:	194 miles	Northern Ireland:	—
Trunk Roads	8,347 ,,		382 miles
Class I roads:	19,797 ,,		956 ,,
Class II roads	17,608 ,,		1,733 ,,
Class III roads	48,982 ,,		2,865 ,,
Unclassified roads:	103,527 ,,		7,923 ,,
	198,455 ,,		13,859 ,,

trunk roads are expected to increase from 1,450 to 2,250 miles. In 1965
there were 12·9m licensed vehicles, inclusive of 8·9m cars, using
100,000 classified miles of road—this represents about 130 vehicles a
mile. Vehicles are expected to increase by a third by 1970, doubling by
1980. The problem of mobility becomes more intense since the
management of the road network in Great Britain is the responsibility
of nearly 1,300 different authorities. About two per cent of Britain's
national income is absorbed by traffic congestion. By 1980, four per
cent of the larger national income then expected will be wasted in this
manner[6]. It has been suggested that one per cent of the national
income, some £7,000m, should be spent before 1980 to give an
adequate road network.

Nevertheless, though the expansion of Britain's roads is slow in
relation to the volume of traffic, the new network of motorways and
trunk roads already considerably affect agriculture and rural planning
problems. This is true not only with regard to the physical impact of
new roads taking farm land and more people using the roads to
reach the countryside, but also to a basic change in planning principles.
Between the wars, due to the increase in house building by private
enterprise without many planning restrictions, ribbon development
became prevalent. Housing stretched along both sides of the road,
linking towns and villages to each other, and leaving wedges of farm
land behind the semi-detached ribbons. Post-war planning attempted
to destroy this pattern and replace it with comprehensive areas of
urban building including in some cases open space for recreation.
This has generally been the policy for new towns. Today, largely due
to the impact of the rise in car ownership, planners and sociologists
are becoming increasingly interested by the concept of linear towns,
as opposed to concentric towns planned round a central commercial
and administrative core which hampers car mobility. This concept
would not repeat the pattern of ribbon development, which is still
concentric in principle, but would allow for the planned dispersal of
development into various social units linked by motorways. An example
of linear development has been proposed in Shankland's report for the
expansion of Ipswich whereby the Gipping Valley settlements to the

North-west would expand, linked by a fast road to Ipswich. More advanced development patterns are based on the concept of linking monorails, moving pavements or other forms of mechanised linear transport, in addition to or instead of motorways. Buchanan has suggested that dispersed urban regions would be one solution[3]:

> There are some people who say it is futile to struggle against this kind of dispersal and that it would be better to swim with it. They say that towns, roughly in the form they have had for centuries, are finished: and that the motor vehicle and telecommunications as now developing would enable us to organise our urban affairs very much more efficiently on a dispersed basis. I am not quite sure what this 'designed dispersal' would be like, and I expect there would be a great deal of low density housing, with fully motorised shopping centres here and there: cleanly laid out industrial estates; parks and countryside reservations so arranged that if you desired you could walk for miles without seeing any development. The whole laced together with a network of super highways. I am not being facetious about this, this is the 'natural' direction in which the motor vehicle would like to take us, and there is a lot of sense in saying that in the circumstances we might as well take it, and make a really good job of it, instead of struggling away with the apparently impossible task of trying to adopt existing cities to a form of transport for which they do, let us admit it, present serious difficulties.

Buchanan did not envisage that designed dispersal could supersede the present urban structure nor had it yet been established that existing towns could not be adapted to new needs for mobility. Nevertheless he suggested that many people and their work would have to move from congested centres to more favourable locations, or mobility might be reduced by planned relationship between homes and work.

Motorways, though not necessarily promoting planned dispersal, do promote mobility. The M1 has helped to link industries in London and Birmingham. It has done more than this, for it has increased mobility in residence and recreation. Dispersal, rather than concentration, is becoming easier. Motorways are changing the pattern of life. Commuting, based on the railways, has been a phenomenon recognised as an essential evil of modern life. Commuting distances of twenty to thirty miles round conurbations, or twice this radius round London, are normal. New fast-service trains make eighty-mile commuting from Rugby and Northampton acceptable. British Rail reported in 1966 that with the Midland electrified service, passenger figures rose within a year by twenty-three per cent at Rugby (with 8,000 London commutors) and by thirty-six–thirty-eight per cent at Northampton, Wolverton and Bletchley. Commuting from Coventry and Birmingham to London is now encouraged. The new motorway complex is extending commuting zones (p133). The problem of rural dwelling for an urban based population, especially in relation to two-house families, is considered in the next section.

It seems certain that motorised, out-of-town regional shopping centres should be developed. A survey has shown that conditions which made them desirable and practical in America are beginning to exist here[7]. Although a shopping centre opened near Nottingham in 1964 had a slow start in turnover, the survey has shown, for example, that a 140-acre site at Haydock, Lancashire, could attract nearly £50m sales by 1971. Total retail sales in the region are likely almost to double between 1961 and 1981. Such a centre might halve the potential sales level by 1971 in Wigan, Warrington and St Helens, also reducing by an eighth centres in Liverpool, Manchester, Preston, Bolton and Crewe. A regional city for $\frac{1}{4}$m people by 1985 at Livingstone with a shopping complex of 600,000 square feet is expected to act as a shopping magnet drawing pressure from both Edinburgh and Glasgow. The prospect of large commercial centres in rural regions, as part of the trend towards increased population mobility, creates its own rural planning problems.

REFERENCES

1 Bagrit, Sir Leon. 'The Age of Automation'. The Reith Lectures. *The Listener*, 12 November 1964
2 *The transport needs of Great Britain in the next twenty years.* HMSO 1963
3 Buchanan, Colin. 'Towns and Traffic'. RIBA *Journal*, August 1962
4 Buchanan, Colin. 'Traffic in Towns'. 1963, HMSO
5 *Britain: an official handbook.* 1965, HMSO
6 Morgan, Prof V. *Economic and Financial Aspects of Road Improvement.* 1965, Roads Campaign Council
7 Kantorowich, Prof R. H. *Regional Shopping Centres in North-west England.* 1964, Manchester University
8 *Roads in England.* 1967, HMSO

3d Rural dwellings

The two decades since the war have witnessed a considerable change in the social structure of country dwellers. With the influx of ex-servicemen, there was a peak farm labour force of 520,000 in 1950. Today there are 200,000 fewer agricultural workers (p291). Similarly the number of separate agricultural holdings has dropped by 40,000 from the region of 380,000 holdings existing in 1950 (p217). It would be expected that a quarter-of-a-million farmhouses and cottages should have become unoccupied in this period. In addition, though the national population rose by about $2\frac{1}{2}$m in the period from 1950, thirty of the ninety-five counties of Great Britain had a reduction in their population and, among the other counties, 500 rural, urban

131

districts and boroughs also lost population[1]. It is well known that there has been a drift of population from the Highlands and also from the villages to the towns, particularly of young people. Similarly the drift of population to the South-east has been appreciated for some years (p86), though this has been checked in the 1961–66 period, except to East Anglia and part of the South-west.

The impression gained from this general decline of rural populations is that rural housing should have become depressed, much falling into decay and ruin. In reality this is only partly true. The Home Counties, acting as a dormitory for London, have always been popular residential districts. There must be few derelict rural cottages in Kent, Sussex, Surrey, Middlesex and Hertfordshire. Today the influence of London on housing is felt in much of Suffolk, Cambridgeshire and even Oxfordshire, Huntingdonshire, Northamptonshire and Wiltshire. Similarly the conurbation of the Black Country has created considerable pressure on all neighbouring counties to provide commutor houses for industrialists. The same effect can, to a lesser extent, be noted in other conurbations. It is only in relatively few areas that, with the exception of the Highlands of Scotland, Wales and parts of England, dereliction of rural dwellings is pronounced. Abandoned cottages for example can still be seen in parts of Suffolk and Norfolk, the Yorkshire dales and areas similarly remote from the main urban centres, but this will not be for long. Due to the Severn bridge, speculators are already buying up cottages throughout much of Wales. As Dower said, 'already much of southern England, the midlands and of the Clyde-Forth belt have become effectively parts of city regions. We have to accept the fact. In lowland Britain at least, the old idea of a slow-moving, self-sufficient rural life is dying if not dead'[2].

It has been noted that urbanization dramatically changes farm ownership and practice. The small family farm has been absorbed by London commutors in six areas between the capital and Hastings[5]. Demand for small residential farms is growing throughout Kent and Sussex. Many are farmed with little labour, enterprises being kept simple. In most districts, owner occupiers now outnumber tenants and in some a third of the farm occupiers have arrived since 1959. One significance of commutor farming is that it can retard farm amalgamation into larger units. This problem could become critical around many urban areas, causing a setback to improved efficiency.

Three factors make it unlikely that dereliction of rural housing will be found anywhere in Britain in a few years' time. Perhaps the most important reason lies in the present steadily rising population unknown for generations plus the increase in the standards of living and wealth throughout the population. Coupled with this, it must be expected that not only will there be continued pressure on housing of all kinds, but the Government policy to promote growth in different

132

regions will have some success in reviving population in the more depressed urban areas. Moreover, as previously discussed, mobility between home and work will continue to grow in popularity, especially with an increase in car ownership (p119). More particularly, during the last few years, the trend towards dormitory life in the villages and country round industrial towns has been extended for a much wider section of people, including factory personnel and workers. For economic and social reasons this is contrary to general experience before the mid-1950s. A County Council survey in Hampshire in 1966, showed that four-fifths of town dwellers would prefer to live in rural regions and that nine-tenths of rural dwellers preferred to remain as they were. Though the trend towards complete social mobility between home and work is still the exception rather than the rule, there seems little doubt that the pleasure of living in rural areas will be appreciated and experienced by a wide section of the population in another decade. This will create pressure on dwellings in much of the country areas of Britain.

Secondly this situation is aggravated and extended by the new motorway and trunk road network. Even though less than half of the motorway network had been opened by 1967, the trend towards dispersed living round the motorways had become marked. An article in the *Sunday Times* made this quite clear[3]:

> We are still in the early days of motorways, with only a total of 300 miles open to traffic, but they are already beginning to have effect. A new pattern of community is beginning to emerge. Businessmen's trains benefited mainly those who worked in the centre of cities—the gain from motorways is being felt by those working in the suburbs or the towns just beyond.
> The Medway motorway, the M2, is perhaps the most clearcut example. It has allowed those working in South London, the Medway towns and even as far afield as Gravesend to move their homes to the orchard country around Sittingbourne and the East Kent coast beyond, and house prices have kept pace with the increased demand.

Estate agents noted price rises for bungalows and semi-detached houses of thirty to forty-three per cent within a year of the M2 opening at Whitstable, and twenty to twenty-five per cent at Sittingbourne. People moving to the district in that year required easy access to the motorway. Similar experience was gained in districts around the M1 north of London. One agent noted price rises of fifty per cent, half of which they estimated were directly due to the motorway, in remote villages north of Luton. Many of the buyers were commuters to Luton. Northampton, too, showed similar changes throughout the country, prices rising perhaps from thirty to thirty-five per cent for small bungalows. Old cottages, worth only a few hundred pounds some years ago, are now being sold at as many thousand pounds. Some London Agents have indicated that the Ross Spur of the M5 between Birmingham and Bristol, which was opened in 1960, has provided a new community area for the Midlands. Consequently, prices in a previously remote rural district have risen by a quarter. In areas north of the Midlands, the effect of the Motorways on commuting has been less marked, though even in these districts, especially round Manchester, country properties are becoming more popular in proximity to the new fast roads. Trunk roads (for example the A1 which has been drastically improved during the last few years for much of its length) also make travel faster over large distances. Since many people are prepared to commute at least one hour, and even one-and-a-half hours, in both directions to and from work, residential areas can without difficulty be eighty miles away from the work areas, provided they are near an entry to a motorway at both ends of the journey. Many suburban people, having to cross a central urban area to work, may waste as much time for a journey of only ten to twenty miles. Once the present network of fast roads has been completed, most of England and parts of Scotland and Wales will be in commutor zones.

The third new influence bringing prosperity to rural areas and rejuvenating remote cottages is the trend for the possession of holiday and weekend retreats, acting as second houses for much of the population. As in the case of commutor houses, the trend is that what was once a characteristic of the wealthier executive and professional class is now becoming widespread throughout much of society. It is an alternative to the method of living as a commutor that there should be two houses. In many cases, one residence is likely to be a flat, possibly in a high-density urban area, which is used for the four-and-a-half day working week. The restrictions of this life are made bearable by the family moving *en bloc* to a country house on Friday evenings for the weekend. Therefore with Bank Holidays and other vacations, at least a third of the year can be spent in the country. The advent of the motorway made distances of 150 miles tolerable between flat and country house. London families have therefore cottages by the Wash, in Somerset, Dorset and Devon and possibly in the Yorkshire Dales or, when the Severn bridge is complete, Wales. Even the Lake District, which can be reached in five hours from London, is not considered too far for a weekend. No cottage in Britain is too remote to be potentially attractive as a weekend home for an urban worker. At more expensive levels, it is not surprising that there should be the enormous upsurge of financial speculation in the beaches of the world. By jet a weekend cottage on the Mediterranean is not absurd and holiday houses in the Caribbean, or even the Pacific, are advertised for sale in most of the Sunday and daily newspapers.

It is impossible to know how many people today own two houses and commute between them at the weekends. Londoners for many

134

years have had their cottage in Kent and Sussex. More recently the pressure for cottages has been noticed in Hampshire, particularly round Petersfield[4]:

> East Hampshire has become a desirable area for the increasing numbers of townspeople who can afford a weekend place in the country, and the price they are prepared to pay is helping to accelerate the drift from the land
> For the rustic couple recently married in the church of the village of their birth the housing outlook is indeed bleak . . . When they enter the estate agent's office they are likely to meet the man with a house and a job in London who has just offered over £2,000 more than they can afford for a primitive house which could be home to them, but which he intends to occupy for no more than two months in every year . . .
> Farm workers reaching retiring age and due to leave their tied tenancies discover that their small savings are unable to compete with the ready money of the townbred beneficiaries of the affluent society who in their speedy cars find this corner of Hampshire so irresistible and so convenient.

Cottages in all attractive areas in the southern half of Britain are in demand and the experience at Petersfield is becoming a normal pattern. It is not surprising to find speculative companies advertising for and buying derelict cottages in any remote part. Prices in these regions are beginning to increase faster than the national average. As long as any policy exists aimed at restricting indiscriminate building in rural areas, the site value of existing derelict country cottages will be high.

There are important social and visual consequences rising from the mobility of urban workers, making it possible for them to live or weekend in rural areas. The decline in population in the countryside and villages is being halted and, in many areas, has been reversed. This will soon be true for all areas. Dereliction of rural property, which was common except in the Home Counties up to the mid-1950s, will disappear. New wealth will become available for rural communities. Some Church officials are beginning to wonder whether the present policy of closing remote and redundant rural churches is too short-term. In a few years it is probable that all rural communities will increase in population and country parishes could be given a new lease of life. But at the centre of rural expansion is whether many of Britain's 18,000 villages can be saved from despoliation. It is probable that the pressure for giant shops, infill housing and peripheral bungalows will be too great to save their scale and character. Several policies should be adopted.

Existing villages, as in West Suffolk, should be listed according to their architectural, historic and environmental value. This has limited use unless there are firm controls to protect those of high merit. The

135

example of Buckinghamshire County Council should be followed. In 1966 the Council commissioned consultants to prepare an appraisal of how selected villages might be developed, such schemes helping local councillors to understand how expansion can enhance even attractive villages. In the same year, Nottinghamshire County Council published a report for East Retford Rural District, outlining the character of villages and landscape and showing why eight attractive villages should have restrained development, major expansion being kept for five unattractive villages. It is desirable that more counties should encourage brand new villages, rather than expansion of attractive centres, such as at Bar Hill near Cambridge started in 1966 to house 8,000 people complete with their own services. Overall the best aim would be to set up rural development areas on the lines of those for new towns, as was suggested at the 1966 conference of the Association of Parish Councils.

Two other factors are worth comment. Weekending in the country creates a split in community life. Urban districts, occupied perhaps for only four nights a week, cannot support much social or communal activity. Most people see such residences as a dormitory and their social life developing round their weekend country house. The converse is also true. Many country villages become dead during the week, a large section of the population being absent. Shops are placed in a difficult position whereby much of their trade is concentrated on Saturday, the rest of the week hardly justifying their existence. Secondly, and of great importance, the dispersal of urban people into rural areas intensifies their desire not only to live in but use and enjoy the countryside for recreation. Since however they are not passing travellers but residents, it is probable that a new rapport can develop between farmer and urban worker. The former must make it possible for parts of the countryside to be used by this new rural population and the latter, more aware of the needs of intensive farming, must develop sensitivity in protecting farmland from damage.

Mobility in the population is a serious threat and also possibly a potential boon to the development of rural life and modern farming techniques.

REFERENCES

1 Childs, D. R., 'Chaos or balance'. *Architects' Journal*, 17 January 1962
2 Dower, M., 'The Function of Open Country'. *Town Planning Institute Journal*, April 1964, p138
3 Limb, M., 'Prices Feel the Motorway Pace'. *Sunday Times*, 8 November 1964
4 'Weekenders Drive Out Villagers: Drift from Land in Hampshire'. *The Times*, 19 September 1962
5 Gasson, R., *Influence of Urbanization on Farm Ownership and Practice*, 1966, Wye College

3e Industry and services

Recent years have been embittered by a growing conflict between farmers and the intrusion of industry and services in and through agricultural land. Many people have been angered by the despoliation of the appearance of the countryside by such development. This conflict will become increasingly intense as the modernisation of Britain, which amounts to a second industrial revolution, increases pressure on land requirements. The Director-General of the Confederation of British Industry has recognised the extent of the expected changes[1]:

> Britain will be reshaped physically during the quarter-century ahead. Britain today is a layer of cake: a mediaeval nation overlaid by the industrial revolution of the late eighteenth century and early nineteenth century; and overlaid once again—but thinly—by the technology of the twentieth century. Nothing is more certain than that Britain of the 1990s will have been completely redeployed. Whole industrial regions that exist today will disappear to be resited in greater concentration elsewhere. The first arteries of the new body of Britain are emerging; the redeployment and development of the nation between the late 1970s and the 1990s will be governed by three considerations—overall zoning geared to amenity requirements, transportation systems and indigenous fuels.

It has been recognised that further land losses will be experienced due to[2]:

> Injury or disturbance to further large areas by industrial installations, by quarries, by the construction of power transmission lines, telecommunications towers and aerials; drainage and water supply works and miscellaneous pipelines, motorways and other new routes and defence installations.

The extent of land lost to agriculture by modern urban and industrial developments is discussed later (p174). The effect of industrial growth in rural agricultural regions is more important than one purely of loss of productive land. Bracy has indicated some of the problems created by the new industrial revolution[3]:

> It is not generally appreciated that Great Britain is experiencing the first stages of a new Industrial Revolution which could have even more resounding consequences on the countryside that the Industrial Revolution of a century and a half ago. Nineteenth-century industry distributed pit tips, slag heaps, slums and grime, almost as it wished, across the face of rural England. Many of us complacently imagine that we have twentieth-century industry much more under our control. But have we? It is true that some of the worst excesses of the

137

late century would not now be tolerated: industrialists are more enlightened; the general public is more alert to the dangers; there is greater Government control.

In the past, much of the countryside was protected from industrialisation by its remoteness. This is so no longer, and, since 1946, we have seen industry invading rural areas from the Solent to Caithness and from Essex to Anglesey.

Defining land as of special landscape value for planning purposes or designating it as a National Park ought, on the face of it, to be a strong enough barrier against industrial development. This is so, if the industry is a small one, but since 1950 we have seen power stations and a refinery approved in National Parks; these exceptions have been made 'in the national interests' . . .

In general, the countryman is appallingly ignorant of present day trends which are going to alter his way of life so markedly in the future . . . The average countryman's ostrich-like attitude would be pathetic if it were not so serious. In the past he got plenty of warning of impending change, today he gets little or none . . . But all the time the face of the countryside is changing. Grid and Super-Grid, Electricity Board sub-stations and CEGB pylons, factories and power stations, refineries and filling stations—these things are happening and will continue to happen . . . Most of the industrial executives we met were rural-urban commuters. They showed themselves more alive to the dangers than many indigenous countrymen.

Bracy is correct in emphasising that parks and other designated areas are not proof against industrial development in the countryside. The National Parks Commission and the Nature Conservancy listed the breaches during the 1950s of attempts to conserve rural beauty in detail. Listed briefly they were as follows[4]:

1 750ft television mast on North Hessary Tor in the Dartmoor National Parks; permission granted 1954.

2 Oil storage depot and jetty for British Petroleum at Milford Haven in the Pembrokeshire Coast National Park.

3 Oil refinery for Esso Petroleum on 900 acres at Milford Haven; permission granted 1957.

4 Iron-ore stocking and terminal area on forty-two acres for Angle Ore and Transport in the Pembrokeshire Coast National Park; permission granted 1958.

5 Nuclear power station and 275 kV overhead transmission line for Central Electricity Generating Board at Transfynydd in the Snowdonia National Park; permission granted 1958.

6 Sand and gravel in the Malvern Hills Area of Outstanding Natural Beauty; permission granted 1958.

7 Nuclear Power station with overhead transmission lines at Dungeness in an area selected for a National Nature Reserve; permission granted 1958.

Perhaps more serious was the permitted loss in 1967 of a unique botanical area in a National Park for the construction of a reservoir at Low Green in the Tees Valley—mainly to serve chemical factories in the area. National interest for industrial development is often deemed more important than social amenity and, in this case, than rare plants. Planning consent for such developments are usually made only after extensive technical and public inquiries. Many applications for development are refused because they would disrupt the appearance of landscape of visual or scientific interest. Nevertheless, these examples illustrate that the 'national interest' can prove greater for development than conservation of landscape, even in areas set aside for special protection.

These extreme examples are not generally those which most affect farmers and agriculture. In contrast, land taken for housing is a perpetual source of anger for the farming community (p175). The creation of reservoirs also takes from agriculture large areas of farmland for each new development (p256). It is the more general intrusion of industry and services which, perhaps, cause the most friction. Stansted Airport, permitted by the Government in 1967, with its loss of 20,000 prime acres of Essex farmland and a noise nuisance estimated for twenty square miles, is the most important single clash between the urgent demands for permitting growth in modern communications and the need for sound regional planning and conservation of good agricultural land.

Motorways and other road improvement schemes sear a ribbon of construction and noise, generally through agricultural land. A new motorway, fifty yards between flanking boundaries, will absorb sixteen acres a mile, plus land required for junctions and service stations. The net loss may be more than thirty acres a mile. It is to be expected that the 1,000 mile motorway programme will need 30,000 acres of farm land. The National Farmers Union was well aware that the motorway network 'would have a dramatic impact on the countryside in general and the farming community in particular' long before the Special Roads Act of 1949, 'equal, perhaps, to the railway era of Victorian times'[5]. The Union won concessions in negotiation with the Government that farm underpasses for implements should be 15ft wide by 14ft high, or, for cattle, 18ft wide by 8ft high, and overpasses should be 15ft wide and capable of carrying twenty-four tons gross. Moreover, field drainage, ditch diversion, piping and fencing to prevent neighbouring farmland being damaged has to be carried out prior to any motorway construction. The government is responsible for the maintenance of fencing. Naturally farmers are compensated for loss of land, though this is often at rates below market values and with minimal allowance made for management disturbance in the farm. During the first years of new construction there was friction between farmers and the government and road contractors. Today most of the problems causing friction have been resolved.

There are nevertheless other problems which affect agriculture, other than the obvious reluctance of farmers to lose their own land. Noise and dust during construction, which can prove particularly serious for livestock, is a temporary annoyance and may be subject to compensation. The main risk is that a viable block of agricultural land may be carved up in such a manner that the separate parts prove uneconomic to manage in spite of overpasses and underpasses. An example has been given in the M1 extension from Crick which passes for four-and-a-half miles through the Garendon Estate in Leicestershire of 6,500 acres in sixty farms, mostly of 100–200 acres in extent. The motorway passes through seven of the estate farms, absorbing 152 acres and splitting the block of land from end to end[6]. In such cases it is probable that the estate needs major reorganisation in management and policy to remain viable. Some fear always exists that a farm might be rendered uneconomic to run and almost impossible to sell at its former value. The *Farmers Weekly* summed up with equability the motorway problem[6]:

> Certainly invasion by motorway may mean the reorganisation of a farm which may not always be convenient. There may be permanent disadvantages. But once the motorway is finished and settled its broad effect on agriculture will not be very much worse than when the railways first came a century ago. Since most farmers are motorists they, too, stand to gain from this 20th-century system for rapid communication.

Pollution of watercourses, which can be a hazard to agriculture, is restricted by the Rivers (Prevention of Pollution) Act of 1961. Aerial pollution, though also restricted to some extent, is more difficult to control and to prevent. Industrial waste is discharged via tall chimneys in several industries, some of which have rural locations, especially those based on mineral extraction. The sulphur fumes experienced from the Bedfordshire brick fields are a local problem. Cement factories can also prove an unpleasant neighbour. Some farms in north Lincolnshire receive 370 tons of dust a month per square mile, against a normal average of ten tons, largely due to a local cement factory[7]. Though these rates vary with wind and weather, one farm receives a total of 800 tons of dust a year for every square mile. The effect on livestock, as well as crops, of fluriodosis poisoning is serious. The danger from steelworks should be overcome in a decade, but that from brickworks is increasing without apparent solution.

The planning of services across farmland is a growing problem which frequently causes opposition from the farmers. Electrical distribution, and in particular the extension of the national grid with its mammoth pylons, is a subject of public concern. The 400kV super grid can require pylons about 160ft high, whereas the basic grid under 90ft, both with basic spans of 1,200ft between pylons. There is an amenity problem of siting and scale. With care the 90ft pylons are not disproportionate in great sweeps of landscape where contours and features are bold. Few English landscapes however can take the super grid pylons without loss of characteristic scale. Individual grid lines are not the real problem except in areas of outstanding beauty. The main problem which seems to be inevitable and a growing menace is that in many districts two or more grid lines, plus intermediate supply lines, convert the sweep of landscape into visual chaos. This is particularly true when lines disperse from a power station across the neighbourhood. The visual problem apart, the grid creates two problems for farmers. Firstly, and becoming increasingly important, the sweep of cables can be a serious hazard, even preventing the use of aircraft for fieldwork. Since aerial spraying is a growing practice for arable farming, the presence of overhead cables cannot be accepted without reserve. Secondly, though farmers receive rent for each pylon or pole, field obstructions interrupt the ease and rhythm of tractorwork and also provide an area for weed growth. The problem of placing cables underground has been considered by the Central Electricity Generating Board to be too expensive, except for a few prestige areas when lines are short. Nevertheless in the future new techniques might make it possible to underground much of the present proliferation of grids across farmland. This is a matter for urgent research, though a breakthrough in overcoming the problem of heat from underground cables now seems possible.

Electricity distribution is not the only service disrupting agricultural land. Davies has recognised that 'pipelines will multiply for the carriage of liquid and pulverized commodities of all kinds'[1]. The Pipelines Act of 1962 created a new era for companies wishing to lay pipes overland. A year later, the Minister of Power allowed the British Oil Pipelines Ltd to have a cross-country oil pipeline for a 300 mile route from the Thames Estuary via the Black Country to the Mersey, with a spur to Nottingham and a branch to Fawley near Southampton. The pipeline is laid for the most part 3ft deep in a trench 3ft wide. The scheme provoked widespread opposition from farmers. Gas, like oil and water, needs piped distribution to satisfy modern requirements; this will become pronounced with the development of gas supplies from the North Sea particularly from Bacton in Norfolk, now permitted as the terminal for supplies to the Midlands with feeder mains also to London and the North, the latter joining another terminal near Flamborough Head. Many new pipe lines will be needed. In addition many farms will have gas stored in underground strata below them. Sarsden in the Cotswolds may hold 10,000 cubic feet of gas if approved by the Ministry of Power. There is a growing need for transporting other materials by pipeline; these will usually be solids immersed in liquid. Coal in particular can be handled in this manner. Grain, too, can be piped. In America grain is sometimes handled over long distances from the silos to the ports. It could be that piped automatic transportation, whether as a liquid flow, pneumatic or mechanical conveyance, will be developed on a national network. There seems no reason why paper could not be handled in this manner, perhaps on an endless belt, provided power was cheap. This might be a basis for delivering mail between cities. There is in any case no doubt that there will be many more pipes laid across farmland and it is essential that these should be developed on a national basis with the co-operation of the National Farmers Union.

Surface excavation of the land is not only a visual problem, since it can destroy landscape beauty, but it may destroy agricultural land (p186). Opencast mining requires 6,500 acres a year, thoughm uch of this is returned eventually to agriculture. Similarly, ironstone extraction absorbs 600 acres a year and gravel and sand a further 2,000 acres. This can be a serious planning problem. The South-east will have a short fall of 20m cubic yards of sand and gravel by the mid-1970s (which could upset such projects as the channel tunnel which will need a vast quantity of concrete) unless 8,000 acres of farmland are sacrificed. This demand causes disquiet to local farmers and permission has been refused by the local authorities. Yet pits are becoming exhausted faster than new land is granted permission for extraction. To bring gravel to the area from the Midlands costs 9d for every ten miles. Surface excavation is in addition required for such materials as cement and brick or china clay. An inherent problem in mineral and other surface working is that their location tends to be inflexible, economic strata for excavation being restricted and sometimes available only in attractive countryside. Some quarries, tips and pits can be transformed after use into a community asset. Lakes for sailing in old quarries have become a feature in some regions. Planting round the perimeter of workings can do much to improve the landscape. Nevertheless, most workings are a visual slum due to poor co-ordination of ancillary equipment with the landscape and contours. Extraction, too, is often in conflict with farming interests. The National Farmers Union keeps a keen watch over surface workings and their protests led to a reduction in opencast mining operations[8].

As farmers emphasise, the land is their basic raw material for food production. The historical and social development over centuries has created the recognised belief that farmers own the land rather than act as its custodian. This is an important distinction since each acre taken from agriculture for other social needs almost inevitably

142

creates an uproar from the farming community who feel themselves cheated of their birthright. From the national viewpoint we are not so rich in farmland, especially good productive land, that we can afford to squander acres. But as Bracey and Davies recognised, the modern redevelopment of the national industrial pattern has liberated industry from the location straight-jacket created in Victorian times, mainly round centres for coal and steam. As Bracey stressed, the appearance of industrial development in rural areas is a feature of post-war Britain, the impact often being sudden and disrupting the rural social environment[3]. Davies has foreshadowed that[1]:

> Plant automation will have reached the point where the presence of men is no longer needed and has given way to remote control from administrative headquarters, perhaps at great distances from the plants themselves . . .
>
> It seems to me likely that within the next decade a master plan will need to emerge for the country as a whole dividing it into: industrial zones, urban administrative and amenity zones, township and sub-urban residential zones, rural and coastal amenity zones and some unclassified zones . . .
>
> Priority in zoning will be given to the preservation of rural amenities or their re-establishment in cases where potential has been adulterated by present-day insouciance. By this means great areas of the country will be safeguarded from deleterious development and cultivated to afford distractions which our leisured, affluent grandchildren will seek. Agriculture will be planned to accommodate itself to this pattern.

It seems clear that Britain will in future have less distinction between urban and agricultural land. If the best productive land is to be retained for food production, if industry is to be forced to locations where economic advantage is gained, and if the population is to be mobile in dwelling and recreation, then the poorer agricultural land should be used for industry, dwelling and recreation dispersed among farming zones. It may be that industry will become a feature of much of the countryside by the end of the century and there will be few landscapes of field, tree and cottage unbroken by modern industrial plant. With discrimination in location, scale, detail and landscaping, this might not be a serious distraction, especially considering the future scale of fields and cultivations needed for factory farming. The alternative, as Davies suggests, is to hold large areas free from all non-agricultural development, but it may be difficult to accept this except in a few areas of outstanding beauty—and even there, as has been shown, such things as power stations tend to be built in 'the national interest'. It is certain that farmers will have to change their outlook and accept the inevitable change in use for much land at present farmed, just as the public will have to accept the vast fields for modern cultivations, freed from hedges and public access.

143

This change in outlook will not be easy as it goes against the inherited, traditional pattern of land use.

REFERENCES

1 Davies, J., 'The Future Economic Shape of Britain'. *The Times*, 15 September 1964, p16
2 *The Countryside in* 1970, p103. 1964, HMSO
3 Bracey, Dr H. E., *Industry and the Countryside*, p208. 1963, Faber & Faber
4 *The Countryside in* 1970, pp176–192. Ibid
5 'Requirements of Agriculture and Motorways'. *British Farmer*, 5 September 1964, p20
6 Gurney, P., 'When the motorway comes to stay'. *Farmers Weekly*, 5 June 1966, pviii
7 Perry, T., 'Dust Clouds Settle over Lines Farm'. *Farmers Weekly*, 14 February 1964, p65
8 *British Agriculture Looks Ahead*, p48. 1964, National Farmers Union

3f Recreation

The provision of recreational facilities has become a planning problem of equal magnitude to urban renewal and traffic mobility. During the last few years some planners have recognised there must be complete reappraisal of the use of land, especially relating to the requirements of food production with leisure. No other single factor is of more importance when the future development of agriculture is considered. In 1963 *The Economist* forecast a radical change in land-use to satisfy the growing demand for recreation in Britain[1]:

> No less is needed than the literal reshaping of large chosen areas—slabs of a hundred square miles upwards—as boldly as the eighteenth-century aristocracy moulded the landscape of their choice. The difficult, but not impossible, end should be maximum possible benefit to the visiting public with the minimum degree of restriction necessary to safeguard the pleasures they come to enjoy. This would have to mean public ownership of these areas under a single authority; and—this is where the radicalness comes in—full powers to change, as well as control, land-use there. Enclosed fields and arable would go; forestry, rough grazing and other pursuits would be fitted in with, but never take precedence over, recreational use. And to be of any real value these zones must be easily reached by those who most need them.

Others have in fact forecast that half the farm land might have to be given over to recreational use by the end of the century[2]. Some planners consider the solution to be a dual use of land for agriculture

144

and recreation. But with few exceptions, discussed later, modern food production is incompatible with multiple land-use.

An American survey in 1962 recognised that the growth and distribution of recreational facilities would have to be based on four main factors[3]:

1 By the year 2000 the population of the United States will double, but the demand for outdoor recreation will treble.

2 Broadly speaking, the recreational facilities are where the population is not.

3 The most popular outdoor activity today is driving for pleasure.

4 The focal point of much outdoor recreation is water.

Dower has recognised that Britain has a similar pattern[4]. Although the British population may only rise by under forty per cent, recreational demands are likely to treble, as in America, since there is leeway to gain in overall living standards and leisure in the rapidly expanding period of early affluence. Like Americans the urban population with ever growing frequency seeks recreation by car in open country or near water, whether sea, river or lake. Present facilities are inadequate for demand, causing congestion and poor standards of hygiene and diet, still less sufficient for future trends. This is a matter of great significance for the position of agriculture in society and the appearance of the landscape.

Outdoor recreation is required for holidays and the single day or weekend trip. A man working a five-day week, with a fortnight's holiday, has about a third of each year off work. Should automation create the four-day week and four-week holiday, as is possible long before the turn of the century, then nearly half the year will be free for recreation. Holidays away from home used to be for the minority, even in the late 1940s. From about 1950 there was a rapid increase in holiday travel. This is indicated in Chart 15.

CHART 15: GROWTH OF HOLIDAYS 1955–1985

	1955	1960	1966	1985 (forecast)
population	49½m	51m	54½m	63m
holidays within Britain	21½m	26½m	31m	36m
average length of holiday	10 days	10 days	10 days	14 days
holidays abroad	2m	3½m	5m	?

Not only is there a rapid increase in the number of holidays taken away from home, both abroad and in Britain; there is an expansion in the number of second or even third holidays of more than four days duration taken during the year. By 1960, these had risen to 5m

E

and this kind of short holiday will become very popular. The duration of holidays has not risen during the last decade, though those abroad average a fortnight, but it is expected that this will increase substantially in the future. Additionally not only do Britons travel in the United Kingdom on holiday, but the number of tourists to Great Britain has increased in ten years by 150 per cent and now numbers nearly 2¾m a year and is expected to rise to 5m by 1970. Foreign tourists are the fourth largest means of gaining foreign currency, being worth £320m a year. Together with expenditure on holidays by Britons in the United Kingdom, well over £1,000m is available in tourist trade income (Britons travelling abroad spend £265m). Tourism is the mainstay of much of Scotland's rural economy and in some counties of England is almost as valuable as the production of food from agriculture (p274). This is significant in rural planning since farming does not necessarily make the main contribution to rural economy and it may therefore be desirable that farmers should not upset the tourist trade by despoiling the landscape that acts as the magnet for tourists.

Pertinent to rural planning is an analysis of travel in Britain during 1964[5]. This shows the holiday pressures growing on the countryside. Not only were two-thirds of holidays concentrated in the July to August peak period, but a fifth of all holidays were spent in the South-west region. The North-west, including the Lake District, is also popular. In contrast, both the Midlands and East Anglia each absorb under a fifteenth of all holidays, though the latter region is now promoting a tourist campaign. In all, 20m people averaged ten days somewhere on the shores of Britain. Methods of travel are also important. Half of all holidaymakers went by car. The rest were equally divided between coach, bus and train. More than half of all holidays were spent at hotels and boarding-houses and a fifth at relatives and friends. The remaining people (significant for rural planning) holiday in camps or the open. About an eighth of holidays, equal to about 4m people, were spent in caravans. It is believed that there are official sites for 525,000 caravans, three-quarters of which are within three miles of the coast[5]. A tenth of holidays are at holiday camps, canvas camps or on boats. The eighty-nine holiday camps absorb six per cent of all holidaymakers, actual camping four per cent and boating, which has become a national pastime, one per cent. Similarly trekking, climbing, hiking, skiing, as well as blood sports, are all growth activities. Rural planning has to provide facilities for these leisure needs, accommodation for holidaymakers, both formal and informal, and transport facilities to and within popular regions.

The pressure of weekend traffic as urban dwellers surge into the countryside or to the coast has become proverbial. In 1963, fifty-six per cent of the population travelled for pleasure over the Whitsun weekend, with ten per cent staying away overnight, twenty per cent

CHART 16: LAND AVAILABLE FOR RECREATION IN BRITAIN[5]

A

1962–63 (acres)
Outdoor Rural Recreation Area, England & Wales

Land classification		Lowland England	Highland England	Wales & Monmouth- shire	Total
National Parks (with access)		nil	30,390	nil	30,390
Nature reserves („ „)		6,000	7,260	4,100	17,360
National Trust („ „)		65,000	146,500	52,500	264,000
Common Lands:	minimum	distribution not known			265,000
	maximum	210,000	820,000	450,000	1,480,000
Woodland:	minimum	287,000	227,000	256,000	770,000
	maximum	1,220,000	640,000	440,000	2,300,000
Total:	minimum	358,000	411,150	312,600	1,366,750
	maximum	1,501,000	1,644,150	946,600	4,091,750
Inland water		96,500	80,000	31,500	208,000

B

Regional Distribution of the Estimated Area of Rural Land in Effective Recreational Use, England and Wales 1962–63

Region	Population 1961	Total Area (acres)	Recreation Area			Improved crops & grass % total area
			Acres	% total area	Acres per 1000 pop.	
North	14,207,075	9,061,975	1,050,000	11·6	73·6	54
Wales & W. Midlands	6,371,886	8,521,954	950,000	11·1	149·1	61
South-west	2,495,137	5,056,514	370,000	7·3	148·3	72
South-east	17,559,091	9,809,906	525,000	5·4	29·9	68
East Midlands	5,375,415	4,892,027	105,000	2·1	19·9	82
Total	46,008,604	37,342,376	3,000,000	8·0	65·1	65

having day trips and twenty-six per cent part-day trips[6]. In fact, forty per cent of all car-owning households travelled for recreation, whereas only twenty per cent of the other people left home. As car ownership increases, coupled to an extension of the five-day week, the pressure of weekend travel will also increase, making extensive demands on land for recreation. As Wibberley has stated the key to satisfactory outdoor recreation, whether as holidays or weekend pastimes, lies in location and access[5]. In the case of rural areas of beauty, such as the National Parks, location is less important than

147

access, whereas in normal areas of countryside round conurbations location is more important than access.

Wibberley has assessed the land area available for recreation in the countryside, which for the most part is in multiple use and does not always have clearly-defined legal access, so that there seems to be between 1¼ and 4m acres available with, perhaps, 3m being the most probable acreage with recognised but not statutory access. This might be divided into 880,000 lowland and 1,350,000 highland acres in England and 800,000 in Wales. In addition, Scotland has 1,107,000 acres of forest or land held either by the National Trust or the Nature Conservancy which is available for recreation, as well as over 12m acres of rough grazing, part of which is let for sport and part available for public recreation[5].

Wibberley has suggested that eight per cent of the total land area of England and Wales is partially available for recreation, but that an analysis of the regional distribution of this land shows that the East Midlands has severely restricted facilities in relation to its population and that generally the South is also limited in recreational area. The effect of those regions with large areas of improved farmland on restricting facilities for recreation is also demonstrated by this analysis. As farming becomes more intensive and as the population rapidly increases, with further land taken for urban development, so will the pressure for extended recreational facilities be frustrated unless a new concept of land-use is developed. Luckily recognition of the growing need for leisure facilities is creating a new attitude to the problem.

The National Parks, created by the 1949 Act, have provided a core of attractive land in which the Government has been able 'to promote the provision of facilities for open air recreation' and also preserve and enhance its beauty. But by the end of 1963, of the ten National Parks comprising 3·4m acres, less than one per cent (30,390 acres) were legally accessible to the public, though large parts of the rest had *de facto* rights of access. Nevertheless since total expenditure, including administration, has averaged only £20,000 a year, it is not surprising that in recent years recognition of the need for a new policy has been generated by the growing problem of leisure. In 1963, the Chairman of the National Parks Commission said[7]:

> We are reaching a turning point in the history of the National Parks ... National Parks, like other parts of the country, have become subject to the explosive force of the contemporary threat by large sections of the public to the beauty and charm of the remaining stretches of wild and unspoiled landscape, and of the overriding technical requirements of modern civilisation.

In 1965, a Standing Committee on National Parks reported that the present laws were inadequate to protect the natural beauty of the Parks and recommended that[8]:

1 Constitution to be revised so that the Ministry of Land and Natural Resources should have preponderant control, with all park authorities autonomous and having their own planning officer.

2 Needs for motor transport in the parks should be surveyed, with restriction of vehicles from special grass lanes when vehicular routes have been provided.

3 Greater control over building, road alterations, ploughing and forestry and so on.

4 Estates should be developed outside the parks providing facilities for gregarious recreation, especially near conurbations, to relieve the pressure for scrambling, caravanning and camping in the parks.

Recreational needs have increased so much since 1949 that it is now realised that promoting recreation in the parks is contradictory to preserving their beauty. Nevertheless, though pressure can be relieved by the provision of special recreational estates, the future seems certain in that the parks will become the playground of a large part of the community. It is essentially the province of the Nature Reserves to protect wild life and scenery. It is probable that the 60,000 acres held in Reserve in 1962 should be substantially increased and that other areas, perhaps in the parks, should become semi-reserves with gregarious public recreation restricted. Similarly land held by the National Trust, when public access is included, has made a real contribution to the provision of recreational land but at the same time has allowed control on development and obtrusive recreation. These three national bodies, two public and one private in control, must be the basis for providing a large part of the recreational land of the future, with that provided by the Forestry Commission (p251). The 1965 White Paper, *Leisure in the Countryside*, by re-constituting the National Parks Commission as a Countryside Commission, with wider powers, has outlined the start of the new era where leisure facilities need national guidance and planning. However, as the council for the Preservation of Rural England stated, the less popular recreations, such as walking, riding and nature study, received less impetus in the White Paper. So far only a quarter of all County Councils have set up countryside committees as outlined in the second 'Countryside in 1970' conference.

The provision of large land tracts, principally in the remoter regions, even if augmented by special recreational estates, is but a small part of the problem concerning agriculture, since for the most part these parks, reserves and forests do not threaten the future of intensive farming. As Dower recognised[4], what is required can be summarised as (and was recognised by Dr Thomas Sharp in the 1930s):

149

numerous limited areas wholly or largely devoted to intensive recreation, linked to each other and to our towns and villages by a deliberate network of linear routes and supplemented by access to the larger areas, primarily used for farming, forestry and water catchment.

The basis for linear recreation at present is fourfold, but could be radically extended in the future:

1 Long distance footpaths, such as the Pennine Way, controlled by the National Parks Commission amounted to 1,180 miles in 1963. These should be extended to form a network across the country.

2 Public footpaths and bridleways are of two types; some are recognised and protected by County Councils, others, though used by custom, do not have official designation as rights-of-way. Some counties, often encouraged by organisations such as the Ramblers Association, signpost and actively control their designated paths, while others, without being subjected to public pressure, do not notice when footpaths are cultivated and fall out of use. Many Suffolk paths, for example, are unrecognisable but will soon be at a premium due to the expansion in East Anglian population. It is vitally important for the future that footpaths are protected to provide linear access, pedestrian or bridle, without recourse to public roads right across England. Roads are generally unsuitable for pedestrians due to physical danger, noise and fumes. Moreover many paths should be co-ordinated and be part of the long distance foot-path network. At the same time, due to the needs of modern intensive agriculture with land farmed in large, unbroken fields and with its environment controlled by sprays, irrigation and other artificial aids, it is essential that some extensive areas should be restricted to any form of public access.

3 Canals provide linear access across much of Britain, both for boats and pedestrians, along their footpaths. Already part of the 2,000 miles of canal are used extensively for recreation and some, such as Stratford, have been saved from disuse by public effort. The canals should be exploited for leisure, being coupled to recreational estates along their routes, to the long distance footpath network and similar access along many of the rivers and streams. Many riverbanks, and even rivers, are restricted by private ownership or corporations and it is probable that many should be opened for recreation in the future.

4 Disused railways could provide, and in some cases already do provide, extra footpaths and are ideal for this purpose, though the spread of weeds onto farmland from their neglected banks is a major problem.

Linear recreation can be extended in many ways and can be coupled to other facilities for leisure. Again, these are basically fourfold:

150

1 The coast, as has been shown, is the most popular of all recreational areas. Though there are 2,600 miles of coastline in England and Wales only about a fifth of this is suitable for holiday resorts, as shown in Chart 17.

CHART 17: CHARACTER OF COASTLINE IN ENGLAND AND WALES

	Coastline in miles
built-up or developed	550
cliffs over 50ft high	867
cliffs under ,, ,,	146
shingle	525
sand dunes	230
marshes	280

Much of the unspoilt coastline is under pressure for development, but the National Trust is attempting to acquire more land round the coast for preservation and it is possible that they may save some of what remains unspoilt. Though at present about thirty per cent of the coastline is within National Parks or areas of outstanding beauty, this does not automatically preserve their natural character. In any case, coastline walks could be integrated in a national footpath scheme. Many coastal resorts may well be transformed into large marina holiday centres, providing an important recreational outlet for many people in concentrated areas. The projected Brighton marina along a half-mile of foreshore to provide moorings for 2,000 boats, as well as shore recreation with a dance hall, casino, pub, restaurant, cinema, theatre, bowling rink, swimming pool and so on is the most imaginative large scale unit of this kind.

2 The $1\frac{1}{2}$m acres of common land, now being examined with regard to their legal rights in use, are a safety-valve in and around many villages and towns. Registration of common land has begun. Commons have survived as an anachronism from the Mediaeval manorial system, protected from enclosure since 1865 by the Commons Preservation Society, but often misused. In fact in 1964 over half were generally neglected, at least a third were scrub and pest infested and a quarter affected by litter or vandalism[9].

Common land is nevertheless a useful national asset, providing local and sometimes regional recreational areas; it might well be linked to the network of paths in a linear plan for recreation.

3 Inland water, whether reservoir or lake, coupled with rivers and canals, should generally become recreational areas, though sometimes restricted to act as wildlife reserves. In many cases, they are already centres for fishing and boating, but much could be done to enhance their usefulness for recreation. The plan outlined in 1965 to extend and develop the Broads as a recreational area has shown what can be achieved on a regional basis.

4 New linear areas could be created to link existing natural routes. The proposal by the Civic Trust to turn the squalid and under-developed, but potentially attractive, Lea Valley, which is administered by eighteen separate authorities, into a linear park stretching from near the heart of London to the country at the North-east is an imaginative attempt to increase recreational facilities within a conurbation. Similarly in rural parts, many landscape faults, whether cliffs or clefts and unsuitable for intensive agriculture, could be used for recreational routes. Regional studies would show how much land could be made available for such purposes and how it could be linked to other routes, whether path or water.

Though linear access through the countryside is desirable and already existing in part, and though recreation is possible in some National Parks or Forests, the policy for green belts round conurbations has been for many years controversial. In 1933 Sir Raymond Unwin recognised the need for checking the spread of London and providing recreational space round the perimeter. Five years later the Green Belt Act made it possible to prevent 25,000 acres round London from being developed, part of which was also made available for recreation. Although Birmingham, Sheffield and Leeds also made some attempt before the war to control their urban sprawl, and in spite of the Town and Country Planning Act of 1947 which made it possible to restrict urban growth by refusing planning permission to develop land, the only formal proposal for a green belt by 1955 was round London. During the last decade, Green Belts have been considered primarily as a means of preventing urban sprawl. The belt round London covers 840 square miles, with proposed extensions to 2,000 square miles. The other main conurbations also have belts, agreed in principle at least, but varying in effectiveness[10]. They have done much to prevent the worst excesses of ribbon development or the linking together of towns in larger conurbations. Nevertheless their existence is continually under pressure from developers and by 1965 the policy for encouraging green belts seemed to be falling apart. Much needs to be known concerning land-use, with its many contingent problems, before urban restraint or green belt policies can prove effective. It does not seem that public opinion understands or endorses the need for checking urban growth, nor has there been any demand for using the belts for recreation, rather than farming, as originally intended when they were conceived.

As *The Economist* suggested in the quotation at the beginning of this section, land patterns may have to be drastically reshaped to satisfy the need for recreation. Similarly it was pointed out that this need was not the same as that for controlling urban growth. In practice, green belts appear to be areas of rural land round conurbations primarily used for agriculture, but this does not ensure freedom of movement or relaxation for the urban population. In fact intensive agriculture and recreational needs are incompatible. Extensive farming, perhaps as a form of ranch farming, is uneconomic on fertile and expensive land. Multi-purpose land used for grazing livestock, rambling or picnicking is realistic in highland or heath areas only and even then the economics of managing livestock are uncertain except under specific conditions. The eighteenth-century landscape principle of having cattle and sheep in parkland has no basis in modern husbandry. Grassland today has to be treated as an important and expensive crop, cultivated as any other, with permanent and largely untreated grassland of limited value. Modern farming requires concentrated control over all physical aspects of the land within its sphere. In contrast forestry at certain stages of tree growth is generally more suitable than agriculture for multi-use, because it is possible to combine recreational facilities with cropping. Water conservation can also have a use for leisure.

It may prove possible to restrict agriculture to more fertile land, thus releasing marginal or poorer land for recreation, without an overall loss in food production due to the increased productivity of modern farming (p207). Wibberley has suggested that, provided urban development does not absorb good farm land, it should be possible to release ample lower quality land from agriculture to satisfy all other needs, including recreation up to 1970, and by inference long after that date[5]. It may in fact prove to be the case that poor grade land will become uneconomic to farm during another decade, absorbing too much capital in the form of equipment, labour and fertilizer in return for below average yields compared with intensive farming. It will certainly be socially desirable to release low grade land near conurbations for recreational purposes. This is fundamentally important in the East, the Midlands and the South since, as has been shown, these areas are restricted in recreational land compared to the population.

As agriculture becomes more industrialised, it becomes clear that urban and farm land must be distinct and, moreover, that recreational and farm land must have a clear division. Thus, there must be green belts round all urban centres, preferably with clear-cut definition. These belts may be agricultural or recreational in character, depending principally on topography, unless used for forestry or water conservation when they may have a dual use including some facilities for recreation. Some highland or heath may be ranch farmed, but allowing public access. If good land encircles an urban area, then recreational land should be further out than the perimeter. Pockets of poor land in the country will in any case be used for recreation, some of which should act as viewing places over intensive farm land to make it possible for the public to see and possibly understand modern farm practice. As many recreational areas as possible should be linked by roads with parking facilities or by linear recreational routes, such as river, canal or path. The basis of such development must come from regional studies, with suitable land being withdrawn from agriculture by public acquisition. The need for recreation is great, is growing and needs new policies for its satisfaction. The problem cannot be left to unplanned and haphazard solution and time is limited before there is a social crisis, frustrating farmer and urban dweller alike.

REFERENCES

1 'Land for leisure'. *The Economist*, 13 July 1963, p14
2 Beresford, T. Farm Management Association Conference. April 1965
3 *Outdoor recreation resources in the United States*. Report of the Review Commission. 1962
4 Dower, M. 'The function of open country'. *Town Planning Institute Journal*, April 1964, p136
5 *British Travel Association Survey* 1964
Wibberley, G. P. and Burton, T. L., *Outdoor recreation in the British Countryside*. 1965, Department of Economics, Wye College
6 *Survey of Whitsun holiday travel*. British Travel & Holidays Association. 1963
7 Strang, Lord, *The future of National Parks. The Countryside in* 1970. p210. 1964, HMSO
8 *The future of National Parks and the Countryside*. Standing Committee on National Parks, 1965
9 Denman, D. R., *Report to the Royal Society of Arts*. 15 January 1964
10 Ministry of Housing and Local Government, *The Green Belts*. 1962, HMSO

154

4 LAND: STRUCTURE

Introduction

The structure of the land of Britain means different things to different people. The geologist and the geographer have already comparatively detailed maps concerning their subject. Though their knowledge becomes more comprehensive, due to new techniques of measurement and survey, drastic changes in their records are comparatively rare. The archaeologist and the historian see their structure of Britain, in which many gaps of knowledge are rapidly being closed due to modern research, as a social rather than a physical fabric. The architect, planner and landscapist see the impingement of history on the geological and geographic fabric in terms of buildings, towns and countryside. The farm agriculturalist, as opposed to the scientist or planner agriculturalist, sees the map of Britain in terms of the distribution of crops and livestock. His knowledge is recorded and demonstrated in specialised atlases with precision and detail. However, in a crowded country, with an expanding population creating enormous pressures on every acre of land that is not completely desolate and rugged, it is surprising and alarming that the planner in land-use has completely inadequate maps and statistics available for his work.

The foundation of any study in land-use lies, naturally, on the area of land available. Overall land areas are known with some accuracy, continually being revised by degrees by the Ordnance Survey Department. Nevertheless few of the maps available are accurate with regard to changes of use and, therefore, of land area as divided into different categories of use. Though agricultural acreage are known for different crops and livestock, compiled from agricultural returns made each year by farmers, these contain inaccuracies due to their method of compilation and do not easily reveal the actual land pattern as farmed. There is moreover considerable fringe land of doubtful, confused or multiple use which is either unclassified or recorded under the wrong category. It is not easy to know how much land is really suitable for agriculture nor where it is distributed. It is of more concern to the land planner that even this knowledge,

155

which is not ideal, is of doubtful value since it is not related to detailed maps of soil structure and terrain. Knowledge of land classification by soil and physical character in relation to farming is based largely on surveys made nearly a third of a century ago. No-one knows the potential fertility of Britain's agricultural land, though maps being prepared will to some extent indicate present fertility. Even worse, no-one can really determine the priorities in land-use for any district or area, nor decide which land should be taken out of farming for urban or other needs. It is impossible to gauge how much undrained, poor or generally infertile land might be made productive by using modern techniques of reclamation. It is impossible to assess how much land is potentially available for intensive farming. It is impossible to estimate how much food the United Kingdom might produce if a determined effort was made.

It is not surprising that since land classification is inadequate there is only partial knowledge concerning annual changes in land-use, particularly with regard to the loss of agricultural land. The present annual loss for urban development may be around 40,000 acres (it may well be about 50,000 acres) much of it being in the lowland regions. In addition 40,000 acres are taken for forestry, but much of it in less fertile regions. Unfortunately not only is the exact total area lost unknown, but the location of loss and, more particularly, the loss by soil classification is not recorded. The real loss to agriculture in terms of potential production is therefore not known. Since it has been suggested that another 2m acres will be needed for urban development before the end of the century, it is important that the character of this loss should be determined. If the bulk of it proved to be fertile land, the consequences could be serious for the nation. By careful planning, the development could be largely diverted on to potentially less fertile land. In addition, large areas of land should be provided for recreational needs, much of it close to urban areas and, therefore, tending to be within agricultural regions. However, again with planning, this could be directed towards land unsuitable by terrain and soil structure for intensive farming even in districts which are predominantly agricultural. This kind of planning is possible only if there are detailed maps and statistics available for the planners.

One of the most encouraging aspects of land-use during the last few years has been the national determination to reclaim much of the derelict land of Britain generated by urban spoliation. The large areas of land laid waste, partly by greed and partly by extravagance, have been a national disgrace throughout this century. Only recently have these areas been recorded. It is possible that this waste will become controlled in the future, many of the derelict areas being restored to agriculture or urban needs. Land reclamation of water, marsh and moor has been a perennial challenge to agriculturalists.

With modern machinery the challenge is easier to accept even though the areas suitable for reclamation have become fewer. Today however, barrage schemes could become a feature of several coastal areas. Feasibility studies are already being made with regard to several estuaries. It is possible that such engineering feats will make a contribution to agriculture in the future equal to the Fen drainage project of the last centuries.

Any land planning not only has to take into account the physical structure of Britain, but must also be based on recognition of the ownership and value of the land itself. This is an important facet of the overall land structure from the planner's viewpoint. The categories of ownership of much of the agricultural land is however unrecorded. Although the division throughout Britain between farms which are owner-occupied and those which are tenanted is known, both sections being about equal in area, the type or status of owner in each case is not clear. Many farms are not owned by individuals. There is growing ownership by companies or authorities of one kind or another. The problem of nationalised land ownership, which is possible if social pressures should change, has created much political dissention in recent years. The change in ownership due to normal economic trends however needs better analysis if land planning is to be useful, with a survey of existing ownership. Vertical integration in agriculture will change the structure of ownership over the next decades, even if land nationalisation does not take place. It is probable that many large companies will, either for food retail or food processing or both, begin to acquire or indirectly control, through contract farming, much of the land. Other land will pass into the ownership of joint stock or limited companies formed by the farmers themselves to counteract the pressure from retail integration into agriculture. Many of the farmers, managers or workers, are in any case likely to become part-time agriculturalists, having other occupations in addition to their farm work. This becomes increasingly possible with mechanisation and specialisation.

During the last few years the structure of farming has been shaken by the phenomenal rise in agricultural land values, which have on average trebled in the last seven years. Whereas traditional farming was, and still is, based on land having a rental value of between £2–£4 an acre, today, with modern land prices, it should be between £15–£20 an acre. On this basis only the most streamlined and intensive farming operations are economic. The full impact of this transition has not yet been felt by many farmers, especially those who have held their land for many years, if not for generations. Nevertheless commercial farmers, working to proper modern costing techniques, have to include their land as a fixed overhead on the basis of its real value. There seems moreover little reason to believe that land values will not continue to rise. Nothing will prompt the development of factory farming so much as recognition that a return from the land has to be commensurate with its real value. This situation will create physical changes in the landscape discussed in the next chapter.

4b Land area and land-use

The total land area of the United Kingdom, though not constant, is known with some accuracy. In contrast the manner in which the land is used for different functions is not known with any precision. No authority makes a regular census recording changes in the national use of land. This is surprising and tragic considering the many demands on land resources made by an expanding industrial society.

England, as is well known, is a crowded country. Within a national division of land, there would be less than three-quarters of an acre, whether mountain, forest, urban or farm, for each member of her population. If however such a share-out were limited to improved farmland, which excludes rough grazings, each person would own about half an acre only. By the end of this century the country will have become much more crowded, there then being within the total land area available no more than just over half an acre for each person due to the estimated population increase. If the agricultural area shrinks by 4m to 5m acres to under 20m acres as may be probable, there would be only about a third of an acre of improved farmland for each member by the year 2000. If the country is to become almost self-sufficient for temperate foodstuffs, as will be desirable if not essential, then each acre of farmland must feed three people. In contrast, if there were no imports of temperate food, which actually account for about one third of consumption, then each acre of improved farmland would at present only support about one-and-a-quarter people.

The situation is hardly better if the United Kingdom as a whole is considered rather than England alone. With an existing total population of 54m there is rather more than an acre for each person within the total land area—about 1·1 acres in fact. Considering improved farmland only, there is about the same area available (that is just over half an acre for each person) as for England with her existing population of nearly 45m. By the end of the century, the total area of improved farmland in the United Kingdom may have shrunk from 31m to, perhaps, about 25m acres, farmed intensively. This estimate takes into account the fact that some of the extensive rough grazing areas, especially in Scotland and Northern Ireland, may have been reclaimed for productive farmland. With the population of the United Kingdom estimated to be nearly 75m by the year 2000, the improved farmland available for each person will be similar to that

158

estimated for England, that is about a third of an acre. The significance of this estimate is considered later (p212). In order however to support the population by the end of the century, agricultural output from each acre would have to rise by 250 per cent if food imports were to be restricted to the present percentage, without allowing for any improvement or increase in nutritional standards. On this basis it would be prudent to husband the fertile land available for food production and sacrifice for urban needs only that land unsuitable for factory farming. Unfortunately there is a general national indifference to the use made of land; few people not only consider it to be the most important of all national assets but are also prepared to accept the sacrifice to individual liberty necessary to make the best use of the resources available. As demands on land intensify, this indifference must precipitate social unrest during the next decades. Lord Holford stressed how the flashpoint is near in the 1967 Maitland Lecture to the Institution of Structural Engineers by saying, 'More and more evidence is piling up to establish a critical population density that a given agricultural and ecological system can support, and at a density of more than 5 % people to the square mile the United Kingdom has already passed the critical point.'

The United Kingdom has a land area established by the Ordnance Surveys of nearly $59\frac{1}{2}$m acres. This area is not constant due to a process of erosion and silting perpetually occurring around the coast, changes in the area of inland water and land reclamation. Moreover discrepancies in surveys occur, especially in the estimate for the high-water tidal position which defines the land area. Estimates of land areas, for example, have been reduced since 1910 by about 40,000 acres. Chart 18 gives the land area established in 1958, excluding the Channel Islands, the Isle of Man and the Scilly Isles, plus the additional areas for inland water, and the acreage of the improved farmland, including arable and permanent grass as well as rough grazings, according to the agricultural statistics for 1961 prepared by the Ministry of Agriculture. The last, as discussed elsewhere, tends to include several grounds for inaccuracy, being based on agricultural returns for all holdings of more than a quarter acre (p218)[1].

It is evident from this analysis that about two-thirds of England and Wales is improved farmland, whereas only about a half of the United Kingdom taken as a whole is similarly either arable or permanent grass. Scotland in particular has less than a quarter of her land in this category, but having instead almost two-thirds of the total area of the country as rough grazing. Only about an eighth of England and Wales and less than a quarter of Northern Ireland is in contrast rough grazing. The category of rough grazing land is generally synonymous with open moors. Agriculture considered as an entity with regard to land-use includes all cropland, whether

159

CHART 18: ESTIMATED UK LAND AREAS IN 1958

	Total Land Area sq miles	acres	Inland Water acres	Improved Land acres	% total
England	50,051	32,034,660	176,640	24,393,695	66
Wales and Monmouth-shire	7,966	5,009,041	32,640		
Scotland (incl: 186 habitated isles)	29,795	19,068,734	393,600	4,308,573	23
Northern Ireland	5,206	3,331,840	161,120	1,935,159	58
Total	93,018	59,444,275	764,000	30,637,427	51

(continued)

	Rough Grazings acres	% total
England, Wales and Monmouthshire	4,960,432	13
Scotland (incl: 186 habitated isles)	12,435,529	65
Northern Ireland	787,460	24
	18,183,421	31

arable, permanent grass or rough grazing. On this basis, agriculture accounts for over four-fifths of the land area of the United Kingdom, ranging from seventy-nine per cent for England and Wales, to eighty-two per cent for Northern Ireland (the general average) and as much as eighty-eight per cent for Scotland.

Agricultural land areas can be considered in two basic but different classifications. In the first place, areas devoted to different crops can be analysed and, since statistics are prepared by the Ministry of Agriculture from the annual returns completed by farmers, this is relatively easy for showing changes in agricultural land-use, provided their tendency to error is borne in mind. Secondly, land can be classified according to terrain and soil and drainage structure. This gives a better indication of potential fertility and the potential value to food production of the land itself. Unfortunately knowledge of how the land may be classified in this manner rests largely on studies made by the Land Utilisation Survey in the 1930s which were published in a summarised form by Professor Dudley Stamp in 1948. However, new surveys should be complete by 1970 (p67). The Agricultural Land Service is preparing maps showing not only the classification of land in five grades but also an output cash value, albeit based

160

on average production, standard management and normal fertilizer practice.

Agricultural returns for June 1964 showed a slight drop in total acreages from those given above for June 1961, but during the last few years they have also shown marked increases in the acreages for wheat and barley, with a decline in other corn crops, a slight overall increase in other tillage crops (particularly certain crops for stock-feeding) but generally a reduction in grasslands, including temperary, permanent and rough grazing acreages.

CHART 19: CROP ACREAGE IN JUNE 1964 IN MILLION ACRES

	England & Wales	Scotland	N Ireland	Total
Corn	7·12	1·05	0·29	8·46
Potatoes	0·55	0·15	0·07	0·77
Sugar beet	0·43	0·01	—	0·44
Other crops	1·25	0·30	0·01	1·56
Orchards, fruit, hops	0·26	0·01	0·01	0·28
Total tillage	9·61	1·52	0·38	11·51
Temporary grass	4·34	0·72	0·62	5·68
Permanent grass	10·43	2·08	1·00	13·51
Total crops and pasture	24·38	4·32	2·00	30·70
Rough grazing	4·86	12·39	0·65	17·90
Total agriculture	29·24	16·71	2·65	48·60

This analysis reveals two factors of significance when considering agricultural acreages. In England and Wales two-fifths of the improved farmland is given over to tillage which is about equal to a quarter of the total land area. One acre in four appears therefore as cornland, orchard, fields of vegetables or soft fruit. In contrast Northern Ireland has only one-fifth of the improved farmland as tillage, equal to little more than a tenth of the total land area. This gives a clear indication of the different agricultural structure of the two countries. The second factor is perhaps more significant when considering the future of agriculture. Even if the rough grazed moorlands are not considered, under a third of the total grass area is ploughed and sown; in contrast, in Northern Ireland only about a quarter is temporary, that is cultivated, grassland. Permanent grassland for grazing has been and still is traditional to generations of farmers.

In England and Wales, even when the rough grazings are not included in the statistics for grassland, more than one acre in every four of the total land area is devoted to permanent meadows and pasture. It is not surprising that many parts of the country give a general impression of a traditional, pastoral landscape with green fields stretching to the horizon, stocked with cattle and sheep peacefully grazing. This is the image gained particularly in Midlands and shires of England. In the United Kingdom there are well over 12m acres of permanent grass. In spite of the great conurbations, the historic hardwood and modern softwood forests, the mountainous regions of north and west, and the vast stretches of rough-grazed downland, every fifth acre in the Kingdom is unploughed grassland. Within this image, created by the facts of the actual use made of the land by farmers, it is difficult to believe that agriculture has changed significantly since the enclosures. Permanent grass, largely due to the inter-war work of Sir George Stapledon at Aberystwyth, is the antithesis of modern intensive farming. Temporary leys, usually of three years duration, are a feature of modern cattle management, especially in milk production. Grass should be treated as a crop, with techniques similar to those for any other crop. Although this is true, grassland management in the country as a whole is still generally treated by nineteenth-century methods. Some modern grass preparations do, it is true, provide weed control and seeding without ploughing, but this is a recent and limited technique, though possessing revolutionary possibilities for the future (p412). The permanent grassland areas are one of the principal and largely unexploited natural resources of the United Kingdom. As Davis pointed out[2]:

> Although England is overpopulated and her agricultural land fairly efficiently utilised, Scotland, and more especially Ireland, have a considerable area of land which is capable of greatly increasing production if sufficient money were available for conditioning, fertilizers and weed control. To quote one example, it has been shown that the productivity of a poor pasture can be raised by 500 per cent with proper weed control. We have, therefore, a large potential source of food on our doorstep which still remains to be developed.

That this example is extreme is perfectly true, because it describes the improvement of a 'weed-riddled pasture in Ireland'. Nevertheless the numerous thistle-infested and generally rank fields still to be seen in England are a national disgrace. In any policy for the planning of rural land, it must be assumed that land is for the most part farmed intensively, or taken out of agriculture for urban or recreational needs. The interplay of intensive and extensive farming patterns is discussed later (p378).

Not all agricultural land is potentially suitable for intensive farming. As previously stated, land can be classified not only by its crop acreages, but also by its general structure according to soil, terrain and drainage. It is in this respect that knowledge is limited.

Statistics are still largely based on the surveys made in the 1930s by Professor Dudley Stamp, published in 1948 as *The Land of Britain—Its Use and Misuse*. A detailed analysis is given in Appendix A. Stamp divided the land area into regions of good, medium and poor quality, sub-divided into ten classifications, plus the urban areas which then amounted to about three per cent of England and Wales or two-and-a-quarter per cent of Great Britain.

CHART 20: LAND CLASSIFICATION SUMMARY OF PRE-WAR BRITAIN

| Land Classification | Percentage of total land area pre-1939 | | |
	England Wales I of Man	Scotland	Gt Britain
First class	5·3	2·1	4·2
„ „ (heavy)	3·3	0·0	2·1
Good	26·0	10·1	20·6
„ (heavy)	13·3	8·6	11·7
Medium (light)	7·0	0·4	4·8
„ (other)	25·0	14·7	21·5
Moorland	12·1	62·9	29·3
Other poor land	4·9	0·6	3·5

nb Isle of Man: 140,986 total acreage.

Thirty years, a major war and an agricultural revolution have passed since the structure of the land was surveyed. How much of the first class or good land assessed by Stamp has been lost to urban development is unknown. Similarly how much land might be upgraded due to improved drainage or reclamation is also unknown. Assessments of land-use, based on out-of-date surveys, must be inaccurate, preventing either a sensible appraisal of the present situation or the preparation of a national plan for land-use in the future. The situation has been improved to some extent by a detailed study by Best in 1959, followed by a further study in 1962 by Best and Coppock[3]. These studies showed wide discrepancies between the assessments of land-use made by the Land Utilisation Survey and those made by other organisations, particularly by the Ministry of Agriculture and especially with regard to assessments of agricultural and urban land. Best was able to study the statistical methods used in previous assessments and collate their results with other published evidence, thereby establishing an appraisal of land-use. He was able to put forward a new classification of land-use for England and Wales, based on the year 1950, which gives an idea of how at that time the land was divided into four major categories: agriculture, multiple and special uses, woodland and urban development.

163

Land-use	Area '000 acres	Proportion of land area %
Agriculture: (land used primarily for farming)		
Arable	13,949	37·5
Permanent grass	10,496	28·3
Rough grazing	3,969	10·7
Total	28,414	76·5
Multiple and Special Uses:		
Common rough grazings	1,502	4·0
Service departments	850 ?	2·3 ?
Water gathering grounds (Water Board)	500 ?	1·3 ?
Opencast mineral workings	150 ?	0·4 ?
Civil airfields	35	0·1
Unclassified	250 ?	0·7 ?
Total	3,287	8·8
Woodland:		
High Forest	1,812	4·9
Small towns and villages (under 10,000 population)	717	1·9
Isolated dwellings	534	1·4
Other Urban land	539	1·5
Total	3,602	9·7
TOTAL LAND-USE	37,676	101·4
Total Land area	37,133	100·0

Best has appreciated the limitations of an appraisal which is not based on modern surveys. His assessment given in Chart 21, already refers to a land classification more than fifteen years out-of-date and it does not analyse the agricultural potential of the farmland available. This important aspect of land classification has still to be based on pre-war analysis. Best has nevertheless helped by his work the study of rural planning in relation to agriculture. His assessment, given in the table below, shows an aggregate area of used land greater than

164

the actual land area available. The discrepancy arises from errors of appreciation as well as from the fact that some land, having a multiple use, will be included in the assessment more than once. Best records that in fact multiple land-use is a growing feature of modern society. Some land used by the services for example, may also have an agricultural function. Similarly water gathering grounds may also be used for grazing or other purposes. Nevertheless an error of about one-and-a-half per cent is not serious for general discussion and has to be accepted until an extensive survey is made.

By 1960, the land-use pattern had changed as further recorded and summarised by Best[4]:

	Land-use in England and Wales 1960	
	Area '000 acres	% Total land area
Arable	13,665	36·8
Permanent grass	10,780	29·0
Rough grazing	4,999	13·5
Total agriculture	29,445	79·3
Woodland	2,540	6·8
Urban development	3,965	10·7
Unaccounted areas	1,180	3·2

In order to plan the future of Britain it is essential to produce a detailed land utilisation survey including ground-use and terrain classification that records changes in every decade with population and industrial studies. There is no indication that the nation is willing to do this, though the Second Land Utilisation Survey being prepared will help to fill the vacuum which has existed since the 1930s.

It seems that only about six per cent of the land, which excludes Northern Ireland, is agriculturally first-class, that is capable of cultivation for prime foodstuffs; a further twenty per cent is good general land suitable for ploughing for grass and crops. Eleven per cent is good heavy land suitable for a restricted range of crops. It would seem therefore that only about a third of the land is generally suitable for intensive or near-intensive agriculture, representing at most 22m acres. Another five per cent, being light but practical for ploughing and equal to about another $2\frac{1}{2}$m acres, might be suitable for semi-intensive farming. It is possible that Northern Ireland might contribute up to another $1\frac{1}{2}$m acres. On this basis, though essentially an assessment from the 1930s, 26m acres are available in the United Kingdom for varying degrees of intensive food production. Some of this land will certainly have already been absorbed for other needs; and new development during the remainder of this century will make

165

further reductions. Any analysis of this kind is, in the absence of accurate statistics fraught with difficulty. Allowing however for land losses, plus compensation from upgraded or reclaimed land, it may be reasonable to assume a land area of about 25m acres available within the whole of the United Kingdom for intensive or near intensive food production by the year 2000. As previously stated, this will be about equal to a third of an acre for each person. This will nevertheless be true provided that urban expansion is directed as much as possible to the medium, but difficult agriculturally, and other generally poor quality land which, excluding moorland, represents about a quarter of the total land area, that is perhaps around 14m acres. This land should be used, for as much urban growth as is practicable, for recreational needs, forestry and water conservation in the form of reservoirs. The rest could be suitable, if selected, for a certain amount of extensive, even ranch, farming as discussed below.

The overall urban character of the United Kingdom, especially England and Wales, is emphasised by the fact that four-fifths of the population live in the larger settlements which have over ten thousand people. In the case of England and Wales, with 35m people in settlements of this size, the land area required for them is less than 2m acres, according to Best's analysis. Only about five per cent of the land area is used for the larger towns and cities. A substantial part of the population lives in the great conurbations created by the first industrial revolution—London, the Black Country, Merseyside, the Pennine cities and Tyneside. The social significance of these city regions and the drift of population has already been discussed (p115). The effect on the countryside in England and Wales of urban expansion in regional areas between 1950 and 1960 has been clearly expressed by Professor Wibberley in an analysis made at Wye College in 1967, shown in chart 22.

Nevertheless the rural areas of England and Wales, which include smaller settlements such as market towns, villages, hamlets and farmsteads, have already a population of nearly 10m, requiring $1\frac{1}{4}$m acres. The overall population density in these areas is approximately half of that in the larger settlements. There are no statistics giving details of the distribution of the population in rural areas, but about a quarter of those in the smaller settlements—approximately $2\frac{1}{2}$m people—live in isolated dwellings and use nearly half the land area needed by all the smaller settlements and isolated dwellings.

It is not possible to establish how many of these isolated dwellings are used by farmers and farm workers. Many farms are situated in hamlets and villages and by no means all farm workers live on the farm land. There are however nearly $\frac{1}{2}$m farm workers, plus perhaps as many farmers, and if each lived in family units of four people (which is above the national average) this would about equal the

166

Standard Region	Urban area 1960–61 % total regional area (incl: inland water)	Percentage Urban Growth 1950–60
London and SE	35·6	2·1
NW England	28·7	1·8
EW Ridings	14·2	0·9
Midland	12·7	1·4
Southern	9·7	1·6
North Midland	7·8	0·9
Eastern	6·9	1·4
Northern	5·9	0·5
SW England	5·0	0·5
Wales	4·4	0·2
Av: England & Wales	10·4	1·0

2½m people known to live in isolated dwellings. If an arbitrary allowance were to be made that an eighth of the farmhouses were not isolated and that a quarter of the farm workers lived in settlements, then about ½m people living in isolated dwellings might have no direct connection with work on the land. It is probable that this is an underestimate. Some of these people, though not farming, would be indirectly concerned with agriculture, working for commercial or social services connected with the countryside. Even if this assessment is inaccurate, it is true that not only are farmers and farmworkers being reduced in numbers by about 25,000 a year but many others are moving from isolated dwellings into the villages and small towns. Similarly, the demand for isolated houses by urban people, either as dwellings or holiday homes, increases every year (p134).

CHART 23: URBAN LAND-USE IN GREAT BRITAIN IN 1950
SETTLEMENTS OF UNDER 10,000 PEOPLE[3]

	England & Wales			
	acres	'000 pop:	acres	'000 pop:
small highland settlements	231,096	3,069	143,590	1,764
„ lowland „	485,677	4,688	—	—
isolated dwellings	534,526	2,586	81,203	588
railways in open country	134,332	—	27,011	—
roads in open country	404,718	—	107,997	—
Total	1,790,349	10,343	359,801	2,352

The hills and uplands present a difficult agricultural problem, though farmers in these regions have received government aid for many years. These regions are of course suitable in parts for forestry and recreation. Moreover, reservoirs and hydro-electric schemes are often sited in the less tractable parts of Britain. Hill farming is generally taken as being at over the 1,000ft contour level where extensive systems for rearing sheep or cattle are practised. Nevertheless, upland areas were taken to include land between 600–800ft and 1,400–1,500ft by the Committee on Hill Sheep Farming in 1944, since this zone could support most crops and livestock with reasonable levels of intensive production. Similarly hill farming is chiefly at over the 1,500ft contour, but extensive systems may be suitable in some areas as low as 1,000ft due to terrain and climate. It is difficult to assess the area devoted to hill and upland farming, but Wibberley and Davidson estimated that it amounted to nearly 14m acres in Great Britain in 1956, farmed at that time in about 40,000 holdings, which was rather less than a tenth of all holdings[5]. They estimated that in 1953, the net agricultural output from these regions was about £40m, including £11m for sheep plus £5m for wool, £6¼m for cattle and £7¼m for milk. This output included nearly £3¼m in direct subsidies or about thirteen per cent of net output. Total subsidies at that time were over £7½m for hill and upland areas. Whether or not this is a high price for supporting marginal farming areas is a difficult social and economic problem, especially since part of the upland agricultural techniques are interwoven with lowland food production. A decade ago, this quarter of the land area produced only four per cent of agricultural output. In 1964, however, the National Farmers Union gave their support for maintaining hill farming[6]:

> The hill farms of this country occupy one-third of the total farming area: they provide a vital source of breeding and store animals for farms in lowland areas. The Union regards it as imperative that the full potential of the hill areas should be developed in order to help meet the increased and growing demand for meat. This means that special facilities for hill farmers should not be reduced.

It is probable that modern technical aids, such as weed control without ploughing, seeding by aerial or spray-gun techniques and new strains of grass, will revitalise upland and hill farming, especially if new management techniques are introduced. For example in 1963 Professor Cooper called for a complete reappraisal of hill land, with dairy farming largely eliminated and sheep grazing limited to five or six summer months coupled with in-wintered housing[7]. On this basis more stock could be grazed on each acre, wool clip could be substantially increased, and lambing percentages and fertility periods improved. Severe winter losses could be avoided, working conditions

168

bettered and the output from each ewe nearly doubled. The future of farming these 14m difficult acres in Britain could be transformed, but it would be essential for large areas to be ranch farmed under single management. Intensive research backed by experiment at farm level is needed to boost farm outputs.

Much needs to be known about the structure and use made of the land. It is impossible to forecast with any precision whether the farmland available will be able to support the future population of the country. Not only is the land area unknown at the present time according to terrain and fertility, but also the amount of good land, suitable for intensive food production, being lost each year. Good land is being sacrificed recklessly for a multitude of projects. This is evident from a study of the national press. Seldom is the assessment of change in land-use ever made on the relevant issues of agricultural fertility, food production and national need. This must be so, due to present ignorance. Nevertheless a rational policy for land-use can only evolve if full studies are made of the basic, national resource— the land of Britain. These studies should be a matter of government priority.

REFERENCES

1 *Britain, an Official Handbook*. 1965, HMSO
Agricultural Statistics for the United Kingdom 1961–62. 1964, HMSO
2 Davis, J. G. 'The Food Industry in AD2000.' *Journal of the Royal Society of Arts*, January 1966
3 Best, R. H., *The Major Land-uses of Great Britain*. Studies in Rural Land-use no 4. 1959, Wye College
4 Best, R. H. 'Recent Changes and Future Prospects of Land-use in England and Wales'. *Geographical Journal*, March 1965
5 Davidson, B. R., and Wibberley, G. P., *The Agricultural Significance of the Hills*. Studies in Rural Land-use no 3. 1956, Wye College
6 *British Agriculture Looks Ahead*. 1964, National Farmers Union
7 Cooper, M. McG. Association of Agriculture Conference. Yorkshire (WR) Institute of Agriculture, Askham Bryan, Yorks, 1963

4c Loss of agricultural land

In recent years the appearance of Great Britain has changed perceptibly, both in town and country. Demands on the use of land have increased due to expansion of the population, industry and modern means of communication. These pressures were discussed in the previous chapter. They have led to increased national awareness that agricultural land is being lost rapidly to urban development. Each time a new town is planned or an existing town expanded, there is an outcry from the farming community that they are being dispossessed of their natural heritage—the ownership of rural land. Each time a motorway is constructed, not only do farmers lose some land, but farms may be split into uneconomic production units. Each time industry builds in the countryside (which for diverse reasons is increasing) not only is there a change in land-use but the social structure of rural life in the district concerned may be transformed.

Since about 1950, urban and industrial absorption of farm land has become pronounced. Suburban sprawl was deplored in the 1930s because it destroyed the natural beauty of the countryside. Many warnings were given, especially in such books of essays as *Britain and the Beast* devoted to prophesying doom unless the nation paused to think again and plan her land resources[1]:

> What are we doing with our inheritance? Every one can answer that sorry question. In the last fifteen years we have gashed it to pieces with arterial roads, trimmed the roads with trash, and ruined several selected areas systematically[a].
> We are making a screaming mess of England[b].
> Part of the price for a saner and more ordered England must be paid for in liberty—not omitting that most cherished private right to do public wrong[c].

Nevertheless the loss of agricultural land today seems to be visibly accelerating at alarming speed, especially in the South-east and round urban areas. In the long term, the loss in food production caused by the shrinkage in land available for this purpose might not prove serious provided the demand for food remained constant and food imports did not diminish. Though factory farming methods, by increasing productivity of each acre, can more than compensate for the annual loss of farm land, even including loss of good agricultural land for building, total food consumption will increase substantially due to the growth in population and consumption per head and the cost of food imports will become disproportionate unless they are reduced. Therefore land losses may soon become critical.

The indiscriminate and unplanned use of agricultural land for other purposes, as largely happens at present in spite of national planning policies, may have far-reaching social repercussions. It is remarkable that in a crowded island little is known concerning land-use or change in land-use, especially with regard to their significance for food production. Britain is however not alone in the problem of losing food producing land at a rate giving alarm. In the United States, as Highbee has observed, the situation could become critical[2]:

> An official of the Department of Agriculture has estimated that though we shall need 40 per cent more food in 1975 than we had in

170

1955, we are losing productive agricultural land to suburbanisation and other development pressures at the rate of one million acres annually. Thus food supply . . . may eventually become a concern in America. Surpluses cannot very well persist indefinitely under the twin assault of human multiplication and farm subtraction . . . Of comparable importance, and of immediate concern to most taxpayers, is the probability that as farm shrinkage continues on the peripheries of major cities, little open land will eventually remain between the suburban outposts of abutting Metropolitan areas. Unless precautions are taken, whole regions such as that between Boston and Washington are destined to become built up complexes of fused cities . . .

America, losing 1m acres of farmland a year, has a population growth of 3m. In the decade from 1950, the central cities gained 1·5 per cent in population, but the suburbs expanded by forty-four per cent since low density suburban life is 'today's tomorrowland come true . . . a pastel-coloured playpen world' which appeals to the American wealth conscious citizen. In Los Angeles the ratio of population to agricultural land in 1941 was 9:1 by 1954 it was 22:1 and by 1975, with an expected population of 10m, it will have become 133:1—this in an urban area of 450 square miles. Already this conglomeration of 6m people (with every other person owning a car) has sixty suburban communities linked by 650 miles of freeways. By 1980 it is expected there will be 15m people and the existing areas of farmland will have disappeared, leaving an urban zone about equal in size to the county of Norfolk, surrounded by mountains to the east and the ocean to the west. This has intensified the pattern of factory farming. Similar urban pressures could be generated in Britain.

America, in contrast to Britain, seems to have limitless space for agriculture and expansion. Nevertheless between 1945 and 1960 urbanisation absorbed a twentieth of all cropland, mainly due to the fact that a half of all tillable soil is located near the growing metropolitan areas. Unless checked by other forces, the present population expansion could increase the existing 180m people to 3 (American) billions by the year 2150. In overall space standards America is today perhaps akin to early-Victorian England, soon to be subjected to the same space pressures and loss of vital agricultural land now prevailing in Britain. During the first half of the century the urban area of England and Wales expanded by eighty per cent, covering an additional 1·6m acres. During the same period, soon after the nadir of agricultural prosperity to the birth of the present agricultural revolution, the net loss of farmland was about seven per cent, including all other factors that is nearly 2¼m acres. It has been estimated that the urban area will continue to expand during the second half of this century by about a further sixty-six per cent. This will absorb another 2·4m acres. In fact Best has estimated that during the twentieth century as a whole, the urban area will have trebled from the 2m acres existing in 1900. This will mean that the proportion of urban to total land area will increase during this century from 5·4 to 16·2 per cent, although the population will have barely doubled within the same period (p86). By 2000 about one acre in six will be urban in character. It is more difficult to predict the net loss of farm land from all causes by the end of this century. However a more detailed understanding of present trends and attitudes can give some indication of future change.

An understanding of the present situation and the changes between 1900 and 1960 has to be based largely on the detailed studies made by Best and Coppock in 1962 and note must be taken that they recognised that the accuracy of their analysis was subject to several limitations rising from the inadequacy of available statistics[3]. In particular during the first half of the century, much land came to be included as agricultural land which previously had escaped enumeration and these inclusions reduced the apparent loss of farmland to other requirements. As stated the urban area expanded by 1·6m acres in England and Wales between 1900 and 1950. In the next decade the urban area grew by 40,300 acres a year and another ¼m acres of farmland were taken. The major changes in land-use between 1900 and 1960 are given in Chart 24[3]:

CHART 24: MAJOR CHANGES IN LAND-USE IN GREAT BRITAIN
1900–1960

	Year	Agriculture '000 acres	%	Woodland '000 acres	%	Urban '000 acres	%	Other '000 acres	%	Total '000 A
England	1900	31,050	83·6	1,900	5·1	2,000	5·4	2,180	5·9	37,130
and	1939	30,180	81·3	2,290	6·2	3,200	8·6	1,460	3·9	,,
Wales	1960	29,440	79·3	2,540	6·8	4,000	10·8	1,150	3·1	,,
Scotland	1900	14,290	74·9	870	4·6	170	0·9	3,740	19·6	19,070
	1939	15,020	78·8	1,120	5·9	>360	>1·9	2,640	<13·8	,,
	1960	15,320	80·3	1,330	7·0	470	2·5	1,950	10·2	,,
Great	1900	45,340	80·7	2,770	4·9	2,170	3·9	5,920	10·5	56,200
Britain	1939	45,200	80·4	3,410	6·1	>3,160	>5·6	4,470	<8·0	,,
	1960	45,240	80·5	3,700	6·6	4,070	7·2	3,190	5·7	,,

Best gave warning that the figures given in this table are approximations and that there can be errors in the main three categories of land-use, especially for 1900, since errors can be absorbed in the acreages given as of 'other' use which includes land unaccounted for in the analysis. The acreages given for agriculture have been based on the agricultural statistics and these are prepared for purposes other than a study of national land-use. By their method of assessment, they cannot give an accurate record of changes in land-use which,

172

on the basis of other evidence, would indicate that the losses of farmland are considerably greater than appears from their statistics. Best has shown that the net loss of farmland between 1927 and 1959 in England and Wales was nearly 1¾m acres, as indicated in Chart 25, whereas the previous analysis would suggest a loss of no more than 1½m acres over the whole period of sixty years to 1960. Comparative figures for Scotland can only be obtained for the post-1951 period and the loss of land for urban requirements is not as dramatic as England. The analysis also shows the effect of the second world war which, for a time, almost prohibited urban growth and caused a temporary loss of land for the requirements of the services.

CHART 25: NET LOSS OF AGRICULTURAL LAND IN ENGLAND AND WALES TO NON-RURAL USE[3]: JUNE 1927–JUNE 1959

Period	Total lost Acres	Average acreage losses for special purposes pa			
		building	sport	services & Govt:excl: forestry	Total
1927/8–1934/4	337,000	37,800	9,000	1,300	48,100
1934/5–1938/9	378,200	50,000	10,600	15,000	75,600
1939/40–1944/5	673,100	15,200	+4,500	101,500	112,200
1945/6–1947–8	+15,200	36,000	8,700	+49,800	+5,100
1948/9–1950/1	69,200	28,100	8,200	+13,200	23,100
1951/2–1953/4	91,500	32,800	3,400	+5,700	30,500
1954/5–1956/7	106,100	35,600	3,100	+5,300	35,400
1957/8	25,100	27,800	2,500	+5,200	25,100
1958/9	35,100	34,300	2,400	+1,600	35,100
Total 1927–59	1,700,100	33,300	5,100	−14,700	53,100

IN SCOTLAND 1951–59

Period	Total lost Acres	Average acreage losses for special purposes pa			
		building	sport	services & Govt:exd: forestry	Total
1951–59	39,900	3,300	500	1,200	5,000

However on the evidence available, it is not possible for any one analysis showing losses of agricultural land to be exact since there is some land which has a double function and other land which reverts back to agriculture after a period of other use.

Best gives an analysis of changes between agriculture and other important land uses, shown in Chart 26.

CHART 26: NET LOSS OF AGRICULTURAL LAND IN ENGLAND AND WALES TO ALL OTHER USES: JUNE 1927–JUNE 1948

Period	Total Lost Acres	Average acreage change per year		
		Total gross loss	Total Recoveries*	Net decrease agricultural land
1927/28–1938/39	942,000	95,600	17,100	78,500
1939/40–1944/45	766,800	186,200	58,400	127,800
1945/46–1947/48	33,300	85,100	74,000	11,100
1927/28–1947/48	1,742,100†	120,000	37,000	83,000

* recoveries including land 'previous use uncertain now designated as agricultural land'
† of this amount, 419,000 acres transferred to woodlands or 21,000 pa

It appears from this analysis, that the annual loss of agricultural land in England and Wales averaged 53,100 acres between 1927 and 1959, with perhaps a further loss of 5,000 acres a year in Scotland. There are differences in tempo of land changes in the three decades between 1930 and 1960 which are worth noting. In the 1930s, 60,000 acres were being taken each year for urban sprawl and another 20,000 by forestry. During the 1950s, the position changed since only 36,500 acres a year were taken for urban requirements, reduced to 32,200 or nearly half the pre-war average due to land returned from service and other departments. With the additional loss of 5,000 acres in Scotland and a doubling of forestry requirements to 40,400 acres, much of it poor land, the total loss of land for other requirements in the decade before 1960 would seem to be nearly 80,000 acres, only about half of which was required for urban requirements. Northern Ireland by comparison of course, is relatively under-developed with 2·8m acres in agriculture, of which a quarter is rough grazing, out of 3·5m acres available. About 0·05 per cent only of the total area is urban districts.

The situation in 1965 does not seem to be much clearer, many conflicting figures for agricultural land losses in England and Wales being quoted. In 1959 Best predicted an annual loss of 45,000 acres during this decade, most of it from the lowlands of England, in the

Midlands and South-east. The aim to build half a million homes a year by 1970 must increase the pressure on farm land. Several new towns have recently been designated, each of which may take more than 5,000 acres and other major towns have authority to expand. The motorways alone average an absorption of about 4,000 acres a year, if schedules are kept. Numerous other road expansion schemes nibble at farm land with considerable cumulative effect. The study for the development from the South-east published in 1964 predicted a loss of 200,000 acres in that region by 1985, that is 10,000 acres a year purely for this expansion. Many believe, that without strict overall planning for this expansion (which was considered unnecessary by this report), land absorption will be higher and not necessarily where an analysis of agricultural needs suggests best for minimising losses of food production. In the autumn of 1965 the Water Resources Board predicted that the bulk of additional supplies must come from surface storage for many decades (p256). Much of this will be on farm land. Universities too have in recent years tended to be sited in rural rather than urban situations. New airports, possibly even new docks, are projected for the immediate future. Industry continues to take isolated pockets of farm land, not only for mineral extraction, but for power and sub-stations, water and sewerage works, petrol stations and refineries as well as for a multitude of small scale projects. The cumulative land lost to pylons is not negligible. The demand for building on farmland has increased since 1960. The Ministry of Agriculture reported a loss of 54,000 acres of farmland in 1963/64, 46,000 being taken for urban use. This is considerably more than the losses a decade earlier. There are of course other losses of productive land. Farmers take over several acres every year for their own new roads, reservoirs and buildings as well as the new status of country residents needing land such as paddocks for horses in the upsurge of such activities as hunting and similar pursuits as a national past-time. Considering all losses for agricultural land, including any gains from reclamation, an estimate of an annual loss of 50,000 acres might not be rash—either now or long before 1980.

Farmers are not unobservant concerning the loss of land and the situation is politically explosive. Social as well as agricultural disquiet at the loss of agricultural land in the past has been mainly local in its manifestation. In recent years the tendency has been for national concern to be expressed as the effects of the change in land-use and multi-purpose demands on land become more apparent. Pressure groups at local and national level preventing development in rural areas have become more powerful. It is a consequence of unco-ordinated change in land-use that social pressures can arise which restrict development for the wrong reasons or in the wrong regions. Social pressures can in fact become confused in an attempt to preserve the countryside so that not only may industry be prevented from development in rural areas, even within those of low agricultural value, but agriculture may be prevented from becoming an efficient industry, which could release more land of low agricultural value not only for industry but recreation. It is not desirable that the industrialisation of the country as a whole should be retarded nor that people should suffer in the wake of its advance.

As previously suggested, farmers are roused to protest at each proposal for a new town—though from a national standpoint new towns are essential for an expanding and modernised Britain. It was social and political pressure from landowners that largely destroyed the chance of Hook, the revolutionary design for a town prepared by the former London County Council in the late 1950s, from being built in Hampshire. If Hook had been built, Great Britain would have led the world in the urban segregation of traffic and pedestrians within high density development long before the Buchanan Report made the importance of such planning popular. Many people considered that the official disregard for the idea of the new town of Hook, which came about for the wrong reasons, was a major setback for radical ideas in town planning—a setback which has taken more than a decade to be partially mitigated by more recent planning and development, such as at Cumbernauld new town near Glasgow. Similarly, since 1965, the National Farmers Union and Buckinghamshire farmers have contested the idea of a new town for up to 150,000 people in north Buckinghamshire, which could absorb 23,000 acres of farmland, with 5,000 acres for a reservoir (p113). A pilot study showed how this new town could be of revolutionary design according to preliminary studies, ahead of the world in its planning of services and community needs. The site for Milton Keynes in North Buckinghamshire was confirmed in 1967, though the farming pressure group managed to get a large reduction agreed to the 22,000 acres of farmland originally scheduled for development. Similarly, in proposals for expanding Peterborough, a reduction of thirty per cent from the original proposals was agreed due to the outcry from farmers. Good planning should not need substantial modifications if all land factors are studied prior to publication of proposals. The new town of Dawley, in Shropshire, which includes much despoiled land within the cradle of the industrial revolution as well as the natural faults of the Severn Gorge, and several thousand acres of medium good land intermingled with urban scrawl, created deep protestations from the farming community. The expansion proposal for Stevenage, which would absorb land between the existing new town and Luton, bringing them within four miles of each other, created opposition from farmers and also from many planners who believe urban areas must be self-contained and isolated from each other by wide margins of open country.

Esso Refinery: Milford Haven, 1963. View from the east with railhead in middle foreground and storage tanks and process area behind. Great care was taken in siting the refinery within land contours and, where exposed, a tree belt was planted on the far side. Sheep are used to graze adjoining land to reduce fire risk. In this case, industry and agriculture are complementary.

1

1 Cement works erected at Weardale, Co Durham in 1966. Extraction industries usually have to be sited in the countryside, often within scenic areas and, sometimes, as here, in non-intensive food producing regions. These works employ 300 people in a depressed area to produce 600,000 tons of cement a year. Large scale industrial architecture can be reasonable when designed and landscaped with care.

Architects, Ryder & Yates; landscape architect, S. Haywood.

2 Oddicombe Beach, South Devon August 1961. The need to preserve sections of unspoilt coastline and allow others to be developed for recreation is obvious. A cove like this is a contrast to Brighton Marina in scale. Coastal recreation helps to keep the pressure from the countryside.

2

Revised model of Brighton
Marina proposed in 1966.
Architects, P. Farley & Partners.
The need to plan for sophisticated
recreation is an urgent problem.
Part of the problem is how to
promote seaside facilities for
recreation without destroying the
remaining unspoilt coastline.
Marina projects, such as this, are
one form. Similar sports centres
in the countryside will also be
needed, for example skiing in
the Cairngorms.

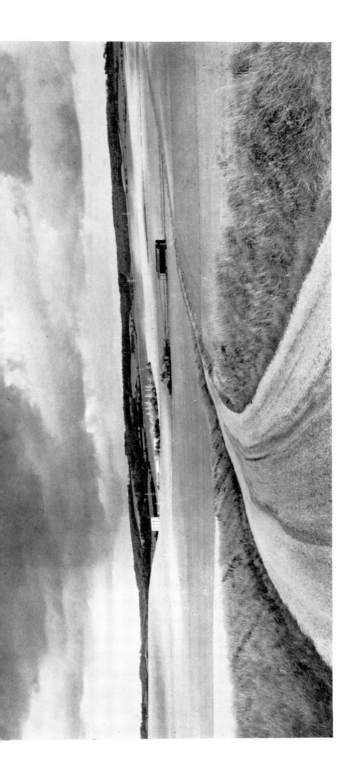

Ipsden Prairie, Oxon. An intensive corn-growing area in South Oxfordshire. Hedges have been removed to allow for maximum productivity. In this case the nature of the agriculture blends with the shape of the land.

1

2

1 A Shropshire Mere 1964. There are many examples of multiple land-use. In this case the mere is a boating and fishing lake, picnic area and nature reserve, but the emphasis is on recreation. Fishing is not commercial and the woodlands, though attractive, are not an economic investment. There are many corners of agricultural land which could be used for recreation where the topography is unsuitable for economic food production.

2 Little Hampden, Bucks. Farmers quite often turn their attention to small specialist enterprises, such as willow or Christmas tree plantations, to use odd corners of land or rough ground. This is a sensible way of making use of derelict acres; alternatively in some situations they could be given over to recreation or camping.

3 Field drainage, Lydiate, Hants 1962. Half the farmland of Britain is still inadequately drained. Modern drain-laying machinery is making it economic to improve this situation. This machine operates at 600 yards an hour, laying drains three and a half feet deep. Other methods use perforated plastic pipes which can be uncoiled into trenches from drums and therefore need less labour.

183

Clywedog Valley Dam, South
Montgomeryshire, Wales 1966.
Work started in 1963 on a £4½m
scheme to form a 200ft deep
reservoir, providing water for
Birmingham, Bristol, Coventry,
Shropshire, Worcestershire,
Gloucestershire and Staffordshire
and controlling floods in the
Upper Severn as well as generating
electricity. A 460-acre farm loses
the best 160 acres in the process,
the remaining hill land being of
poor quality. In 1966 the Severn
River Authority surveyed twenty-
nine possible reservoir sites in
Montgomeryshire, involving 360
farmers, and prepared a map
showing about a third of the
county under water.

Other developments, as well as new town designations, keep the farming press in ferment. The pipeline from the Thames to the Mersey, as discussed previously, aroused considerable anger (p141). The proposal to take a motorway across the Berkshire Downs caused widespread dissatisfaction; in the first place because it was thought that it would despoil the downland (the viewpoint of country lovers) and in the second if sited to avoid the downs, it would disrupt good agricultural land. The conflict between absorbing agricultural or scenic land, which may be the same thing in some cases, seems irreconcilable under the many pressures for development. The efforts to save Dedham Vale on the Suffolk/Essex boundary from urban expansion in 1965 is of some importance. Local residents, by appeal to the Minister, have saved further intrusion of housing into an area of Constable countryside of scenic beauty. At the same time this is an area of countryside, though attractive as a Vale and reasonably lush as meadowland, which is neither noted for intensive agricultural production nor particularly available for relaxation and enjoyment by the public. It is difficult to be sure of the exact motifs and benefits to be gained by protection from development when the scale of priorities is obscure. However, a survey for the area was published in 1967 with proposals for restricting development, major land-use change, and access to agreed viewpoints and footpaths. More encouraging in this predicament is the land resources study set up by the Country Landowners Association in Dorset during 1965, including representatives from other organisations interested in land preservation, suggesting to the County Planning Authority how to balance the needs for modern planning and development with those who live by and on the land. In particular their interest is to study the impact of the proposed new town near Shaftesbury for 60,000 people and the expansion of four other Dorset towns to 30,000 people. In South Buckinghamshire another group has been formed to unite existing organisations and co-ordinate objectives in terms of planning and preservation. At County level this could be valuable and constructive for relating land-use planning to the needs of conflicting requirements.

These examples are but few of many changes in the countryside which cause social unrest. The pressure to develop the countryside to meet the demands of industry and modern social requirements is becoming, and will become, more intense. Farmers are well aware that under present conditions obscurities and anomalies abound. The timing and organisation, still less the period for compensation, for official development are not always sympathetically handled in relation to the social and business needs of the farmers. For decades there has been no attempt at national level to alleviate the social disturbance and co-ordinate development. Each authority has contributed to piecemeal development, individual aims and requirements frequently being opposed to each other. Local interest and opposition can confuse the real issues for a national land policy. Only recently have Government and public opinion begun to change in their recognition that a national scale of priorities for land-use should be established. For example, the first report of the Northern Economic Planning Committee[4] has specifically stated that land in urban areas should be used before further encroachment on farm land, including the reclamation of all derelict land. At present the average annual loss is 5,700 acres, of which 4,300 are for urban needs, 800 for mineral working and 600 for sand and gravel extraction. Moreover, the report urges that agriculture and tourism must be integrated, a Rural Development Board should be appointed, and production and marketing co-operatives should be promoted, backed by further farm amalgamations, modernisation and drainage. This is the first serious agrico-social report on land-use for regional planning, making an important stride in rural balance. Moreover, in contrast, at National level the Country Landowners' Association began a pressure group in 1967 to see that:

1 Agricultural considerations should be featured at an early stage in all new plans,

2 The Ministry of Agriculture should have maximum opportunities for stating the case of farming,

3 Greater efforts should be made to develop derelict land.

But even this change is not yet sufficiently radical for a fully co-ordinated policy to be socially or politically acceptable. Not only must social opinion become more clear in the need for change and controlled change, but this must become strong enough to curb the excess pressures of private enterprise and the powers of individual government departments. Farmers can only be reconciled to changes in land-use if they are convinced that the overall consumption of agricultural land is guided into urban and social development without waste of their one basic raw material. This means that land taken should be wherever possible within areas of poor or medium food producing potential; land remaining in agriculture should be within viable units, protected from vandalism, and compensation paid should be commensurate with the value of the land, and equally important with the disturbance or hindrance in farm management. No priorities can be established until there is greater knowledge available, both statistical and social, concerning the existing use of land with the changes, and the inter-relation of these changes, occurring at the present time. The only alternative is a long period of social unrest, discord and bitterness, with Britain's most valuable asset frittered away by a process of desolate and despicable erosion.

REFERENCES

1 Williams-Ellis, Clough, *Britain and the Beast*, p4. 1937, Dent
Forster, E. M. 'Havoc.' Ibid, p44
Marshall, H. 'The Rake's Progress.' Ibid, p164
2 Highbee, E., *The Squeeze*, p4. 1961, Cassell
3 Best, R. H., and Coppock, J. T., *Changing Use of Land in Britain*, chapter 8. 1962, Faber & Faber
4 *Challenge of the changing North*. 1967, HMSO

4d Land reclamation

Land can be reclaimed from the sea, unproductive marsh, scrub or moorland or derelict areas of waste land. Once reclaimed, such land can be used either for food production and forestry or for urban development, including recreation and other social needs. Reclamation is a small, but important, part of planning land resources. It has always appealed to the pioneer, but recently it has become part of the planners', and perhaps even the national, consciousness.

The spate of the Industrial Revolution caused much land to be laid waste. The Civic Trust showed that in 1964 coal tips, shale heaps, gravel pits and abandoned quarries accounted for more than 150,000 acres[1]. At present, this area extended by 3,500 acres each year, often including good farm land; but by 1970 4,000 acres a year will become derelict. Existing waste land includes 36,000 acres within urban areas, two-thirds of which is in spoil heaps, the other third being partially excavated ground. The remaining 114,000 acres are in less populated areas, much being incapable of economic reclamation. 12,000 acres are taken each year for mining or spoil tipping, but about 8,500 acres are restored for farming. In 1965, it was expected that 1,375 acres of sand, clay and gravel pits, 980 acres of mineral surface workings and 1,250 acres of coal and other tippings became derelict. As Senior suggested, better regional planning with an expenditure of about £1m could prevent further waste and reclaim much present dereliction for agriculture, building or recreation.

One outcome of the Civic Trust report was that in 1965 the Minister of Housing asked Local Authorities for full details of land damaged by industrial and other development, needing treatment to be of use. Thereafter annual returns from Planning Authorities should help to record progress in land reclamation and any further losses. Swansea County Borough Council, for example, financed by the Nuffield Foundation, produced a report in 1967 surveying the derelict areas and recommending how the lower Swansea valley could be improved over an area of four square miles, at present a barren wilderness. Reclamation of industrial waste land may be promoted on a national scale, but the War Department is known to hold consider-

187

able areas of derelict and unused land amongst the half million acres in Great Britain used for military purposes[2]. Authorities are reticent about land areas used for service requirements, especially about waste land under their control. Nearly 120,000 acres are used by the War Department in the National Parks, but the National Parks Committee believes in particular that the 17,000 acres in areas of scenic beauty should be reduced[3]. Local Authorities in the West Country, among others, have expressed concern at the retention of derelict buildings on wartime sites, twenty years after the end of the war. For example, 3,365 acres of derelict airfields still existed in 1964 at Lindsey in Lincolnshire[2]. Disused camps and aerodromes are a national problem.

The Ministry of Housing published a report in 1963 to show how modern equipment made it possible and economic to reclaim land, provided Local Authorities had the necessary determination[4]. However land reclamation is a national problem requiring direction and co-ordination, though several instances of successful renewal of derelict land can be quoted without such organisation. The Electrical Board, though frequently disfiguring the landscape with pylons, has done much to reclaim land, especially in an attempt to dispose of fuel ash and waste. The Central Electricity Board produce about 7m tons of ash a year, increasing to about 10m tons by 1970 and, perhaps, reaching 20m tons a decade later. The ash waste can be used for lightweight concrete blocks, road embankments and land reclamation[5].

The CEGB plan to restore 2,000 acres of derelict brick quarries near Peterborough with ash waste from the new Trent Valley power stations, perhaps using 52m tons during this century. The ash is to be handled by rail to a terminal built specially for the purpose at Peterborough, at a rate of ten 1,000 ton train loads a day, when it is mixed with water and pumped as a slurry to the pits. The plant will cost £3m and filling another £6m; reclamation will cost therefore around £4,500 an acre or more than ten times the present value of top-class land. It may prove possible to provide topsoil from washed beet at a local sugar factory, after which the land could be returned to agriculture. It has been shown that clovers are the best pioneer crop to use on ash, which is deficient of nitrogen and has high alkilinity, but within a few years the land becomes suitable for roots[6]. Similar reclamation to the Peterborough brickfield is taking place elsewhere. For example, from Dunston Power Station in Tyneside, six-and-a-half acres of bogland have been reclaimed. Between 1956 and 1959, a depth of 14ft of ash slurry was laid, which drained until 1960 when it was ploughed and cultivated[7]. In the Dee Estuary in Flintshire, at Connah's Quay, ninety acres of saltings have been recovered and another eighty acres will be fertile by the mid-1970s at a cost of about £1,000 an acre and over 1m tons of ash infill[8].

188

Current production of fly ash from power stations is 5m tons, but this may rise to 15m tons by 1975[13].

The National Coal Board has reclaimed much land after their opencast mining operations. H. E. Collins, addressing the conference on 'The Countryside in 1970' on behalf of the Coal Board, stated that complete rehabilitation of land after opencast workings could cost £1,200 to £3,400 per acre. Though this cost seems high in relation to the value of agricultural land, it is a fractional part of the value of the extracted coal. The land is restored with its own topsoil, but an extra benefit is that it is possible to rationalise the field layouts.

Land reclamation of moorland, scrub or other natural districts has been pioneered throughout history. A third of the land surface of England and Wales is not classified as improved farm land, though part of it is used for rough grazing; in fact almost a quarter of the total area, representing $8\frac{1}{2}$m acres, has no agricultural use. In the whole of Britain, nearly forty per cent of the total agricultural area is rough grazing, producing only about five per cent of the country's agricultural output[9]. Hill farms are considered to produce about two-thirds of their potential, which should be increased in the future but could never represent more than about seven per cent of total present output. Nevertheless the future of hill farming is uncertain, though the possibility of ranch farming, as is practiced to some extent in North Scotland, could be an important development. Control of grazing land without ploughing, which makes farming steep slopes easier, could change the economics of hill farming which at present are not encouraging. Reclamation of moorland is hard work, taking many years, and it seems unlikely that there will be substantial reclamation of further hill land for agriculture, since it is expensive and does not dramatically increase national food output, though reafforestation should absorb many more waste highland acres. As long as farming is a private concern, there will be farmers willing to tackle the hard life of farming the marginal uplands, though it is possible that there may be a reduction in hill farming acreages during the next years. With new techniques available, it might be foolhardy to cut back on hard won land by not helping the hill farmers; the cost to the country in helping them is relatively small.

Much fenland and bogland has been brought into productive use this century. The work of Lord Iveagh is renowned for its success. In Norfolk two farmers are reclaiming 260 acres of marsh at Brancaster which have been undrained since Telford erected a sea wall to protect them[10]. Another group of Norfolk farmers intend to lower the water table over 30,000 acres of bleak land to improve its grazing fertility. During the last thirty years, 360 acres of saltmarsh have been reclaimed on the Wash near Boston. In Berkshire two farmers have recently drained 120 acres and 176 acres of rough grazings at around £18–£20 an acre gross[11]. Throughout the country modern methods for trenching and piping have made it possible to drain and reclaim many low lying acres at an economic cost. Similarly, many acres of scrub, copse or woodland are being cleared for agriculture (p251).

Coastline reclamation or enclosure of the sea can prove profitable and bring many acres into productive use. In some cases no more than the control of tidal erosion, the drainage of salt marshes or the stabilising of sand dunes is required. For example an area of 320 acres of tidal marshland is being reclaimed by W. H. Mouland for his farm on the Medway in Kent. Such land, once reclaimed, can prove very productive. C. S. Smith has estimated that 47,500 acres on the coasts of England and Wales and about 42,000 acres on the coast of Scotland could be reclaimed in a similar manner[12]. These areas include 3,750 acres in Kent, as much again round Southampton Water, about 8,000 acres in Essex, perhaps 14,000 acres round the Wash and North Norfolk coast, over 27,000 acres along the west coast from the Dee to the Solway as well as another 2,000 acres around the Humber. From the national viewpoint, most of this reclamation could be a valuable investment.

Interest has recently developed in major schemes for reclaiming sea within some of the estuaries, particularly the Wash, Morecambe Bay and the Solway Firth. The Wash has always roused speculation about the possibility of its enclosure and reclamation. Since 1846 4,000 acres have been reclaimed and a further 21,000 are reasonably suitable. In the spring of 1964 the Crown Estate Commissioners announced they were prepared to spend £50,000 a year over the next few years on reclaiming land round the Wash. Reclaiming all 80,000 acres of the Wash has been estimated to cost £150m, or about £2,000 an acre. There is greater interest at present in the possibility of forming river barrages across the Wash and Morecambe Bay to provide vast fresh-water reservoirs. Such schemes could do much to save farmland from being taken to form new reservoirs (p266).

Even without the grand schemes for estuary barrages, in the region of 200,000 acres of derelict or unreclaimed land, which excludes any improvements to rough grazed land, could be turned into productive farmland unless used for recreation. An increase of 200,000 acres in England and Wales would add about 0·7 per cent to the area of improved farmland. The cost of reclamation would be high, being disproportionate to the land value. Nevertheless on a long-term basis with the threat of inadequate sources for food imports and a growing urban demand for land, the need for land reclamation on a national basis seems critical. Moreover once the situation becomes acutely critical, reclamation schemes might prove too late to ease the crisis.

REFERENCES

1 Senior, D. (editor), *Derelict Land*. 1964, Civic Trust
2 'Clean-up campaign on derelict acres.' *Farmers Weekly*, p54, 17 September 1965
3 Report. *The Times*, 6 August 1964
4 Ministry of Housing and Local Government. *New life for dead land.* 1963, HMSO
5 Report. *The Times*, October 1965
6 'Waste ash will rebuild the lost acres.' *Farmers Weekly*, p72, 29 November 1963
7 'The good earth is ash.' *Farmers Weekly*, p83, 14 June 1963
8 'Lagoon now—land later.' *Farmers Weekly*, p50, 30 October 1964
9 Wannop, A. 'Are we wasting Britain's Land—the hills and moors.' *Farmers Weekly*, p81, 26 February 1965
10 Turff, A. 'Neighbours link to crop the marshes.' *Farmers Weekly*, p44, 22 January 1965
11 Hope, H. 'Winning good land from wet.' *Farmers Weekly*, p89, 8 October 1965.
12 Smith, C. S. 'Are we wasting Britain's Land.' *Farmers Weekly*, p87, 26 May 1965
13 Barber, E. G., *Win Back the Acres—Ash and Agriculture*. 1963, Central Electricity Generating Board

4e Land ownership and values

The Ministry of Agriculture, by means of the compulsory Annual Returns which are compiled by farmers, is able to prepare useful statistics concerning much farming. Information is available with regard to the size and distribution of farms, crops, stock and labour and it is possible to assess changes in farm practice and food production. Nevertheless the Domesday Book of 1086 is the most recent survey of land ownership and the distribution of wealth in relation to ownership. Fragmentary knowledge has partially brought the subject up to date, due to valuations made for rating purposes in 1873 and the National Farm Survey of 1942, but neither of these gave comprehensive knowledge of land ownership.

It is not surprising that the Ministry of Land and Natural Resources has been handicapped by lack of adequate statistics concerning the people or organisations owning land. This is an important facet of the land structure of Britain. No national policy for land-use can be rational without knowing who owns the land and how one of the most basic of natural resources is divided in ownership. In a crowded country with an increasing population the use made of every acre is of vital concern.

The structure of farm capital and incomes is discussed in Chapter 6. As indicated the market value of farm land in Great Britain by 1965

191

may well have risen to over £6,500m. In addition, it has been estimated that the working capital invested in stock, crops, equipment, feed and fertilizers may be nearly £2,500m at any one time (p282). On this basis, all improved farm land in Great Britain represents on average about £250 of tied capital for each acre. Such assessments do not account for specialised land used for horticulture, including orchards, forestry or fisheries and game. The value of farm land has risen with dramatic speed in recent years and there is growing pressure for farmers to have their land rated—factors discussed in this section.

LAND OWNERSHIP

Throughout this century, there has been a radical change from tenanted to owner-occupied farms. At the turn of the last century only fifteen per cent of farms were owner-occupied. By 1950, forty-three per cent had become owner-occupied, increasing to almost fifty per cent during the next decade. Similarly between 1950 and 1960 the area of owner-occupied land had increased from about 10·8m acres (thirty-eight per cent) to about 14m acres (forty-nine per cent), tenanted land dropping from 17·6m to 14·5m acres in England and Wales. It is expected that by 1975 owner-occupied land will have increased to seventy per cent. In Scotland change is slower, though in 1950 seventy-five per cent of farms were tenanted representing only fifty-seven per cent of the agricultural land. It has been thought that most of the 3¼m acres taken out of tenancies in the decade after 1950 represented land taken in hand by private landlords, though some would-be tenants bought their previously rented farms, rather than change to farms let by official organisations[1].

It is approximately true today that half the farms and agricultural land of England and Wales is owner-occupied. However among farms of over average size tenants still predominate. As the National Farmers Union has recognised[2]:

the tenancy system can no longer be described as the characteristic pattern of tenure in England and Wales, though there are still substantially more tenant farmers than owner-occupiers of farms of 50 acres or more.

At the same time as there has been a shift away from tenanted land, there has also been a marked growth in the number of farm partnerships and joint stock companies. Some agriculturalists believe that this development is the best solution as modern food production becomes an industrialised process. However statistics are incomplete on the extent of this change which not only effects owner-occupiers but in many cases tenants, though many landlords are reluctant to permit tenant companies since the prospect of regaining possession at the death of the tenant is not encouraging[2]. Not only is the average size of a tenanted farm greater than that of the owner-occupied, but

192

the size of owner-occupied estates is considerably less than those of private or public companies. As Denman indicated in 1959, of owner-occupied farms only two per cent are in estates of over 2,000 acres while a quarter of all land owned and occupied by companies and miscellaneous bodies is in large estates of this size[3].

A survey of milk production in 1963 showed that almost a quarter of milk producers were in partnerships and companies, but that these firms produced almost a third of the total milk output[4]. Nineteen per cent of producers were partnerships with twenty-three per cent of total output. Two per cent of producers were companies with seven per cent of total output.

The registration of partnerships and companies is increasing steadily. The same development is recognised to be occurring throughout agriculture but statistics are not available. However Ashton and Cracknell in 1959 made a survey of the census parish lists in order to establish the legal status of the occupiers of each holding, though this does not indicate the status of ownership[5].

CHART 27: LEGAL STATUS OF OCCUPIERS OF HOLDINGS IN 1959

Individuals	314,571	holdings
Partnerships	31,786	,,
Executors and trustees	1,734	,,
Joint stock companies	7,035	,,
Other corporations	304	,,
Government and public bodies	865	,,
All other categories	962	,,
	357,257	holdings

It is significant that whereas most types of occupier have remained the same in relative proportion to each other since 1943, partnerships have increased by almost fifty per cent from 21,500 and joint stock companies by well over fifty per cent from 4,150, to nearly 32,000 and over 7,000 respectively. At a different level, it is believed that about a fifth of the 56m acres of Britain is now owned by companies and trusts.

Denman studied the ownership of let land in England and Wales in 1959 at a time when there were 15m acres of tenanted land in approximately 120,000 holdings of fifteen acres or more[3]. The survey covered twenty-nine per cent of these holdings with an area of nearly 4¾m acres. Under half the tenanted land was in private ownership, representing just over a third of the owners. More surprising is the fact that nearly a quarter of the tenanted land was in public ownership, whether government or local authority. This means that when considering agricultural land at least an eighth to a tenth of England and Wales is in effect nationalised, though Denman warned that his figures might be on the high side since information from these sources was easier to obtain than others. His study also showed the distribution of tenanted land in estates of various sizes:

Estates with under 1,000 acres	: 10 per cent
„ „ „ 1,000–4,000 acres	: 25 per cent
„ „ „ 4,000–10,000 acres	: 25 per cent
„ „ over 10,000 acres	: 40 per cent

Considering owner-occupied land, on restricted evidence, Denman believed ninety per cent of the acreage was in private ownership, 6·6 per cent was owned by companies and the rest by miscellaneous types of owner. Privately owned land was mainly in small estates, ninety-five per cent being under 1,000 acres and forty-six per cent under 250 acres. During the years since this survey there has been a shift towards larger estates and away from private ownership.

CHART 28: OWNERSHIP OF TENANTED LAND IN ENGLAND AND WALES[3]

	Percentage of total					
Type of Owner	England		Wales		England & Wales	
	Acreage	Holdings	Acreage	Holdings	Acreage	Holdings
Private persons	45·4	37·4	49·1	48·5	45·8	38·9
Companies	10·9	9·2	4·1	3·1	10·2	8·4
Trustees	12·0	9·7	11·6	9·8	11·9	9·7
Charities	9·3	6·3	0·4	0·4	8·3	5·5
Local authorities	8·9	24·9	17·9	23·7	9·9	24·7
Govt depts	13·5	12·5	16·9	14·5	13·9	12·8

Apart from agriculture the Forestry Commission with its 2½m acres is the largest landowner in Britain. The National Trust owns over ¼m acres, much of it farmland, as well as having restrictive covenants over other land. As a landowner it is in a similar position to private owners except that it is exempt from income tax and death duties. The Queen owns 239,000 acres, including the 140,000 acres of the Duchy of Cornwall. The Crown Estates, which include Windsor Park and other basically non-agricultural land, extend to 180,000 acres. The National Coal Board holds 300,000 acres and British Rail 250,000. The Ministry of Defence has 622,000 acres. Among other large landowners are some of the well-known inherited estates held by the Dukes and other nobility, though they often include tracts of infertile land. For example the Duke of Buccleuch owns

194

336,000 acres, the Countess of Seafield 197,000 acres and Lord Lovat 190,000 acres. Both the Church Commissioners and the Cambridge and Oxford Colleges are large landowners. One of the largest estates in England and in one county is the 80,000 acres belonging to the Duke of Northumberland.

Death duties affect land ownership. The duty on land is forty-five per cent as against eighty per cent on other wealth. Many estates have been broken up to pay death duties, especially when two owners die within a short time of each other. The threat of death duties often precipitates ownership into younger hands, since, as is well known, a man escapes duties on his estate if given away five years before his death. This encourages the elderly to renounce their control over land. At the same time, placing land into a company of trustee ownership can evade death duties. Moreover many industrialists have bought land in order to avoid full duty on other estate and this has led to an increase in one-farm landlords.

A major political debate in recent years has been whether all or some agricultural land should be nationalised. Agricultural land is a basic raw material of the nation which, it can be argued, like steel or coal or electricity, should be in public ownership and control. As in all other cases public ownership can lead to management rationalisa-tion, allowing amalgamation of many small units into their critical economic size for maximum productivity. Centralised control can, but does not necessarily, lead to more effective use of the basic resources of the nation. Political priorities apart, most planners would acknowledge that land nationalisation would be a more difficult exercise even in theory than nationalisation of other resources, such as the railways where the organisation was already managed in large units with control centralised. The fragmented and diverse nature of British farming makes it a difficult problem for public ownership. Nevertheless the National Union of Agricultural Workers stated that a reformed Land Commission should buy and operate experimental estates demonstrating the benefits of State control and should eventually acquire all farms so that farmers would become tenants of the State[6]. The National Union of Agricultural Workers believes that 'a rational distribution of farm units and the provision of adequate fixed capital investment will only be obtained through public ownership of land' and that 'the pattern of land ownership is today too complicated for this process to be carried out effectively'. Like most statements of this kind it is both true and false. Many agriculturalists agree that a large part of agriculture is not rational in its unit size, is inadequately financed and has too many owners. But public ownership of land has not been shown, even in theory, to give better results and it is probably true that the speed of amalgama-tion, of investment and development is at present nearly as fast as the capacity of farm management and expertise can absorb. Many

195

more highly trained personnel would be required for modernisation to be superimposed from above. It would moreover seem that vertical integration, as discussed in Chapter 7, may rapidly do much of what the Union desires, though it will be private monopolies rather than the state which precipitates the change.

A number of large state farms, well administered and experimental or advanced in policy, linked to new marketing and processing techniques would be valuable. Similarly, as Dower said, limited public ownership is desirable to assist positive planning of the countryside, especially in relation to the development of resources for leisure[7].

Two other factors which affect land ownership should be discussed. The number of farm businesses are considerably less than the number of recognised holdings due to multiple holdings, as officially listed, being under one business management. Secondly not only is the structure of farm land divided by two classes of farmer—tenants and owner-occupiers—which affects the rate of change in farming patterns, but there is a further distinction between full-time and part-time farmers.

1 MULTIPLE HOLDINGS

In 1958, there were about 360,000 holdings recognised by the Ministry, each holding being over one acre in size but not necessarily being always productive units to be included in the Census (p218). A scrutiny of the occupiers' names showed that 30,368 holdings, though individually recorded, were in fact farmed by 13,444 occupiers having two or more holdings each and being managed as unified businesses except for the census returns. The breakdown of these holdings into farm sizes has been given in Chart 29[5]:

CHART 29: MULTIPLE HOLDINGS IN ENGLAND AND WALES 1958

Acreage of Holding	Size distribution in relation to no of Holdings	
	a	b
Under 20	8,577	1,294
20 – 49	6,005	1,829
50 – 99	5,289	2,454
100 – 149	3,153	1,707
150 – 499	6,276	4,363
Over 500	1,068	1,797

a Size distribution of individual holdings forming parts of multiple holdings.

b Size distribution on assumption that holdings forming parts of multiple holdings were merged.

It seems that about $3\frac{1}{2}$m acres of farm land may be in multiple holdings and that $1\frac{1}{2}$m acres of these are probably merged into larger business units than indicated by the census of individual holdings. A full survey might show three per cent less farm businesses than actual holdings recorded and, moreover, the average farm size would be then greater than officially listed.

2 PART-TIME FARMERS

Farming does not have to be a full-time occupation in order to be profitable or make the best use of resources. It is not easy to distinguish between full and part-time farming. Not only do business men own and work farms, but many manual or trade workers are also farmers. A standard of 275 man-days a year (based on labour requirements for eight hours of adult male labour a day) has been taken as the break-point between a part time and a full-time farm assuming average efficiency[5]. It is agreed that this assessment does not necessarily give a true basis for judgement, but accepting the limitations an analysis of the 370,000 holdings existing in 1955 indicated that 180,000, or almost half, were part-time farms. A further survey of holdings in 1958 examined 116,000 part-time farms, which excluded holdings which had ceased to exist since 1955 (13,000), those with less than twenty-five man-days (48,000), multiple holdings aggregating over 250 man-days (5,000) and holdings with 251–275 man-days being within the limits of the Small Farmer Scheme (6,000). The analysis made by Ashton and Cracknell of the part-time farms gives an interesting appreciation of the farm structure of Britain. Occupiers of the part-time farms had in some cases full-time jobs elsewhere, but over 10,000 were totally dependent on the farm for their living[5].

CHART 30: SOURCES OF LIVELIHOOD OF PART-TIME FARM OCCUPIERS

	Number	Per cent
Occupiers with full-time jobs	41,000	35·4
part-time ,,	13,100	11·3
other sources of income	29,300	25·3
no other income but with more than 250 man-days	5,600	4·8
Institutions etc not primarily for agricultural purposes	10,700	9·2
Multiple holdings	5,800	5·0
Occupiers with less than 250 man-days solely dependent on their holdings	10,500	9·0
	116,000	100·0

Considering the large number of part-time holdings, particularly the fact that 41,000 or almost twelve per cent of all holdings in 1958 were occupied by farmers with full-time jobs outside farming, it is not surprising that over 20,000 had no dwelling and nearly 13,000 had no farm buildings. In fact, eight per cent of the part-time holdings were used solely for horticulture and ten per cent solely for poultry. Holdings with horticulture mixed with pigs and/or poultry accounted for another eleven per cent and holdings with pigs and/or poultry, but without horticulture, a further seven per cent. As indicated by an analysis of the occupations of these with jobs outside farming, it is clear that a wide section of the population desire to have a stake in agriculture[5]:

CHART 31 : PART-TIME AND FULL-TIME NON-FARM OCCUPATIONS

Occupation	Full-time %	Part-time %
Farm workers	14	34
Agricultural contractors	2	3
Haulage workers	3	2
Forestry workers	2	–
Producer/Retailers (milk, fruit, veg)	–	8
Builders and decorators	10	3
Catering, accommodation, publicans	3	4
Retail trades & distribution	17	19
Quarrymen and miners	5	–
Professions & civil servants, etc.	9	–
Business executives	7	–
Other	28	27
	100 (40,950)	100 (14,500)

As Wallace observed, part-time farming tends to be ridiculed by the fifty per cent of full-time farmers. Nevertheless, though seldom recognised in the British official policies, the part-time farmer is becoming a major figure in most western official farm programmes[8]. Though some part-time holdings are inefficient or semi-derelict and though there is a social stigma against part-time work in Britain, many make an important contribution to food production and help those wishing to start full-time farming by building up capital. Part-time farming can be useful for the nation, moreover part-time farmers can work within co-operative or contract farming as successfully as those full-time farmers who work in this manner. Even in America a third of all farmers are part-time farmers.

198

Land ownership has always been considered a good investment, being the basis for much power, status and wealth. The rise in land values generally has proved an insurance against inflation. Speculation in land potentially suitable for urban development has in some cases inflated land values. Such special cases apart, the sudden upsurge during the last few years in agricultural land values has changed the pattern of farming and, within the next decade, must affect the whole structure of rural life.

The average freehold price of farms with vacant possession was £83 an acre in 1958. Five years later it had doubled to £168 an acre and, by the first half of 1965 it had trebled, then being £250 an acre. An increase within seven years in the value of farmland of 200 per cent has been a remarkable capital gain for those holding farms since 1958. Farms are in fact now worth seven to nine times their pre-war value. There does not appear to be any real sign of the increase in values slackening and, if the present trend continued, farms within another two decades would cost an average of £1,000 an acre. Though this seems improbable, unless massive national inflation also occurred, values are increasing much faster than would be proportionally natural in relation to the depreciation in the value of the pound. The effect of the Capital Gains Tax on agricultural land values is not yet clear, but it is possible that this will inflate values, sales rising appreciably to yield approximately present values plus a proportional allowance covering the tax. If this proved to be the case, prices could average between £400–£500 an acre within another year or two.

The Oxford Agricultural Economics Research Institute studies farm sales to assess the cost of agricultural land with vacant possession. On this basis average prices are obtained and published. For example during the first half of 1965, four per cent of all sales (some 600 farms) were covered in the analysis. This would suggest about five per cent of all holdings change hands each year.

Although farmland by 1965 was averaging £235 an acre, good land could often fetch around £350, with specialist land costing much more than these figures. Poorer land or land needing drainage and development could be bought for much less than £150 an acre. The rapid rise in average prices for farms has several important implications. Tenanted land should have rents commensurate with the land value. Due to national economic problems, causing a restriction in obtaining loans, it is not surprising that land prices were checked in their rise during 1966.

The Agricultural Land Service conducts an annual inquiry on the rents for 30,000 farms covering 3¼m acres, with 400,000 acres let as County Council smallholdings. This equals a quarter of all rented

IN £ PER ACRE

	5–50	50–100	100–150	150–300	over 300	Av 5–300	Av all
1958	134	93	80	83	66		
1959	166	110	100	89	83		
1960	206	135	122	101	106	132	123
1961	197	136	113	111	108	132	124
1962	196	139	130	118	124	139	134
1963	264	148	145	148	170	168	168
1964	300	207	210	206	194	224	214
1965	338	250	233	192	228	239	235
1966	256	236	224	218	230	235	234

land. In 1966 average rents rose from £3 11s 0d to £3 16s 0d with those in England being mainly around £4 and those in Wales around £2 5s an acre. Though many rents are still under £4 an acre, based on traditional lettings, yielding three-and-a-half per cent gross on the capital required to purchase land at £250 an acre would need a rent of £9 an acre, and at £400 of £14. Similarly if a five per cent gross was required rents of £12 10s and £20 respectively would be required. Annual overheads on land of around £10 an acre prohibit traditional farming practice. For example, at two acres of land used to keep each cow averaging 800 gallons, the land represents 6d for each gallon produced, which would be uneconomic. If a 1,000 gallon cow can be kept on one-and-a-quarter acres, comparable with good modern practice, the land represents only 3d a gallon.

In pig rearing on traditional extensive systems, about four sows might be kept on each acre. With modern land prices this could represent about £60 a sow, plus equipment and land maintenance. A new specialised building with all equipment might cost £240 a place, each place being used about four times a year. Thus the capital required for each method for each sow would be very similar, but the specialised unit would be more attractive for other reasons, such as economy in labour, feed and management, as well as increasing the numbers of piglets successfully reared.

The cost of land is one of the principal reasons why intensive farming becomes essential. Any farmer buying land at £250 an acre or above and costing the capital at around £10 an acre—and some economists believe that at least £15 an acre is nearer the economic allowance for good land—must farm intensively to be solvent. This is a fundamental reason why livestock have to be housed permanently, or principally, in intensive units rather than graze the land. In those cases where land has been inherited or let on traditional assessments, it is possible to farm extensive systems of stocking or cropping; however this is so only because the true economic situation is not taken into account. Denman has shown that, in fact, 'prices of freeholds in farmland keep closer in step with farm incomes than with farm rents', and that 'freeholds with vacant possession moved upwards faster than prices of freeholds subject to farm leases from 1939–55 and slower thereafter'. Incomes rose 525 per cent between 1939–55 but only sixteen per cent between 1955–63, while freehold land subject to farm leases rose 118 and 187 per cent; during these two periods respectively rents rose only seventy-two and 129 per cent[9].

CHART 33: INDEX OF PRICES OF FARMLAND, FARM INCOME
AND RENTS 1939–63

Year	Farmland Prices		Farm Income	Rents
	With Possession	Let		
1939	100	100	100	100
1955	252	218	625	172 ('56)
1962	541	627	725	301

A further implication of present land prices is the considerable capital required to buy a farm of a size suitable for modern labour and machinery utilisation. For example a corn enterprise needs to be at least 250 acres to be economic and this requires a capital outlay for land alone of at least £60,000 and, probably, £75,000. Similarly, running a dairy enterprise for one full-time cowman should be based on at least 100 cows, with perhaps one-and-a-quarter acres each, and this would need between £30,000–£35,000 for the land. Buying, equipping and stocking most farm enterprises on an economic scale to employ two full-time men will seldom need less than £100,000 in capital outlay to start. As a rough assessment, most farm enterprises based on modern techniques will have something in the order of £50,000 of tied capital for each person in employment.

The cost of land is the crux of all modern agricultural techniques; intensive food production is essential to cover the vast amount of tied capital.

RATING

For most of this century, agriculture has been the poor relation of industry, supported by the taxpayer and exempted from many controls and restrictions. Local Government is largely supported by finance collected from householders, commerce and industry. Agriculture became so depressed that in 1929 the Government in the Local Government Act of that year freed agricultural land and its buildings from rates, though dwelling houses were still assessed. Land used for arable or pasture, or poultry when exceeding a quarter of an acre, has been defined as agricultural land. Similarly buildings which are on agricultural land and used solely for operations cultivating the soil or rearing livestock have been defined as agricultural buildings.

These definitions seemed intelligible and fair at a time when agricultural techniques were based on centuries of custom and when change was a slow, gradual process. Farming in 1929, though depressed, was a way of life based on the power of the horse with the diehards stirred to anger and scorn by the introduction of steam traction engines. Agriculture, thirty-five years later, is at the crossroads. It has become one of the most efficient of modern industries with under four per cent of the working population producing over four per cent of the gross national product. It is forseeable that within a generation, due to the decline of those engaged in agriculture coupled with increased productivity, about one per cent of the working population might produce considerably more than four per cent of the nation's gross income. At present however, though farming is generally efficient and in some places very efficient, it includes a large number of farmers who make a living only because of their grants, subsidies and exemption from rates. Agriculture is two-faced; one face projects an image of efficiency second to none while the other of an industry, like the social services, requiring public support in order to exist.

During the last few years, because of the two-faced image of agriculture, rating has become a matter of political controversy and legal complexity. It is now possible to produce food in buildings not on agricultural land. It would be technically possible to produce all meat and dairy products and much other food, with exception of cereals, legumes and roots, in buildings or under plastic covered fields. Moreover, it is difficult today, due to the use of modern materials, to define the meaning of the word 'building' still less establish what is a 'building on agricultural land used solely in connection with agricultural operations thereon'.

The cost of Local Government, with its many social responsibilities has risen dramatically in recent years. By 1965, rates collected had become more than £1,000m a year and widespread concern was felt that the whole system of rating should be re-assessed. In some quarters, strongly resisted by farmers, pressure to rate farm land increased. The County Councils in 1954 had argued that agricultural land and buildings should be rated to provide a new source of revenue and, if assessed on twenty-five per cent of the annual value, at that time might have yielded about £8¼m. Farmers escaped from any form of rerating even when the Rating and Valuation Act of 1961 changed the basis of assessment in other spheres. In the summer of 1965, the Association of Municipal Corporations attacked the farmer's freedom from rates by recommending that all agricultural and forest land should be fully rated, since if farmers needed financial support 'this should be given by means of state subsidy and not by erosion of the basis of rating'. On this basis, it was estimated that farm land would add an excess of £100m to the valuation lists, yielding perhaps about an additional five per cent to Local Government income from rates.

It is probable that rating property is an unbalanced system for modern society, especially when improvements to property incur heavier assessments. It is also possible that rates should be a form of income tax, which is considerably easier and socially fairer to assess and to which farmers would make their own proportionate contribution. However under present methods of assessment, since all industry except agriculture contribute to Local Government, the reasons why agriculture was originally freed from rates no longer apply since farmers recognise they are engaged in the country's biggest single industry, with an annual turnover now of nearly £2,000m, which has proved to be one of the nation's most valuable assets[10]. Nevertheless, farmers are against their land being rated and the National Farmers Union is 'adamantly opposed to any extension of rating to agriculture'[10]. The reasons for this opposition tend to be based on doubtful social values.

The National Farmers Union believes that rating farm land is illogical since it 'is the farmer's raw material, and it would be just as logical to attempt to rate the sea which is the raw material of our fishermen'[11]. This argument is fallacious since fishermen do not own the sea whereas farmers or their landlords own agricultural land. There could be an illogicality between having most rates based on building areas and amenities and a minority on farm land, especially when building sites are exempt, among other anomalies in present assessments made more on buildings than land. This difference would make it more sensible to rate farm buildings rather than farm land, a factor which is discussed below. The second main argument against rating farm land is that 'the money would have to come from somewhere . . . leading to higher food prices', thus being 'a tax on the housewife's food'[11]. It is true that the proposals would lead to increased costs in food production, being an additional farm overhead. These costs however could either be absorbed by increased productivity or could be passed to the consumer in higher food prices. Already food costs must be inflated by rates on food processing factories, storage buildings and shops. There is no logical reason to exempt farmers, rather than processors and distributors, on the basis of the cost of food. Local Government has to be financed and rates should be equally assessed for all groups of people with similar functions.

Two minor arguments are also put forward by farmers against supporting the cost of local Government from farms. It is suggested that making rating assessments would be difficult and costly, requiring a large number of officials. This is equally true for all assessments. Rating is a costly procedure, which is an argument for basing rates on income rather than exempting the agricultural industry. Secondly farmers do not necessarily gain the same benefits as other industrialists out of local government funds. It would be necessary for rates to be graduated in relation to benefits as they are to some extent at present.

The main difficulty in rating farm land is twofold. As indicated above, this would be fundamentally different from most rates which are related to premises and not to land. Secondly farm land varies in value due partly to locality, terrain and structure but also to the value of its crop. Land used for sugar beet, potatoes or corn is much more valuable than that used for grazing. Thus a flat rate on all land by area would seem to be unfair while one by cropping, particularly due to rotations, practically impossible to assess.

These comments are not equally true in the case of buildings. With the development of broiler and battery hen housing during the last decade, many valuers have felt that such buildings should be rated since they are not necessarily or directly used in conjunction with farm land. The legal position is not clear, no case having been taken to the House of Lords, especially when intensive housing is used partly in conjunction with farm land, and rulings tend to vary between regions. A test case was taken to appeal by the Lands Tribunal in the spring of 1964 when a farmer, backed by the National Farmers Union, contested a rating assessment on three broiler houses which he claimed were an integral part of his mixed farm. The 100 acre Cheshire farm produced eggs, broilers and arable crops, manure from the poultry being used for the crops. The appeal was lost and rates on the broiler houses upheld. In Herefordshire, by the autumn of 1964, seventy buildings for intensive poultry housing had been rated with only one appellant exempted on proving his poultry production was an integral part of the farm land. But in Shropshire in the summer of 1965 a rating assessment on a battery house was rejected by the Lands Tribunal on the basis that the building was used solely for the production of eggs which was the objective for which the agricultural land was occupied.

Demands that other intensive livestock buildings, if not all farm buildings, should be rated as well as broiler houses are often made by valuers. When animals never, or rarely, leave their buildings food production has ceased to be in the form known in 1929. Production is similar in technique to many industries. Buildings owned by more than fourteen members in co-operation are rated, but those owned by machinery syndicates are not. Sites for milk vending machines are rated, but potato packing sheds on agricultural land are not, though other industrial packing units are rated. The situation is difficult and confused. Rating all farm buildings would pose several problems. All buildings not in use, or in partial use, would have to be pulled down, and this would put an end to many half-used traditional buildings, in an attempt to evade assessment. Buildings, even if fully used, do not have the same effective value in relation to area. It would be as hard to assess buildings as it is to assess land. Moreover, rating on this basis would fall hardest on the small, efficient, modern farmer.

Although there are no social or economic reasons why agriculture should not contribute to rates, the difficulty lies in devising a simple and effective basis for assessment. It is probable that a system could be developed, and as farming becomes more efficient and industrial in technique should be so. But such arguments evade the basic problem which is to establish a completely different basis for rating whereby Local Government costs are borne more equally by society.

REFERENCES

1 de Ramsey, Lord. Country Landowners Association Conference. April 1965, Cambridge
2 *Tenure of Farm Land*, p9. 1963, National Farmers Union
3 Denman, D. R. 'Who owns the land?' *Farmers Weekly*, p72, 20 November 1959
4 *The structure of dairy farming in England and Wales.* 1965, Milk Marketing Board
5 Ashton, J. & Cracknell, B. E. *Agricultural holdings and farm business structure in England and Wales.* 1961, Agricultural Economics Society
6 *Farming for the future.* 1965, National Union of Agricultural Farm Workers
7 Dower, M. 'The function of open country.' *Journal of the Town Planning Institute*, April 1964
8 Wallace, D. 'Part-time farming.' *Farmers Weekly*, p77. 23 October 1964
9 Denman, D. R. *Land in the market*, p14. 1964, Institute of Economic Affairs
10 *British Agriculture Looks Ahead*, p6 & p80. 1964, National Farmers Union
11 Report. *Farmers Weekly*, 13 August 1965

4f Land required for food production

The principal single use made of the land is the production of food. Yet as discussed previously the land actually required for agriculture has never received systematic study. This is true not only in regard to long term forecasts but also to a short term period such as a single decade. The area of land used for farming is governed for the most part by casual fluctuations in the economics of food production together with those of urban pressures developing farmland for other purposes. Politically there has always been greater concern for resources other than land, such as manpower and capital. Nevertheless in the last analysis these are less critical, perhaps, than the conservation or dissipation of land resources. It is only recently that political, if not national, consciousness has begun to be aware that social and economic wellbeing is related directly to the balance made between urban requirements and food production. It was not until 1964 that any modern critical assessment was made concerning the relationship between the future requirements for land and food, when Professor Wibberley published a brief study on the changing rural economy up to 1970. This is discussed below. A decade earlier in 1954 Wyllie made an analysis of the land required for food production up to 1950[1].

Wyllie summarised previous studies of a similar nature which indicated that prior to the Great War three acres of crops and grass were required to feed one person. This was reduced to two-and-a-half acres by 1926. Wyllie then assessed that each person needed a million calories a year, which prior to the Second War could be obtained from 1·85 acres of crops and grass, shrinking to about 1·28 acres for each person by 1950. The population fed from United Kingdom crops and grass rose in the decade from 1940 to 1950 from 17·3 to 23·8 million. These computations excluded land used to grow feedstuffs for livestock. The actual land areas required (including the production of animal feedstuffs) would be considerably greater. Today caloric consumption has increased to nearly 1·2 million for each person a year. In 1944 Wibberley approached the problem of farmland requirements, using different criteria than Wyllie's. He put into perspective the issues governing the land required for agriculture as being the product of several inter-related variables[2]:

1 The growth of population and significant changes in its composition.

2 The growth of personal incomes, with the consequent effects on the consumption of food.

3 Changes in the physical productivity of agriculture.

4 Changes in the proportion and character of food supplies imported into the country.

Wibberley analysed each of these four factors in order to produce a range of possibilities that could occur within each of the variables. He was able to make projections showing land area requirements which would satisfy forecasts at different levels of change up to 1970. Changes, forecast by different authorities, were taken for the projections which included the minimum and maximum growth expected for each variable[2]:

1 Population growth of 0·75 per cent a year.

2 *a* Real income growth of 3·2 per cent a year (0·5 per cent of this may be taken by increased savings).

b Food expenditure is weighted so that for each £100 rise in real personal incomes it is assumed £16 of it would be spent on livestock products and £14 on crop products.

3 *a* Gross agricultural output growth of three per cent a year.

b Output growth weighted to suit probable yield increases from 0 per cent for beef cattle to three per cent for apples represents 1·28 per cent a year unit growth rate.

4 Reduction of imports if proportion of total imports to home production drops from fifty per cent, allowing for increased productivity, by six per cent or twelve per cent.

The estimated acreage required for food production, based on these forecasts, is, as Wibberley stresses, 'fraught with hazard'. Nevertheless, though the situation could be changed overnight by political action, such as war, or by disease and other forms of disaster, the range of variables taken are sufficiently broad to give a reasonable indication of requirements. The projections Wibberley made were based on the presupposition that no rapid change would occur in the organisation of farming; but since the projections are only taken to 1970 this is not significant. The projections given in Chart 34 are based on calculations by simple proportions, expressing the percentage of land in the United Kingdom required for agricultural purposes in 1970, taken in comparison with that required in 1960 as an index of 100 per cent[2].

These projections show that only ninety-five per cent of the agricultural land held by farmers in 1960 will be required by 1970. This assessment allows for a reasonable increase in population, incomes and agricultural efficiency. Increased agricultural productivity is outstripping the rising demand for food. Thus, in the 1960's, theoretically on this assessment 1½m acres of average farmland, or ¾m acres of good farmland, could be released for other purposes. This would be more than adequate for all other land-use requirements, especially if the poorer agricultural land were to be mainly used for various urban developments. This analysis and projection was reasonable in 1964 when considering the needs for food up to 1970. 1970 is now sufficiently close to be of only relative importance considering the long term needs of this century. Wibberley recognises rightly that with the kind of projections used it is important that they should not be taken too far into the future. There are many subsidiary factors impinging on the main variables which could rapidly make the projections invalid over time spans of more than a few years. In fact since the analysis was made one of the main variables has changed. Population growth, according to more recent surveys, suggests a rate

CHART 34

A Land Requirements: 1970: assuming no changes in productivity or %
imports

% increase pa in population	% Annual increase in personal income (real terms)			
	2·0	2·5	3·0	3·5
0·50	108·2	109·1	109·9	110·8
0·65	109·7	110·5	111·4	112·4
0·75	110·8	111·6	112·6	113·3

B Land Requirements: 1970: increased agricultural productivity:
population increase 0·75% pa

% increase pa in personal income	% Annual increase in agricultural productivity			
	1·0	1·5	2·0	2·5
3·5	102·7	97·8	93·0	88·6
3·0	102·0	97·1	92·3	88·0
2·5	101·0	96·3	91·5	87·2

C Land Requirements: 1970: reductions in imports of temperate food
products: population increase 0·75% pa personal real income increases
3·5% pa

% increase pa in agricultural productivity	% Annual decrease in food imports	
	6	12
1·0	108·7	115·0
1·5	103·6	109·5
2·0	98·5	104·0
2·5	93·9	99·2

of 0·8 per cent a year, rather than a maximum of 0·75 per cent taken
by Wibberley. It is now becoming politically expedient to reduce
food imports by at least fifteen per cent as soon as possible, that is
by £250m a year. In addition, there is a growing awareness that
Britain could become a food exporting country. Excluding the last
factor, the other two changes to the projections made in 1964 would
indicate that little or no land should be taken from agriculture
during this decade, especially no good land. Half a million acres of
farmland will have been taken out of food production during the
decade from 1960.

The situation during the period after 1970 could become serious.
It will certainly become critical as the need to expand home food
production becomes more obvious. The only compensating factor is
that agricultural productivity is, or could be, increased at a faster

rate than assumed by Wibberley in 1964. Wibberley acknowledged that he was allowing for a reasonable and not an excessive assessment of improved agricultural efficiency and that as the allowances for population and income were increased agricultural productivity tended to rise.

There is an urgent need to set up a research department financed by the Government to examine the land requirements for food production in relation to forecasted demands and changing agricultural methods. This department might be organised in conjunction with one of the existing universities which specialise in land-use problems. To some extent, the survival of the country will pivot on reducing food imports. Food imports should not increase to cater for the increase in population or the increase in nutritional demands for each person. For preference, the existing food import bill of about £1,600m a year should be reduced to help the balance of payments. The problems of assessing food requirements and agricultural productivity and acreage are so 'fraught with hazard' that, without the backing of a specialised department, it is dangerous to make any assessment. Not only are the variables analysed by Wibberley complex in themselves to assess, and even more complex in relation to each other, but other potential changes in food technology could alter the situation so drastically by the year 2000 that existing concepts of agricultural land-use would be meaningless.

Food technology is changing rapidly. In the first place, it is now generally recognised that caloric intake is insufficient as a guide to nutrition. In fact, though calorie intake in the United Kingdom is about 3,200 calories for each person a day, an average of 2,600 might be sufficient if balanced in a mixed diet but containing adequate animal protein and plant oil. This puts prime emphasis on eggs, cheese, milk, meat, poultry and fish as the most valuable foods for nutrition, with the first three particularly favourable on economic and humanitarian grounds. Two fundamental changes to diet could change the existing agricultural pattern. Fish farming and marine harvesting have barely started (p392). Fish provide good quality protein for consumption, and algae or other sea-foods are exceptionally nutritious. There seems little doubt that intensive sea farming, coupled with factory methods on inland water, will do much to close the gap between nutritional requirements and food supply by the end of the century, not only in the world as a whole but also within the United Kingdom. It is impossible to gauge how much of the food required in this country will come from water rather than land. Microbiological and synthetic foods could cater for a large part of the diet without making any demand on land resources.

Davis has stated that 'the possibilities of food production by micro-organisms are tremendous. They can be very economic, easily controlled, can use a variety of waste materials, are independent of season and climate'[3]. For example, it has been shown that a ton of paraffin can yield a ton of yeast which 'is more efficient than the cow on a weight basis for this biological transformation'. Similarly microorganisms have been used to purify sewage, producing food suitable for cattle; and a by-product of moulds grown for anti-biotics can yield at the same time an animal food which can liberate soya meal from their diet for human consumption. Foods produced by artificial chemical processes are already possible, the synthesis required for fats and carbohydrates being fairly simple though that for protein being more difficult. By the year 2000, foods artificially produced, but resembling nature in the chemical processes for their manufacture, could be available not only for human consumption, but more particularly for livestock feeding, releasing 'vast quantities of roots, green vegetables, cereals, seed proteins and oils' for man's diet as well as increasing the capacity of producing dairy and meat foods without heavy demands on land resources.

With the advent of rapid progress in the development of fish and marine foods, microbiological and laboratory-controlled foods, and completely synthetic foods it is particularly dangerous to equate future demands and requirements for food purely with the capacity of food production from agricultural land. It seems clear that these non-land-based foods will be implementing the diet by 2000. They will be particularly valuable in the undernourished countries. But it is difficult to believe that they will take a major place in the diet of the United Kingdom within the next thirty-five years. It is probably not rash to predict that non-land-based foods, which include salt and fresh water fish, will represent between ten to fifteen per cent of food consumption and, in dire emergency, could have been increased beyond this level.

Changes, other than those discussed, could fundamentally alter the technique of using agricultural land for food production. The present processes of improving strains of crop, weed control and cultivation methods will continue over the next decades, in many cases substantially improving yields. But other changes could be more revolutionary. There is a possibility that one day weather control may be more than science fiction. Similarly the use of leaf protein is in its infancy. Though generally inferior to animal proteins, the addition of certain amino acids to leaf proteins can make them of comparable quality. At present millions of tons of leaf protein are produced each year and wasted. A ton of green leaf or green vegetable waste could yield the equivalent of about a ton of milk, but of inferior protein value[3]. Protein milk extract has already been produced experimentally and proved difficult to distinguish from cow's milk. Besides any direct change in food itself, due to new techniques such as leaf protein extraction or the importation and development of plants from other and warmer continents for temperature cultiva-

210

tion, variations in diet habits can alter agricultural methods. There is no guarantee that future generations will want foods in approximately the same proportions as at present, even allowing for greater emphasis on proteins. It could be that, as on the Continent today, mutton might become unpopular or veal rather than beef might be preferred. Such changes in diet could alter the amount of land required to satisfy the new market. Already long life convenience foods protected by one of the new techniques, deep freezing, freeze-drying or sterilisation by heat or by irradiation, (the latter being now restricted) are creating new diet patterns. By 2000 much of the national diet may be satisfied by convenience foods. Natural, untreated foods, which begin their process of decay at harvesting or at slaughter, may be considered unhygenic.

There will be change in food technology and this change is likely to upset any estimate of agricultural land requirements by the end of the century. Nevertheless, rather than built up an estimate of land requirements on the basis of diet, it is also possible to consider the land which may be available for agriculture irrespective of the needs of food production. The former estimate is difficult to make, though an example might be taken in milk production. It has to be assumed that milk imports—as all food imports—would be discouraged. The possibility of milk exports, which could prove an important trade to tropical countries, has to be discounted as an unknown quantity. Today, rather less than five pints a week are bought as liquid milk for each person. It is possible that the campaign for consumption of a pint a day may be attained. On this basis, the United Kingdom would need about 3,400m gallons of milk a year. At present, between 800–850 gallons are needed for manufacture into butter, cheese, powder, and so on, representing about half of the liquid sales. It would seem probably that the proportion of milk required for manufacture in relation to liquid sales will increase, perhaps arbitrarily, to two-thirds. A total of about 5,600m gallons of milk would be required each year in the United Kingdom.

It is difficult to estimate the acreage required to produce 5,600m gallons of milk. The main difficulty lies in not knowing whether milk will in the future be produced mainly from grain or from grass products. It could be that the former might replace the more traditional grass dairy farming. Even with a mainly grass diet, it is to be hoped that at least 1,000 gallons will be produced from each acre, including that required for growing the corn supplementary diet, by the end of the century. Productivity might be greater, though this seems doubtful on present knowledge, but could be lower. On this basis milk production alone would need about $5\frac{1}{2}$m acres of intensively farmed land. In addition the youngstock replacements for the national milking herd might number around 2m calves and heifers. Though many of these might be reared indoors, it is to be expected that at least another million acres would be required for their food-stuffs. Similarly, if animal corn is to be home grown rather than largely imported as at present, it is probable that these acreage allowances should be increased. Perhaps, about 7m acres of factory farmed land will be required for the milk industry by the end of the century. As previously discussed, there might only be 25m acres available in the United Kingdom for this kind of intensive farming. The milk industry could therefore require about twenty-eight per cent of the farm land area available. In later sections land requirements in terms of agricultural productivity are examined further.

It is clear from this example that if the United Kingdom is to become mainly self-sufficient in her temperate food requirements, as seems desirable, and is to support 75m people by the end of the century, agricultural land suitable for intensive farming will become precious. If the estimate of a reduction of farmland during the next thirty-five years to about 25m acres is correct, which would release some 6m acres of improved farmland of varying quality for other purposes, then care should be now taken to keep as much fertile land as possible for food production. The quality of the 25m acres will be critical, since it will have to be farmed with factory methods and precision. Each third of an acre will have to feed one person. Even if food imports were allowed to continue in the present proportion, that is at one-third of temperate food consumption, each half acre would have to support one person. Because between 40,000 and 50,000 acres are taken from farming each year, much of it in lowland Britain, it is to be expected that much of it is on good or potentially fertile land. If only little more than 25,000 acres of potentially fertile land are absorbed each year for urban requirements, this would be equal to nearly one million acres by the end of the century. This is an area which could be needed to feed three million people, that is about the national population growth for nearly one decade, allowing for the average of a third of an acre being available for each person.

Even allowing for immense strides being made in intensive farming methods, it is possible that a third of an acre will prove completely inadequate for feeding each person. Agricultural output for each acre would have to increase at least fourfold to make this possible. Since at present much of Britain is farmed with traditional methods, some of it on an extensive system of low output, productivity can be increased substantially. Attaining near self-sufficiency for the future population will depend on intensive farming which, in turn, depends on fertile land of suitable terrain. The less land available in the future, due to urban development on suitable land of this kind being permitted, the harder the task of self-sufficiency will become. There will be only two alternatives to make good a deficiency in land. Foods from non-land production will have to be increased or food imports will have to be raised. Both tend to be unknown quantities,

212

one in social and the other in economic terms. The only basis for successful land husbandry would be for accurate land classification to be made as soon as possible.

REFERENCES

1 Wyllie, J., *Land requirements for the production of human food.* 1954, Wye College
2 Wibberley, G. P. (a) *The changing rural economy of Britain,* pp41–55. Report of the Town and Country Planning School. 1964, Town Planning Institute, (b) *Pressures on Britain's land resources.* Tenth Heath Memorial Lecture. 1965, University of Nottingham
3 Davis, J. G. 'The food industry in AD 2000.' Journal of the Royal Society of Arts, pp84–93, January 1966

5 LAND: APPEARANCE

Introduction

The appearance of the landscape will change during the rest of this
century, perhaps more drastically than at any other period of history
within the span of one generation. Urban growth, coupled to increased
facilities for mobility and recreation, has already been discussed. This
growth will leave its terrible mark on the countryside, especially in
relation to those excesses of suburban despoliation which no planning
seems able to contain. If the future is judged by the record of the
immediate past, then there is every reason to despair. Lionel Brett has
emphasised in *Landscape in Distress* that, in spite of the planners'
best intentions, random urban expansion through the small towns
and villages has devastated much of the inherited beauty of south
Oxfordshire, even into the heart of the rural countryside, and the
little which seems to remain is in danger of being engulfed. What is
true in Oxfordshire can also be seen in much of Britain. The urban
pressure for ravaging rural Britain has barely started; mobility and
leisure will carry the plague into the remotest parts with all the banal
and mediocre impedimenta of modern society. Much design is
created by people unskilled and untrained in functional or visual
disciplines, and lack of co-ordination and comprehended unity
bedevils much urban growth. It is no wonder that many farmers,
conscious of the blight they create on the landscape with their own
endeavours, to some extent out of economic necessity, retort that it is
but a pinprick compared to the urban plague which, on one pretext
or another, seeps into the countryside.

Change there will be—both in regard to the physical structure of
land-use and the visual structure of the landscape. Modern forestry
and agriculture are already conducted on vast scales of production,
but they are only as yet in minor key. The society which is now
emerging will make new uses of the countryside, creating a different
emphasis in the visual relationship between nature and man's control
of its resources. The greatest of the changes to come will be of scale.
The image of a rural and rustic Britain, with its landscape of gentle
contours broken by a network of tree-decked hedgerows, of copses

214

and neat farm courtyards intermingling with a scattering of hamlets, villages and market towns drawn together by the fine thread of narrow and flower-banked country lanes is dissipated by the mechanics of a machine age, only now making a real impact on its inherited beauty. Mechanisation and increased productivity must be the hallmark of the future. The new landscape could have its own attraction, if the period of change is treated with sensibility, but its beauty will be drawn from a different relationship of scale from that known during the first half of this century. Preservation of the countryside in its present pattern is valueless as a basis for planning. Conservation of the resources of nature is desirable, governed by a new concept of control and development in land-use.

The change in ownership of farmland and in the distribution and size of the farms themselves is of profound social and visual significance. Not only may much farmland pass out of the ownership of the traditional farming families, descendants of yeoman stock, but the farms will be amalgamated into large production units of a scale unknown in the past. By degrees, the average size of all farms has increased from fifty to seventy-five acres. But, more significant, is the rapid growth in farms of more than 300 acres. In 1950, there were less than 13,000, but today there are nearly 15,000 and, by 1980, there could be over 17,500 farms of this size in England and Wales. Land farmed in units of over 300 acres could in fact increase during the second half of this century to represent an increase from about a quarter in 1950 to two-thirds in 2000 of the improved farm land area. This, in itself, will change the scale of the landscape since, with management in large units, the distribution of fields, windbreaks, roads and buildings have to be altered to suit a different and enlarged concept of capital investment, production and mechanisation. Amalgamation of farms, at present at a rate of almost 4,000 a year, is, perhaps, the greatest change in the social fabric of rural Britain since the breakdown of the fuedal systems.

Mechanisation, coupled with the process of amalgamation, has a tremendous effect on the landscape, creating changes which are now only in their infancy. The innumerable small fragments of land suitable for hand tillage and the power of the horse, the traditional five to ten acre field, will be swept away. Already hundred acre fields are not unknown, though most large modern fields are of forty to fifty acres. Before the end of the century, 2,000-acre fields may be too small for arable farming and grassland and, if still predominately used for livestock, may be in units of hundreds, even if not thousands, of acres. It is certain that hedgerows, field trees and many copses will be eradicated, creating profound changes in the ecology and soil structure of Britain. It is possible that these elements will cease to be a recognisable feature in much of the landscape.

Forestry has already made a considerable impact on rural Britain,

215

not only in the highlands but also in many parts of lowland Britain. At present, increasing at the rate of 45,000 acres a year, the sweep of conifers, though still considered to be alien, is becoming a feature of the landscape. If wisdom prevailed, the parsimony of recent governments to reafforestation would be replaced by a crash programme to at least double the present acreage of commercial timber before the end of the century. The need to conserve water, also, will have its effect on the countryside, reservoirs not only being created among the hills of north and west but also today in areas of rich farmland round conurbations, as well as in small units on many farms for irrigation. Trees and water must become an important basis for much of the planning for future recreation, sometimes utility and leisure having a dual function in land-use. The use of trees and water will change the scale of the future landscape.

Many of the existing and charming agricultural buildings, built with materials indigenous to their locality, will disappear as a feature with the passing of the traditional landscape. Many of the modern buildings are, for a variety of reasons, no more than shacks. The best are neat blocks clad with asbestos-cement, though specialised units of metal and glassfibre have a real contribution to make in the storage of crops, and others are long, low and compact timber buildings for intensive pig and poultry housing. The scale of the new buildings are unsympathetic to the old, being far larger in size, cruder in colour and detail and no longer grouped in attractive courtyards. It is possible that a change in the methods of processing and selling food could, in the future, remove many of these buildings for ever as individual blobs in the landscape, grouping them together in regional centres, with allied industries, near to road and rail networks.

It is clear, from this introduction but with the issues discussed in more detail in this section, that change, dramatic in its social and visual implications, will radically transform the face of rural Britain. Many will resent this change. It may be, probably will be, for the worse. It could be, if the issues are seized by a society sensible to their implications and sensitive in their realisation, that the future landscape will have its own attraction, albeit different in scale and function from that which is loved today.

5b The amalgamation of farms

Each year, nearly 4,000 farms in England and Wales cease to exist as separate holdings. In the decade since 1951, this reduction which has come about by the amalgamation of holdings into larger units rather than by a reduction in the area of land farmed, represented a decline of eleven per cent in the total number of farms. During that period, the number of holdings recognised by the Ministry of Agriculture from an analysis of the agricultural returns completed by farmers fell by 38,903 to a total of 338,295 in 1961. By 1965 there were well under one-third of a million holdings in England and Wales, although in the United Kingdom there are 450,000 officially listed.

If the rate of amalgamation remained constant by 1980 there would be about 265,000 holdings in England and Wales, declining to less than 190,000 by the end of the century. In the second half of the century the number of holdings will have been halved by a natural process of amalgamation. It is probable that not only will the rate of amalgamation increase, at least during the next two decades due to a natural shift towards big business farming, but that this process will be accelerated because of financial incentives made by the Government. Throughout North America and Europe, the trend is towards amalgamation and the OEEC has recognised that to improve economic growth the number of farmers in Europe must be drastically reduced. Common Market countries may soon co-ordinate their measures to aid amalgamation[1]. Some agricultural economists believe that amalgamation in Britain is not only inevitable but should perhaps be accelerated by state intervention rather than by financial incentive alone. Nevertheless during recent years some farmers, finding it difficult to remain independant and make a living, have attempted to get national intervention to restrict production on the more efficient farms, especially those which are farmed with factory methods or are owned by tycoon businessmen, so that the trend to greater amalgamation would be checked. One result of the policy of subsidising and aiding farmers in recent years has been to make it possible for many basically uneconomic farms to remain in production, thus retarding the rate of amalgamation, but the introduction of grants and pensions to encourage amalgamation should help to restrict the natural desire for small farmers to remain independant.

The change in the size of farms managed as individual units will have a profound effect on the structure of agriculture as well as on the appearance of the countryside. Amalgamation makes it possible to get a better return out of labour, machinery and buildings, so that less capital for each acre need be invested to provide the same return. Alternatively it may become economic to increase the investment for each acre since the potential return on capital may be proportionally greater. Amalgamation may make it desirable and feasible to reorganise the pattern of field layout, improve fertility and drainage on the land, and centralise buildings to suit a different management policy. The last may in turn make many existing traditional buildings redundant and uneconomic to retain.

It is surprising how little in fact is known about the structure of farm size and layout, especially in relation to different types of management. The ministry statistics are not necessarily related to the actual structure of farms as production units, particularly to self-

H   217

contained production units. The census includes all holdings of more than a quarter of an acre and a holding need not be a productive farm. Land which is used solely as an amenity to a country house for riding, shooting, fishing or as orchards or as rough grazing for non-commercial production can be counted as a holding. Though small holdings can be extremely productive, especially if they include intensive livestock units, it is probable that many of the holdings of less than twenty acres and some of more than this area are not farmed commercially. If, for example, all farms of under twenty acres were excluded from the census, there would be only 190,532 holdings recognised in 1962 and 25,947 of the 38,903 holdings amalgamated in the decade since 1951 were of under twenty acres. The rate of amalgamation for all farms between June 1951 and June 1961 was 3,890·3 a year, that is a reduction of one farm in nine during the decade, but for farms of twenty acres or more only 1,295·6 a year, representing a reduction of one farm in fourteen over the same period. In the year June 1961 to June 1962, 3,846 farms of all sizes ceased to exist, but of those of twenty acres or more 2,085 were amalgamated, which is considerably greater than the average each year over the previous decade. Rough grazings are excluded from the statistics, but holdings of this description dropped by 380 from the previous year to a total of 6,049 in 1962.

The change in the number of farms of less than twenty acres between 1951 and 1962 in England and Wales, which includes the two smallest groups of holdings recorded by the Ministry, are given in Chart 35[1].

CHART 35

		No of holdings of under 20 acres
Year	1951	171,625
	1961	145,678
Reduction	1951–1961	25,947
Reduction	1951–1961 pa	2,594·7 pa
Year	1962	143,917
Reduction	1961–1962	1,761
% of all holdings in 1962 under 20 acres		43·1%
% change 1951/62		16%

The chart shows that between two-fifths and a half of all holdings are of less than twenty acres. Many of these units may be completely unproductive, others may be farmed at a loss and most of the remainder would show a poor return for the capital and labour involved in their management. A few may be farmed intensively and the basis for farming on a factory scale within a small acreage is discussed elsewhere (p311). But as a general rule it is doubtful

218

whether the inclusion of such small holdings in a census is sensible when considering the structure of farm size in relation to modern agricultural techniques, since although their total number is unknown, small factory farms are comparatively rare. In contrast, Chart 36 shows an analysis of farm size for those of twenty or more acres. A decision to take twenty acres as the smallest productive holding is arbitrary. It must be realised that the total number of holdings can fluctuate not only by amalgamation of farms within the number given, but either by holdings of less than twenty acres amalgamating to make one of more than twenty acres or by a larger holding being split into two country houses with paddocks, each of less than twenty acres.

CHART 36: NO OF HOLDINGS OF 20 ACRES OR MORE (EXCLUDING
ROUGH GRAZINGS IN ENGLAND AND WALES

				Acres					
	20–50	50–100	100–150	150–300	300–500	500–700	700–1,000	over 1,000	Total
Year 1951	68,203	60,012	31,185	33,510	9,110	2,097	957	499	205,573
1961	59,893	56,886	29,092	32,646	9,643	2,563	1,189	704	192,617
Reduction 1951–61	8,310	3,126	2,093	864	+533	+466	+232	+205	12,956
1951–61 pa	831	312·6	209·3	86·4	+53·3	+46·6	+23·2	+20·5	1,295·6
Year 1962	58,557	56,348	28,765	32,441	9,784	2,662	1,245	730	190,532
Reduction 1962	1,336	538	327	205	+141	+99	+56	+26	2,085
% of each group in 1962	30¾%	30%	15%	17%	5%	1⅓%	⅔%	⅓%	100%
% of each group in 1951	33¼%	29½%	15%	16¼%	4½%	1%	½%	¼%	100%
% change in each group 1951–62	−13%	−7%	−9%	−3%	+7%	+26%	+30%	+46%	—

Approximately a third of the holdings of twenty acres or more are under fifty acres in size, a third of between fifty and 100 acres and the rest of more than 100 acres. The average size of farm in Britain increased in the decade until 1963 from sixty-four to seventy-three acres. In contrast, in the Common Market countries more than seventy per cent of farms average less than twenty-five acres each[1]. An analysis of the size of farms can, by itself, be misleading since although there are more small farms than large ones the total acreage of cultivated land represented by farms within each group is disproportionate to their number. For example, though half the farms are of less than seventy-three acres, together they represent not more than a fifth of the cultivated land area. Similarly, although only about seven per cent of all farms are of more than 300 acres, together they include a quarter of the cultivated land area. The importance of the large farm in England and Wales (those of more than 300 acres) is therefore evident by the fact that nearly seven million acres of cultivated land is farmed in units of this size. Though at present nearly 15,000 farms average more than 300 acres each, it is expected that there will be more than another 2,500 farms of this size by 1980[3]. This is contrary to the general impression that, numerically, the country is made up of small farms.

The analysis of farm sizes indicates three important trends. Firstly, as discussed above, farms are being amalgamated at an increasing rate into larger units. In 1962, over 2,000 farms of more than twenty acres ceased to have individual existence, whereas the average during the previous decade was under 1,300 a year. Secondly, up to 300 acres, the number of farms is declining in all size groups, whereas farms of over 300 acres are becoming numerous in all size groups. The numerical change seems to have increased in each group in 1962 when compared with the average for the previous decade. Though the number of farms in the 150–300 acre group continued to decrease in 1962, the proportion of farms by groups to the total number of farms only declined in the groups under 100 acres, remaining constant in the groups of 100–150 acre and increasing in all groups of over 150 acres. Thirdly, the proportional change in the number of farms within each group between 1951 and 1962 was a reduction of under ten per cent for farms of fifty to 300 acres and a gain of under ten per cent for farms of 300–500 acres. The decline in the number of twenty to fifty acre farms in the same period, being thirteen per cent, was more dramatic, but the increase in the number of farms in the groups of more than 500 acres was startling. By 1962, there were nearly fifty per cent more farmers holding over 1,000 acres each than in 1951. To some extent this may reflect the fact that in recent years farmers working two or more farms as a single unit have been asked by the Ministry to make only one return.

The change in farm size has regional characteristics. As is well known, most of the big farms are grouped together into one or two regions. For example, over two fifths of the farms of more than 1,000 acres are in Lincolnshire and Norfolk, 115 being in the former in 1962 and ninety-three in the latter. In the same year in Hampshire, there were sixty farms of more than 1,000 acres, whereas in 1951 there were only forty-two. The increase is close to the national average for the increase of farms in this size group over the same period. The adjoining county of Wiltshire had nearly as many farms of the same size, there being fifty-three in 1962. The greatest number of reductions in the number of farms naturally occur where there are many small

220

farms, principally in the North and West. Frequently the losses have occurred in these regions because of dairy farms going out of milk production and being amalgamated into adjoining farms. In other cases, numerous losses in the number of farms occur in the counties where there has been a swing to big farming units. Examples of the reduction in the number of holdings of over a quarter of an acre between June 1961 and June 1962 in individual counties are given in Chart 37.

CHART 37: REDUCTION IN NO OF HOLDINGS BY SAMPLE
COUNTIES

	1961–1962
Devon	226
Cornwall	202
Lancashire	201
Norfolk	184
West Riding	152
Somerset	115
Shropshire	115
Northumberland	107
Leicestershire	3

In Devon, where 226 farms disappeared from the records in one year, most of the amalgamation occurred in farms of under fifty acres. In contrast, Leicestershire, which traditionally has been a county containing above average-sized farms, only lost three farms from a total of 4,817 in the county. In Huntingdonshire, in the same year, there was an increase of thirty-two in the number of farms and in Surrey of thirty-one. In the last case all gains were in holdings of under fifteen acres. It is probable that with the national increase in wealth, the improvements in roads and the extension of facilities for leisure, with all their social consequences, there will be an increase in the number of country properties, qualifying as holdings, but being non-productive. The Ministry of Agriculture has attempted to eliminate non-productive holdings from their records in recent years. If a better understanding of land-use is to be encouraged in the future, it will be essential to have accurate records of productive and non-productive holdings, showing in the former case some assessment of productivity.

Hampshire is a county where the change has not been untypical of the country as a whole, though there has been less shift in farms of between 100 and 1,000 acres than elsewhere, mainly perhaps because of the change which occurred in corn growing techniques during and immediately after the war. Similarly big dairy producers were becoming established before 1951, though dairying is not the major enterprise.

CHART 38: NO OF HOLDINGS IN HAMPSHIRE

	acres					
	under 20	20–100	100–500	500–100	over 1,000	Total
1951	5,188	1,794	1,198	168	42	8,390
1962	4,216	1,597	1,079	183	60	7,135
Reduction 1951–62	972	197	119	+15	+18	1,255
% change 1951–62	−18%	−11%	−10%	+9%	+43%	−15%

In contrast to Hampshire, Cardiganshire is a county of traditionally small farms. In the depression between the wars, there was a considerable decline in the number of holdings. This was caused to a small extent by amalgamation but more generally by a reversion of farm land to rough grazing. Since 1939 there has been a slight decline in the number of holdings of less than twenty acres, partly by amalgamation and partly by reversion to rough grazings, and a slight increase in the number of holdings of more than 100 acres, though the total number do not equal the pre-1913 number.

CHART 39: NO OF HOLDINGS IN CARDIGANSHIRE

	acres				
	under 20	20–50	50–100	over 100	Total
1913	3,419	1,238	1,066	751	6,474
1939	2,459	1,162	1,163	632	5,416
1959	2,020	1,153	1,148	708	5,029
Reduction 1939/59	439	9	15	+76	387

Cardiganshire is not typical as a county, though in Wales eighty-three per cent of holdings average less than fifty acres, but it does represent the pattern to be found in hill farming districts, hit by the depression and only partly recovering with the modern trend to mechanised farming generally more effective on the lowlands. Devon, which has the same tradition of small, independant farms, has been more fortunate in its transition towards amalgamation into productive units. As recorded in Chart 37, 226 farms, mostly of under fifty acres, were amalgamated into larger units in 1962. Devon has been fortunate in another respect since the Teign valley was the centre for the Nuffield Foundation's Farm Project undertaken from 1959–1963[5].

222

The Project sponsored by the Nuffield Foundation with a grant of £25,000 was to increase the ratio of farm advisors to the number of farmers, with the co-operation of the NAAS, from the usual average of one for every 700 farmers to about one for every 200 farmers in the selected area of Devon and to assist the advisor by making it possible for him to follow up his advice with a certain amount of practical help. The detailed analysis of results has not been published. However, within the five years of the project, the 198 farms were reduced by twelve, or by a little over six per cent, so that the average farm size increased from eighty-five to ninety-two acres, an increase of eight per cent. More significant perhaps is the fact that incomes were increased by about sixteen per cent on a small proportion of the farms where the accounts were analysed over five years. In addition, some co-operation in the use of machinery and labour developed in the district.

More recently a study of the Northern counties, as analysed in Chart 40, has shown that in this region not only has there been a substantial increase in the number of farms of over 300 acres, but farms of over 500 acres have increased by more than a third during a decade. In Northumberland four-fifths of the agricultural land is now in units of more than 150 acres. The area considered includes Northumberland, Durham, Cumberland, Westmorland and the North Riding of Yorkshire[6].

CHART 40: AMALGAMATION IN THE NORTHERN REGION 1953-63

Size of farm: acres	0–20	20–50	50–100	100–150	150–300	300–500	500+
No ,, ,, 1953	9,644	4,946	6,045	3,634	3,993	877	258
No ,, ,, 1963	7,663	4,038	5,602	3,384	3,974	944	353
Change 1953/63	−1,981	−908	−443	−250	−19	+67	+95
% Change	−21	−17	−7	−6	−½	+8	+37

This analysis shows a greater trend towards amalgamation into large units than is general in the country as a whole.

In 1965 both government and public opinion changed its outlook radically. The introduction of a Land Commission to help reshape the national farm structure and, in particular, to encourage the amalgamation of such land which cannot provide a reasonable livelihood into viable and well equipped holdings is a departure from previous policy. Retirement grants as an annuity for farmers over sixty-five and as capital for those over fifty-five should do much to accelerate the natural process of amalgamation perhaps, as some economists wish, to eliminate 100,000 of the 450,000 holdings in the United Kingdom during the next decade. In England and Wales, this might increase the present rate of amalgamation by twenty-five per cent to give over 5,000 less holdings each year.

From the national and farming viewpoint it is desirable that farms should be the optimum size to promote maximum efficiency. Optimum size is not clear-cut, especially since factory farms can be economic on a very small acreage. Such factors as factory farming apart, optimum size is obviously influenced by soil, terrain and climate. The choice of location, for any particular enterprise, which is influenced by these factors, must also be determined by the economics of capital investment especially in relation to the balance of labour and equipment to the yield of the product concerned. Each skilled man and each expensive machine must be used to capacity and the basic yardsticks for this are rapidly being increased as equipment improves. Today one man can look after 100–120 cows, or 600 highland ewes, or 1,000 fattening cattle, or 100 sows or 2,000 fattening pigs or poultry[7]. Similarly one man can cultivate 200 arable acres. These factors have to be balanced with other machinery potential. A medium combine-harvester can therefore manage at least 250 acres and any farms with a smaller corn acreage tend to be over-equipped unless harvesting is by contract or by a co-operatively owned machine. A large combine-harvester can handle 500 acres, but a two-combine unit is more efficient, making 1,000 acres economic. If the land is light, so that continuous corn is undesirable, then a four to one rotation would mean that the farm unit should be of 1,250 acres; including a break crop this might be a seven-man farm. Alternatively mechanisation means that sugar beet should be in 150–200 acre units and potatoes in forty-to-fifty acres. A dairy farm with good grassland holding 120 cows might normally need 150–200 acres, though some could manage on 100 acres; if followers to the herd are included, another fifty to eighty acres might be needed. Here again, a two-man unit is needed for efficiency, which could carry a third man acting alternatively as relief milker for each herd. A good dairy farm should probably be of 350–400 acres in extent. Amalgamation should be directed to produce farms of economic size for each enterprise in relation to labour and mechanisation rather than to size unrelated to production requirements.

Though a certain amount is known about the size of farms in the country from the Ministry census, even though these are known to contain some misrepresentation being based on returns made out by farmers, the analysis is confused by lack of knowledge about co-operation between farmers. In the past this was not significant except perhaps on the large estates. The traditional farmer, due largely to the historical development of agriculture (p31), gained a reputation for being independant, relying on his own resources and distrusting both the Government, since it did not protect his interests in times of need, and his neighbour, who was his commercial competitor in buying and selling in the market. Co-operation between farmers was almost unknown except in times of national or local

224

disaster. The greatest change in agriculture during the second half of this century may prove not to be the tremendous technical development, leading to factory methods of production, but the far reaching social implications of co-operation between farmers which has become evident during the last few years. Co-operation between farmers has principally taken two forms. The most dramatic has been the growth of marketing groups in which farmers join together to sell their goods instead of each being in competition with his neighbour. This has made it possible to secure better terms as a group than could be obtained by individual farmers. Marketing groups are discussed in Chapter 8. A second form of co-operation which has recently developed has been direct assistance to each other by a group of farmers in the production of food and in the management of their farms. This may be a simple matter in that a group of farmers might buy an expensive machine and share its use. For example the machine bought and used by the group might be a combine harvester or a hedger and ditcher. Alternatively there might be a more elaborate form of co-operation in that a number of farmers might erect and manage a grain drier and storage plant. Machinery syndicates, as these co-operatives are usually known, are also discussed in Chapter 8.

Co-operation can obviously affect the structure of farm sizes in a manner which may not be revealed by a normal census. Amalgamation of tenant farms on the big estates, will in normal circumstances, be reflected in the returns made to the Ministry of Agriculture. It may be easy for an estate to re-arrange its leases and to redivide the land into larger and more economic units. An arrangement of this kind would depend on the existing structure of the estate, on the nature of the leases and on human relationships between landlord and tenant as well as on the feasibility of forming a more economic group of farms. Several amalgamations of this kind have been reported in recent years. Four examples are given below:

1 *Burdon Estate, County Durham*[8]

The eleven tenants of the estate formed an estate-tenant company in 1962 at the instigation of the landlord, Major A. A. M. Gregson. Six tenants, being suitably placed, were interested in developing a central bulk storage building. The tenants, as a group, could arrange bulk purchasing and could have machinery and equipment as a syndicate. By these arrangements, though the farms were not amalgamated, centralised buildings would change the structure of the estate.

2 *Claydon Estate, Bucks*[9]

The estate of 4,757 acres, owned by Mr R. Verney, former president of the Country Landowner's Association, had thirty-four farms in 1947. By 1963, these had been reduced to twenty-seven. The owner is promoting amalgamation as the opportunity arises. On the present amalgamations, both productivity and rents have been increased.

3 Birch Hall Estate, Essex[10]

The estate of 3,300 acres, owned by Colonel J. Round, with at present twelve farms, will be replaced by three 1,000 acre units within twenty years under a plan made by the owner to create the most efficient and economic unit for landlord and tenant. The farms will specialise in grain and root production and will have a central general purpose service building.

4 Codlands Estate, Hampshire[11]

The possibility of re-organising three farms on the estate was discussed by Mr M. P. Jones, the County Agricultural Officer for Hampshire, at a meeting in the autumn of 1963. The three farms of 316, 237 and 185 acres could make a 738 acre unit which could be used for grain and milk production more efficiently than the three separate farms. Labour on the estate could be halved, and output for every £100 of labour and for every £100 of machinery invested would be substantially increased. The plan would include a 120-cow Ayrshire herd with followers, using 340 acres, and 360 acres devoted to grain. A dairy building and a grain drying-and-storing plant would be erected, placed centrally for each enterprise. Fewer field machines would be required than at present. The annual building charge for the new buildings would be covered by the savings in labour and equipment. The existing and proposed investments are summarised as follows:

	Existing farms:			Existing total	Amalga-mated unit
	316 acres	237 acres	185 acres		
Acreage: total	316	237	185	738	738
as corn	91	95	31	217	360
as cows	68	36	59	163	120
Labour force	7	5	5	17	8
Total cost	£2,894	£2,881	£2,286	£8,061	£5,400
Machinery invested	£3,543	£2,900	£2,913	£9,356	£6,700
Running cost	£2,513	£1,708	£1,226	£5,447	—
Gross output/ £100 labour	£382	£418	£366	—	£526
Gross output/ £100 machinery	£302	£542	£486	—	£557

It is evident that amalgamation of farms into larger units in the big estates is possible and sometimes economically desirable. It is

226

clear that several estates are tackling the problem with the owners giving encouragement to their tenants. Amalgamation of individual farms not owned by such estates takes place by normal purchases made when the ownership of a farm becomes vacant. However, another form of co-operation which does not technically alter the structure of farm sizes, but changes their structure as production units rather than their ownership, are management syndicates. The most dramatic example of this has been the recent formation of the Mallingdown Farming Syndicate based on Piltdown in Sussex[12]. In 1962–63, fifteen farms in four counties holding 2,000 acres and £¼m of capital formed a management syndicate. Eleven of the farms were near Piltdown, but others were in Wiltshire, Somerset and Lincolnshire. Within two years by January 1964, the membership had risen to nineteen partners farming 3,000 acres, divided into 500 enclosures or fields, in holdings of mainly 100 acres, but with a few of 200 to 300 acres. Within the syndicate it is possible to have heavier stocking and cropping for each acre and make better use of labour, equipment and buildings. Administration is centralised and bulk buying and centralised reserves are possible. Youngstock for dairy and fattening enterprises on several individual farms can be reared on one specialised farm. Specialisation of all kinds is easier. The 3,000 acres are treated as one estate, in 1963 there were 1,000 acres of cash crops, 200 acres of grass, kale and roots, with 500 cows in nine herds, 200 calves as well as sheep, pig and poultry enterprises. In 1967 the syndicate was reformed, acreage being cut back to 1,200 to come within the terms of the Agriculture Bill of that year permitting grants towards co-operation.

The difference between the Mallingdown Syndicate and most modern groups for marketing or centralising equipment or youngstock is in the financial arrangement. Most groups are composed of independant farmers entering into a limited agreement to share equipment or grow produce on contract. The Mallingdown Syndicate has partners who draw a salary, have shares and combine their business assets under an elected management committee, even though legally each farm is owned by a partner in the syndicate. Co-operative syndicates of this kind, which could be an important development in management in the future, make it difficult to establish the true size of a holding. In the past holdings were clear-cut, being owned and managed by a farmer or being farmed by a tenant. Each holding was independant. Today this is no longer true. Co-operation between farmers can lead to the position where several holdings are, to all intents and purposes, under centralised management. Amalgamation of holdings can take place to form large production units, though legally the holdings are still separate farms. It is probable that in a study of the structure of farm sizes and the amalgamation of farms some account must be taken of production units rather than holdings. The management of holdings for a common purpose is perhaps of equal importance, of even of more importance, than the strict definition of one farmer to one holding as an independant farm.

It is not surprising that in the various schemes for amalgamation many of the farms concerned are of 100–200 acres. Though on the basis of present trends in amalgamation as discussed above farms of 150–300 acres have remained almost constant in number, whereas those of 100–150 acres have dropped, it is the 100–200 acre farm which will in future be difficult to manage economically. As Wallace said[13] it is farms of 150–200 acres which are going to be forced out of business since they are the most vulnerable to changes in market prices and cost and need nearly as much mechanisation as farms of over 300 acres. Farms of about 350–400 acres particularly are sought after when sold since they are suitable to manage in terms of labour for each acre and machinery for each acre. Though many small farms of 40–70 acres are being amalgamated, partly because there are many farms of this size, they can be economically resilient if farmed by a farmer and his family using second-hand equipment. As an alternative, farms of 50–250 acres are particularly suitable for co-operative or syndicate ventures. The economic stresses which occur in agriculture, now and in the future, will make co-operation for many farmers an attractive alternative to amalgamation in order to retain their identity as individuals.

At the beginning of this section it was suggested that, on the basis of the statistics of the last decade, there would be 265,000 holdings of all sizes by 1980 instead of the present number of under a third of a million. It is probable that this rate of amalgamation may increase and it could be that there will be less than a quarter of a million farms by 1980. Perhaps more important, there will probably be a dramatic drop in the number of farms of less than fifty acres, from 202,474 at present to a little over 150,000 in 1980; secondly, the rapid increase in farms of over 300 acres will continue so that whereas there may be nearly 15,000 at present there will be about 17,500 by 1980. If by 1980 the average farm size were to be 600 acres for farms of more than 300 acres, whereas at present it is more like 500 acres, then $10\frac{1}{2}$m acres would be farmed in units of this size (about two-fifths of the improved land in England and Wales) compared with the present 7m acres. By the turn of the century there might be 20,000 farms of more than 300 acres occupying nearly two-thirds of the improved acreage existing at that time. Such a change would have profound economic, social and visual affects on the country.

REFERENCES

1 Williams, M. 'Prospects—or a pension?' *Farmers Weekly*, p59. 9 April 1965

2 Based on statistics published annually by the Ministry of Agriculture from an analysis of the official returns made by farmers every June.
3 Walston, Lord. National Power Farming Conference Report 1964. *Farmers Weekly*, p53. 14 February 1964
4 Jones, P. M. T. Country Landowners Association Report. Hampshire Conference 1963
5 Charlton, R. 'The grass is greener but . . .'. *Farmers Weekly*, p80. 31 May 1963
6 *Appraisal of Agriculture in the Northern Region* 1953–63. 1965, Ministry of Agriculture
7 Garner, F. H. 'The right size for British farms.' *Country Life*, p36. 1 July 1965
8 *Farmers Weekly*, p47, 30 March 1962
9 ,, ,, , p48, 12 April 1963
10 ,, ,, , p37, 12 July 1963
11 ,, ,, , p83, 18 October 1963
12 Attlee, P. 'Fifteen farms link-up for more profit.' *Farmers Weekly*, p48. 25 January 1963
'Farm syndicates to cut costs.' *The Times*, 9 January 1964
13 *Farmers Weekly*, p57. 6 March 1964

5c Hedges and field boundaries

A feature of the landscape which many consider to be an important part of our heritage of scenic beauty is the pattern of small fields bounded by hedges and hedgerow trees that is typical of much of Britain. The familiar field pattern is of comparatively recent origin. Man's use of the earth's surface has always been in a state of flux. The Mediaeval, the Georgian and the Victorian countryside were all markedly different in appearance.

Hedges have existed on well-drained soils from Saxon times, but for the most part the Mediaeval landscape was one of open strip fields. In some cases, these strips were formed by the ridge and furrow cultivations still visible in many Midland fields. Occasionally they were divided by turf walks and corner stones or more rarely the edges of fields were marked by wattle fences. A pattern was created of large open fields round each village interspersed with rough common and scrub land. Lying beyond the boundary of each community were the woodlands and untamed forests which covered much of Mediaeval Britain.

The enclosure movement of the sixteenth to nineteenth centuries was the outcome of the breakdown of a strict feudal society. Many of the strip fields were divided by fences into small enclosures and by degrees scrub and hedge intertwined with these fences. With the growth of population and trade during the reigns of the Tudors and Stuarts and with the rise of the yeoman farmer much scrub and wood was cleared and new fields created. The enclosure movement became national policy, rather than a local expedient, by the middle of the eighteenth century when private acts of Parliament overrode the interests of individuals. When Victoria came to the throne the enclosure of the open cornfields was nearly complete, though further enclosure of common land continued for some decades. It has been estimated that 180,000 miles of hedge were planted during the eighteenth and nineteenth centuries.

The enclosure of land was not uniform throughout the country, since most of the acts concerned counties south of Yorkshire through the Midland shires to Salisbury Plain. Much of the fertile land of Wessex had been enclosed from earlier times; similarly the Downs and moorlands of the North and West remained largely open as extensive pasture. For example more than half of Northamptonshire was enclosed by the acts but, in contrast, less than a fiftieth of Northumberland.

The Victorian landscape was established by the early part of Victoria's reign, but as the century progressed agriculture prospered until it reached a peak during the last decades. Timber was felled and scrub cleared, the pattern of fields were organised to suit not only new agricultural techniques but also the great compact estates leased in large farm units to tenants employing labour. Hedging and ditching became an established winter art providing work during the slack months when field cultivation was impossible. For the most part, the enclosures were designed to provide the maximum number of small fields to suit the new forms of livestock husbandry made possible by improved pastures and the use of hay and roots for winter fodder. During this period pedigree livestock became established and was grazed in the enclosed pastures.

The hedged fields, mainly of five to ten acres in extent, provided shelter for the livestock and made it possible to rotate production with maximum flexibility round each farm. Small fields were particularly suitable, since they could define the frequent undulations in ground and changes in soil characteristic of much of England, making it possible in addition to drain the land along the field boundaries. Ditching and hedging are activities usually considered complementary to each other. An important side effect of the pattern of hedgerows has been the support they have given to wildlife, especially to the variety and number of birds found in the country, also to animals and insects. For example although 100 acres of moorland will support less than twenty pairs of birds of probably not more than ten species and open fields a greater number of birds but probably from fewer species (principally partridge, lark and lapwing) ordinary farmland of the same acreage will support, because of the hedgerows, 100–250 pairs of birds of up to fifty species[1].

Hedged and fenced fields have had an important bearing on the

230

County	Area in sq miles	Boundaries in miles	Miles of boundaries per sq mile	Percentage of total mileage: hedges:	timber:	other:
Ross and Cromarty	2,533	3,635	1·4	0	74	26
Argyll	2,695	5,315	2·0	1	70	29
Cumberland	1,520	20,456	13·5	50	28	22
Westmorland	789	11,019	14·0	33	13	54
Yorks (NR)	2,128	29,650	13·9	53	20	27
Yorks (ER)	1,172	15,406	13·1	64	28	8
Warwick	938	14,375	14·6	74	18	8
Montgomery	797	12,060	15·1	69	28	3
Herts	632	9,494	15·0	65	25	10
Essex	1,528	18,677	12·2	77	16	7
Devon	2,612	52,724	20·2	86	7	7
Total	17,389	192,811	11·1	65	20	15

development of agricultural techniques and still have a profound effect on the economics of food production. They form a region where, over the last few centuries, a complex association of plants and animals have given rise to an ecological balance with the farming activities within them. Their variety is a course of great beauty, appreciated by an urban population living mainly in cities bereft of wildlife. In these circumstances it is surprising how little is known about the hedges round the fields, especially since their value in modern farming methods is debatable.

The extent of the hedgerows is largely unknown and has never received a systematic study. In 1955 the length of the field boundaries in the 24½m acres of improved farmland in England and Wales was estimated to be under 2m miles, on the basis that to enclose the land in five-acre fields would require 1,700,000 miles of boundary and in ten-acre fields 1,200,000[2]. Therefore a mean could be taken representing about 1½m miles, to which had to be added an additional mileage on account of the ¼m miles of roads, 20,000 miles of railways and 2,000 miles of canal estimated to exist in the 1931 census, most of which passed through the countryside.

Recently the Forestry Commission made a sample survey of field and other boundaries[3]. In the first instance an aerial survey was attempted, but it was found to be impossible to differentiate between the many types of boundary. This method having failed, a ground survey was taken from samples in eleven counties representing 17,389 square miles or 20·2 per cent of the land area, excluding most of the outer islands. The samples themselves covered 93·8 square miles, or 0·54 per cent of the total area. Therefore though the survey is by no means exhaustive, it does give a more reliable indication of the length of boundaries than previous assessments. The survey was summarised as follows:

a The estimated length of field and other boundaries in Britain, excluding those in urban and suburban areas, is 954,000 miles, representing an average length of eleven miles for every square mile of land area.

b Of this total 616,000 miles are estimated to consist of hedges, 146,000 miles are fences composed of materials other than timber and 192,000 miles are composed either wholly or partly of timber.

About two-thirds of field boundaries are hedged and a fifth are based on timber construction, including post-and-rail and post-and-wire fences. The remaining types of boundary include walls and banks, as well as metal or concrete posted fences. The importance of the hedgerows is evident from this analysis, generally increasing in density from north to south, with Devon having the greatest mileage of boundary, particularly of hedge, for each square mile. Though many varieties of hedge exist, the greatest mileage is composed of hawthorn, with localised areas of elm, beech, hazel and blackthorn, and, to a lesser extent, of holly, elder, ash and other plants. Within the hedgerows are intermixed trees of great value to the wildlife which also provide shade for livestock. In a survey by the Forestry Commission in 1951, hedgerow trees of oak, ash, elm beech and sycamore were estimated to represent a fifth of the nation's standing timber.

As Way and Davies pointed out, few detailed ecological studies have been made of hedgerows, even though they form one of the largest wildlife habitats remaining in the country, except for some recent surveys made by the Nature Conservancy[1]. It is easy for the ecological balance between hedge and field to be upset, for:

In some instances the field crop has proved more attractive or abundant than the food plants available in the hedge, and insects and birds normally resident in the hedge have outstripped their predators and become pests. This has happened for instance with a number of aphid species in the neighbourhood of root and horticultural crops, and of bull-finches in fruit growing districts. Some crop diseases, notably the mildews and rusts, have secondary hosts in hedges, whilst some hedgerow plants find field conditions suitable for their growth and become weeds.

The inherited pattern of hedgerows, created in days when fields were ploughed by horse and most herds were small, frustrate the development of modern agricultural techniques and the use of modern field machinery. Throughout the country, hedgerows are

232

Wimbledon Common. 1½m acres of common land are now being registered. Common land close to or within built-up areas is a vital inheritance and it is essential that more commons are provided for recreation before the year 2000. Some common lands can be remote, some informal and others with built-in amusements.

1

1 Dunston Power Station, Co Durham. Pulverised ash is pumped into bogland to raise the level by fourteen feet to reclaim six and a half acres between 1956 and 1960 for intensive grassland. Waste from generating stations can be used for reclamation of old quarries, gullies and bogs.

2 Blackwater Estuary and Mersea Island, Essex. There have been plans to reclaim this land for over a century. The maze of creeks and silted flats round this area could yield several thousand acres of good farmland.

3 Lincolnshire coast of the Wash, near Freiston. Reclaimed land round the Wash is fertile and suitable for intensive farming with large field patterns. An earlier line of sea wall is visible half way to the present one, beyond which are undrained and enclosed saltings. The Wash reclamation, damming and forming into a reservoir, presents a major challenge to the next two decades.

1

1 Annat Point near Fort William, Inverlochy and Ben Nevis. Commercial forests and modern pulp and paper mill bring new industrial life to the Highlands.

2 Kielder Forest, Northumberland 1950. Foreground Kielder Forest; background Deadwater Fell. With 47,000 acres of woodland, this is Britain's biggest man-made forest and is a major part of the Border Forest Park. There is an urgent need to drastically increase the commercial woodland area.

Cross Lanes Farm, Northallerton, Yorks. 1966. In 1962, the farm had seven small fields. Today only one 120-acre field set on

remains. The field is used for barley, part of which is used to fatten beef and part sold, the work being managed by the

Stithians Dam, Redruth, Cornwall 1967. Designed to hold 1,200m gallons behind a seventy foot high and nearly 800 foot long dam, due to drown many acres of farmland. Stithians Dam is one of many urgently required in low as well as in high land before the year 2000.

1

2

1 Farm reservoir, Suffolk/Essex border near River Stour for Sir Joshua Rowley Farms, covering nearly fifteen acres and holding 40m gallons.

2 Agricultural irrigation has become an important part of modern farming. In 1965 over a quarter of a million acres were irrigated. Eventually, $1\frac{1}{2}$m may artificially irrigated, mainly by spray guns, contributing to considerably higher crop yields.

being grubbed out and field trees felled. This practice, developed in the first place with the introduction of the combine-harvester in the corn growing regions of East Anglia and Lincolnshire, has today become widespread for a variety of reasons. The extent of hedge removal is unknown, since no records are kept at national or regional level, (though individual studies for some areas are recorded by the Natural Environment Research Council) but estimates have been made suggesting that within the last twenty years in some parts of the country as much as a fifth of the hedges have been removed[1]. In Devon there were 28·6 miles of hedges per square mile in 1951, but less than twenty by 1962[9]. It is certain that before the end of this century many others must be cleared if agriculture is to become efficient and economic. It is possible that at the present rate of clearance they may cease to be recognisable features of the landscape. Many people consider that the long term effect will have disastrous consequences, though this is by no means certain.

The economic value of hedge removal has been clearly demonstrated by one progressive farmer, Mr J. J. Rainthorpe, with 2,300 acres near Lincoln, who has cleared forty-eight miles of boundary hedge and tiled and filled eight-and-a-quarter miles of open ditch. The original eight farms, having 135 fields with an average of fifteen acres each, have been amalgamated into one farm with only thirty-three fields averaging sixty acres each. This has helped the planning of an all-arable farm, half with heavy land having a rotation of nine years of corn to one change crop and half with light land having a rotation of four years of corn to one change crop, manned as one unit with only one man for every 150 acres[4]. Hedge clearance has many benefits and in this case annual running costs are estimated to be 32s an acre, less due to field rationalisation, and sixty-five acres of wasted land have been made productive, representing about three per cent of the farm[5]. Benefits, which are of general significance, can be summarised, though the economic gains are particular to one farm in 1964:

1 Land gained from the removal of hedges and ditches, very approximately, is equivalent to one acre for every mile run. In this case, sixty acres were gained for cropping, worth perhaps £15,000 or, with interest at six per cent, £900 a year.

2 No hedge trimming required: representing on forty-eight miles a maintenance saving of £1,440 a year (12s 6d an acre).

3 No ditch maintenance: representing on eight-and-a-quarter miles a saving of £240 a year (2s an acre).

4 Larger fields reduce the need for internal roads. In this case six-and-a-quarter miles of road were reduced to three miles, releasing five acres of land with a value of £1,250 or, with interest £75 a year.

5 Rationalisation of field size and shape—bigger fields with parallel sides—reduces overlap in fieldwork and saves inevitable double application of fertilizers, seeds and sprays. On 136 acres, this represented £375 a year.

6 Increased machinery efficiency, with reduced idle turning-time because of awkward corners and with less damage to implements through the elimination of obstructions.

7 Better control of weeds, which soon spread from hedgerows, and reduction of vermin and insect population always harboured in hedge bottoms.

8 Scenery may or may not be improved, but the view is unimpeded by hedges, giving fewer blind corners—a considerable safety factor with narrow winding lanes.

This summary emphasises the main reasons why hedge removal has become increasingly desirable with mechanisation. As machinery becomes larger and as more stock are winter-housed, hedges become a liability. The labour force required for field cultivations on the more advanced arable farms has declined perhaps from a more traditional average of one man for every fifty acres to one man for every 150–200 acres. This is possible only with powerful machines and simplified field layouts. For example, on one 900-acre farm at Great Munden, Hertfordshire, the fields have been reorganised by the reduction of ten miles of hedges since before the war, which has released many acres for production[6]. Two of the fields are now more than 100 acres each in size. This makes it possible to use a combination roller, with seven eight-foot wide rolls, covering more than fifty feet on each run or a twenty-four-foot wide drill capable of seeding at a rate of fifteen acres an hour. This is typical of progressive practice in which machines become larger. Though most combine-harvesters have about ten-foot cutter-bars, giant models have eighteen-foot and it is possible that future machines might be devised to cut twenty-five or thirty-foot swathes. Not only are all field machines, tractors and their implements, as well as combines, becoming larger, but aerial spraying, and even sowing, is on the increase and, in experimental work, hovercraft and robot-controlled equipment has left the realm of science fiction in agriculture. This is discussed later in chapter 9. It is clear that future machinery will become increasingly hampered by hedges and trees.

At present, though hedge and field boundaries have been removed with greater effect and frequency in the East rather than in the Midlands or the West Country, the trend to specialised farming will increase the rate of disappearance in all districts. The traditional pattern of mixed farming, usually requiring a rotation of crops interspersed with livestock grazing, is on the decline. Stockless arable farms have proved practical and economic and are becoming more prevalent when, in most cases, piped field drainage and shelter belts are more important than traditional hedgerows and ditches. Similarly, even on livestock farms, the trend is for indoor intensive housing for poultry, pigs and beef cattle with interest developing in similar methods for dairy cattle and even for sheep. Whether the stock are fed corn or roots or conserved grass products, the aim is increasingly to have large open-fields suitable for intensive mechanised cultivation. Even when the fields are grazed, which is still the case in much of England, anyway during the summer months, strip grazing between moveable electric fences in large cultivations is more economic for intensive production than traditional grazing in small fields. It is not only on arable farms where hedges prove redundant.

Hedging is no longer a winter art, practised during a time of slack labour requirements, even though the annual national competition for hedging and ditching reveals that these skills are still attained and praised. But manual hedging is uneconomic and modern machinery, though keeping hedges trim, does not keep hedgerows clean so that coarse vegetation round the roots is not removed. Annual and biannual plants are choked and do not become established and, due to the rank thicket that prevails, the animal population declines. One factor has retarded a universal acceptance of mechanical hedging and, in some cases, has prevented any removal of hedges. Frequently traditional hedging, that is cutting and laying a proportion of the hedges each year, is a condition in a lease granted to a tenant farmer, especially on mixed or stock farms. This condition is a source of contention since it is claimed that, provided a hedge has a good foundation and has been laid at least once, regular mechanical trimming will maintain a hedge as stockproof for up to twenty years. Moreover a tenancy may preclude hedge removals, even though their presence renders a particular farming system uneconomic, since a landlord may consider that a future tenant might require the hedges for a different system. The National Farmers Union has suggested a more liberal approach to hedge maintenance in a lease[7], but it is still probable that the rate of change will be retarded in tenanted farms, whereas it will accelerate in owner-occupied farms.

Even with mechanised hedging, the cost for each acre of maintaining hedgerows, which may be about £30 a mile a year is a drain on farm finance unless the hedge has a real value in a farm plan. The headland creates unproductive land along the sides of two hedges to each field. In Hertfordshire, for example, which has fifteen miles of boundaries for each square mile, there are nearly 9,500 acres of headland representing about fifteen square miles of unproductive land or 2·3 per cent of the total agricultural land in the county. Of course the headland is unproductive only in the case of cultivated land, so the wastage would be less allowing for permanent pasture.

It is clear however that if a fiftieth of a farm is unproductive because hedges have been inherited from a former agricultural system, which may be no longer relevant, their continued existence must be questioned. It is claimed that, on a large farm, the cost of converting a traditional 10–15 acre field layout into one of 40–60 acres will be about £7–£10 an acre after all financial support has been received[8]. At ten per cent interest, this capital would represent an increase in rent of £$\frac{3}{4}$–£1 an acre for these improvements, which is far less than their potential value in increased efficiency and land-use.

Hedges and other field boundaries will diminish in importance within the landscape. In some districts the effect will be similar to the prairies, as is becoming the case already in parts of Lincolnshire and East Anglia. As has been said, in the future[5]:

> The forward speed of tractors pulling implements designed for high speed will be automatically adjusted to maintain the engine at its most satisfactory load—75 per cent of maximum hp . . . we can expect more attention to springing air-conditioned cabs with radio and television to be looked at, when the automatic pilot is on control and meals will be taken in the comfort of the cab without stopping the tractor. On account of the high cost of these machines a three-shift system will be necessary . . . Four-wheel drive tractors of 300 hp with a yearly appetite of 3,500 or more acres of ploughing and cultivating are possible today, and probable tomorrow . . . Today it could be argued that the minimum size of arable unit for optimum economy is about 100 acres, but the machine dictates and tomorrow 2,000 acres may be too small.

If the number of field boundaries are reduced to a third of a million miles of hedges and a third of a million miles of bank, fence and wall by the end of the century, which may well be the case, then the ecology and appearance of the landscape will change profoundly. Already duststorms in parts of Norfolk due to a hedgeless landscape are not unknown. Concern is expressed in many informed quarters that the overall effects will unbalance nature even if, as is unlikely, no dust bowl is generated similar to American experience. At present farmers can change their landscape without cognisance of changes in their neighbour's farms. Piecemeal depredations of the existing hedgerow network are occurring without relationship to each other or to their cumulative effect on a regional ecology. Within a few years districts can change their physical character before even the agriculturalists are aware of it. Fundamental changes can be generated which, possibly, are not in the national interest. It is vital that the loss of hedgerows are recorded and that their widespread uprooting is sanctioned by the nation. It is essential that the effect of these physical changes are studied regionally and locally by experts so that, should there be any danger to the conservation of natural resources, change may be directed into safe channels. It will be suicide unless shelter-belts are planted to replace the loss of hedgerows. Change is essential and hedges must be sacrificed to further agricultural efficiency, but tomorrow will be too late in knowing whether nature has been unbalanced.

REFERENCES

1 Way, J. M., and Davis, B. N. K. 'Hedges as a feature of our Countryside.' *Agriculture*, p565. December 1962
2 Stamp, D. *Man and the Land*, p.96. 1955, Collins
3 Locke, G. M. 'A sample survey of field and other boundaries in Great Britain.' *Quarterly Journal of Forestry*. April 1962
4 Leonard, D. 'All down to arable.' *Farmers Weekly*, p100. 26 April 1963.
5 Rainthorpe, J. J., *The future outlook for arable farming in Britain*. Nineteenth Oxford Farming Conference Report, p57. January 1965
6 Report. *Farmers Weekly*
7 *Tenure of farm land*. National Farmers Union, p62. December 1963
8 Report. *Farmers Weekly*, p69. 14 May 1965
9 Hooper, M., Journal of the Devon Trust for Nature conservation, p263. 1965

5d Forests and woodlands

For a country liberally endowed with trees, it is surprising that almost ninety per cent of the timber required in the United Kingdom is imported. In 1964 Britain spent £216m on foreign timber, that is nearly five per cent of all imports. After food timber is the second highest item in the overseas trading bill. This discrepancy between production and consumption appears greater if the import of timber by-products, such as paper and chipboard, are considered. Trees are used in many forms, both for timber and its by-products, and requirements are increasing not only in the United Kingdom but throughout the world. Forests in many countries are being exploited on the crude assumption that their resources are limitless; few nations are planning long term planting programmes to cope with future needs.

It is probable that as the standard of living rises in the many rapidly developing countries, and as the population increases throughout the world, the demand on timber resources will outstrip the natural capacity of the forests for regeneration and the few efforts being made to replant them. This has already occurred in some parts of the world with devastating results. New deserts are being formed and existing deserts extended. The twentieth century rape of the earth will have profound and disastrous consequences for the future of mankind. It is doubtful whether, in these circum-

245

stances, the United Kingdom should rely for all time on imports for most of its timber requirements. By the end of this century, timber may become an expensive commodity. The Food and Agriculture Organisation has forecast a growing world shortage of timber. In Europe, consumption is expected to double between 1950 and 1975 and, by the end of the century, it is expected that Europe's timber requirements will be short of 3,500 to 5,600m cubic feet a year from her own forests[1]. Even if an attempt were to be made now for reafforestation on an international basis, plans would have to be made to suit forecasted demands for the end for the first quarter of the next century. Sixty years, or even twice as long for some hardwoods, must elapse before a seedling will produce commercial timber.

The great Mediaeval forests of England were dissipated by the agricultural clearances and the demand for timber to make the warships of earlier ages and later fire the furnaces of the industrial revolution. By late-Victorian times few of the forests remained except as shadows of their former glory to be found in such places as the New Forest, Sherwood Forest and the Forest of Dean. Nevertheless much of the landscape is wooded, particularly in Sussex and the Shires, and hedgerow trees as well as those marking rivers and other watercourses add to the appearance of fertility and beauty.

In commercial terms the wooded appearance of the countryside is an illusion. It is only in the case of forests tended by the Forestry Commission and a few progressive landlords that timber is grown scientifically with full use of the technical resources available. Most of the woods and copses represent overgrown tangled environments in which timber becomes rank and useless, forgotten by landlord and farmer. They remain as small islands of gross uncultivated land, even amidst progressive farms. Sometimes they hide or cover steep changes of ground contour useless for agriculture. In some cases their retention is deliberate since they provide natural windbreaks, protecting stock or crops; in others, they remain as a breeding ground for game when sport is more important than agriculture for their owners. Their continued existence is desirable, if not essential, since they contribute to the creation of micro-climates, sometimes beneficial to fertility, to the retention of moisture, to the prevention of erosion and to the provision of humus for future generations. In addition in their support of wild-life, they contribute to the balance of nature traditionally considered essential for successful farming and they can in some cases provide a recreational area for the urban dweller. At the same time, their continued presence can retard modern farming, being wasteful of land, restrictive to the use of machinery and a source of pests.

As in the case of hedges, little is known concerning the actual relevance or importance of the woods, copses and hedgerow trees to the long-term ecology of the land on which modern farming must be based. It is known that their complete removal will precipitate the loss of moisture from the ground, causing erosion and dust-bowls. It is difficult to relate this knowledge to indicate what effect might occur should any particular wood be removed. It is probable that many derelict woods could be removed from any one district without appreciable change occurring in the soil structure. It is certain that much could be gained if random woods and copses were replaced by plantations providing useful timber for future generations, and which, if planted with care, could create microclimates and provide shelter to large, commercial fields more successfully than at present. Ignorance pervades the subject of micro-climates, though the power of hedges and trees to retain warmth from the sun after the surrounding land has cooled is known—as is the cause of frost pockets. But the balance and condition of climates occurring over small areas of land is largely unknown except as uncritical observation on the part of individual farmers. Much research is needed before the presence of trees in the landscape could be planned to create better farming conditions. This is discussed further in the next section (p267).

There is also ignorance concerning commercial aspects of the existing woodlands. Interest developed in estate forestry at the end of the last century. An examination of the agricultural returns prior to the 1914–18 war reveals incidental information regarding the increase in woodland areas, but it was not until the Forestry Commission was created at the end of the Great War that statistics became available on which a national forestry policy could be based, with a census in 1924, 1938 and 1947 showing the rate of growth as given in Chart 42.

CHART 42: ACREAGE OF WOODLAND AREAS

Year	England	Scotland	Wales	Great Britain
1871	1,314,316	734,530	126,625	2,175,471
1913	1,667,574	852,120	216,494	2,736,188
1924	1,630,987	1,074,224	253,461	2,958,672
1938	1,809,800	1,076,300	315,000	3,201,100
1947	1,865,046	1,266,838	316,478	3,448,362

When the Forestry Commission was created, ninety-seven per cent of the woodlands were privately owned, with only three per cent belonging to the Crown. Today more than a third of the forests belong to the Commission, which has planted or developed 1½m acres of woodland in less than half a century, the bulk of which is

247

conifer. Its analysis of the woodland areas made in 1961 and given in Chart 43 emphasises this remarkable achievement:

CHART 43: '000 ACRES IN 1961

Woodland	Forestry Commission	Private	Total	Per cent Total
Conifers: high forest	1,207	655	1,862	45
deciduous ,, ,,	137	756	893	21
coppice	28	296	324	8
unproductive	86	999	1,085	26
Total	1,458	2,706	4,164	100
per cent total	35	65	100	

During the last half century the woodland area has been increased by about fifty per cent to over 4⅛m acres, representing approximately seven per cent of the land surface. Unfortunately whereas only a fifteenth of the woods owned by the Forestry Commission are unproductive, about a third of those privately owned have no commercial value. In fact on the basis of these figures not only is a quarter of our woodland unproductive but nearly two per cent of the land surface is wasted in this manner, much of it in fertile regions. A new census of private woodlands is due to be published by the Commission at the end of 1967.

Although the achievement of the Forestry Commission is excellent, in recent years the reafforestation programme has failed to keep to its schedule. By the end of 1953 the Commission had planted 1,821m trees, ninety per cent of which were conifers. A few years earlier, in 1947, their aim was to increase the rate of planting to attain 5m acres of productive woodland by the end of the century, including 3m acres of afforestation and 2m acres of existing woodland. A decade later only sixty-one per cent of their target for the first ten years was attained. This included seventy per cent of the target for afforestation of new lands, but only forty-nine per cent for replanting existing woodlands. In 1957 it was hoped that the original target of 5m acres would still be achieved by the year 2000. This began to appear improbable by the summer of 1963 with the government statement that only 450,000 acres, mostly in hill areas, would be afforested within the next ten years, representing a slight reduction on the acreage of the previous decade. At the mid-point of the original plan the Commission may only have about 2m instead of the intended minimum of 3m acres by 1975, and, at this rate of planting, little more than 3m at the end of the century.

The reasons why the Commission will fail in its post-war pro-

248

gramme are varied, but for the most part the reasons have one common factor. On the national scale of expenditure, successive governments have had incessant problems in finding sufficient money to meet all demands for modernisation and development. These problems have been made painfully acute by the recurring crisis in the balance of export to import payments. It is not surprising that when economy has to be made in some sectors of the national expenditure it should be made in forestry, since in forestry the return on capital invested takes sixty or more years. It is easy, for immediate political reasons in order to gain temporary relief to a financial crisis, to restrict investment in a sector where few living people can hope to gain advantage from it. The cumulative and long-term result of this policy, accepted by each government in turn, is unfortunate and possibly disastrous. In reality the financial reasons for the failure of the nation to invest in forestry are obscured by other factors.

The original incentive for a national forestry programme was the Great War, when timber, like food, was needed for national survival. The Second World War intensified this argument, leading to the fifty-year programme for reafforestation. In a nuclear age however, and with the development of such products as plastics, the argument based on the needs of the nation in future wars has less pertinence. The peace-time need for timber is less dramatic, since it seems easy to import softwoods from Canada and Scandinavia and hardwoods from Africa and Asia. The acquisition of land for planting on the scale required by the Commission, and in the areas where forestry can be successful, has proved difficult and expensive. In fact in 1965 new land acquired by the Commission dropped to some 3,500 acres in England and Wales and under 28,000 in Scotland. Taken together these reasons for restricting the Commission have proved an easy bait for governments attempting to save money. Though private owners are encouraged, and even helped financially in planting programmes, their efforts can have but little effect unless the incentive for investment is commensurable with that in industry. Such incentive could be stimulated by further grants, tax relief, and, perhaps particularly, by allowing death duties to be avoided where long-term investments in forestry are made. In return it might be expected that the nation should have a share in the profits from the enterprise.

A decision to restrict tree planting, by not providing the money required, has to be based on the doubtful premise that timber will always be plentiful in the world and cheap to import. The evidence is that this cannot continue to be an economic policy. Unfortunately by the time it is clear that the forests of the world cannot give sufficient timber to meet demand, it will be too late to create a national source of timber on the scale required. Naturally it is equally spurious to base a major reafforestation policy on the imprecise indication that timber will become expensive, or even prohibitive, to import. Of the two policies restricted forestry is the more dangerous, particularly since there is little reason why forestry in this country should not only be economic but profitable. To be profitable, it must be conducted on a large scale, employing mechanisation and scientific control of all aspects of production. It is probable that only the Commission could tackle the problem and only then if it has adequate financial backing. It must be remembered that the investment so far made by the Commission has not had time to show an appreciable return, since planting only began in the 1920s. Nevertheless by 1970 sales are expected to reach 100m cubic feet (Hoppus) with thinnings and the first trees reaching maturity, manufactured mainly in large modern factories, with production expanding rapidly after 1980[3]. It is now necessary for the Commission to embark on marketing as well as planting as part of its national policy.

Reafforestation in this country has had an unfortunate legacy to contend against, since the unproductive and beautiful woodlands and hedgerow trees, mostly deciduous and with seasonal changes of colour and texture, are considered to be part of the national heritage of scenic splendour. Not only are conifers, though profitable, alien to the soil, but they have remained alien to the national consciousness and their appearances on the bare hillsides of the North and West have been decried. Each new enclosure of moorland is greeted with the same hostility as were the enclosures of common land in the eighteenth century.

The aesthetic problem is not easy since the matter is of personal judgement. But it must be acknowledged that the general opinion is against the Commission on the basis that their forests are regimented and ugly and alien to the moorlands, spoiling their beauty. To some extent the Commission has shown itself sensible to this problem; there are cases of careful planting to suit the contours and skylines of a district, and of the use of deciduous trees to mask the perimeter of plantations, particularly along roads[8]. In many cases the existence of hillsides dark with trees give scale and contrast to a landscape, lacking in the bare heath and outcrops of rock. There is grandeur and beauty in fertility, in the sense of a conquest over nature's grim barrenness, in order brought from chaos. There is beauty in the great sweep of trees following the contours, interspersed with rivers and highland roads. There is beauty in the trees themselves at all stages of growth. It is a matter of opinion. What is clear is that not all the moorlands should be planted, that even the great plantations should be contrasted with open hillsides and that care must be taken in landscaping.

If wisdom prevailed, which is improbable, so that the nation realised that the future depends on using all land to advantage, then great forests would be planted. It is certain that the post-war aim of

250

having 5m acres of state forest by the end of the century, still less the probable achievement of a mere 3m acres, is inadequate. Perhaps a concentrated national effort could create a total of 8m, or even 10m acres of useful forest by 2000 in the United Kingdom. Even this might be inadequate for the needs of the next century. Such an aim would transform the economy and appearance of the landscape. It is in any case probable that the state forests of the future will be different in character for it is recognised that[3]:

> There is no doubt at all that as our first generation forests become ripe for regeneration so will they steadily become far more mixed as to age, distribution and in many places also as to species.

National forestry has two further important contributions to make to land-use other than in the provision of timber alone. It has always been the intention of the Commission that forestry should contribute to rural industry, encouraging population to remain on the land. At present the Commission employs 12,000 people. This has been important, especially in introducing new industry to remote parts. For example the largest industrial development in the Highlands since the war has been the new £15m integrated pulp and paper mill, unique in the United Kingdom, opened in 1965. This provides work for 700 in the mill, to be increased when a second paper machine is built, and for 2,000 in the surrounding forests by Lock Eil, Inverness-shire, from which 10,000 trees will be cut every day[4]. Secondly it is the Commission's intention that much forestland will be available for recreation. There are already seven Forest Parks in which camping, caravanning and exploration is allowed and 'camping nights' increased from 171,000 in 1956 to 395,000 in 1962. By 1970 there will be several more Forest Parks and extended rights for hiking and trekking in other forests[3]. But for the fear of fire, it is easier for multiple use to be made of forest rather than farm land. It is essential, as the need for recreation increases, that access is extended into woods and forests (p153). There is also a relationship between water conservancy and forestry.

As discussed in the previous section, not only hedgerows but copses are sometimes cleared for improved agricultural purposes. For example on a 1,000 acre farm near Newick, Sussex, forty-six acres of woodland and two miles of hedgerow were cleared in 1964 at a cost of about £4,500, but yielding £800 for timber. Within a season, after soil analysis and dressing, the reclaimed land produced over one-and-three-quarter tons of barley from each acre and the farm layout had been replanned for streamlined corn production[5]. Tree planting, other than for commerce, is important for the landscape, especially as hedgerows are cleared for agriculture, as new motorways sear through the countryside and new towns are built. There are cases of farmers planting new avenues and copses, more commonly than is realised. Much could be done to encourage tree planting. Some schools, as recommended by such societies as the Men of the Trees, encourage children to plant and tend new trees. Planting by farmers could be made obligatory should they remove hedgerows. County Councils, such as West Suffolk and Norfolk, have a keen policy for rural tree planting. The Ministry of Transport recognises its landscaping responsibility round new motorways. During 1963–64, 400,000 trees were planted for this purpose. The 1960s have witnessed a breakthrough in transplanting methods for mature trees, even of sixty feet in height, at a cost of a few pounds each. This may make a considerable difference to the future landscape, especially since trees could be stored for transplantation in national tree banks and farmers could create mature windbreaks without waiting for a generation[6].

Farmers, too, sometimes conduct small commercial tree planting schemes in odd acres unsuitable for agriculture. Willow and christmas tree plantations in particular are economic on small acreages when soil conditions are suitable. This is a small, but important, sideline to ordinary farming, as is the provision of shoots on agricultural land, usually in conjunction with the presence of woods and copses. The Game Research Association records that from 350 shoots covering just over a million acres (which may be representative of 15m acres, mainly of lowland agricultural land, used for shooting), an average of 239 pheasant and forty partridge for every 1,000 acres were shot in 1962, an increase of over twenty-five per cent and 66 per cent respectively above kills for 1956, with birds reared for release similarly increased in numbers[7]. It is considered that 25m acres of agricultural and small woodlands, plus 2m acres of forestland, plus 2m acres of rough grazing are potentially suitable in Great Britain for holding lowland game, with 10m acres suitable for grouse and other moorland species. Perhaps seventy per cent of suitable land for game is not at present preserved in any way for that purpose. Rents of 10s an acre are common for productive shoots and up to £500 a gun for each season for a syndicate shoot. Game farmers have sales for eggs and birds worth £½m a year and the cash value of shot game exceeds £1m. Therefore especially with the increase of all sport for recreation, shooting is an important sideline to agriculture and it conditions a landlord's attitude to farming and land-use. Shooting, to some extent, is the antithesis to intensive agriculture and, in some areas, it is a principal reason why farmland is extensively farmed and woodland allowed to remain. It is uncertain to what extent this conflict of purpose will be resolved in the future. Much intensively farmed land will be without game. Some, perhaps ranch-farmed land, could be dual-purpose, providing profitable shoots. This could be combined with a policy for green belts round conurbations (p115).

REFERENCES

1 Scott, C. W. British Association Conference, Cambridge 1965
2 *Britain: an official handbook*. 1965, HMSO
3 'Britain's Forests in 1970.' *The Countryside in* 1970, p262. 1964, HMSO
4 Report. *The Times*, 6 August 1965
5 Report. *Farmers Weekly*, p59, 10 September 1965
6 Report. *The Times*, 28 September 1963
7 'Conservation of Game as a Natural Resource.' *The Countryside in* 1970, p241. 1965, HMSO
8 Crowe, S. *Forestry in the landscape*. 1966, HMSO

5e Water resources

Water is the life-blood of agriculture. It is a basic raw material for the nation required not only for human consumption but also for many domestic and industrial functions. Annual requirements for water have outstripped existing methods of conservation and supply. The national water shortage has become serious for any year with below average rainfall. The three years 1962 to 1964 were the driest recorded this century, highlighting the urgent need for new methods of conservation, while in contrast the wet summer of 1965 provided more than adequate resources. Though Britain is a country with high humidity, rainfall is unpredictable, fluctuating rapidly between periods of drought and excess. In some districts excessive rainfall quickly leads to flooding, since much of the river network is unable to cope with sudden concentrations of stormwater.

It has been calculated that England and Wales on average have 40,800 million gallons of rainfall a day (mgd) which, theoretically, could be conserved and used[1]. At present, an eighth of this amount is required, but consumption is increasing at the rate of about four per cent a year. Total water consumption in 1964, excluding requirements for cooling water, was 5,000 mgd. Industrial consumption represents about sixty per cent of present total demand, but is rapidly increasing, and by 1980 it is predicted that industry alone will require nearly 10,000 mgd which is almost a quarter of theoretical yield. In addition to these industrial requirements, power stations need vast quantities of cooling water, though this can be reused; but, with the growing overall generating capacity, this demand may upset fresh-water supplies for other purposes unless most future stations are sited near the sea. Domestic requirements consume 1,400 mgd, representing about thirty gallons a person. With increased sanitation and automatic washing machines, the daily average is expected to rise to fifty gallons a person which, with an increased population, could amount to 2,700 mgd by 1980.

In recent years, water requirements for agriculture have increased

253

with the development of irrigation. At present, excluding irrigation, about 200 mgd are required for stock and such functions as cleaning yards, equipment and washing vegetables. This amount is likely to increase due to new agricultural methods, especially with more intensive stock housing, but would rise substantially should Britain increase livestock numbers to be almost self-sufficient in meat production. Nevertheless overall consumption would be unlikely to rise to much over 300 mgd. More serious will be the effect on local water resources as livestock, especially beef cattle, are concentrated in large numbers on individual sites. This has been demonstrated by the experience of the British Beef Company in their Suffolk beeflot.

The beeflot, aimed to hold 10,000 cattle, needing 100,000 gallons of water a day, was started without planning approval, though this was granted retrospectively with some conditions in the summer of 1965. Nevertheless, when about 4,000 cattle were housed on the site in the spring of 1965, water requirements rose considerably above an informal allowance of 14,000 gallons a day granted by the Local Rural District Council. Realisation that requirements for the beeflot were to rise to 100,000 gallons a day, with the intention that this should be drawn from a proposed 350 foot borehole, came as a shock to the local water authorities, from whom no consent had been requested for a project of this nature[2]. Since East Anglia has a population rapidly expanding in a district with far from adequate water resources even for present requirements, a new private borehole drawing 100,000 gallons a day was considered a threat to public supply. If too much water is abstracted from the mid-Suffolk catchment area, then there is a risk that the water table will fall to a level when seawater would penetrate into the water-bearing strata. Abstractions from the Gipping catchment area, the relevant district for the beeflot, amounted to over ten mgd in 1964. The beeflot, therefore, would require about one per cent of present consumption and this was considered an unnecessary burden since requirements for domestic needs were projected to rise to eighteen mgd in 1981. The Local Authorities considered that the beeflot water consumption might strain supplies, prejudicing the desired domestic expansion for the district. Fears were not relieved when the Minister of Housing and Local Government gave planning consent for the beeflot, with its water requirements, until 1975. The moral is clear. Large intensive livestock units should only be developed if water resources are sufficient, not only for them but for other development in the areas concerned.

Soon after 1960 agricultural irrigation, as opposed to irrigation for horticulture, came to be recognised as economically worthwhile to obtain optimum growth for many crops, including grass, corn and vegetables. In particular irrigation generally may be economic for one year in two in an area south-east of a line from Hull to Torquay,

254

increasing to nine years in ten round London, and this occurs in a region basically short of water for other purposes. By 1965 some 266,000 acres on 7,000 farms were irrigated in England and Wales, double the area irrigated in 1962. Irrigation has been encouraged by a government grant of forty per cent to the cost of forming reservoirs. It is predicted that by 1980 ½m acres will be irrigated. On average seasonal applications of water may be four inches an acre, requiring overall 50,000m gallons per annum, but with peak demands of nearly 1,000 mgd. In 1961 a government enquiry under the Yates Committee suggested that eventually about 1½m acres could benefit from irrigation with a seasonal total demand of 130,000m gallons, but with peak demands of 2,700 mgd. The second would be more than half the present average daily need for all purposes. At peak periods require- ments for irrigation can be well over 20,000 gallons a week for particular acres, but this amount would never be required at the same time for all irrigated fields.

It would seem that by 1980 water required for all purposes other than for cooling may be around 14,000 mgd during peak periods, which is nearly treble present requirements. By the end of the century, consumption could have exceeded 20,000 mgd during the summer months, that is about half the mean daily yield. Consumption at such levels would seriously reduce water tables and empty rivers and streams without vast quantities of water being obtained from the sea or conserved from the winter months. During the last few years, the decline of natural resources of water has become marked. The water table in the home counties had sunk by over 100 feet and even in the wetter South-west some wells, which had never been known to fail, ran dry during the 1964–65 winter[3].

The appearance of small reservoirs on many farms will be a feature of this decade and has already made its mark on the landscape, especially since irrigation is indicative of intensive cropping tech- niques, often coupled with enlarged field layouts. Most of these reservoirs average about an acre in extent, holding perhaps 1m to 2m gallons each. In 1965 a 40m gallon farm reservoir, covering 14·7 acres, was constructed on the Suffolk/Essex border in order to irrigate 400 acres of sugar beet, potatoes, currants and grassland. It is expected that the system will work only nineteen out of twenty years since occasionally there will be inadequate water during the winter to replenish the reservoir. Even a reservoir of this size can be lined with a welded plastic sheet, formed from half-acre rolls costing about £500 apiece. In 1967 another Essex farm completed a three- quarter mile long reservoir covering thirty-two acres to hold 100m gallons drawn from the River Ter, with two smaller holding reservoirs down river each holding another 5m gallons. Irrigation will be for 353 acres of potatoes, 165 acres of sugar beet, 290 acres of peas and beans, seventy acres of grass and fifty-seven acres of fruit, though a total of 2,800 acres could be reached by that system. The latter has cost £½m for reservoir and irrigation and is expected to yield an extra £30,000 of food each year during the next decade. It is obvious that reservoirs of this size make a notable contribution to the landscape and will no doubt change the local microclimate near them. Plastic lined reservoirs are not suitable for dual-purpose activities, such as sailing, since the plastic could be punctured.

Farm water conservation has been encouraged by government grant, though now only registered farmers will be able to draw water to replenish the reservoirs. The development and conservation of water resources in England and Wales is now governed by the Water Resources Board, authorised in 1963, and extraction of water from the surface or the ground is permissable only by licence. At last water supply and consumption has been co-ordinated and the same Authority also controls polluting discharges. There has been in the past a real risk that large underground sources for water could become contaminated from industrial waste, in particular radio-active elements, or from salination due to sea infiltration caused by a fall in the aquifer. Some wells have been known to become polluted because of contamination underground.

Farmers may have two major conflicts with the water authorities. In the first place, water is needed for irrigation and livestock, often in quantities and location where supplies are inadequate for their needs without endangering the sources for urban consumption. Regional river boards, responsible for various catchment areas under the Water Resources Board, can charge for water extraction. This could lead to rationing by price during shortage, making irrigation uneconomic except for the most valuable crops, thereby reducing yields[4]. With proper conservation, this need not be necessary. The second and equally serious danger for farmers is that reservoirs for urban needs occupy land. In the past reservoirs have been constructed mainly in mountainous areas, but today they are often required within valuable agricultural areas. The flooding of farm land has caused much bitterness during the last few years. In the spring of 1965 sixty farmers in the Vale of Aylesbury, Bucks, fought a proposal for a twin reservoir which would drown 6,000 acres of grassland, each holding 25,000m gallons and supplying a total of fifty to 100 mgd intended to satisfy a projected increase from sixteen to eighty-eight mgd in the Buckinghamshire area when a proposed new town has been built. The loss of farmland for these reservoirs has been estimated to equal a production loss of 4m gallons of milk or 10,000 tons of grain or 3m lb deadweight of meat[5]. In 1966 the Water Resources Board warned 'that on strictly economic grounds we should look to further surface storage to meet requirements over most of the county for many decades to come'. By 1975, however, considerable yields should be obtained from underground storage,

Burleigh Farm, near Langley, Herts. A traditional courtyard farm at the end of a farm road. The high granary and the lower stock buildings are formed to give protection to stock yards. The farm house is set in yards to give control. Modern buildings of a different scale are set clear of the older layout.

257

1

2

nall farm building in
estershire set against contours,
;e and hedging is a reasonable
ision in the landscape. This
tograph won a prize for a
Atcost building in 1966. The
ilem of scale, silhouette and
g is fundamental to modern
i buildings, with materials and
r junctions contributing to the
all success or failure.

2 Modern farming methods
can create agricultural slums.
The squalor of this
farmstead and shacks is quite
unnecessary.

3 A comparison with 1 and 2 is
this bubble building which forms
a new and exciting addition to
the countryside.

Dairy unit, Casalpalocco, Ostia,
Italy, designed by U. Luccichent.

ancillary rooms. Manure is
shovelled through hatches to

the ground floor is an implement
store. A ramp at the far end gives

Estate farm, Birkeneck, near Munich, designed by F. Kiessling. New buildings for a missionary apprentice training estate of 345 acres, replacing those destroyed by fire, include four linked blocks against the plain containing cattle on the ground floor and fodder storage above. The square block round a centre yard has a farrowing and a fattening wing, linked at the left by a feed preparation unit and at the right by a tall square chaff silo, beyond which are a group of manure silos.

Pig and Dairy unit, Limerick, Eire, designed by B. Christensen. A three-storeyed piggery has accommodation for eighty sows on the ground floor and 400 fatteners on each upper floor. In the foreground are two manure tanks. At the right is a cowhouse for 125, with two silos at the back and a linking unit for a milking

Cattle unit, Agricultural Research Institute, Justus Liebeg University, Giessen. The tall block, from which wings project, contains feed preparation, storage, offices, examination rooms, and so on, on two levels. The three wings contain housing for beef and dairy cattle, including bulls and calves.

Lichtenberg Estate, Bavaria, designed by F. Kiessling. A 400-acre stock farm in the foothills of the Alps has a single storey house for sixty-six cows linking a large hay store in the background and a dunghouse in the foreground. The cowhouse has a low loft in which straw is stored. The reinforced concrete construction is unusual for farm buildings.

263

Hyde Farm, Temple Guiting, Glos 1963. Specialisation in modern farming is essential. This 212-acre farm grows one crop, barley, and only sells one product, by two men. Farm buildings tend to 'grow' by accident, thus appearing to be small shanty towns. In this case rebuilding was planned round the two storage

particularly in the chalk of the Thames basin and East Anglia. The first borehole in a three-year test in the Lambourn valley of Berkshire was operating by 1967. It is hoped the total scheme will produce 270 mgd (which could save thirty-one square miles of farm-land from flooding as new reservoirs) at a cost of only £8m, saving £70m over conventional storage costs. Between 1975 and 2000, further developments of upland storage sites coupled with water transfer in river channels should help to meet national requirements[9].

The situation in the South-east is serious. Most of the water resources in Essex and the Lee Valley are fully developed, as are much of those in Suffolk. Several water undertakings in Essex were considering additional reservoirs during 1965, which could mean the loss of another 5,000 to 6,000 acres. The Diddington reservoir in Huntingdon, planned five years ago to supply forty-five mgd was considered adequate until 1980. Consumption has increased so rapidly however that the reservoir will be inadequate soon after 1970 and further sources will be needed. It has been thought that during 1963–64, 4,000 to 5,000 acres of farm land, among the 54,000 lost that year, were taken for reservoirs (p175). The 1964 White Paper on the South-east region asked for detailed investigation of sites for surface water storage in East Anglia and the estimated cost for the additional $3\frac{1}{2}$m people in the South-east by 1981 is expected to be £65m for water schemes alone. Ten new reservoirs are being studied as outline proposals. No detailed study has been made to indicate the overall loss of farmland, by the end of the century, which may be required in the provision of reservoirs. Unless alternative methods of water supply are created, the loss of farmland will be considerable. On average, fifty acres may be needed for each extra mgd of water supply. If half the possible additional supply required by 2000 came from new reservoirs, that is 7,500 mgd, then well over a third of a million acres would be needed, much of it being taken from agri-culture. Fortunately, there are alternative possibilities for new sources. These have been summarised as 'reuse of sewage effluents, pumped storage, ground-water recharge, desalination of sea water and the construction of barrages to store fresh water in estuaries'[1].

Domestic sewage effluents are particularly suitable for irrigation, especially when they contain nitrogenous matter. It has been estimated that sewage effluents in Britain contain enough nitrogen for a third of the fertilizer requirements. There is little doubt that present sewage disposal is wasteful—and possibly dangerous when pumped out to sea. Brunswick, for example, with over $\frac{1}{4}$m inhabitants, supplies about twelve mgd effluent to a collection point north of the city from which, via four pumping stations, 10,000 acres owned by 750 farmers receive organic irrigation producing additional food for 7,000 people at a capital cost in the mid-1960s of £1·6m and an estimated running cost of £60,000 a year[6]. The wasted fertiliser and

I

liquid values by pumping sewerage into the Sea (apart from the hygenic offence) is a major loss. Municipal compost could be a great agricultural benefit for food production. Techniques and costs are now being studied at the Soil Association.

Pumped water supplies from upland reservoirs are cheaper than desalination methods. The Clywedog Valley scheme for example will trap 100 mgd from the headwaters of the River Severn and five extra dams, if built, could contribute a further 250 mgd from the Severn Basin. Surplus water could be pumped from the Severn into the Thames to supply the South-east as Thames water is already taken by tunnel to Essex. A plan proposed in 1967 for Essex was to bring 24 mgd by tunnel and pipe from the Ouse. This was part of an imaginative report published by the Water Resources Board, aimed at saving much South-eastern farmland from drowning as reservoirs. This could reduce the need for ten new reservoirs demanded three years previously as the only solution. Similarly there have been suggestions to take 1,000 mgd by canal from Newcastle, via Manchester, to Ipswich, with branches from Wales. The canal would be 100 feet wide, seventeen feet deep and would extend for 1,400 miles along the 310 foot contour at an estimated cost of £600m[7]. The canal requires 8,500 acres compared to about 20,000 acres for conventional reservoirs.

Recharging underground supplies during the winter was attempted by the Metropolitan Water Board several years ago, but only thirty per cent of the water was recovered, the rest percolating into other areas. With all water under national control percolation from area to area has less significance. The Netherlands recharge ground-water to a considerable extent. Desalination experiments are well advanced in Britain, but, at present are considered to be uneconomic. One plant in Venezuela produces six mgd, but at a cost of 8s a 1,000 gallons. Desalination by flash distillation or osmosis, freezing and electrolysis, could be vitally important in the future[3].

Present studies for estuary barrages across the Solway Firth, Morecambe Bay or the Wash show further hope for the future, which would save farm land being wasted by reservoirs. At present the ideas and problems have not been resolved. Pilot studies have shown that Morecambe Bay could produce 500 mgd within five years for a cost of £28–35m plus a running cost a year of equal amount, and that Solway Firth could yield 585 mgd within four years for only £6m a year. The former could also give 16,000 extra acres due to drainage and another 15,000 by reclamation. The Wash would provide 100,000–150,000 reservoir acres, holding up to 1½ billion gallons or thirty times the size of the Buckinghamshire reservoir proposed. Estimated costs vary between £100m and £600m but might be less than traditional reservoir construction of the same capacity. Though it would take twelve years to construct, therefore not meeting short-term needs, it would do much to mitigate present discontent by farmers at

266

the possible long-term loss of land for water conservation. There is still concern that the Government has not carried out a proper survey of the Wash.

The problem of providing adequate water supplies for Britain will not be solved easily or cheaply. It is obvious that solutions will change the visual appearance of the landscape both by small irrigation reservoirs for farms and, in the short term anyway, many large new reservoirs for urban use. The last, though taking valuable farm land, could have a dual purpose use for recreation. In the long term barrage schemes could change the appearance of several estuaries, as generating stations will mark the coastline. What is little known is the effect water conservation will have on local microclimates and ecology. The presence of water is known to have profound local effects, as also woodland plantations, and extreme cases have been noted in America. The Hydraulics Research Station started a long term experiment in 1963 covering seven square miles of north Buckinghamshire to find out where the rainfall goes. The area is taken up by seventeen per cent woodland, sixty per cent grass and the rest as arable, buildings and roads. Short-term calculations suggest that of 1·2 inches of rain on the area, 0·5 inches were lost by evaporation and transpiration, 0·1 inches by surface run-off and 0·6 inches by percolation into the soil. Such results are dependent upon temperature, soil, season, crop cover and so on[8]. It is obvious that the national mean yield of 40,800 mgd could be changed by differences of temperature and cropping, both factors being altered by changes in land-use. It is known, for example, that woodland will increase rainfall retention at the expense of evaporation. It could be that forestry would play considerably more part in water conservation plans, reducing quick run-off and evaporation. Far too little is known at present concerning the relationship between rainfall, ecology and other pertinent factors. Important research has still to be done concerning the true effects of changes in land-use.

REFERENCES

1 Issac, P. C. G. 'Making the most of our water.' *The Times*, 1 May 1965
2 'Beeflot finished if water appeal fails.' *East Anglian Daily Times*, 8 May 1965
3 Mills, J. L. 'Britain's water supply shortage.' *Farmers Weekly*, 9 April 1965
4 'Wanted—a water plan.' *Farmers Weekly*, 31 July 1964
5 'Farmers say "no" to new lakes.' *Farmers Weekly*, 19 February 1965
6 Scharff, E. 'The use of sewage in irrigation.' *International Asbestos-Cement Review*, July 1958
7 'Water for the east.' *Farmers Weekly*, 14 May 1965
8 Laurence, H. 'Finding out where the rain goes.' *Farmers Weekly*, 4 October 1963
9 Second Report. 1966, Water Resources Board

5f Farm buildings

The appearance of the countryside is changing; the change is revolutionary and rapid. The future structure of the landscape will not seem rural and rustic, as in the traditional image of Constable or Turner. It will be industrial and streamlined, without its former old-world charm. Many may accept, albeit with regret, the modern prairie field, stockless and trim with crops and with much wildlife banished for ever. But few can accept with any pleasure the shack-like, asbestos-clad buildings which have erupted across the face of rural England. Change in the appearance of the traditional farmstead has been catastrophic during the last two decades, particularly since 1957 when the Farm Improvement Scheme was started. This momentum of change is yet in its infancy. Within a few years much of the inheritance of traditional farm building will have been swept away.

It is essential to be clear that this will be, must be, so. Equally it is essential to understand why the priceless heritage of buildings, indigenous in material to their localities, blended by tradition and time to their environment and sympathetic in scale to the pastoral England of former renown must be lost for ever. It is essential to ponder what will replace the traditional farm buildings, since their modern counterpart present an intractable aesthetic problem. The loss of the traditional farmstead cannot be accepted but with regret. Similarly realignment of many rolling, reeling and rambling country roads or the transformation of old market town centres for modern, motorised commerce must be regretted with some bitterness since beauty gives way, in each case, to the ruthless economic forces of modern life.

Before discussing the modern development in farm building, two points are worth emphasising. As considered in more detail later (p396) future farm buildings may not be dispersed in small groups, a few to each farm. It is possible that many farm buildings, if such they may be called, will be grouped in regional centres, coupled with industries for food processing, storage and distribution, as well as allied industries handling their by-products. Should this prove to be so, then much of the present aesthetic problems will be transitory. Secondly, as the *Architects' Journal* stressed, it is essential that a survey is made of unwanted farm buildings to list those worth preserving[1]. Many buildings now being demolished give a factual record of changing social, as well as agricultural, custom from Mediaeval times until the modern agro-industrial revolution. They help to illustrate England's history. Many demonstrate the development of rural craftsmanship and the use of local materials in building. Many are important examples of new technical ideas, essential steps between early tillage and modern mechanised agriculture. Many are

268

just attractive, singly or in groups. Unless a record is made now, preservation orders enforced and national finance made available to retain the best buildings for posterity, this inheritance will be gone. In this matter tomorrow will be too late.

There is no simple answer to the problem of how modern farm buildings should be improved in function and appearance. That there is a problem is recognised not only by architects, but by many farmers and manufacturers. In the winter of 1965, the Farm Building Association held a conference to discuss this problem. This Association is perhaps unique. Probably no other type of building, whether industrial, domestic or social in function, has generated an organisation similar to the Farm Building Association, devoted to the better understanding of a particular building-type. An association which can be a mutual and informal meeting-point for designers, clients, manufacturers, officials and research workers related to a particular building-type, without being dominated by sectarian interests, is invaluable. That the Farm Building Association, in partnership with the Royal Agricultural Society, has been able to promote a Farm Building Centre, in the absence of government sponsored research and development in farm building, is remarkable; from such interest may come better building. In 1962, the Council of Industrial Design published a report which emphasised that much of the problem of farm buildings, with regard to their poor function and appearance, has been created by badly-designed components and poor sales literature provided by manufacturers[2]. This report stated that, coupled with these factors, the situation was aggravated by farmers being unspecific in their requirements causing manufacturers to provide unnecessary components. Though these comments are true today, the issues are confused by other factors not examined in the report. There are indeed many separate, but inter-related, factors which confuse the efficiency of modern farm building design. These are considered under six headings.

1 PSYCHOLOGICAL DIFFERENCES

Lionel Brett has clearly summarised the basic difference of mentality that splits agriculture, with its visual image, into two diametrically opposed groups[3]:

> Farmers, like landowners, come in all sizes, from do-it-yourself small-holders living in open-air attics to big businessmen rocking the balance of Nature. The two kinds of visual damage are quite different. The small man is not the rural craftsman you might imagine . . . he tends on the contrary to be a sucker for small ads and travellers and accumulates junk in penny sizes . . . rusting cars and tractors lie about waiting to be cannibalised, old prams and radios foul the dewpond, old sheets of tin or bedsteads fill the gap in the hedge . . .

269

This is one extreme of dereliction. The other is the fully mechanised factory-farm, its hedges mechanically trimmed or bulldozed out of existence, its hedgerow trees chain-sawn, its vast fields chemically fertilized and mechanically combined, baled, ploughed and drilled. There is no use in such agriculture for the isolated farmstead or row of low-ceilinged cottages. Labour is better off in a bungalow, animals under asbestos, implements in a garage. We are up against the brute fact that the countryside of great elms and thatched cotts and barns like churches and churches like little minsters is as pretty and pointless as a sailing ship. This summer, many farmers demonstrated their contempt for it by putting a match to large parts of it.

2 BUILDING DEPRECIATION

The speed of change in farm management and techniques is rapid and the crux of the design problem. This is best illustrated by the example of grass conservation and dairy cattle housing. Grass is conserved primarily as a winter feed for cattle and by tradition it was cut and dried in the field on tripods to form hay, which was handled loose with forks. After the war mechanisation meant that the grass was cut, tedded and baled; alternatively it was cut and dried loose with air from high temperature furnaces. Later, since grass drying proved laborious, baled hay was dried by low temperature fanned air. In the mid-1950s, the art of silage making was rediscovered and it was found that cattle could self-feed at the silage pits in the fields. Pits soon became clamps in silobarns and a major break was made from the traditional cowshed plus hay feeding. In the early 1960s, a trend developed towards wilting the grass, chopping it and blowing it into tower silos. In large layouts, this could be coupled with mechanised feeding via augers. Other forms of conservation developed at the same time, for example chopped, dried hay which could be self-fed. Different types of feeding became the vogue, by 1962, especially for beef fed on rolled barley, harvested and stored wet in sealed containers, whereby no grass was required. In 1965 silage kept in sealed plastic sheets, with the air removed by vacuum, gained many adherents. With this method, once again, grass conservation requires no buildings. All this has taken place within fifteen to twenty years and future policy is open to new ideas especially since straw plus additives rather than grass could be the winter diet for future cattle.

Equally drastic have been the changes in dairy cattle housing. By tradition, cows were tied in cowshed stalls where they slept, ate and were milked by hand. Mechanical milking speeded one operation, being introduced just before the 1939 war. Milking parlours, fully equipped, reduced labour in the 1950s, the cows going to the milkers instead of vice versa. At the same time, self-fed silage was introduced and cowsheds were converted into semi-open strawed yards for loose housing. By 1960 the cost and labour of straw handling encouraged the use of slatted floors instead of bedding. By this time parlours were becoming more sophisticated. By 1962, cubicle housing became popular, requiring buildings not unlike cowsheds but with the cows untied. In many cases feeding became mechanised. Buildings have sometimes been altered for new housing systems three or four times within fifteen years. Similarly whereas one man previously looked after fifteen cows, within the same period he may now manage 120 or more cows—an eight-fold increase.

It is not surprising that farmers no longer want permanent buildings but wish to recover capital invested in buildings within five to fifteen years. On average buildings are depreciated within ten years. Unfortunately it is not possible to use materials and construction, quite often for buildings with exacting functional requirements, which have a life of only ten years. For this reason, farmers would like buildings to be made of components which can be taken down and reassembled in new forms. At present, this is not possible generally and therefore converted buildings predominate, seldom being satisfactory in utility and appearance. Obsolescence in farm buildings is a serious problem, structures lasting much longer than their functions warrant. Buildings erected today, even if functional and attractive, will, almost without exception, be knocked down or converted long before 1980. Some large framed barns or tower silos will remain, but will probably be used in a different context. Even if well designed now, there is no guarantee that buildings will still be reasonable by 1980. There is a natural tendency for buildings to be put to a use alien to their original function long after their real economic life is over. In this respect there will tend to be a perpetual running sore of buildings, often with unsympathetic excrescences, on individual sites. From a planning viewpoint it is difficult to counteract this trend once it has started and equally difficult to prevent it starting due to the stringent laws of economic food production. In contrast, for the same reason of continual change, in some cases existing shacks or misshapen buildings will be swept away long before 1980 and completely new layouts erected. Existing visual problems will therefore sometimes prove to be of short duration.

3 MATERIALS AND CONSTRUCTION

Traditional materials, as in all industrial buildings, seldom have relevance today. Similarly factory-produced components and sheet or slab materials are as desirable on a farm as on a factory. Physical requirements giving stability against thrust, whether from livestock or produce stored in bulk, or providing environmental control, or withstanding chemical and mechanical action can be demanding. In such cases materials and construction tend to be expensive, a tendency contradicted by the problem of rapid obsolescence, and sitework, as in all building, is also expensive. Prefabrication is therefore desirable. Unfortunately there is practically no co-ordination between different components used in farm building. This limitation cannot be corrected by time-consuming craftsmanship on the site—as in traditional building. The result is that buildings tend to have ungainly junctions between different materials and detailing generally is crude. That co-ordination is limited is illustrated by the fact that most framed buildings, whether of steel, concrete or timber, by an accident of tradition, have bay spacings of fifteen feet. In contrast the most common cladding material for framed buildings, asbestos-cement, has a linear module of three feet four inches, suitable for ten feet, thirteen feet four inches, sixteen feet eight inches or twenty foot bays. The only hope for better farm buildings, both in function as well as appearance, is for components to be co-ordinated and this will not come about until the functional requirements are more specific.

4 FUNCTIONAL REQUIREMENTS

As the manufacturers claim a serious problem preventing better design is that farmers seldom know what they really require. The rapidity of change in agricultural techniques reflect and perpetuate the state where functional requirements are imprecise. There is no hope at all for an improvement in the design of farm buildings until requirements are analysed, tabulated and variations reduced to a minimum. The most satisfactory of present day farm buildings are to be found when requirements are precise and design is co-ordinated, usually under one manufacturer. The individual, independent designer can only hope to be better than average in the buildings he produces. It is almost impossible to produce good and economic building on the one-off basis. The best examples of modern farm buildings are most tower silos, some grain plant and intensive live-stock buildings for poultry and sometimes pigs. Unfortunately not all manufacturers given the opportunity rise to the occasion and design buildings co-ordinated in function, material and detail.

The investment in buildings, new and converted, amounts to over £60m a year in England and Wales. The amount spent by the Government on direct building grants amounts to over £13m a year, plus specialised grants for such things as water supply. The amount spent on farm building research by the Government, as opposed to agriculture (though some of the latter is relevant to building design) is very limited. The experimental farm building scheme has been essentially pragmatic by its terms of reference and has not initiated and developed new ideas. Further official research, in agricultural machinery for example, is pertinent to building design. Commercial research is for the most part unco-ordinated, though the Farm

Building Centre acts as a clearing house for ideas and information. In these circumstances, it is not surprising that design requirements are confused by lack of knowledge. It is probable however that as big business begins to reorganise and control agriculture, farm building design will receive an impetus towards precision and co-ordination as has happened in the poultry industry. This, with the possibility of big business organising the purchase of buildings in bulk and over sufficiently long periods to encourage manufacturers to develop co-ordination of components, is the best hope for improved farm building design.

5 SITING AND SCALE

At present comparatively few farm buildings are erected on completely new sites. Most are extensions of existing farmsteads, and in many cases extensions or conversions to individual existing buildings. At a guess, most building work of over £1,000 in value will be in the ratios of 1:25 as new sites to extended old sites, and 1:10 as new buildings to extended or converted old buildings. This poses two main design problems—of siting and scale—as well as the obvious one of using materials unsympathetic to traditional building.

The modern farm usually requires a linear layout, that is one based on the movement of the tractor and its various attachments. In this respect buildings need to be sited in relation to an axial service road and, in some cases, need access on two or more sides. Openings into buildings for mechanical equipment need to be large. In contrast, nearly all traditional farmsteads have a courtyard plan, designed to give protection from the wind, with the high granary to the north; with livestock buildings, east and west, opening into the courtyard; with low buildings to the south so that the winter sun can reach the central livestock yard; and with the farmhouse placed to control the layout. The modern mechanised building is alien to the courtyard and nearly all sizeable new developments have to destroy the spirit and tradition of existing farmstead layouts.

The second problem is one of scale. Traditional buildings were designed on the scale of truss construction carrying slate, tile or thatch. Spans are, with few exceptions mainly twenty to twenty-five feet. Headroom, except in the main barn, is kept to eight to ten feet. Door openings, except for wagons and threshing, are under four feet wide. Such buildings are seldom much use for modern requirements. Spans today usually need to be forty to eighty feet, sometimes even up to 150 feet without internal supports. Internal headroom seldom needs to be under twelve feet and should often be round twenty feet, except for specialised livestock buildings when the internal volume should be kept to the minimum to provide a satisfactory environment. In the case of pig and poultry buildings, eaves height may be no more than five feet.

1*

The character of modern buildings, with regard to siting and scale as well as material, is inevitably alien to the existing farmsteads of Britain. In nearly every case, new development has to destroy the harmony and rhythm of traditional design. In principle it is usually better to build on a new site, rather than disrupt existing courtyards, even if the latter are left as redundant structures. This does not often happen, since most farm developments are piecemeal, new buildings being added as the need arises. Long-term planning is the exception, mainly due to the uncertain nature of food production in the national and political scale of priorities. Building in the farmstead can save the cost of extended roads, drainage and other services. Though conversions may save a quarter to half of the capital required for a completely new layout, in many cases this can prove to be false economy. Nevertheless many new developments, based on conversions, are built which include inconvenient or inefficient techniques of food production since their economic appraisal will have been based on false assumptions, whereby minimum capital cost is given top priority rather than the return which may be yielded for each pound invested.

6 PLANNING CONTROL

As has been previously discussed (p60), planning control for most new farm buildings is non-existent, primarily limited to those which have areas of over 5,000 square feet. Bye-law control is, for the most part, cursory in practice with the exception of drainage. There is however growing concern, by planners and the public, that many new farm structures are such a blemish on the landscape that control should be extended. At the same time farmers are worried that further control could cause expensive delays and difficulties in improving their methods of food production without, in fact, making the new buildings any better in appearance. External directions made by planners on matters of appearance, whether in siting or detail, farmers believe would increase the cost of building, perhaps rendering their developments uneconomic. Not only are these fears to some extent genuine, but further control could be costly and frustrating to the farmer. It is equally true that the landscape is a national asset with an economic value that can be measured against the frustration and expense to a farmer restricted by further controls.

The value of the landscape as an attraction for tourists has been emphasised by the County Planning Officer for Somerset who said[4]:

> The tourist industry in Somerset is worth between £10m and £15m a year, excluding day trippers. The total value would be a sizeable proportion of the estimated £43m value of agriculture in Somerset. The raw material of our tourist industry is scenery. Spoil the scenery and you spoil the tourist trade.

In Warwickshire the County Planning Officer has requested that planning control for all new agricultural buildings should be introduced in given parishes to preserve the panoramic views across south Warwickshire. Such requests create opposition from farmers in the areas concerned to any form of stricter control, especially since they often consider they are victimised when others create ugliness in the countryside without planning control on a scale unknown to the agricultural industry. One Somerset farmer has had to treat his new asbestos-cement building to satisfy the planners that it will tone with the landscape, but to his exasperation across his boundary is a vast aircraft factory which is a far worse blot on the landscape, dwarfing his farmstead, and apparently without such directions concerning its appearance[4]. There are many authorities permitted by law to erect, without planning control, what they wish within the landscape. Railways, gas, water, electricity, among other services, can despoil the scenery and reduce the attraction for tourists, without the Planning Authorities having any control on their developments. In such circumstances farmers are justified in feeling that stricter planning control is for them meaningless. Nevertheless the extent to which the landscape could be ruined by indiscriminate farm building has been emphasised by the suggestion that agricultural expansion and the amalgamation of farms into larger units, now encouraged by the Government[5]:

> ... could bring a wave of farm building such as we haven't seen since the Victorian model farms were built after the enclosures. If our scheme is really comprehensive—with a target of around 120 acres as a minimum—some 50,000 new sets of farm buildings could be needed.

It seems certain that investment in new farm buildings will increase, and it may be that annual expenditure on fixed equipment and works will soon increase from the present £60m to £80m a year. This will create a remarkable change in the appearance of the landscape by 1980.

It is desirable that farm building design should be controlled to safeguard the landscape from the effects of changes of this magnitude which, if indiscriminate, will prove disastrous. Further control should however be based on the following conditions:

a All structures, both of Statutory and private development, should be governed by the same criteria concerning their impact on the landscape.

b Farm buildings should be under the direction of special panels, composed of agriculturalists as well as planners, affiliated to regional planning authorities, but permitted to give quick, and sometimes verbal, decisions when issues are not important. These panels should have full-time operators, not being once-a-month meetings as normal under present planning conditions.

c Regional planning authorities should be available for the consideration of all aspects of land-use, even weighing the merits of agricultural expediency against tourist attraction, and capable of designating regional areas of districts where landscape is an important amenity.

d Tidiness rather than arbitrary asthetics should be a major consideration governing aesthetic control.

e Long term control over design should be undertaken, by a government sponsored research station, for co-ordination of requirements and components, since this is more important when considering the appearance of farm buildings than restriction of individual designs.

REFERENCES

1 'Bigger Farms in a Shrinking Countryside.' *Architects' Journal*, 11 August 1965
2 Report on Prefabricated Farm Buildings. 1965, Council of Industrial Design
2 Brett, L., *Landscape in Distress*. 1965, Architectural Press
3 Report. *Farmers Weekly*, p54. 3 September 1965
4 Leader. *Farmbuildings*, p9. Summer 1965

6 FARM MANAGEMENT RESOURCES

Introduction

Modern farming depends on skilled management. This is principally the science of co-ordinating agriculture's three MS—money, manpower and machines. Management, obviously, also requires expert knowledge of stock and crops, soils and fertilizers, and climate and seasons. All farmers must know how to grow plants or rear and fatten livestock. Such knowledge is basic for working the land. Today however even if a farmer has advanced technical knowledge in these matters, it will be inadequate for a profitable business. Basic skills in growing crops or stock have to be disciplined in a farming system, within a co-ordinating policy for the three MS.

Farming systems have existed throughout history, becoming more technical as theories concerning cultivations developed into a science. The rotation of crops has perhaps been the most important single farming system to be practised. The balanced deployment of money, manpower and machines is today an exacting science to which factors concerning stock or crops have to be disciplined. There is, of course, a fourth M in modern agriculture. Marketing is equally important to the other three, but is considered in later sections.

Farmers have always been concerned with money, both for the sake of earning a living from agriculture and for reinvesting in their farms. Personal income has become a matter of acute anxiety for farmers in recent years. It is claimed correctly by their spokesmen that their level of income is rising more slowly than in other sectors of the community. The top farming strata are rich men with large incomes, but half the holdings receive annual net incomes of under £700. This is a poor return in terms of hours worked and capital invested. It is recognised that income will rise due to two main factors. Greater intensification, requiring more capital to be invested, and amalgamation into fewer and larger, but more viable, units could provide a better income to less farmers. This is coming about slowly due to natural economic pressures, and to some extent may be encouraged by direct government policy.

Personal income is only part of the importance of money to farmers. By normal post-war practice, at least a third of gross income should be ploughed back into each farm to improve the farming system. Even this sum is inadequate for modern levels of improvement. It is essential that farmers seek external capital to help finance better systems. Part of this capital comes directly from the Government in payments protecting the market price of food and, more important, in grants improving land, equipment and buildings. Bank loans and other sources for credit have increased dramatically in recent years, but still only cover about fifteen per cent of present land values. There is a major source of potential credit which could be tapped to release the extra £120m of working capital required each year for some time to come, in order to improve and extend farming systems. If this capital is to be released, mainly in terms of mortgages, it is essential that development plans for each enterprise are prepared to show that increased capital expenditure can be recovered within a fixed term of years and with a reasonable level of interest.

The reduction in the national farm labour force at the rate of 20,000 a year is well known. Similarly the need for skilled technicians and stockmen, rather than general labourers, is also established. At the same time the farmers themselves have to become specialists and businessmen with the same degree of managerial training and acumen found in any modern industry. The method of training these men, managers and directors is far from clear. Educational systems for agriculture today need urgent rethinking to cope with the future structure of the industry.

Skill in farm management and work should be remunerated properly and such skilled personnel may cost, including their overheads, at least £1 an hour for stockmen and tractor-drivers and £2 an hour for managers or top foremen, At such rates they will earn their keep only if their productivity is commensurably high. To this end modern farming has to eliminate traditional systems which tended to rely on seasonal fluctuations between peak and slack labour requirements. Modern labour must be productive all the time, except during the rest periods which should be planned within the work routines as for any other industrial process. Unproductive work or slack periods must be eliminated. Expensive machinery can frequently be justified for mechanical handling of farm produce or waste to save back-breaking and time-consuming work. Similarly equipment for automation or automatic work can be justified, especially in stock-keeping where feeding can become a push-button operation. Machinery to reduce physical labour can become a heavy capital burden for a farmer, yet without it he will not be able to

278

obtain or employ efficiently a skilled labour force. It may be that the basic mechanical aids purchased to make each man more productive may even double the real labour cost. For example a cowman usually needs a tractor to himself, plus mechanical aids for pushing or lifting materials. The latter will make it possible for the cowman to look after more cows without assistance. The cost of a skilled cowman, plus his tractor and attachments, which creates a super-cowman, will be equivalent to a farm cost of at least £1 10s an hour. This can be justified only when the super-cowman is looking after at least seventy, and probably ninety, cows.

British farms are the most mechanised in the world and the rate of investment in machinery continues to increase. The average expenditure on machinery and vehicles represents nearly £4 a year for every improved acre of farmland. It is obvious that any farm system must co-ordinate men and equipment into a balanced work routine. Both must be related to their hourly cost. Capital cost in itself has little meaning when developing a farming system. The annual depreciated cost for machinery and other equipment, such as buildings, is the essential factor, further divided into its cost per working hour. The latter cost is reduced the longer the equipment is used each year. Men and machines are a team, the power unit of modern farming, yoked to the same control which is the money factor.

Modern management, skilled, technical and specialist as it must be, must also know how to translate capital resources into an integrated farming system. The canker of much farming today is that many enterprises are uneconomic in scale related to the capital invested in manpower and equipment. Low-cost farming systems can be viable, where less produce is obtained for lower capital investment, though these may not make the best use of national land resources. Even these systems must balance money, men and machines into a consistent farm plan to be viable. At the other end of the scale, the intensive farmer with more capital invested for every acre, for each man or for every enterprise, will be successful only if each pound invested is reflected in a balanced team of men and machines. Management today can only co-ordinate its resources if each farm, each enterprise and each product is fully costed. The complexity of attaining a balanced system is such that calculations, sifting the data to produce the most economic policy, have become the province of computers.

6b Farm finance and productivity

Financing agriculture is an act of partnership between the nation and farmers. Practically every developed country supports the income of its farmers. In few of them does such support place so heavy a burden on the taxpayer as Britain. The principal trustees for the two parties in the United Kingdom are the Minister of Agriculture and the President of the National Farmers' Union. Each spring, as if by ancient rite, they meet together with their technical and economic advisors. By haggling, as toughly as in any market place, they establish the level of national support for the ensuing year necessary to guarantee a 'stable and efficient agriculture' as decreed by the 1947 Agriculture Act. In spite of this support, the average British farmer has a low income compared with his urban counterpart. He tends to become suspicious and bitter of his partner, believing that the economic decisions in the price review are governed by biased political motives. The future of this partnership between nation and farmer is far from clear.

Within the last decade British taxpayers have ploughed nearly £3,000m into agriculture. This support, via a mixture of price guarantees, production grants, improvement grants, and research and advisory work, represents approximately £100 for every acre of improved farmland in the United Kingdom since 1957. A cursory examination of agriculture hardly reflects a national investment of so large a sum. Much of the less intensively farmed land does not suggest it has been improved by £100 an acre within the previous decade. Much of this support is neither a direct investment in land nor specifically for improving stock and crops. It is equally difficult to see how £3,000m has substantially helped farm incomes, though it is worth noting that England received less financial assistance per £100 turnover than Scotland, Wales and Northern Ireland together. On average, instead of this support, each farm business could have been given a direct income of about £1,000, or each holding one of slightly less than £700, every year since 1955. But in practice, about half the holdings, anyway in England and Wales, have net incomes of less than £700 per annum.

Agricultural productivity has risen dramatically in recent years, though there are wide extremes of efficiency. Agriculture is among the first five industries for its productivity record, especially in relation to output per man, with an annual growth of nearly six per cent. In fact, it is expected to equal 8·3 per cent per annum between 1964–70 against the 3·2 per cent rate for all industries. It is surprising that neither land nor farm incomes truly reflect a national investment averaging about £10 an acre a year. The main benefit, especially in relation to the price guarantees which represent up to two-thirds of the annual support, has been in lower food prices for the consumer. This was dramatically illustrated in 1966 by the last president of the National Farmers Union who compared the cost of food in three capital cities for the same shopping list of meat, dairy foods, bread and some non-temperate produce including tea and coffee. In Paris these foods cost over half as much again as in London and in Rome just over double the London price[1]. The British cheap food policy has become politically and economically suspect in that it obscures the real incentives for improving agricultural efficiency. It has also been a major obstacle to joining the Common Market.

The crux of the second agricultural revolution lies in the structural and financial reforms which face the industry. The need for increased capital investment is of paramount concern, both for the nation and farmers, if the growing population is to be fed and food imports reduced. The situation was made clear by a statement of the National Farmers Union at the outset of 1966[2]:

> It will be impossible, unless the economic situation is strengthened, to maintain the pace of development and meet the never-ceasing demands for new capital which accompany the introduction of new techniques and the provision of new fixed equipment, plant and machinery, and the building up of increased livestock numbers.

It is certain that more capital must be tied up in farming and the sources for this investment must be varied. Exchequer support reached a peak of almost £343m in 1961, but dropped by practically £100m in 1965 when price guarantees totalled £135·6m and grants and subsidies £108·1m. The former included a large sum of £43·5m for cereals and one of £54·5m for livestock, including cattle, sheep and pigs, with a further £16·9m for eggs. Government support in 1966 was basically similar. These payments are superficial in that they do not directly increase efficiency but only bolster fluctuations or deficiencies in market prices. In contrast fertilizer subsidies which cost £31·3m in 1965, help to improve fertility and calf subsidies, at £22·9m, help to some extent improve the national herd. More important are the direct grants for improvements in buildings, equipment, drainage and against disease. Any tampering with the national financial support for agriculture causes political storms, especially from the poorer farmers who need this support to survive. However most economists believe that help should be directed at easing many of the less viable holdings into amalgamation by the provision of pensions for the dispossessed. This was in fact the aim of the 1965 White Paper. In addition, financial support should be aimed at improved output in terms of quantity and quality, preferably obtained with reduced production costs. Considering long term national needs, more government investment is required for increased productivity rather than for cheap food, as such, or for keeping a status quo in the structure of agriculture.

Farmers have to provide their own capital or raise it on loan for most of their improvements. In all business part of the gross income must be reinvested. Many farmers plough back all they can afford after supporting their families. On average there has been a reduction in the amount reinvested in recent years from a third of income in 1950 to a sixth today[3]. This in itself seems to reflect an unsatisfactory trend. It can however mean greater reliance on other sources for investment, which is taking place, plus a greater percentage of income being taken for personal needs. A survey of 350 farms by Cambridge University showed that a third of farm income, which averaged £2,669 in 1963, was still being reinvested but that this was not significantly increasing income[4]. It is comparatively easy to make improvements without sufficient planning, thus failing to gain an economic return.

It is probable that the total value of farmland today, inclusive of fixed equipment such as buildings, may be worth £6,500m. Perhaps at any one time a further £2,500 is invested in stock, crops and their ancillary field requirements (p192). Livestock represents nearly half the latter value, cattle alone being worth round £720m in 1964. In addition sheep represented about £155m, pigs £72m and poultry £57m. These investments have to act as securities, especially of land, in obtaining loans. As a source for raising capital for investment to improve agriculture, farmers are not yet over mortgaged. The future of the industry must depend on the use of normal business methods for finance, with greater participation by the banks in making loans, with farmers preparing proper long-term development plans for submission to their bank managers. Too few farmers, partly due to insecurity caused by political fluctuations, have sensible plans for more than one, or at most two to three, years ahead. Modern industries have to be based on five to ten year development plans, with rather hazier projections further into the future, and agriculture should be no exception.

By degrees farmers are using their own resources for raising capital. Loans from the major banks rose from a total of £221m in 1955 to £503m in 1965. Although this represents more than a doubling in bank loans within a decade, land values in the same period trebled. Capital for improvements is also obtainable from the Agricultural Mortgage Corporation and the Lands Improvement Company, as well as private sources. The average loan made by the AMC doubled between 1960 and 1965 to almost £12,000, which also indicates the willingness of farmers to seek external capital. The total of all loans, whether short, medium or long term, from banks, mortgage companies, merchants and auctioneers was estimated to be £1,125m in 1966[9]. It would seem that about fifteen per cent of land values at present are used to raise capital or only about ten per cent of the total value of all land, stock and crops.

Loans are required for three main terms of repayment. There are long term loans to purchase or reclaim land. AMC loans, for example, may extend for sixty years. Most loans for improvements for buildings and fixed equipment are for up to ten years. In the decade up to

282

1964, £1,200m was invested in buildings, some of which would need investment loans. Finally seasonal loans are required to cover seed or fertilizers until a crop is sold. Farmers spend about £1,000m every year on animal feed, fertilizers, fuel, seed and other such commodities, much of which is aided by short-term credit.

Shortage of credit restricts expansion in food production or modernisation of agricultural methods. Progressive farmers are always short of working capital for improvements. Sir Harold Woolley has estimated that occupiers' working capital, as distinct from landlord's or owner's capital tied in land and buildings, must increase by £600m in the five years from 1966[5]. Such increased capital is essential if food imports are to be reduced. The capital required to prepare agriculture for its future role is such that private farming must diminish. It is becoming increasingly difficult to finance farming development from its own profit margins. The formation of joint-stock companies in agriculture is becoming inevitable for future development. Alternatively there is growing pressure for medium term loans to be made on low interest rates from a National Land Bank on Continental lines[6]. In France, for example, about two-thirds of all development capital is financed by their state-supported credit system.

Though British agriculture is one of the most highly capitalised industries, the present rate of investment is inadequate. As Sir Paul Chambers recorded, the total fixed assets for every employee in agriculture in 1960 were £6,500 or, excluding land and buildings, £3,500[7]. In contrast the average of all manufacturing industries was only £2,100 and only in highly specialised industries such as in chemicals or oil did it become £8,000–£11,000 for every employee. In spite of the high level of capital invested in agriculture when related to manpower, the output per man is probably only about £1,000 a year which is only equal to the average in the manufacturing industries. Although an assessment of agricultural output is obscured by the subsidies and grants, the recorded output per man increased by eighty-four per cent in the period 1948–62, whereas manufacture as a whole including agriculture only expanded by thirty-six per cent. Increased farm productivity, when related to labour, reflects the high level of capitalisation and the continual increase in investment which is taking place at a rate of about £180 for every employee a year.

Total output from British farms was worth over £1,800m in 1966, with net output at £885m. By 1970 gross output should exceed £2,000m. Almost three-quarters of present output is for livestock products: less than a fifth is for crops and horticulture. Net output is already double pre-war levels and fifty per cent above 1945 production. This expansion of food production is, as farmers believe, a credit to their efficiency and progressiveness in trying new techniques. Nevertheless an expansion of output by a half in the two

283

post-war decades is only equal to that of the country as a whole. But the return for this expansion in income has been less favourable for farmers than for the community as a whole. Considering the decade from 1955, farm output increased by a third, whereas that of the community only increased by a little over a quarter. In contrast, income in real terms for farmers only rose by five per cent in this period, whereas income for the community rose by thirty-nine per cent. The price index for all farm products, including subsidies, paid to farmers fell by 1·5 per cent, whereas retail food prices rose by thirty-three per cent. At the same time food production costs had risen by thirty per cent. It is not surprising that farmers are dissatisfied members of the community nor that, in 1962–3, two-thirds had incomes of under £1,000 and over two-fifths of under £600[8].

Total farm incomes are about £420m net, which represents about £1,000 a holding or, perhaps, £1,500 a farm business in the United Kingdom. There are wide differences in farm incomes, and though two-thirds of farmers earn less than £1,000, the top ten per cent are comparatively wealthy men. Land, in itself, provides additional benefits to actual income in terms of status of residence and protection against inflation and death duties. But in spite of agriculture being a major national industry with £10,000m in one form or another locked within its enterprises and with an annual turnover approaching £2,000m each year, its financial situation is both unsatisfactory and unsettled. It is unsatisfactory mainly due to its historical fragmentation into small units and the pre-war depression which has exaggerated a national policy for cheap food imports. It is unsettled due to political uncertainties, which have tended to prevent long term development plans being prepared with any faith that national policies for any particular food would remain stable. Even today, no farmer can prepare a five year, still less a ten year plan, for developing an enterprise and be reasonably certain of an established market for his produce during that period.

The expansion of British agriculture, which is essential, needs considerable further financial investment both by the nation and farmers. This can only be realistic if the nation accepts a consistent attitude to food production and expansion and, at the basis of such attitudes, there must be a complete reappraisal concerning food imports. Production, to be economic, must be from viable units to established markets. This, in turn, means not only that enterprises must be related in size to their output but that farmers must be controlled to a greater extent by the processors and distributors of food. Farm enterprises must be related to their economic potential as attained by the correct balance of land, labour, mechanisation and investment. No one of these resources should be wastefully used in relation to the others. Similarly farmers should not produce food according to

284

their own predilections, either in quantity or in quality, relying on their market adroitness to attain a satisfactory income. Most food production may well be on a contract basis in the future and this will help to create stability and conditions favourable for further capital investment.

REFERENCES

1 'Britain's food is cheapest.' *British Farmer*, p12. 8 January 1966
2 Woolley, H. *British Farmer*, p9. 12 February 1966
3 Legge, T. 'Profit in the red?' *Farmers Weekly*, p49. 7 January 1966
4 Bullock, S. 'Ploughed back.' *Farmers Weekly*, p61. 16 July 1966
5 Report. *Farmers Weekly*, p46. 28 January 1966
6 'The case for a land bank.' *Farmers Weekly*, p75. 9 October 1964
7 Chambers, S. P. *Agriculture's place in an industrial Britain*. Oxford farming Conference Report, 1965
8 *British agriculture looks ahead*, p15. 1964, National Farmers Union
9 Hooper, S. G. *Sykes Memorial Lecture*, 1967, Institute of Bankers.

6c Farmers as specialists and businessmen

Agriculture depends for growth as an efficient industry on the capacity for skilled management among farmers. Business skill is of course essential for all modern industries. Training for top-level management has become an important facet of adult, industrial education. Most of the major industries, except agriculture, promote senior executive training as an essential part of their organisation. The growth of advanced business schools has been a feature of this decade.

Traditionally farming was based on skills attained from a combination of a countryman's inherited insight of nature, folk-lore repeated by each generation and lives spent working the land with the sons copying their fathers' practice. Skill was considered born, not made, though maturing as each farmer grew older. With this pattern, education and bookwork were unnatural and innovations in techniques were slow to be adopted. These attitudes still persist, but were the norm a generation ago when a preponderately feudal farming structure was based primarily on the horse for cultivations. Within two decades, since the end of the 1939–45 war, traditional techniques have been generally replaced by those of a mechanised, adaptable modern industry. It is not surprising in so short a time span that agriculture still includes considerable trace of pre-mechanised mentality with wide extremes, not only in terms of efficiency, but also in language and outlook. Nevertheless, the rapid change in agricultural concepts during the last twenty years, among those farmers who are mentally mobile, is a remarkable social

285

phenomenon. The new men of the post-war generation, coming both from farming families and urban backgrounds, accept that skill needs training and education and that managerial and business knowledge is essential for good agricultural practice.

Today farming techniques change so rapidly that five years may out-date a complete system and a decade is a time-scale of historical significance. Long before 1980, the old ways of farming which caused farmers to be almost entirely self-reliant, distrustful of their neighbours and market hagglers will have gone, perhaps completely.

In 1965, a farm management association was inaugurated. This is a sign of the times, especially since its membership and policy have already expanded rapidly: the association reflects the recent change of attitude among farmers towards business co-operation and education. A few years ago, such a venture would have failed. Similarly, the last few years have witnessed a proliferation of firms specialising as farm management consultants with fees commensurate with industrial practice. Such firms were largely unknown before 1960. Since advice is provided free by the Ministry of Agriculture, including many aspects of management, the growth of consultants for farmers is significant. Top-level agricultural business schools have not yet come into being, but it is probable that such post-graduate training will become an essential part of future food production.

The traditional farmer, for various economic and geographic reasons, mixed his enterprises to suit an agricultural theory of crop rotations and, permitting sudden expansion or contraction within each enterprise, to suit market fluctuations. Mixed farming still predominates, many farmers having six or more enterprises even on small acreages; specialisation is still comparatively rare considering the total of a third of a million holdings in England and Wales. In many cases, the enterprises may not even be costed separately. For example, grain may be both grown and fed to livestock on one farm. The farmer may not cost each job, only knowing the income from the fatstock when sold; yet it might prove more economic to sell the grain and have no livestock or, vice versa, to buy rather than grow grain for the fattening enterprise. This cannot be known without costing each enterprise separately. Modern farm business methods, in contrast, are based on fully-costed specialist enterprises rather than on such mixed-farming methods.

The specialist farmer concentrates his resources. He develops his skill within limited and circumscribed enterprises. He may have only one, or at most two or three, enterprises even on large acreages. Within each enterprise, every item of expenditure will be recorded and analysed. Moreover, each enterprise will be completely pre-planned. Though disease and weather can wreck even well established plans, the unknown variables, which predominate in traditional mixed farming, are reduced to the minimum. Each stage in the

286

process of food production will be controlled as much as possible and the limits of such control are continually being extended. This is the basis of modern farm management, practised by the new generation of farmers.

Modern farmers may be so technically competent that they enter into contracts to sell produce of accurate specification, in prescribed quantities and at prestated times. Vagaries of traditional marketing are eliminated to permit planned food production on schedules equal to those in any efficient industry. This is, perhaps, the major break-through of this decade into new concepts of agriculture in relation to society. It is now possible for the processors and distributors of food to dictate, even if not control, the methods of food production. In future it will be less easy to divorce farming from marketing and the term 'farmer' may become imprecise. The man who organises the policy and technique of using land for food production, traditionally known as the farmer, may be today an industrialist with an urban rather than a rural background. Similarly the man with an agricultural background may become a management tycoon concerned with matters extended far beyond work actually conducted on farmland. It is certain that the future farmer will be a specialist and a business-man and may not, in the traditional sense, have mud on his boots.

It is increasingly difficult to define a farmer by his work. For example, at one extreme, there is the outsider, who controls or influences large sections of agriculture, such as Carl Ross. Though Ross bought his first trawler in 1935, today the annual turnover of the Ross Group approaches £100m, including £2½m exports. In 1964, when turnover was £76m, sales included frozen foods at £21½m, fish at £18½m and poultry at £18m. The group has a fleet of over sixty trawlers, an army of transport vehicles and garages, and a chain of frozen food wholesalers and retail fish shops. Though this is hardly the enterprise of a farmer, the group is the largest producer of chickens in Europe. In 1964 they controlled one out of every four eggs sold in Britain and as many as four out of every five broilers. Oven-ready chickens were sold at a rate of a million a fortnight. Similarly the expansion of John Eastwood's chicken empire is well known. The firm of W. & J. B. Eastwood Ltd has breeding, hatchery, broiler, processing and feed mill complexes in Nottinghamshire, Lincolnshire, Norfolk, and others planned for Carmarthenshire and Yorkshire, each costing about £1½m and aimed together to produce about 30m broilers a year by 1970, that is roughly a quarter of the United Kingdom market. The world of chicken and egg production is not yet typical of all farm enterprises, though it is an illustration of the trend for the future, where business tycoons and vertical integra-tion fuse the role of farmer, processor and distributor into a new agri-businessman.

Much of the total farm output comes from England (seventy-five to seventy-six per cent), while only eleven per cent (worth £196m in 1965) comes from Scotland, with six to seven per cent each from Wales and Northern Ireland. More important is the concentration of output from few holdings. In 1964–65, half of the 400,000 holdings in the United Kingdom produced ninety-two per cent of total output (thus, the other eight per cent, worth under £150m, came from the remaining 200,000 holdings). More dramatic is the fact that £925ms of output came from a mere 40,000 holdings, those employing at least four men.

By 1965 a total of ten per cent of farming output, that is £200m in annual sales, was controlled by 1,800 tycoon farmers—representing approximately a half per cent of all farmers. Twelve per cent of all barley production was controlled by under 1,200 barley barons, even though a total of 100,000 farmers grow barley. Milk production is concentrated even more dramatically. Twenty per cent of milk was produced by 6,600 farmers, though again like barley, nearly 100,000 farmers have cows. Throughout agriculture, production is being concentrated into larger units, producing an era of tycoon farmers almost unknown before 1960.

Arthur Rickwood, who died in 1965 aged seventy-five, started farming at fourteen with a one-acre fen plot. He became a tycoon, with 9,000 acres in five counties growing 1,000 tons of produce each week and employing 650 permanent and casual staff, many of whom worked in mobile units moving from farm to farm. Rickwood in particular was famous for his carrot production from 2,000 to 2,500 acres yielding 25,000–30,000 tons a year, with as many as 300 tons a day being harvested in season. In addition, he held 3,000 acres of corn and 1,000 acres each of potatoes and sugar beet, as well as growing parsnips, sprouts and celery and fattening 5,000 baconers and several hundred beef cattle every year. Frank Arden, though starting as a farmer with fifty-six acres in 1936, now owns 12,500 acres in Lincolnshire, Yorkshire, Shropshire, Buckinghamshire, and Perthshire. His empire is organised in five companies with eight managers and a regular staff of 350. He produces about 40,000 tons of dried grass a year, equal to two-fifths of the total national production. He farms his land in large blocks and orders over fifty tractors a time at intervals of about fifteen months. He has approaching a quarter of a million laying birds and large acreages of corn and potatoes. Several of his farm buildings are ex-aeroplane hangers. Rex Patterson started farming with 60 acres rented in 1929. Today he farms 7,000 acres in Hampshire and owns another 1,500 acres in Wales. He produces 2m gallons of milk a year from 2,600 cows, managed in small units of sixty cows on a low-cost production basis. David Taylor started a small pig farm in 1952 with two pigs. Today, his Dorset unit has 10,000 pigs, fifty a day being despatched to Walls. In addition from feeding his pigs he has developed a £35,000 feedstuffs factory with sixty vehicles and twelve representatives with a wide local market. Arthur Crichton, once an agricultural educationist, managers 14,000 acres in Norfolk, half of which are devoted to cereals. Frank Sykes, the exponent of agribusiness techniques, farms 2,500 acres in Wiltshire. Ronald Ward, with 180 acres alone devoted to potatoes in Shropshire, has developed a prepacking plant, employing a staff of nine, and handling 2,000 tons of potatoes a year to supermarkets.

The men quoted above are the tycoon farmers who are able businessmen, much respected in agriculture, and who are of profound importance for the nation. They represent the specialist farmers of the future. Although all these men are farmers it is easy for them to become concerned with processing and marketing. As discussed in detail later (p351), some farmers are attempting to counteract the big-business pressures of the new markets on farming by direct sales through their own outlets. This is sometimes attempted individually or in small groups and sometimes in large co-operative movements.

The farmer of today cannot be parochial in his interests. The leaders of the industry must be men of vision. They must understand the nature of food production on an international scale, seeking to establish an integrated policy for feeding the vast population of the world by making the best use of all natural resources. They must be prepared to encourage the direction of individual gain to the urgent needs of the community at large. All farmers must understand the intricate business of feeding the nation, including the production, processing, distribution and cooking of food. They must appreciate that production is but one link, and financially a minor link, in the chain. They must be prepared to work within a team of specialists, each in charge of one aspect of food technology. They must even seek partnership within a process of vertical integration in the food industry and not remain hostile and segregationist in their attitudes to the industry as one complex, but co-ordinated, unit. In their own immediate field they must be financiers capable of translating capital into realistic patterns of investment. They must also know how to choose and handle some of the most technically skilled men in modern industry—that is, the field and stock workers needed to serve the agri-business of today and tomorrow. Equally they must be experts concerning mechanisation, in the selection, use and maintenance of all modern farm equipment, including an appreciation of automation and computer aids to the industry. Finally, of course, they must have their basic knowledge of stock, crops and land, including such diverse matters as climate and chemistry.

Farm management, and, therefore, the nature of farm managers both in temperament and in training, is rapidly leaving the mediaeval world of agriculture and rural life which existed into this century.

Agri-business is a term coined to denote the new agriculture coming rapidly into being due to the present agrico-industrial revolution. Farmers, today, must look to the managerial techniques used in other successful industries to be able to cope with their own changing situation. The image of Farmer Giles must pass for ever from the scene of British agriculture.

6d Farm labour

The total labour force has declined in numbers over many years. The reduction in numbers has been so remarkable that it has been termed 'a drift from the land'. This phrase can be misleading. The exodus has not been caused by artificial pressure, such as redundancy sackings, except perhaps during the depression when some workers may have been forced from their chosen livelihood. For the most part, farm workers leave the land today on account of retirement or due to the attraction of urban pay and working conditions. Some quit agriculture since they forsee no hope of promotion to worthwhile management positions.

Statistics regarding the labour force tend to be difficult to define. There are several classifications. The total labour force in England and Wales in March 1967 numbered over 375,000. This included both male and female labour, regular full-time and part-time labour, as well as temporary seasonal labour. Quarterly labour returns made to the Ministry of Agriculture reflect seasonal fluctuations. As an indication of the trends in the labour force, the number of full-time male workers is normally taken. In March 1967, there were just under 260,000, that is just over half of the total labour force available. The breakdown of the labour force into its classifications was as follows:

ENGLAND AND WALES: FARM LABOUR FORCE: MARCH 1967: '000

	Full-time	Part-time	Casual	Total
Male	259·2	29·5	20·8	309·5
Female	23·6	24·4	17·7	65·7

These figures exclude the occupier of each farm, that is of each holding exceeding one acre, his wife and all school children. In Scotland the labour force in June 1964 only totalled about 68,500, including nearly 50,700 full-time male workers. Similarly the figures for Northern Ireland were about 40,000 and 20,000 respectively. The full-time male farm labour force in the United Kingdom is at present about ½m. There are, of course, at least as many farmers as men but half of these are known to be only part-time farmers.

Four decades ago, in 1925, there were about 662,000 full-time male farmworkers in England and Wales, considerably more than double the present number. From 1925 numbers declined by about 14,000 each year until the 1939 outbreak of war. This annual decrease dropped to about 4,000 due to the wartime boost given to food production. An influx of servicemen after the war created a peak force of 520,000 men in 1950, that is about equal to numbers employed in 1934. Since the peak year of 1950, nearly a quarter of a million men have quit agricultural employment. The rate of those leaving farmwork is increasing, now being about 20,000 full-time men each year, representing a six per cent annual decrease in the labour force. Few people are worried by the rapid shrinkage in the number of farmworkers, since mechanisation is able to replace their work capacity and, in fact, increase the total farm output. In 1965 the Government recognised that it was desirable to accelerate the transfer of labour from agriculture to urban industries in order to reduce the forecasted manpower shortage in industry for 1970. The National Economic Plan for these five years is aimed to reduce the numbers engaged on farms, as farmers or workers, by 140,000. Many agricultural economists believe the labour force could be reduced by at least this amount and that the present total could be more than halved.

Professor Colin Clark has suggested that a total labour force of 150,000 could be practicable. Agricultural requirements could be attained by 60,000 men on dairy farms at the rate of one man for seventy-five acres, mainly within a limited area along the south and west coast. About 20,000 men would be needed on arable farms with each man working about 450 acres and with most of the cereals being grown in the dry eastern counties. An additional 70,000 men would be required on general livestock farms at the rate of one man for 250 acres. In this estimate, $4\frac{1}{2}$m acres would be needed for dairy products, 9m for arable products and $17\frac{1}{2}$m for other livestock requirements. Thus, a total of 30m acres could be managed and worked by 150,000 men. If this appraisal is projected further into the future, acknowledging a reduction in farmland, an increase in intensive livestock units and full mechanisation, then all arable and grassland managed at an average rate of 350 acres per man might be worked by not more than 65,000 farmworkers. Livestock units, comprising basically indoor work and automatic controls, might only need a further 35,000 men. It is conceivable that 25m acres of land plus intensive livestock units could be managed by 100,000 highly skilled and paid men backed, of course, by scientists, engineers and other specialists.

The present distribution of labour is neither uniform in relation to farm size nor to locality. In theory, each holding of more than a quarter of an acre could employ one full-time worker, either male or female, in England and Wales. Similarly if only holdings of over twenty acres were considered, then each could have at least two full-time employees. Since only 100,000 holdings actually employ farmworkers, with more than half of all holdings being worked by a farmer on his own, comparatively few farmers control the full-time male labour force. In fact, a mere 17,000 farms employ about half the farmworkers in units of more than three men to each holding. Another 50,000 holdings, which is half of those having full-time employees, only have one man in addition to the farmer himself and a further 22,000 holdings have only two men. The small size of labour units is considered one attraction of farmwork. There tends to be a direct and personal relationship between a worker and his boss. It is however equally true that as the labour force is reduced, teamwork becomes rare. Many men spend isolated working lives. The physiological significance of this factor, considering the exacting and monotonous nature of modern farmwork, has not been fully examined. Nevertheless it is important when considering the structure of rural society and the compensating amenities which should be provided for the men and their families.

The age structure of the full-time male labour force is of importance. At present, about three per cent continue working when over sixty-five. Almost ten per cent are youths under eighteen and a further six per cent are aged between eighteen and nineteen. About eighty per cent are aged between twenty and sixty-five. This seems reasonable. It is of more concern that nearly half of those quitting agriculture each year are aged between twenty-five and forty-five, being 'trained experienced men in the prime of life, in whom the industry has invested a good deal of time and money'[2]. The principal loss is among those in their early thirties. This suggests that the structure of agriculture must be unsatisfactory in that young men, having worked for ten to fifteen years in farming, quit for other occupations.

There is a direct relationship, obviously, between the decline in the labour force and the increase in mechanisation. Since the end of the 1939–45 war, the full-time male labour force has dropped by about forty per cent. Nevertheless farm production has increased by almost seventy per cent in the same period and output per man by nearly 250 per cent. This change has been made possible by increased mechanisation, new techniques, improved livestock genetics and seed, better technical management and increased skill in the labour force. The relationship between labour and mechanisation becoming more numerous, it is also becoming more efficient and powerful as well as used to better effect for longer hours.

A survey by the Ministry of Agriculture has shown a remarkable increase in productivity for less work in the six years between 1956 and 1964. The manhours worked on each holding dropped by twenty-three per cent in this period, from a national average of

292

18·4m a week to one of 14·2m a week. During these years, output per worker rose by sixty per cent and the overall net output by twenty-five per cent. The revolution in mechanisation is nowhere near complete and productivity per man will continue to improve at least at this rate for some years to come. Equally significant is the fact that the increase since 1945 in productivity per man in agriculture is more than double that in the manufacturing industry as a whole, including agriculture, and is even considerably greater than in the chemical and allied industries, which are well known for their efficiency.

McCrone in 1962 studied the remarkable achievement of the farm labour force in the United Kingdom compared with other countries[4]. Only one in twenty-five of the working population of the United Kingdom works on the land, whereas in other advanced countries the proportion is at least one in ten and often more than one in fifteen. The contrast between the United Kingdom and other countries in 1962 is shown in Chart 44[4]:

CHART 44: PERCENTAGE OF POPULATION WORKING IN AGRICULTURE AND NATIONAL VALUE OF AGRICULTURAL PRODUCTION IN 1962

	A	B
United Kingdom	4·1	4·2
Belgium	10	7
Switzerland	15	7
Netherlands	12	10
Sweden	18	6
West Germany	17	7
Denmark	17	16
Norway	18	7
France	26	14
Austria	30	12
Irish Republic	38	32
Italy	32	21
United States	12	5
Australia	19	25

A: population working in agriculture as percentage of total working population.
B: agricultural production as a percentage of the Gross National Product.

The late Professor Nash has clearly demonstrated how production per man in the United Kingdom is better than in the Common Market countries, each person engaged in agriculture (as opposed to farmworkers only) cultivating five times the area, with the exception of France where it is only three-and-a-half times the area. More important is the value of the produce attained by each person. Each person in the United Kingdom produces between sixty-five and 400 per cent more in the value of food output, though such comparisons are difficult to make and different emphasis can be given when equating values.

CHART 45: PRODUCTIVITY COMPARISON: UK TO COMMON MARKET COUNTRIES IN 1962[5]

	Farm population (millions)	Agricultural area (m acres)	Acres/ worker	Gross farm output (m dollars)	Output per man
Belgium/ Luxemburg	0·5	4·6	9	992	1,990
France	5·0	85·5	17	7,326	1,470
w Germany	3·8	35·4	9	5,005	1,320
Italy	6·4	51·8	8	5,479	860
Holland	0·7	5·7	8	1,393	2,000
UK	1·2	49·2	41	4,031	3,360

Even allowing for some artificiality in the assessments, it would seem that the United Kingdom's productivity is considerably better than on the Continent. This is partly due to greater capital investment in machinery and equipment and partly to geographic and historic reasons.

As the farm labour force declines, the number engaged in auxiliary occupations related to agriculture continues to increase. Unfortunately it is impossible to be precise concerning the allied industries. The latter include the services directly related to agriculture, including all the distributors of machinery, seeds, and fertilizers, with their salesmen, representatives and engineers. There are also as many engaged in advisory, teaching and research capacities related to agriculture as actually work on the land. There are, of course, in addition those who work in the factories and processing plants handling food products. Food production and processing, including bakeries, confectioneries, dairies—as well as the meat, fish and vegetable processors (excluding catering)—is one of the largest industries employing 600,000 people. About a further four per cent of the working population are required to distribute food and drink which again equals the number working on the farms. As an approximate estimate it is probable that about twenty per cent of the working population are more or less directly engaged in the food industry, excluding those indirectly concerned such as factory workers making

294

tractors or building workers erecting farm buildings. It is important that as those directly working the land drop in proportion to the total working population from the present four per cent to under 0·5 per cent at the end of the century, and as those engaged in auxiliary trades increase that the total manpower for the food industry is assessed and integrated. It is easy to make great strides in improved agricultural manpower efficiency, only to waste it by inefficient services allied to the farm.

In spite of the remarkable productivity per man, the apparent low wages for farmworkers seem unreasonable. A minimum income of little more than £10 a week lags behind other industries. The minimum wage, though more than doubled since 1945, is paid to only one in five workers. At least four-fifths receive a premium ranging in 1962 from an average of 11s a week for general workers to over 53s for foremen[6]. A third of the labour force earned at least 20s a week over the minimum wage. In fact farmworkers often earn more than farmers. As recorded by a Midland Survey in 1962, a quarter of the farms studied with less than 150 acres yielded less than £500 for the farmer, averaging as little as £266, though there could be hidden assets such as wages paid to family members and a house free of rent or mortgage. A few skilled stockmen can earn £20–£25 a week, sometimes with other assets such as free or subsidised housing. Nevertheless, as the skill and training demanded of the labour force is increased, with the responsibility required, the smaller number of workers must command a much higher wage. It is not far-fetched to see that they eventually may have the status and pay of any skilled technician.

The continual decline in the numbers of farmworkers engaged on the land, with the decrease in the numbers of farmers, is the basic reason why intensive farming is becoming evident, though other technical and social forces also create similar pressures. It is obvious that farmland cannot be managed with a small labour force without some dramatic change occurring in its appearance.

REFERENCES

1 Clark, C. Oxford Agricultural and Economic Research Institute. Report of Conference at Nottingham University. *Farmers Weekly*, p45. 11 January 1963
2 Barber, D. 'The Men we Need.' *Farmer & Stockbreeder*, Supplement, 2 March 1966
3 'The Wages Bill grows, Yet the Workers Leave the Land.' *Farmers Weekly*, p72. 19 June 1964
4 McCrone, G., *Economics of Subsidising Agriculture*, p24. 1962, George Allen & Unwin
5 Nash, F. 'Farming in the Common Market.' *Dairy Farmer*, p83. February 1962

6 Giles, A. K., and Cowie, W. J. G., *The Farm Worker: His Training, Pay and Status*. 1964, University of Reading
7 Farm Management Notes no 27. 1962, Department of Agricultural Economics, University of Nottingham

6e Education for modern agriculture

The purpose of education, with its administration, structure and finance, needs constant reappraisal. This is vital in an age of rapid technological and social change. Today theories about education are keenly debated. This is true of all forms of education and at all levels, whether primary, graduate, professional or adult. Agricultural training is no exception; in fact its purpose seems more confused than for most skilled work. The distinction between worker, manager and farmer tends to be imprecise. Similarly there is little real distinction in training, temperament or techniques between those engaged in farmwork and those within many ancilliary organisations.

Two traditional types of farm personnel have no modern relevance. In the past the slow-witted child educated in the village school was sure of adult employment as an agricultural labourer. There will soon be no place for unskilled workmen in farming, except occasionally for seasonal casual work. Secondly the cartoon image of Farmer Giles with knowledge based on an instinctive cunning, which has matured through generations of inherited experience of the land, is an anachronism. The modern agriculturalist, whatever his level of employment, must be highly skilled. Every farm worker today may be equipped with buildings or machinery costing perhaps £25,000 and he may manage stock and crops worth £15,000 a year. A farm manager of a medium sized estate may be in charge of investments representing at least a quarter of a million pounds of tied capital. Industrial tycoon farmers are concerned with multi-million pound businesses. Management miscalculations or mistakes can have serious financial repercussions, being avoided only by constant observation, analysis and reappraisal of all factors within each enterprise—a matter of skill and efficiency at all levels of employment.

In 1964 the Bosanquet Committee examined the future needs of agricultural education for the Minister of Agriculture. They recognised rightly that modern food production must be based on a large corps of agricultural scientists in order to increase cultivation, fertility and yields. Agriculturalists, statisticians and economists, as well as physicists, chemists, bacteriologists and engineers, are among those required as skilled personnel of exceptional calibre to serve the industry. Nevertheless in 1961 there were only 10,000 people holding British degrees in agriculture or similar qualifications in related fields, and of these only three-quarters were using their qualifications

296

for food production[1]. This represents a ridiculously small number of skilled and qualified workers serving an industry with an annual turnover of nearly £2,000m. The Agricultural Research Council alone now needs eighty new graduates a year, but between 1958 and 1962 their annual intake was only a quarter of this number. Similarly the Ministry of Agriculture has difficulty in obtaining specialists of sufficient calibre to staff their various departments. Agricultural degree courses include training in applied sciences, but there are inadequate post-graduate courses available to create the standards required for specialised research. This is serious considering the future demands on agricultural land and food. In 1966 an Agricultural, Horticultural and Forestry Training Board was set up by the Government to establish priorities and methods for future training in the industry.

Two types of worker are required for the modern industrial farm. There is a clear distinction in aptitude and training between the fieldworker and the stockman. The former must be a skilled tractor driver, interested in machinery and capable of handling a wide range of cultivation tools with precision. He must have skill in judging weather, soil and crop conditions. His work is exacting and often monotonous. He must frequently work alone all day and every day but sometimes he will be part of a small team of skilled men. On some arable farms he may be responsible for 250 acres of crops. On stock farms he may manage a large acreage of grassland. The stockman, in contrast, may have to use a tractor, milking machinery, milling plant or other expensive machinery, but he should not essentially be a mechanic by temperament. He must have a sympathy for animals, being observant and patient, sensing their needs almost by instinct, even though handling hundreds of animals at a time. But instinct must be backed by detailed knowledge of genetics, nutrition and disease. He must be meticulous in recording details of his stock and he must withstand the monotony of a repetitive job. Like the field worker, he usually works alone, but sometimes as part of a team. In addition to these two distinct types of farmworker, there is a limited demand for full-time mechanics, clerks, building tradesmen and other skilled workers on the larger estates.

The various skills of field and stock worker, where farms include several men, may be supported by a foreman as intermediary to the manager or farmer. On small farms the manager or farmer will work with his men, combining management with his trade or craft skill, but this tends to limit his capacity for research, analysis and forward planning. Larger farms, supporting more staff, may mean that the manager or farmer will only do physical work at peak times or as relief to his men. There are relatively few farms which can support a leader devoting all his time to management, though this will be the trend in the future.

K

Agriculture is still largely based on a labour force without technical education. The traditional farmer believes that critical thinking is his responsibility and prefers his men to be trained by himself. Advertisements for farmworkers in the *Farmers Weekly* in the decade from 1952 increased from 704 to 863[2]. In spite of great changes in educational facilities during this period the demand for trained employees barely increased, being still less than two per cent of all advertisements in 1962. The lack of demand for technically trained men is unsatisfactory for a modern, skilled industry, where work routines incur increasing exactitude and responsibility. Nearly a third of the advertisements were for general workers, without specific skills[2].

CHART 46: QUALIFICATIONS REQUIRED AS % OF VACANCIES: 1952–62

| | General workers | Tractor drivers | Stockmen | | | | Total |
			cattle	poultry	pigs	sheep	
1952	0·7	—	0·9	—	—	—	0·7
1962	1·6	0·8	1·3	3·3	3·7	4·3	1·7

Though qualifications may not be requested by advertisement, it may be that their possession increases the chance of selection for a job. Similarly many jobs, particularly at top level, may be filled by personal recommendation and not by advertisement. These comments are a matter of conjecture. Nevertheless this analysis hardly reflects a modern, technical industry demanding trained skill in its operatives.

The same report, however, indicated a substantial increase in the demand for qualified managers. Though the situations advertised dropped from forty to thirty over the decade, requests for qualifications in this sense included training in agriculture or allied skills and not specifically in agricultural management. Manager situations in practice may sometimes prove to be little more than superior foremen positions. Another analysis of advertisements in the *Farmers Weekly* during 1963 showed an average demand for 4·6 managers a week, only a fifth of which were for trained personnel[2]. It is possible that no more than 500 manager positions fall vacant each year, most being filled by unqualified people and practically none by those with training in agricultural management. It is estimated that there are about 3,000 salaried farm managers in England and Wales and, in comparison, relatively few in Scotland or Northern Ireland[3]. In all industries managers need to be trained in modern techniques of management, as well as in some basic skill related to the industry. This is equally true in agriculture and, moreover, once trained, managers need regular refresher courses to keep abreast of new techniques.

There are three types of institution providing full-time agricultural education—universities, agricultural colleges and county farm institutes or, in Scotland, farm schools. Twelve of the universities in the United Kingdom include post-graduate agricultural training. Graduate courses are for three years and most of the abler young farmers will have graduated or gained a three-year diploma. Most college courses, however, are for two-year diplomas. Eight of the national colleges train people specifically for specialised work, such as the National College of Agricultural Engineering. The institutes provide one-year courses which, in practice, only include sixty days practical and ninety days theoretical training[3]. Every year about 20,000 young people enter farming, and at present a total of about 3,000 students attend university, college or institute[4]. In addition, the institutes cater for 10,000 students on day release from three-year apprenticeship schemes to local farmers, providing a minimum of sixty days classwork. It has been estimated however that in future a replacement rate of only 10,000 a year may be needed[6].

Agricultural education is not providing an adequate framework for the future of the industry. The institutes and colleges tend to confuse their training courses as being suitable simultaneously for general workers, who are still in demand by farmers, skilled field or stock workers, foremen, managers and farmers. Many of those trained become merchants, salesmen, advisers, teachers and research workers, but have the same course as the agricultural worker. University training does not necessarily aim to produce potential managers or farmers, specialised for particular enterprises, backed by top-level understanding or modern business and managerial techniques. The courses generally produce graduates suitable for mixed farming, with limited knowledge either of food production, marketing, processing and distribution as an integrated system for feeding the population, or land-use as a social responsibility, or industrialised business techniques.

Agriculturalists appreciate that even with good qualifications, the chances of a young man becoming a farmer are remote unless he is backed by substantial capital. A 250–300 acre arable farm, which is the minimum to be equipped and managed economically, may need £100,000 in capital. A smaller farm for eighty cows could need half this sum. Farms to rent fall vacant comparatively infrequently, compared to those put up for sale, and they command many applicants for the tenancy. In one issue of the *Farmers Weekly* in 1964, sixty-five farms were for sale, but none to let[5]. There were in the same week 380 advertised jobs in farming or allied industries. These included seven farm managerial and three assistant managerial positions. Only fifty-four jobs were for specialist jobs, including stockmen, mechanics, foremen and even two secretaries. More than half of the advertisements, totalling 200 jobs, were for unspecialised work. There were fourteen vacancies for skilled men for relief contract work by specialist firms. Farmwork by agencies contracting to farmers is a growing concern. Equally important there were twenty-eight vacancies external to farming for salesmen and technicians within allied industries and marketing, nine for teachers, advisors and research workers and a few for others for work abroad. This analysis of weekly advertisements is typical of the present position. It does not provide a healthy framework for the 1,000 or more students qualifying with degrees or diplomas each year. The opportunities for specialised advancement in agriculture are slender. There are more opportunities in the allied industries, but the basic agricultural education is not suitable for work in these fields.

To serve the future industry a new training system is required, with a distinction made between skilled specialist workers and managers or farmers. Both groups need a general agricultural basic training, possibly of two years duration, supplemented by further specialist training to take them beyond the traditional mixed-farm mentality. The managers and farmers would need additional training to cover modern business techniques. Training for managerial positions might attract skilled workmen of any age as well as those having recently finished their basic training plus practical experience. Those intending to join the allied industries to farming would attend the basic agricultural training, then have a further course appropriate for salesmen, merchants, engineers, or whatever was their particular business. For the time being, those intending to remain as general and unspecialised farmworkers would only do the basic training. It is possible the institutes might have courses at two levels, one course would be to attain a basic diploma, possibly including some apprentice students; the second course would be for those aiming either for advanced diplomas or degrees as specialists, but going to colleges or universities after finishing the institute course.

The urgent need is for an integrated and flexible educational system, aiming to produce as many specialists as possible and channelling some students to post-graduate research and top-level management both for the larger estates and for allied trades. Dovetailed into the system must be various refresher courses to keep the specialists up-to-date with new techniques. The aim must be to produce skilled technocrats capable of serving a modern industry. There is a long way to go before the educational system comes to terms with the needs of the future industry, producing specialists and businessmen.

REFERENCES

1 'Farmers will need more trained brains.' *Farmers Weekly*, p39. 31 July 1964

2 Giles, A. K., and Cowie, S. J. G. *The Farm Worker: His Training, Pay and Status.* 1964, University of Reading
3 Willis, S. J. 'Wanted: a Robbins for farming.' *Farmers Weekly*, p77. 24 April 1964
4 Barber, D. 'The men we need.' *Farmer & Stockbreeder*, Supplement, 8 March 1966
5 Legge, T. 'The farming ladder.' *Farmers Weekly*, p69. 21 February 1964
6 Report on future of agricultural education. June 1966, Department of Education and Science

6f Mechanisation

British agriculture is highly mechanised. The machinery invested, in terms of each worker and acre farmed, is greater than in other countries. Because of this mechanisation, output is equally higher than normal elsewhere.

The trend in farm mechanisation continually shifts. The development of the tractor has been the one machine to do most to revolutionise farming. In the immediate post-war years, due to increased use made of tractors, arable farming became the centre for new techniques in agriculture. Productivity levels, impossible when power had been related to the horse, rose sharply and were later increased with the advent of the combine-harvester. All forms of cultivation equipment were improved to suit the new tractors. By 1955 interest in machinery research became centered on improving material handling techniques as the next step in mechanising agriculture. This interest is still unabated, manpower requirements in handling materials at all stages of food production being rapidly reduced. By 1960, though farm electrification had expanded for many years, the need for electrical power in farm buildings and fieldwork, especially for stock fences, became apparent. Similarly mechanised livestock farming only reached serious consideration after 1960, being coupled to electric power for many of its requirements. By 1965, though all machinery continued to be improved and mechanical aids introduced, research attention began to shift towards computer planning, automation and remote control. It is probable that the mechanisation of farming methods is, if not in its infancy, not yet of mature stature.

In 1939 there were over half a million working horses on farms in England and Wales and only 55,000 tractors. It is surprising that numbers of horses and tractors were about equal at the time of the Festival of Britain in 1951, a little over a quarter of a million each. Even today working farm horses are not extinct. Tractors of all kinds, however, now exceed half a million with well over a third of a million being wheeled vehicles in excess of ten horse-power. This represents about one main tractor for every 100 acres of farmland or

301

one for every farmworker. The modern tractor is very sophisticated compared with those known two decades ago. In recent years powerful tractors have become an essential part of farming and represent a considerable investment. A seventy horse-power tractor, plus its basic equipment of plough and cultivator, may cost £1,500. But larger tractors are not unknown, those of 100 horse-power being relatively common and of 120–140 horse-power becoming accepted. Tractors in this category can cost well over £5,000 with their basic tools. Average tractor power sold by dealers doubled in the two post-war decades.

A 100 horse-power tractor is a powerful and expensive tool. It needs skill in handling. To be economic it may need 400–500 acres to cultivate. Alternatively if one such tractor can be used instead of two, then one man's work will be saved and this can make the powerful tractor worthwhile. Tractor mechanisation has to be related to the overall farm plan, its size being matched to the task. Increased power can permit faster work and improved cultivation techniques, without necessarily sacrificing quality of fieldwork to speed. It is worth noting the work capacity of the larger tractors compared with those of more conventional size. Ploughing can be undertaken at rates of four acres an hour with a large machine, against a standard yardstick of only a half acre an hour. Cultivation is even more dramatic, being eighteen against two acres an hour respectively and even drilling can be three times faster, being six against two acres an hour. Speed in fieldwork can be vital, especially considering unpredictable weather conditions, but also for improving productivity for each worker. Heavy tractors need to work at least 1,200 hours a year to be truly economic, and preferably up to 1,500 hours. This means working between 150 and 190 eight-hour days a year. On most farms this would prove to be too high a proportion of the working year. Shift working is likely to become more commonplace in the future, whereby at peak work seasons tractors would be used round the clock. This can justify the high capital expense and becomes practical, even for small farms, where work is co-operatively managed.

The tractor and its operator is only part of the work unit and field cultivation only part of its scope. The attachments which can be added to a tractor are legion. Only in the realm of grain harvesting has the move been away from the tractor as the power unit towards self-propelled combine-harvesters. The hydraulic power of the tractor has become the mainstay of most field work and much farmstead work. The tractor is used, of course, for ploughing, harrowing, drilling, thinning and all other cultivation work. It is used for fertilizing, spraying and manuring. It is used in all stages of grass conservation from field to barn or silo. It is used for much of root and vegetable harvesting. It has become, with its various types of trailer, the general form of farm transport for most materials. Fore- and

302

rear-end loaders and even fork-lift attachments have made the tractor the jack-of-all-jobs. The capacity to lift from a half to a ton loads to heights of ten feet have made mechanical handling a normal facet of tractorwork. The tractor can also power much other machinery, including fans and augers, by a process of power take-off couplings from the engine. It is also used for maintenance work, such as hedge-cutting, ditch-cleaning and even for drainage pipe laying.

Considering the versatility of the tractor and its widespread use for much farmwork, it is surprising that little attention has been paid to its ergonometrical design. The Max Planck Institute in Germany has given the matter considerable study, and within the last year or two the National Institute of Agricultural Engineering has begun to do likewise. But vibration, with observation and control of rear-mounted equipment, is known to lead to spinal disorders. Controls are not always placed for easy manipulation. Noise too can be a major stress factor in modern tractor-work. Protection cabs against the weather have only recently become more than a freak structure on the fringe of farming. Though deaths from overturning tractors are numerous in accident statistics numbering forty a year, crush-frames are seldom seen. Even the design of tractor-seats has had limited attention. Most farmers consider working comfort, not as an essential ingredient of industrial efficiency, but as a luxury which cannot be afforded. There is little doubt, in spite of the many innovations in tractor design in recent years, the modern tractor will appear primitive within another decade or two (p414). The need for a tractor is questioned. With increased sizes and loadings, essential for efficient work routines, soil damage can become a serious consideration. Hover vehicles might replace the conventional tractor. It is possible that future cultivation techniques will rely on chemical, rather than mechanical, processes, (p412).

For some years to come, whatever its ultimate future, the tractor will remain the centrepiece of a wide range of equipment. Until recently tractors have generally been used in conjunction with equipment and for tasks never conceived in their original basic design. In particular hydraulic power has been a limited, though useful, adjunct to tractor design, but a variable delivery pump for external hydraulic power or separate hydraulic systems for direct power take-off will become essential features of future tractors. The tractor and attachments will be designed as one entity and not as separate mechanisms for different functions. The trend is towards comprehensive design, but much remains to be done before the tractor has reached the end of the process for research and development.

The need for heavy powered machines in fieldwork, which is transforming the pattern of all arable farming and, more recently, of grassland management, has not been confined to tractors. The trend to giant machines was first noticeable with the design of combine harvesters. Although early versions were introduced in the 1930s, there were only a little over 3,000 of all types in use by the end of the war. Numbers expanded rapidly to about 30,000 by 1955 and to 46,000 self-propelled harvesters by 1965, plus 12,000 tractor-drawn harvesters, though the latter are now rapidly declining in numbers. The size of combine is normally related to the length of cutter-bar, most being round eight to ten feet. Some are much larger models, having fourteen feet cutter-bars, with one recent giant of eighteen feet. Moisture content of the crop affects speed, but these larger machines can have harvesting rates in excess of ten tons an hour. Speed also depends on large fields, unbroken by hedges or other obstructions. The sight of teams of combines at work in the open landscape of the eastern counties can be majestic. Though grain harvesting methods were originally pioneered as a new concept in bringing crops from the land, sugar beet harvesting today is nearly as efficient and even crops like potatoes, though more difficult, and peas can be lifted and transported on factory lines of production. In fact the real aim in crop harvesting must be to create a free flow of produce from the field to the factory. Peas for freeze-drying in particular, must reach the factory within a few hours of harvesting. Floodlit fields, during harvest, with shift work round the clock, is the modern and necessary technique for food production. This is factory farming in its most obvious form.

The forage harvester for cutting grass crops, developed within the last few years, has transformed cattle husbandry. Coupled to tower silos and mechanised feeding, grass can now be harvested, stored and fed by machines requiring little labour. Even bale handling, either for hay or straw, has been mechanised so that manual operations need be limited. A single man can in fact lift, transport and store 3,000 bales in a day. In the trend for simplified handling, recent developments in chopping and blowing are, perhaps, the most probable systems for the future since semi-solids, such as chopped materials, are easier to handle than solid bales.

The supply of electricity to farms, except for a few very remote districts, is now complete, though a decade ago only two-thirds of all holdings had electricity. This, with the rapid increase in the number and power of electrically driven farm machinery, has increased consumption within that period by sixty per cent to total 2,700m units in 1965, averaging 9,250 units a farm. Equally important is the estimate made by the Electrical Development Association that consumption will increase by a further seventy per cent to a total of 4,600m units by 1972. Livestock housing is expected to account for about a seventh of this amount.

Mechanical ventilation is required for much poultry and pig housing and, more rarely, is being used for cattle. As intensification

304

in housing increases, so does the need for controlled environment. Youngstock usually need electric heaters for warmth, and under-floor electric heating may be used, particularly for piglets and sometimes for pig fattening. Mechanised feeding usually requires electric motors and some of the power requirements can be high. In fact mechanical handling by belt, auger, blowing or suction, now common for many materials on the farm, all need electric power. Similarly, fan drying either with warm or chilled air for grain, potatoes, hay and other produce can be expensive, though economically justified. The use of electricity for mechanisation and in the future, for automation, is likely to be considerably greater than at present. Electric fencing is desirable where cattle, sheep or pigs are allowed to graze. As permanent housing becomes prevalent this will decline. The possibility of buried leader-cables to guide tractors and other equipment without manpower, especially in orchards, but equally practical for some farm crops, is being examined. This could considerably increase electrical consumption for fieldwork in the future. The implications of automation for farming are considered later (p414).

The expansion of the agricultural industry, coupled with the rapid decline in manpower, obviously depends on this trend in mechanisation and automation being continued. The planning of mechanisation on the farm is a skilled job. In order to attain maximum profitability and productivity in relation to manpower and machinery, the size which is economic to manage as a unit has become critical. The most urgent national need in the agricultural industry is the elimination of under-sized enterprises which are unbalanced in their ratio of land to equipment available. This reorganisation, creating viable units, will require redistribution of much of the present structure of farms into larger units. Progressive grain farmers, for example, appreciate that production should be at least in multiples of 250 acres. For preference, a 650–750 acre, two-combine unit is easiest to plan and work. Small fifty to 100 acre corn enterprises, though still prevalent, are not economic in terms of national, or even individual, resources. Mechanisation planning for corn, and all other products, has become critical. Recognition of this factor caused in 1959 *Farm Mechanization Management* to replace *Farm Mechanization: Costs and Methods* as the standard text-book on the subject[1].

As the era of integrated mechanisation (that is with each food considered as a single process and machinery dove-tailed throughout each stage of its production) and also of automation evolve into the late-1960s, so must farm management techniques be transformed. Few farmers are at present trained to plan mechanisation on factory methods. Even fewer can grasp the implications of computer planning and critical path analysis. Modern planning techniques are becoming essential as the co-ordination of capital, land, manpower and machinery becomes more complex. An age is coming when a farm

K*

system will be determined, to gain the maximum benefit in relation to a team of men and machines as a single investment, and then a block of land to suit this team will be selected. In the past, and even today, the converse is true. A block of land is acquired (selected is too precise a term) then a farming system is chosen to suit that land. Almost inevitably this leads to less efficient men-machine teams being used.

REFERENCE

1 Culpin, C., *Farm Mechanization Management*. 1959, Crosby Lockwood

7 MODERN MARKETING

Introduction

Barter, as a means of trading, is primitive and inefficient. The introduction of coinage proved equally important for the growth of civilised societies as the cultivation of crops and the breeding of livestock. The development of marketing techniques of monetary policies marked the rise of civilisations as surely as armed conquest and centralised government. Just as agriculture is now being transformed by radical changes in the methods of farming, marketing is equally undergoing a revolution as intense as at any period in its history. The pressures making it essential to farm on factory lines are being generated both from within and without the agricultural industry. The individual farmer has to streamline his management and husbandry, introducing intensive production methods, to compete with his neighbour and counteract the rising cost for labour and raw materials. No matter how industrious and efficient the individual farmer becomes, he has to sell the food he produces to suit current market requirements and the social climate of the day. Marketing methods are also becoming streamlined; the farmer has therefore less scope for manoeuvre in selling his produce as trading techniques become integrated with production and distribution. Changes in marketing organisation are fundamentally significant when considering the future of rural planning, since they affect all farm operations and methods.

Agricultural markets for the sale of stock of produce to merchants developed over the centuries from the medieval fairs. By the eighteenth century country market towns were a feature of social life throughout Britain, each indigenous in character with the agricultural pattern and architectural style of the district around it. Today the traditional market town atmosphere is coveted by commuters, dwelling away from their industrial workplaces, and tourists. Many of the smaller markets no longer exist, even though the towns which housed them at the turn of the century still retain a social structure based on agricultural trade. Some markets still having weekly meetings, are relatively small and local in character. But several of the larger markets have been rebuilt during the last few years, often on important central sites in towns now largely industrial in character. Market day has still a strong aura of custom and tradition for a large part of the population. It has woven around it a pattern for business transactions, technical discussion and social intercourse far removed from the actual trading of stock and crops. Yet marketing by auction, time-honoured though it is, may have ceased to exist by the end of the century.

The growth of vertical integration is the crux of all the many changes facing farmers. It should be the basis of any discussion concerning either the future of agriculture or planning. The system of linking production, processing and distribution from manufacturer to customer is a feature of the second half of this century throughout much of industry. It is a change in the organisation of society of profound importance, the ramifications and outcome of which is only dimly understood. Vertical integration in the food industry is becoming evident, though its true nature has only to a limited extent affected farmers.

Nevertheless within a few decades integration of food production, which can be a two way process, will have changed the structure of agriculture as it has been known for centuries. The basic problem concerning farmers at the present time is whether they can remain their own masters against the pressures of big business. Food to the customer costs approximately three times the price paid to the farmer. In the trend to an integrated food industry, production is not the dominant financial consideration. Processing and distribution are concentrated in large business organisations to a much greater extent than production. Farming retains to a considerable degree its medieval fragmented structure. In such circumstances farmers are weak competitors in the battle to control their industry. The chance that urban industries will control, if not own, much farmland within another generation is a real threat to present day farmers.

Farmers may organise themselves to counteract these external pressures over their control of production. The traditional system by which farmers have grown produce on speculation, taking it to auction markets in the hope of gaining a good price. is inefficient and archaic. Traditional marketing makes production a gamble and makes it unlikely that farmers will concentrate their resources into well planned and intensive systems which, though efficient, tend to require more capital than extensive and mixed farming policies. Modern retailing cannot survive sudden fluctuations in quantity or quality in the food displayed for sale. It requires a constant flow of standard and planned foods to suit a predicted market outlet. To this end precision is essential in production methods and, to get precision, farmers have to control as many of their raw materials and environmental factors as possible.

This means two things. Production must be controlled and farm resources must be directed at all stages to yield a product of a predetermined specification. Timing is essential and random selling, causing delays between farmers and processor or packer, cannot be tolerated. Stock and produce suffer setbacks to quality each time they pass through an auction market. To gain full control in the flow of produce to the customer there has to be a guaranteed throughput at each stage and, to enforce this throughput of food, contracts may be formed between retailer, processor and producer. Thus contracts rather than auction marketing is the logical outcome of vertical integration, farmers planning production to suit a known market outlet.

Contracts for meat and produce, controlling all stages in food production, is the outcome of the phenomenal growth in the supermarket and self-service trade of recent years. The nature of the contracts, that is whether individual farmers contract to a retailer or whether groups of farmers are in contract to a co-operative, which in turn may be in contract to a retailer, may prove in the end to be of only academic and relative interest. In either case, the effect may be the same. Intensive and large scale specialist units, grouped efficiently for transporting produce to the processor, will predominate. This will in turn change the appearance of the landscape from a small-scale mixed agricultural character into the factory farms now becoming evident. The management of food production will pass from the whim of individual farmers to marketing policies laid down by those at least one stage removed from the land itself. At the same time the historic character of market towns and market day social customs will disappear and a more regional pattern of agricultural administration will take its place. In future marketing managers will be the pipers calling the tune for farmers to obey.

7b Vertical integration

Farmers, who have been their own masters for centuries, are concerned that the control of agriculture may soon pass out of their hands. An era of vertical integration threatens their time honoured status; agriculture could by 1980 have new masters.

Sir Frederick Brundrett, Chairman of the Agricultural Co-operative Association, speaking at the end of 1962 gave farmers the following warning[1]:

> The rapid growth of vertical integration and contracts may bring farming enterprises under control of external financial and business interests, and farmer-owned organisations may be taken over by outside groups.

At the same time, the *Farmers Weekly* in a leader was pinpointing the inherent weakness of modern agriculture[2]: 'Marketing is the biggest issue facing farmers . . . our production techniques are the best in the world, but our marketing is haphazard and chaotic . . .' and warned against 'the appearance of the commercial fieldsman, the contract system, the integrated food industry.'

Vertical integration and contract farming are twin changes which will revolutionise the structure of farming, the appearance of the landscape and, by their influence in retailing, the nature of society itself. Few are aware of the social implications, in all their ramifications, now coming about within the food industry. Vertical integration concentrates the control of production, processing, distribution and selling under one management. It can extend from the farmer to the consumer. Sometimes, in contrast, the various stages in the farming and marketing complex do not become specialised branches within one company. Individual businesses may retain their technical independence, but enter into contracts with other organisations within the chain of stages which form the food industry, cumulating in the sale of food for consumption. In effect, since the contracts may be rigid, there may be little real differentiation between vertical integration and contract farming, except, perhaps, one of vanity in a nominal independence. The benefits of integration at these levels are gained only when the units handled are large. There is thus for those drawn into the vortex of a rationalised food industry, a tendency for farmers to have to specialise and concentrate their efforts within large enterprises. As a corollary, when units are small farmers may enter into a horizontal integration with each other to attain a level of production attractive to their marketing masters. Similarly, to retain complete independence, a process of horizontal integration may make a group of farmers financially so powerful that they can seek their own markets without being committed to a production contract. Contract farming within a process of horizontal integration is considered later (p322).

Vertical integration made its mark in the growth of the broiler industry, particularly from the early 1950s in the United States and about a decade later in the United Kingdom. Today in both countries broiler production is almost completely integrated from hatching the egg to the wrapped bird in the supermarket, by contract if not always by common ownership. The process of forming specialised and integrated food industries has expanded from broilers to eggs, bacon and pork, and, to a limited extent, beef, as well as some horticultural and vegetable produce. In America, 'vertical integration is being accelerated by today's improvement of technology and the industrialisation that brought vast consumer demand'[3]. The situation had developed in Britain to such an extent by the summer of 1965 that the *Farmers Weekly* considered that[4]:

The struggle for control of farm trading beyond the farm gate looks

310

like becoming a race between the co-operatives and vertical integration interests. At stake are hundreds of million pounds of our business. How much of it can be kept under our own control, not to mention how much might be saved for our own pockets, depends upon who wins. We still have the chance to decide who does. This is a matter of concern to every farmer: the outcome may well determine the future trading pattern for much of our produce. The danger is that too many of us will stand idly by, each on his own little rock, ignoring the tide of change that may engulf us before we realise what is happening.

The leaders of the farming industry are more than aware of the problems facing them. Early in 1965 a special study group in the National Farmers Union reported on the implications of vertical integration for farmers. The National Farmers Union recognises that the wind of change in the food industry cannot be reversed and that farmers must take a positive and constructive attitude to the new techniques:

> The growth of large-scale operations in the retail trade and the development of the supermarket will continue to lead to demands for larger and larger orders for good quality produce and it is inevitable that these organisations will insist upon contractual arrangements. We do not believe, even if it were possible, that anything should be done to halt this process. We feel, in fact, that the industry must take a positive attitude and find ways and means of adopting modern techniques to its advantage and should not try to prevent such developments occurring.

From the farmers' viewpoint, not only is there the threat of marketing interests moving in to control farming, but also of the development of 'concrete farming' for intensive livestock units, requiring no land other than for access around their buildings. This threatens to create a new type of agribusinessman without a real stake in rural farming. The National Farmers Union report recognises that large scale intensive production 'requires little agricultural land and much capital rather than vice versa', a factor lending itself to non-agricultural investment. Already in egg production more than half the groups are under non-farmer control. The term 'agribusiness' was coined in America to describe the close relationship between agriculture and its suppliers, together with those interests which process and distribute its products[5]. Similarly Davis and Goldberg estimated that between a third and a half of the whole United States investment is now in agribusiness. The scale of such investment is vast and as its organisation integrates into fewer units its effective power in the national economy is without equal. No similar calculation has been made for the proportion of national wealth invested in British agribusiness. The proportion is probably lower than in America, but it is unlikely to be less than a quarter and might well be over a third of the national investment.

The tendency is for agriculture to be integrated within the food industry complex. There is a tendency for non-farmers to operate certain intensive food production units. The authority of farmers to decide their farming policies diminishes as the centre of power shifts to the industrial financier and away from themselves. In terms of profit, unless run on high-powered factory principles, farming itself may be the least important part of the food industry complex. As it becomes essential, in order to make profits realistic for an industrialist, to integrate production and marketing, so does the need to preplan all stages within one common aim. Selling is only a part of the planning operation, which must include a central policy for the 'what, when and where' of production. This is necessary in order to keep the retailers supplied with produce in the standard quality and quantity essential for the mass-selling lines in the supermarkets and other high-powered stores. It is only a small step for the industrialist to control the 'who and how' of production, that is the other two critical factors examined by business specialists at the outset of an enquiry to streamline industrial processes. It is easy to forsee a time when the farmer himself is but a small voice in the agribusiness complex. It is no wonder that the National Farmers Union is concerned. Sykes suggested that in Britain only about a quarter of the agribusiness value may be a net farm product, the remainder being an off-farm product[6]. There is a third, and for British farmers perhaps more sinister, tendency within the vertical integration movement. In modern industry, matters of finance rather than of nations form the boundaries for expansion. International agribusiness has begun to rear its head. It is not too far-fetched to forsee that a substantial part of British agriculture could have its control governed by international business. Geoffrey Sykes, the pioneer in interpreting the agribusiness potential for Britain, has forecast that the day will come when fifty companies will control fifty per cent of the breeding and fattening of livestock in Europe. With poultry the process has begun. Honegger Farms Ltd, for example, with egg hatcheries in thirty-eight countries, began to operate in Britain in recent years. British Beef Ltd, which started a beeflot in Suffolk in 1964, is a subsidiary of an American based international company (p70). The grocery trading group, VG Ltd, operates in eleven European countries (p328). The Ford Motor Company is of course international in its agricultural machinery operations. The American firm, Armour & Co, which is a giant international meat trader, has fifty depots in the U.K. to which many farmers are under contract. Big international business in food processing has been established for many years. Numerous packaged foods are household names almost all over the world. Internationally operated food producers are yet in their infancy. But it is probable

312

Glentworth, Gainsborough, Lincs 1962. A converted hangar, 230 feet x 126 feet, housing 65,000 hybrid layers in batteries twenty-six stacks of cages, part of Frank Arden's farming empire. Two views of the battery cages showing access between cages and the ends of cages with automatic belt-cleaning from cages.

1

1 Pre-war lunch break, September 1939. A pastoral scene typical of a former age in contrast to modern farming where men mainly work alone and travel by car to their homes for the mid-day break. Modern farming has little companionship.

2 Swaythorpe, Driffield, Yorkshire 1966. Three four-furrow ploughs, followed by discs, harrow, drill, harrow, cover up to twenty-four acres a day planting winter wheat after a clover lay. Much modern farmwork is by solitary workers, but 'crash' fieldwork depends on team operations with a battery of equipment pointless without large fields.

1

2

1 Southburn Estates, Yorkshire 1962. Feed is mechanically conveyed from a provender mill at left to pig pens in each of the three houses. Feeding and cleaning is a push-button job.

2 German fifty foot wide 'air-blast' drill used for precision sowing and fertiliser broadcasting. Large-scale arable equipment suitable for giant fields now being formed are a feature of all types of fieldwork, changing the pattern of the landscape.

3, 4 W. and J. B. Eastwood Ltd's poultry unit Attleborough, Norfolk 1965. This £1½m Norfolk factory produces 127,000 birds a week in twelve sites, each with six sheds on 1,300 acres, 1,000 acres of which grow barley. Each shed, 253 feet x 60 feet, holds 22,000 birds based on a twelve week cycle of production. There are four breeding sites, each holding 24,000 hens, and another holding 24,000 chick replacements for breeding. The processing factory is near the group of sites.

317

1

1 Manchester abattoir showing road-rail network, control office in foreground, circular meat market and chill room, by-products area and lairage beyond. A well organised layout, but should be nearer production areas.

2 Hereford market 1958. In traditional farming animals, especially cattle, travel from far to farm via auction markets during various stages of their lives. A great many man-hours are taken by this process and the stock suffer stress setbacks.

3 Livestock transporter 1964 Cor wall and Devon Pig Producers. P preference, animals should not b

2

3

erded or transported. If they
ave to travel an air-conditioned
ransporter as used by this pig
roducing group is desirable to
aintain an equable environment
imilar to that the pigs have
nown in their specialised houses.
n the photograph the lift is
aising a batch of pigs to the
econd of three floors.

1

2

1 Covent Garden Market. For decades Covent Garden has been chaotic, a prime example of an inefficient layout in the wrong situation for modern requirements. Proposals to rebuild the market at Nine Elms raises the question whether in view of the growth of contract farming this kind of market will be required twenty years hence.

2 Control panel of Home Grown Fruits Ltd, Canterbury. Modern marketing can be based on a central office in close contact with packing stations for produce and markets or retail outlets throughout the country. A network of information regulating supply with demand is essential for modern food production.

that over the next two decades, as vertical integration becomes manifest in Britain and many other countries, there will be a substantial growth in international control of food production itself. A farmer in Devon or in Lincolnshire may have his grassland or arable policy decided in a committee room thousands of miles away.

The threat of international integration has become so alarming that the Sheep Development Association recognised, in the spring of 1965, that large commercial concerns might soon take over the sheep breeding industry, which, in turn, was threatened by a bid for control by American interests[7]. In industry even the symbol which heralds each spring, the new-born lamb, is not sacred, being threatened by integration into an international chain of business. It is not surprising that concern is being expressed by farmers that full management of food production may soon pass from them. It is ironic that the one chance for independence farmers possess may well prove their undoing. A fragmented industry, with each farmer attempting to plan and market his produce independently of his peers, cannot hope to influence the bargaining power of the merchants, the wholesalers, the processors or the supermarkets. Similarly the small farmer cannot compete on equal terms with the big operator to gain the best marketing terms. Group farming in itself becomes attractive for the take-over bid.

In the spring of 1964, the *Farmers Weekly* commented on the need for farmers to organise their marketing powers[8]:

> The only practical step producers themselves can take is to join production and marketing groups, greatly strengthened and reorganised so that they are big enough and efficient enough to meet the competition of the large operator.

In grain production, for example, 200,000 sellers sold, via merchants, to a dozen compounders and millers. The compounders and millers are in a strong bargaining position. During the last few years, the legacy of thousands of independent town merchants has been disappearing by amalgamation into powerful trading groups. McDougall reported later in 1964 that[9]:

> Merchanting is in the throes of an even bigger revolution than farming itself, and the movement to bigger businesses has made sweeping changes which have yet to show their true colours when rationalisation and integration are completed by their new owners . . . The prize is the £500m business done by merchants. But no one hides the real reason for the recent purchases. It is to give more certain control over the marketing of home grown grain . . .

It has been predicted that the big companies in grain merchanting, which only had a fiftieth of the trade in 1961, but which had captured

321

a fifth stake by 1964, will control almost a third by 1969. The co-operative has been expanding, but more slowly, perhaps to control a quarter of the total market in 1969. The independent merchants, who owned four-fifths of the trade in 1961, will have no more than round a two fifths stake eight years later. Farmers have to sell their produce to powerful trading groups. They can only compete if they co-operate among themselves to present a united front.

The National Farmers Union report in 1965 on vertical integration summed up their position:

> The real solution to our problems, and the one which will obtain the maximum benefits for the producer, lies in integration—but integration under the control of the producer . . . He must become part of a larger producers' organisation which, on a co-operative basis, will be able to obtain for him the benefits of large-scale preplanned buying of his feed and requisites. A co-operative organisation, of which he will be a member, must also be responsible for marketing his produce and that of other members, so that the industry can sell to the large buyer from a position of strength. To do this will mean the individual farmer will have to accept control and discipline, both on the buying and selling side . . . the pattern we forsee is one built on a much wider farmer-to-farmer system of marketing, eliminating unnecessary costs during the production process. We forsee a contract system developing at each stage and, finally, between the producer group or co-operative and the wholesaler or processor. Production and marketing in this way must be the most economic method, and it is the only way in which we can hope to compete with large-scale intensive producers who have all the separate operations under their own control.

This is essentially a plea for horizontal integration in farming. Just as the merchants have recently been integrated horizontally, so does it become necessary for farmers to co-ordinate their policies and marketing. It has been suggested that farmer-owned organisations should aim to control at least a third of their total market outlets to counteract the threat of vertical integration[10]. The threat comes from a dozen firms actively integrating vertically through agriculture in recent years, with perhaps as many again prepared to operate in the same manner. Not only are farmers worried at losing their independence but, if dominated by the supermarket trade, it is possible that their produce would be used as a 'loss leader' in the stores, that is priced low to attract custom to more important counters. In such circumstances farmers might also be paid a low price. However as farmers form efficient groups to give themselves a good bargaining position, so do they become desirable for absorption into bigger industrial complexes. As quoted at the beginning of this section, the head of ACA is aware of the danger. Other industries have found that it is natural and unavoidable that both declining and expanding

322

businesses can be absorbed by larger and more powerful concerns. Since farmers must attract more capital into agriculture from outside the industry, with company farming in trading groups beginning to be essential, so does the threat of the take-over become real. It is probable that long before the century has passed, the effective ownership of farming and the centre for policy formation in food production will have shifted from its traditional position amongst farmers on their own farms.

REFERENCES

1 Report. *Farmers Weekly*, 2 November 1962
2 Leader. *Farmers Weekly*. 24 November 1962
3 *Contract farming and vertical integration in agriculture*. US Department of Agriculture Bulletin no 198
4 Leader. *Farmers Weekly*. 23 July 1965
5 Davis, J. and Goldberg, R., *A concept of agribusiness*. 1957, Harvard Business School
6 Sykes, G., *Poultry: a modern agribusiness*, p20. 1963, Crosby Lockwood
7 Report. *Farmers Weekly*, p45. 2 April 1965
8 Leader. *Farmers Weekly*, 10 April 1964
9 McDougall, A. 'Merchants merge.' *Farmers Weekly*, p69. 2 October 1964
10 Morley, J. A.C.A., Chief Executive Officer, Notts Farm Institute. Marketing Conference, February 1965

7c Marketing meat

Marketing, the fulcrum by which farmers seek better returns from the housewife, is in a state of flux. Like agriculture the structure of marketing is basically mediaeval. Both are severely strained by the recent introduction of modern, streamlined business techniques. Both have a traditional and powerful core which is fighting a rear-guard action against loss of independence. The crux of the present situation is to decide whether marketing is necessary. Marketing, even if its traditional methods are made more efficient, by its nature is wasteful of time and resources. Nevertheless its supporters are unwilling to lose their apparent independence, which marketing permits. In recent years many livestock markets have been rebuilt and others are planned. In contrast, contract farming, possibly within a system of vertical integration, can make marketing almost completely unnecessary.

In the introduction to the 1965 *Price Review*, it was stated that the 'Government believe there is an urgent need to improve the marketing of home grown produce'. As stated in the last section, the *Farmers Weekly* has expressed the opinion for several years that 'marketing is the biggest issue facing farmers'. John Winter, acting for the British Farm Produce Council, stated that[1]:

Farm produce is a marketing expert's nightmare. Its inherent characteristics of natural variation, perishability and seasonality present problems of supply, preservation and promotion which are unknown in the marketing of most manufactured products . . . The problem facing the promotors of any agricultural marketing operation is how close can they get to an ideal, which, in the very nature of things, is unattainable. Add to this inherent obstacle the excessively fragmented structure of the production side of the industry. Many hundreds of producers may share in the supply of one item of food for the town . . . In an era of slick and sophisticated selling techniques, it is useless for farmers to imagine they can get adequate returns for their products by old-fashioned methods.

By tradition farmers grow food according to their own judgement and then attempt to sell it by auction. In most cases the commodity is bought by wholesalers who, in turn, sell it to processors and retailers. In each stage elements of luck are as important as those of judgement. Market conditions can fluctuate so swiftly, and for unpredictable reasons, that the purpose and method of production may be invalidated after its inception and for no real fault of the farmer. The process is a gamble. Even if the farmer achieves a good quality product, he has no idea what his return will be until after an auction. This makes it difficult, in fact impossible, to know how much may be invested to produce the food. In such circumstances, the farmer tends not to commit himself to the hilt in streamlined production methods, normally requiring high levels of investment, but to perpetuate less efficient techniques.

Livestock markets are part of the social fabric of Britain. Buying fatstock on the hoof is a ritual deeply ingrained in the farming consciousness. Judging live animals by visual inspection at the market for fattening or for their value as joints for the housewife is a skilled, but inexact, art. Farmers continue to take their stock to market in the hope that their sales will prove high. Moreover market day is not only for selling stock, but is also a time for other business, discussion and barter. Market day has been the foundation stone of all country market towns, acting as a magnet for general trade in an agricultural region. Around it has arisen a tradition of custom and folklore. But the herding of animals into trucks, the penning of animals into livestock markets, and the general driving, chivying and prodding of stock, with their transportation sometimes over long distances, is the antithesis of modern livestock production. The science of genetic selection and the conversion of coarse foods into flesh is becoming precise and predictable. For efficient production sudden fluctuations in climate, feeding, and environment, with sudden emotional stresses, are to be avoided. Traditional markets create these conditions. The movement of stock through this ritual of marketing tends to create conditions of hardship and deprivation for the animals and sometimes physical cruelty. Certainly the confusions and disturbances of market day causes obvious distress. Though modern legislation, particularly in requiring livestock to be under cover in their market pens, has done much to mitigate some of these stresses, the principle of livestock marketing is wrong in business terms. The setback to the animals caused by these disturbances, since there can be several days delay before slaughtering after leaving the farm, may reduce weight and upset the flesh structure for grading.

Stress factors in the animals are but one of the inefficiencies caused by livestock marketing. If stock go direct from a farm to a slaughterhouse, not only is one journey sufficient but their despatch at both ends of the journey can be planned to have the minimum delay. This is both kinder and more efficient. Marketing, on the other hand, means as a minimum double instead of single handling on to and off transporters and handling animals is costly. The need to attend an auction is excessively wasteful in time for the farmer and the wholesaler, not to mention the auction staff themselves. Marketing is basically unproductive work. It creates a chain of journeys and middlemen between producer and processor, increasing overall costs. In such circumstances it is not surprising that two trends are apparent today. In the first instance there is growing appreciation that it is better for stock to be auctioned when dead rather than live. This makes it possible to grade the carcasses and for precise pricing to replace speculative judgement. Secondly there is an increasing practice for bypassing the market by farmers entering into contracts with wholesalers or distributors.

In the autumn of 1964, G. T. Williams, now President of the National Farmers Union predicted that Britain's cattle markets would lose more and more of their fatstock trade and that farm production planning and contracting would have a greater effect on markets than any other factor over the last half century[2]. For example in the same autumn West Cumberland Farmers, a large co-operative group, were negotiating a direct farm-to-slaughter scheme for beef and lamb on a considerable scale. During the last few years the Fatstock Marketing Corporation, with their own slaughterhouses and prepacking plant, act as contractors between farmers and supermarkets for an expanding market. Direct trading with retail outlets has attractions other than planned production for the farmer. The producer can attract a share of the wholesaler's costs, can have a closer contact with the customer and can form a stable relationship with the retailer. It is not surprising that a large proportion of stock already by-pass the markets. Poultry is almost never handled in livestock markets. Today the idea seems absurd that poultry should ever have been sold by this method. By 1966 a steady decline in live pig marketing over several years had reached the stage when only a sixth of the total pig population in the United Kingdom passed via these markets[3]. Contract selling, moreover, as opposed to deadweight sales, is increasing for all kinds of pigmeat. Even with beef and sheep about a third of all sales are by deadweight and a small, but growing, part of this stock by-pass the auctions on contract.

In England and Wales, there are 450 auctioneering firms selling livestock, of which about fifteen per cent sell only fatstock[4]. Most of the trade is for youngstock or stores passing from farmer to farmer, though some of these auctioneers, particularly near urban regions, are more interested in estate than stock. There is a wide range of types of firm acting as auctioneers. Though Produce Studies Ltd showed that twenty-eight per cent of the largest firms accounted for forty per cent of total turnover in store stock sales in 1963, there was in fact less concentration of business to the larger markets than expected. Auctions still tend to be local affairs, often owned and managed either by local families or firms, especially estate agents, or sometimes by farmer co-operative societies. So far horizontal integration is almost unknown. The tendency is still for auctions to draw on a radius of fifteen miles, with a declining influence up to about thirty miles. There are, of course, some markets at particular times which have a national, or even international, bias. Youngstock or stores may sometimes be purchased by farmers from distant markets. Breeders from all over the world attend the top sales for stock. In general the trend in marketing livestock in Great Britain is from West to East and from North to South. In 1964, for example, the number of cattle and calves passing through livestock markets was approaching 3m and the value of the total store trade alone represented £130m a year. In such circumstances it is not surprising that livestock auctioneering, principally for cattle and sheep, still seems a flourishing concern. It has been sufficient for numerous large towns, such as Chelmsford, Shrewsbury, Ipswich and Gloucester to invest in recent years in new livestock markets, and others are likely to be built during the next decade, often on costly central sites. Though some of the smaller livestock markets have been closed since the war, the day of the livestock market is not over. Nevertheless the writing is on the wall for their continued existence in the future.

The principle of sending youngstock or stores to market is as wrong, is in fact worse, than selling fatstock by these methods. The stress factors are more critical while the animals are young and unfinished. The store trade, in which it takes several farmers to fatten stock in stages, passing them as each stage via markets, is detrimental to efficient food conversion ratios. Nevertheless the store trade still flourishes. Youngstock, in particular, suffer setbacks at a crucial moment of their short lives by breaks in their routine. There seems little point in applying intensive and expensive methods of stock husbandry if their life cycle is disrupted by passages through the markets. Farmers contracting to sell youngstock for others to

326

fatten can help to overcome the stress of marketing. Many weaners are now reared on such contracts and even eight per cent of calves sold in 1965 were known to pass from rearers to fatteners via farmer organisations and groups, rather than via traditional auctions.

It is probably not rash to predict that livestock auctions will have ceased to exist by the end of the century. It may prove that the existing structure of auctioneering will have collapsed within another ten to fifteen years. Once trade at an auction begins to decline, the process spirals, as has happened in some Welsh markets, so that the market disappears within a short period after the first signs of weakness have appeared. Disease, above all other factors, is sufficient to bring traditional marketing methods into disrepute. It is sensible when such diseases as foot-and-mouth have appeared in the country, that marketing is forbidden by national policy as being too risky. Even less dire diseases can be spread by the contact of animals passing through the markets. As farmers become more disease conscious so will they come to rely on segregationist, or contract, policies for selling stock. As farmers become more expert in nutrition, so will they tend to prevent lengthy disturbances within the life cycle of stock. As genetical and stock performance studies mature, so will sales be by records rather than eye. The many livestock markets, so recently built, could prove to be white elephants by 1980.

The future of livestock production, and therefore of marketing, lies in genetic, environmental and nutritional control, combined with the elimination of disease. The hub of the production processes must be the slaughterhouse, processing and packaging complex. These units must be integral with each other. The animal by-product processing plant should be planned in close association. The overall design becomes a giant factory-abattoir. A modern £3½m unit of this kind was started in 1962 in Manchester[5]. It includes on a twenty acre site, between rail and road services, a production line technique for handling, killing and processing 100 cattle and 650 sheep an hour, plus a small number of pigs, with all modern dead-market facilities and all by-products other than hides being processed. Although wholesalers can buy meat in the efficient dead market provided, in the future the factory might also cut and pack meat ready for the retailer. But, though the Manchester abattoir is one of the most modern in the world, its urban site may not be the pattern for the future.

For decades the structure of the meat trade and slaughtering methods in Britain have been mediaeval. Professor Crossley described the situation in 1962[6]:

> To a large number of farmers rearing animals is added a large number of butchers cutting up carcasses in thousands of shops. In addition, the bones—which comprise about twenty-five per cent of the total weight—are transported about the country and even sold to the

327

customer, who does not want them, merely because they happen to be inside the meat.

During the 1930s, when there were over 1,200 slaughterhouses, there was severe criticism concerning abattoir conditions. Controlled slaughtering in the war reduced the licensed abattoirs to 600, but these increased to 4,500 by the late 1950s. By 1961 there were still 3,326 slaughterhouses, though these will be reduced to about 2,800 when the 1958 legislation on their standards has taken full effect. At present only a little over 150 are publicly owned. Though overall numbers are large, fifty-eight per cent of the 1961 trade was taken by only five per cent of the slaughterhouses, indicating that the large abattoir is important in the organisation of the business. The basis for estimating trade is taken as the 'cattle unit' (one cattle = three calves = five sheep = two pigs) and the annual turnover of all slaughterhouses is 7m cattle units. Poultry have their own units. About a twentieth of the abattoirs handle more than 50,000 cattle units each, averaging almost double this figure. In spite of the size of trade handled in large units, standards of meat control are so low that continental buyers normally require their own ante-mortem inspection to check against diseased animals being slaughtered. The problem of the correct siting for slaughterhouses is as acute as attaining good standards of design and providing livestock control for killing, but has received far less study than these factors.

The siting of future slaughterhouses is crucial both for planning livestock production and also for town and country planning. Generally it has been assumed that abattoirs and meat marketing are urban occupations, especially for factory scale units planned on modern lines. Not only is the Manchester complex an urban factory, but Smithfield, when rebuilt after its fire, was based on the assumption that meat wholesaling should be a central London occupation. The problem of location for these units has received little study. Planning may be considered on a basis of 200 cattle units for every 1,000 head of population. A modern, medium sized and efficient abattoir, handling 100,000 units a year, would serve a population of half-a-million. A large factory, on Manchester lines, might serve a conurbation of a million more people. Size of unit is critical to efficiency and economy. Most existing slaughterhouses are small, being of only 5,000 cattle units a year, with even more established urban abattoirs handling no more than round 50,000 units. Though the size of unit is critical, the handling costs for cattle and carcasses are also critical in planned production. Though these matters are important for good national planning, the Oxford Agricultural Economics Research Institute is one of the few organisations to examine the cost structure. The figures quoted below are based on their analysis.

Transport costs for live animals rise at present as the size of abattoir is increased, since the radius from which stock must be brought also increases. Though the individual cost of transport drops from 4s 4d a mile for every head of cattle for five mile journies to 3s for twenty-five miles, the cost for every cattle unit rises from 18s 4d for transport to slaughterhouses having a 50,000 unit throughput a year to 26s 7d for those with double that capacity. Economies in handling large numbers must offset the increase in transport costs of about 8s for every cattle unit, that is of about forty per cent, as the usual sized urban abattoir becomes a super factory on modern lines. Two factors could help to reduce this pattern of increased transport costs as abattoir units become larger. Handling could become more efficient, with larger transporters working to better routines. Secondly, as Berg suggested, slaughterhouses should be strategically sited in the main producing parts of the country, where livestock has the minimum distance to travel from farm to abattoir[7]. This must be the basis for the future. A rural abattoir factory, with maximum size for economy in operation, should be sited close to a rail and road network. The size would be at least 300,000 cattle units a year capacity, serving a conurbation of $1\frac{1}{2}$m people. Alternatively, the factory would serve five medium sized cities or population regions, each of between a quarter and half a million people. Each factory would be complete with a prepack unit and processing plant for the by-products. Within a radius of ten to fifteen miles round the factory would be the intensive fattening units or feedlots for cattle, sheep and pigs. In turn round the fattening units would be smaller centres for breeding the stock for them. Raw foods for the stock might be grown on the intervening land round the breeding centres and feed-lots. Alternatively some of it might well be grown elsewhere in more suitable parts of the country, being handled in bulk from the grass or grain producing areas.

The factory abattoir would be at the centre of a chain of contracts between producer and retailer. Its centre would tend to be as close as possible to the producer, though distribution to its retail outlets should not exceed twenty to twenty-five miles. At present the average cost of transport for each beef carcass can be as much as about 21s 3d a twenty mile journey. Bulk handling prepacked joints, excluding bone, would substantially reduce this excessively high cost in bringing meat to the consumer. It is clear that planning beef production must take account of the transport cost from fattening unit to abattoir and from abattoir to retailer. It is equally clear that whole-saling either live or dead stock can have no place in a streamlined system of contract meat production, which is essential for feeding the expanding population cheaply and efficiently, using as little land as possible. Wholesalers would become organisation men, arranging and managing the contracts. The factory units, sited centrally to several city regions in an agricultural belt, would attract a nucleus

329

of subsidiary industries thriving on the by-products from the abattoir. Thus it could be that the small market town, as it exists today, deprived of its market for status and trade, might become the centre of this industrial complex, provided it was central to a population of 1½m people and provided it had a good rail and road network to serve that population.

The problem of the meat industry, to satisfy the needs of the population from a restricted national land area, is intense. Its present structure, though being reformed to some extent by the new Marketing Board, is not designed to streamline production and processing in the manner essential for future needs. The matter is critical for good rural planning and the national economy. It is however a problem which needs intensive research before an adequate policy could be formed.

REFERENCES

1 Winter, J., *Agriculture's Role in Produce Marketing*. 1965, British Farm Produce Council
2 National Association of British Market Authorities Conference, Morecambe, 1964
3 Hicks, N. 'What price contracts?' *Farmers Weekly*, p67. 11 February 1965
4 *The Marketing of store stock in England and Wales*, vol 1, p19. 1965, Produce Studies Ltd
5 'An abattoir with a big future.' *Farmers Weekly*, p54. 16 March 1962
6 Crossley, E. L. Association of Agriculture lecture. March 1962
7 Berg, M. 'The role of the wholesaler in the meat industry.' Oxford Farming Conference, 1965

7d Marketing produce

Some years ago, American agricultural experts recognised that: 'Frequently in integration the wholesaler and the large central market are entirely by-passed. The product goes straight from the processor/packer to the retail chains'[1]. Contract farming, not only for meat but for all produce, is becoming accepted in Britain. As long ago as 1956, for example, Marks and Spencer Ltd, decided no longer to buy in the markets since the quality, condition and price of produce for sale varied too much for their streamlined, high quality food counters. Instead they adopted a system of trading direct with selected growers, guaranteeing in advance a fixed price for produce conforming to a set standard. The quantity of produce handled by Marks and Spencer, which in 1963–64 alone increased by £10m to a total of £45m, represents an important retail outlet. Other big stores, equally, like to have a guaranteed supply of good produce on contract. But, the supermarkets and stores are not alone in wishing to avoid traditional wholesale market techniques. Some producers, too, recognise the value of a contracted outlet for their produce. Bedfordshire Growers Ltd, indicative of the changing outlet on marketing, was inaugurated in 1963 as a producer marketing group for fruit and vegetables, aiming to attain direct contracts with the main retail chains, thus by-passing Covent Garden, and hoping to have a turnover of £1m within their first decade. Other producer groups, too, have sought contracts for their produce in recent years, helped to some extent by government grants intended to encourage cooperative marketing.

In spite of a trend towards contract farming, it is believed that at present only about five per cent of produce is taken by direct sales. Many farmers and groups are wary of being fully committed to one or other giant retail outlet, since they fear becoming vulnerable to unfavourable economic pressures which such chains could generate. This has created a climate which seems to support the existing structure of wholesale markets, even though these may come to serve producer groups and retail chains rather than primarily large numbers of individual farmers and grocers as in the recent past. The former Horticultural Marketing Council, though recognising that distribution systems for produce had become more complex and that quantities of produce handled had increased substantially, still believed that large wholesale markets would be the pattern for the future[2]. Considerable expenditure of time and money is continuing to perpetuate new markets in important city centre layouts.

By 1963 only Coventry in 1955 and Sheffield six years later had built new wholesale markets in post-war Britain. The improved facilities in Coventry had made its market popular throughout the Midlands, winning trade from older markets such as Leicester, twenty-four miles away. Pressure throughout Britain for improved markets has grown in the last few years. Leicester itself published plans in 1963 for a remodelled central market, including an imaginative pedestrian piazza, based on the conception that small traders would continue to compete with the chain store complexes. Wholesale markets developed as local affairs, based on horse traffic, close to town centres. Nearly all of them have become congested, with antiquated handling methods, creating traffic bottlenecks and increased costs for producer and customer. No market has generated worse conditions than Covent Garden, transformed by the railway age from a local to a national market. Its inefficiencies are believed to cost £3m a year. Its trade is still expanding, increasing in volume by ten per cent between 1960 and 1965, when it handled over $1\frac{1}{4}$m tons of produce worth more than £75m, half of which were imported foods. Plans are well advanced to build a new market at Nine Elms, south of the Thames and close to a rail and future road network, but also suitable for river transport.

The assumption that large central wholesale markets have a future after the next decade is dangerous. The structure of modern farming and marketing suggests that unplanned food production can have little relevance for future generations and, in particular, the gamble of transacting food sales and purchases via individual stalls is inefficient and the antithesis of intensive agricultural practice and supermarket prepacked food display. Even if wholesale markets should prove relevant by 1980, their form is likely to be considerably different from that of today, even when made efficient with modern handling techniques. Handling perishable foods is, indeed, a difficult problem; and central to this problem is the need for organised, high-speed market intelligence. Even if contract farming did not become prevalent, the need for efficient market intelligence methods alone will change the scope of traditional wholesale markets. Market intelligence is a two-fold problem. In the first instance it is a matter of controlled pricing of produce based on proper trade bulletins. But secondly, and more important, it is a method for integrating production and marketing.

Markets have to clear their produce quickly. Prices fluctuate rapidly throughout each day, reflecting not only changes in quantity and quality but also in supply and demand. But market prices today are not a local or even a regional problem, rather they are a national matter with international ramifications. In America market intelligence is well organised. The Federal Market News Service collects and broadcasts information at producer and wholesaler levels on a national basis twice a day, infilling with local information. This creates, in effect, a radio public auction at a national level, since prices react quickly to the information given all over the country. In Britain, markets are based on less speedy information services, though the example of Home Grown Fruits Ltd, based on Canterbury, has important implications for the future. Early each day, reports from seventy wholesalers throughout the country confirm details of trade the previous day. By the afternoon reports from twenty-one packing stations in the group give information about quantities of produce ready for despatch. Plans are thus issued by the evening allocating from the packing stations produce in over 400 grades to be despatched to markets where the demand seems high[3]. A network of information, regulating supply with demand, is essential for efficient production and marketing. It is not difficult to envisage a closer link in the organisation of food supplies from farm to customer.

A conference on marketing in 1966 stressed the importance of integrating production and distribution[4]. As then emphasised, 'marketing is a planning operation, of which selling is only a part and the two should never be regarded as inter-changeable terms'. The basis of sound marketing, its first stage, is a decision of what, when and where to produce. This decision has been taken 'for too long by

332

too many farmers in isolation from the decisions about what, when and where to sell'. Closely connected with such issues may also be a decision as to who should produce and how a crop should be grown. Obviously if production and marketing is to be integrated to this degree it cannot be a seasonal matter. Long term plans are needed and, by implication, a system for co-ownership or for contracts is essential. The logical development of a close-knit organisation between producer and retail outlet suggests the elimination of traditional sales in wholesale markets.

The present trend seems to be for producer groups to work through selected panels of wholesalers. The latter organise the disposal of produce direct to selected retailers, acting as agents, and such produce never passes through the market premises. The rest of the produce, usually the inferior grades, is sold in a normal manner. Producers employ the wholesalers as agents and market intelligence exports. It seems probable that the percentage of produce sold via stalls will decline as the system of wholesale agencies develops. Similarly, the wholesale agents, knowing the requirements of established outlets, will tend to tighten up the standards from the suppliers. Other producers, not seeking the semi-freedom of these methods, will enter into firm contracts. In either case, a closer link between producer and customer will tend to eliminate the gamble of production for an unspecified market via the hazards of traditional market stalls where prices fluctuate rapidly.

It is true that horticultural markets have a place within the immediate future, perhaps for another decade. Their survival until the end of this century is doubtful. Investments made by many cities for new produce markets close to their centres is likely to prove a series of white elephants. If Covent Garden is rebuilt it may prove to be redundant within a generation. Even if markets did continue to be necessary, their present form is questionable. They might need to be in the form of warehouses, that is temporary transit bases between producer and retailer, with free sales a limited part of their operation. Alternatively, one market complex handling all foods close to, but not necessarily centrally within, the main conurbations might buy better than several specialised markets in different places. Since many supermarkets now decentralise their depots into surburban areas, a ring of smaller wholesale markets close to these suburban depots round the conurbations might be even more suitable than large central units. If these were linked to an efficient radio intelligence network, combined with close links between producer groups and markets, considerably less congestion might result with greater efficiency in getting produce to the shops. Since most produce will have to be prepacked to suit future requirements, the basis of sale from farms via markets will decline. Prepack units need produce of standard quality, size and throughput passing through their factories

333

otherwise, like any industry, machines and manpower are used wastefully.

With the growth of car traffic, growing numbers of producers sell direct to the customer at the farm gate. The wayside stall for fruit, vegetables, cream, eggs and other produce, even oven-ready packed chickens, is a feature of the age. Egg and milk vending machines in the countryside are no novelty. They represent a form of modern sales technique, all of which helps the smaller farmer stay in business. Farm-gate shops, perhaps including refreshments, can be profitable, especially when managed by the farmer's family, since the middlemen are cut out of the sales. Some farmers have extensive delivery rounds for their produce to neighbouring settlements, selling on the doorsteps. Prepacked fruit, vegetables and eggs may often be sold in this manner, even from moderately large farms. It seems probable that localised direct sales will become a permanent part of modern marketing, acting as a relief valve to the high-pressure supermarket methods. Direct contact between urban dweller and farmer satisfies the psycological needs of the former.

Interest in marketing methods is at last being taken by many farmers. The National Farmers Union in 1964 recognised that[5]:

> The industry is faced with a new challenge in finding effective means to meet the growing demand for supplies geared to the requirements of new distributive patterns. It becomes increasingly important that products come forward in a flow which meets consumer requirements as regards volume, phasing, type, quality and presentation.

The National Farmers Union is seeking means to ensure that improved selling methods for produce should remain under farmers' control. Their Marketing Development Department and Agricultural Market Development Executive Committee, the latter making grants to help producers sell their wares, have done much in the last few years to change the former indifference shown by farmers in marketing. With the recent inauguration of Chairs in Marketing at Wye College and Durham University, and the grant in 1966 for a marketing department at Aberystwyth University, concepts for agricultural marketing have attained serious academic recognition as a new science. It is obvious that under the stimulus of big business pressures from the supermarkets, of academic study and farmers' fear for their livelihood, changes in marketing techniques are bound to rise in the next few years. The need for considerable increases in food production from a diminishing land area makes efficiency in production and distribution not only desirable, but critical.

Government direction or control in marketing, as well as in the amounts of food produced, is a difficult political and practical problem. The creation of the Milk Marketing Board in 1933 did

334

much to save agriculture from total collapse after the Depression. The board has done much during its thirty or more years to promote quality and bulk collection in milk supplies as well as ensuring a reasonable level of return for the many producers. At the same time it has been clear of political domination and of enforcing producers to limit their production to a predetermined quota. The early success of MMB led to numerous other boards being created for potatoes, pigs, hops, and so on, many of which have not survived, though others have come into being, or have been reborn, within the last decade. In some cases where commodity prices are protected or subsidised, such as for sugar beet, government quotas restrict levels of production and penalise producers who over-produce. In addition there are times when small farmers, in particular, cry out that quotas should be enforced for other produce to protect themselves from the success of intensive factory farming. Extending governmental powers in farming is anathema to almost all producers, even though they seek financial aid and protection from the nation. Marketing boards stir up fanatical opposition or support from all sides of the industry concerning their future. The implications of entry into the Common Market on British marketing techniques and national marketing boards are far from clear.

It is impossible in this study to discuss the political problems of future marketing or the national structure of marketing boards, still less any national policy for controlling levels of production. It is clear that produce marketing, as well as meat, is in a period of revolution. It seems probable that big business processing and distribution techniques cannot be efficient with a haphazard, free-for-all marketing arrangement between farmer and wholesaler, as has existed for centuries. It seems likely that marketing will become a co-operative operation, partly on contract and partly on a semi-contract basis, with only a small sector of produce available in a free-selling market, and with especially in holiday areas, some produce being sold direct to the public at the farm gate. As food production becomes critical to the nation's welfare, in a more serious relationship to the economy than at present, it would seem natural that the Government will need to be involved more directly in the organisation of the production, marketing, and distribution of food. It may be that this will remain a delicately balanced matter of financial support which, by influence, promotes or retards production. However, it seems good land-use will become so crucial to national survival, with the correct deployment of industrial resources, that the need for the nation to direct, though not necessarily control, food production and marketing will be clear long before the end of the century. Even should this not be, traditional freedoms in growing and selling food on the whim of individuals will pass away under the pressure of efficient, big business in the food industry.

REFERENCES

1 'Contract farming and vertical integration in agriculture.' us *Department of Agriculture Bulletin no* 198
2 Chambers, J. H., *Wholesale markets for horticultural produce in cities and towns*. 1963, Horticultural Marketing Council
3 Fraser, D. 'Computer Marketing.' *British Farmer*, 2 November 1963
4 *Towards better marketing*. Conference, Nottingham Farm Institute, 1966
5 *British agriculture looks ahead*. 1964, National Farmers Union

7e Supermarkets and retail food patterns

It is the housewives, who to some extent, control the future development of farming and therefore of the landscape. In recent years their individual and collective spending powers have increased. New techniques in the processing and packaging of food have made it possible to market more prepacked and standardised products than ever before. Shopping by accredited label rather than visual judgement suits modern society. Speed in shopping permits more women being able to go out to work or alternatively more leisure. The growth of supermarkets and self-service stores, which depend largely on prepacked foods, has been a phenomenon of the last decade. This growth has been termed a 'revolution in the high street' but is far from complete. It has already helped to change social habits and act as a pressure point on the structure of agriculture, helping to create conditions favourable for contract farming and vertical integration.

The supermarket industry started in the United States during the depression of the early 1930s. Today America has one supermarket for every 1,356 households[1]. When the first supermarket in Britain opened in 1953 most people considered that this method of shopping would be alien to the British housewife. During the next few years supermarkets were slow to gain ground and by 1960 there were only 300 retail outlets of this kind. During the next six years, expansion was rapid and an average of about one new supermarket opening every working day to give an overall total of 2,600 by mid-1967. The proportion of supermarkets to households is now nearly a quarter of that prevailing in America. If growth followed the American pattern, saturation point in Britain would be between 10,000 and 12,000 supermarkets. The Supermarket Association predicts that due to psychological and geographic reasons, the ceiling in expansion may prove to be 7,000 in number, equal to one for every 10,000 head of population, with the halfway mark reached by 1971–2[1].

Supermarkets are clearly defined. They must have a sales area of at least 2,000 square feet or a minimum annual turnover of £100,000.

336

They must be principally self-service, carrying a broad range of foods, the value of which must exceed that of any non-foods stocked, such as household goods. On average supermarkets are about double the minimum size, with 4,000 square feet of sales area and a further 2–3,000 square feet of preparation rooms and storage[1]. To justify their usual prestige siting in the main shopping streets and town centres, a large turnover in trade and first-class management are essential. It is possible that future trends will be towards off-centre sites, with lower overheads, provided parking facilities are ample adjacent to the store. Since concentrated shopping in one store is popular, there may be a greater trend towards stocking diversified products other than food. Similarly the pattern of future supermarkets may broaden since some products sell better with an assistant in charge, such as meat, and there is also a demand for refreshments to be provided. Nevertheless in the main prepacked foods of accepted quality, though not necessarily of prime flavour, will be increasingly required.

By 1965 annual supermarket turnover had reached about £400m, that is fourteen per cent of the total grocery trade in Britain, increasing to over twenty per cent in 1967—against eighty per cent in America. Sales of different foods vary within wide extremes, especially since the proportion of non-foods in each supermarket vary between ten and fifty per cent of turnover. On average dairy foods and provisions represent twenty-two per cent of trade, with fresh vegetables and fruit accounting for only seven per cent and frozen foods for a bare three per cent[1]. Meat is, perhaps, the most unpredictable commodity, accounting for between three and twenty-four per cent of turnover in individual supermarkets. Though on average it accounts for as much as eleven per cent of turnover, no more than four per cent of the national meat trade passes through supermarkets. Supermarkets have captured a reasonable share of the dairy and to some extent, of the vegetable market, but have hardly affected the 60,000 butchers. A research survey showed that only 2·3 per cent of housewives in 1965 bought most of their meat prepacked, though another 20·6 per cent bought some in that form[1]. It seems probable there has been a recent break-through into prepacking meat, due to prolonged research by the Fatstock Marketing Corporation, so that joints remain attractive for long periods. This could extend the supermarket control of the meat trade, though it is probable that expansion will not be as rapid as for other produce.

New marketing techniques could make supermarket food sales more efficient. At present they absorb almost two-thirds of sales area, yet yield not much over a third of total profits. The Supermarket Association believes that much can be done by increasing mechanisation and trading efficiency before their aim is attained, which is the mass merchandising of food with the lowest possible distribution costs. However, even the supermarkets can be challenged by the growth in direct-sales. For example, the Ross Group started selling frozen foods in 1967 direct to those households owning deep-freeze cabinets around Southampton. At present, nationally, only less than one per cent of families have a deep freezer, but this is a growth industry which might reach the fifty per cent ownership now prevailing in America.

In the same general trend of prepacked food sales are those of the many self-service stores on the fringe of the supermarket groups, but outside their definition. In addition to the supermarkets, of which only eight per cent are not owned by multiple or co-operative groups, there are 16,000 self-service stores of which almost a third are independent, twice the number four years ago. Supermarkets and self-service stores combined now handle almost half of the total grocery trade. The cumulative effect of this growth has been to reduce the total number of retail outlets and concentrate the management of the rest. Though there were still about 150,000 main outlets for groceries and provisions in 1966, with a somewhat smaller number of other types of food retailer, eighty per cent of the grocery trade passed through no more than 1,600 buying points[1]. In 1950, in contrast, a mere forty-three per cent passed via 2,800 central buyers. Centralised marketing and retailing effects both consumer and farmer, since standardisation of produce is essential.

With growing rapidity, the small, family food shop has been disappearing. Though the change can be noted in all parts of the country, the main growth centres for self-service trade have been in urban and industrial regions, as to be expected, rather than in the market towns and villages. One survey showed, for example, that between 1960 and 1964, though total population increased by 3,500, almost fifty food shops disappeared in Bromley, a market town twelve miles from the centre of London[3]. The remaining small retailers in the country are fighting for survival, often by diversifying their trade. Many food shops today look like the traditional village store, displaying a wide range of products other than food. The sharp definition between trade shops has been blunted.

Though the independent shops still control over half the total retail trade, by 1965 26,000 of these retailers (representing almost a quarter of the small retailers) traded in voluntary groups, attracting some of the discount benefits of collective merchandising. Together they controlled about two-thirds of the total independent's trade, representing a quarter of the national retail grocery business. Combined with the supermarkets and self-service stores, almost two-thirds of the total grocery trade is in group buying systems. There are about seven main voluntary trading groups and VG, one of the largest in Britain has 30,000 grocer members in eleven european countries. VG aims to concentrate its buying into a limited number of selected

338

international brands of food, which will be sold throughout its 30,000 outlets. International trade at this level means that vast bulk orders can be placed with individual food processing firms, perhaps commanding the complete output of factories of considerable size. Collective trading in this manner, though it may help individual grocers to survive in competition with the supermarkets, increases the pressure for standardised foods. This in turn must force standardisation in production methods. Farmers must submit to marketing pressures of this magnitude unless they too group themselves so powerfully that they can impose their own conditions at this level.

Prepacked food is part of the modern revolution in food technology, new processes changing the concept of the future national diet (p210). By 1962 more than 500m prepacks were marketed in Britain through 10,000 self-service stores by farmers, farm co-operatives and wholesalers, whereas no more than eight years previously prepacking was almost unknown. Over a third of eggs and four-fifths of chickens sold are prepacked. By 1961 however a quarter of potatoes were prepacked, but other vegetables varied between only negligible quantities and a twentieth of total sales in this form. In contrast over half of all strawberries and raspberries are prepacked and about a third of other soft fruits. The trend towards prepacked vegetables and horticultural produce continues. In 1964 for example Geest Industries Ltd, opened a streamlined prepacking plant increasing their output of $2\frac{1}{2}$m prepacks a week to 10m, with a distribution system capable of selling Lincolnshire vegetables within a day of harvesting in supermarkets on the other side of the country. Speed of packaging and distribution is essential for perishable produce. Similarly controlled production, yielding a standard quality, is equally important. Geest Ltd, who control over ten per cent of the British fruit and vegetable trade, to a large extent bypass the wholesale markets[5]. The relationship between farmers and markets is discussed elsewhere (p356).

The modern pattern of retailing, working through bulk ordering systems, relies on a regular flow of standard quality food. There is a trend towards having most products as convenience foods (p92). The traditional farming system of selling produce at irregular times and of irregular quality is anathema to modern retailing. Should the traditional farming market fail to supply the right produce at the right time, it is possible that the big retail outlets might acquire a stake in farming to control the method of production. In 1963 Sykes believed that this was improbable in the immediate future[6]:

> Much speculation takes place in Britain and in North America on whether the big retail chains will work back into agribusiness, developing more of their own food processing and packaging and buying themselves right back into the farming sector. For example, in England it must look quite inviting to some of our big retailers to

start up their own table-egg packing plants and farms, to ensure that they have adequate supplies of fresh eggs at a low cost. This type of development, on an extensive scale, is unlikely in the next two or three decades. The retailing of food is going through a tremendous revolution. The building of new supermarkets, new self-service stores and completely new shopping centres will absorb the capital-raising potential of the food retailers to the maximum. Furthermore, agribusiness is likely to become so competitive that the retailers may probably decide that their investment return from retailing in the future is likely to be higher than they would earn if they went in for large-scale farming or processing.

Two years later Lord Sainsbury, whose firm controls 259 shops and stores in his retail organisation, said[7]:

> We have no intention of entering primary production to supply our shops . . . we feel it unwise to specialise in too many trades and occupations. It is better to leave production to the farmers.

At present it appears that the supermarkets and other large retail outlets will not make a substantial attempt to purchase farms. With growing competition and the need to streamline all stages of food production, processing, packaging and distribution, the possibility of the retail outlets eventually wishing to control the sources of their supply cannot be dismissed. Recently in America a move in the other direction has occurred with a plan by the American Farm Bureau Federation to buy the A & P food chain, which has 4,500 retail shops. The move to vertical integration can be a two-way process, as has been previously discussed (p310). In either case the effect for the housewife is the same. Prepacked produce, standardised in quality, is available all the year round.

Standardised food for the mass market, cheaply produced and distributed, is one of the benefits of modern society. It is also one of the faults. Mass merchandising usually means an acceptance of a tolerable, but uniformly mediocre, quality in the products sold. Breadth of choice and prime quality are both diminished. With food flavour may be diminished. If high standards of hygiene are required, as they should be, much flavour may be removed. Flavour is in part a product of decomposition in food and the margin between what is safe and what is dangerous to eat is too fine for the mass market, especially since it cannot afford a high level of wastage in its lines for sale. Other aspects concerning flavour are only partially understood, but the intensified farming systems, relying on artificial fertilisers and antibiotics, are accused of diminishing flavour. It is not surprising that there is a partial consumer revolt against modern, high-pressure food production and marketing. It is no accident that, as an antidote to the supermarket technique, there has been a small but significant growth in health food shops and organic farming.

The interest in organic farming, as a philosophy opposed to modern agricultural practice, has grown with the rapid strides made by the latter. An experimental farm at Haughley, Suffolk, was started in 1938 by Lady Eve Balfour. Since 1947 it has been administered by the Soil Association to demonstrate the benefits of organic farming by comparing the long term effects of organic, conventional and stockless farms. At the end of their first quarter-century the farm has shown that organic farming could lead to better stocks, crops and yield, that the fertility of the soil could be enhanced without the addition of artificial fertilisers and that the food produced had a higher nutritional value and flavour[1]. In 1967 more extensive trials started to show a factual assessment between the benefits or hazards of artificial aids to food production when compared with organic methods. The expansion of health food shops (there were over 400 throughout the country by 1962 supplied from a hundred farms) demonstrates that many people do find produce from organic farming preferable to mass produced foods in the modern manner. Few people would dispute the case for organic farming, though many might place different emphasis on its relative nutritional value. The Haughley experiment has not made a study of the economic comparisons between the different farming methods in terms of production costs or of output per acre. Organically produced foods cost considerably more than their mass produced rivals and cannot be a basis for feeding the population.

The future will probably sharpen the distinction between mass production and organic or specialist flavour foods. Most food will be for the mass market, prepacked, hygienic and of reasonable and uniform quality. Such food will be relatively cheap. In contrast specialist food shops, including health foods will increase in number and turnover. Many farmers will contract themselves to produce specialist foods for this market. It is probable that comparative prices will rise and that specialist foods will cost, perhaps, some three to four times more than those for the mass market. It is impossible to predict how much food will be required for the specialist market. With increasing standards of living and with greater interest in the art of cooking, it is probable that at least ten per cent of temperate foods will be within this category by the end of another two decades. It is possible that the market might expand to as much as twenty per cent by the end of the century, though the former estimate seems, at present, more probable. There is a place for the specialist farm working with opposite techniques to those normally accepted for factory farming.

REFERENCES

1 Stephenson, R. W., *The Supermarket Industry*. 1965, The Supermarket Association of Great Britain Ltd

2 Mills, J. L. 'The butcher, the producer and the supermarket user.' *Farmers Weekly*, p115. 3 December 1965

3 'The vanishing food shop.' *The Times*, p7. 13 April 1966

4 'Shopping revolution.' *The Times*. 5 June 1965

5 Mills, J. L. 'Geest, groups and go-it-alone. *Farmers Weekly*, p75. 11 December 1964

6 Sykes, G., *Poultry: a modern agribusiness*, p211. 1963, Crosby Lockwood

7 Lord Sainsbury. Report to Eastern Counties Farmers Ltd, 1965

8 *The Haughley Experiment* 1938–62. 1962, The Soil Association

8 CO-OPERATIVE FARMING

Introduction

The co-operative movement in farming was born in mid-Victorian times along with other urban consumer societies. It is now a hundred years old. It has had a long turbulent history. There have been periods of acute financial crisis. Many individual societies failed to make the grade, collapsing among unco-operative attitudes and economic difficulties. There have been times of serious political stress. The movement has been crushed between opposing forces with the natural Conservative associations of traditional landowners grinding against the Labour inspired Co-operative Party principles. It is difficult to keep the simple idea of farmers grouping together to buy and sell goods as a non-political act. Although co-operative purchase of requisites is relatively easy to organise, group marketing means that farmers have had to overcome their basic suspicions of each other as business rivals. With the creation of National Marketing Boards the range of goods which can be sold on a group basis has been narrowed. The century old movement has had its times of trouble, its future is far from certain. During the last decade co-operation in agriculture has taken a new turning. Although the whole of the food industry, including farming, is in a ferment of change, indeed in revolution, nowhere is this change more significant than in the realm of co-operation.

In the need for co-operation farmers are having to reexamine their whole position in society and their basic function in the food industry. The root to the problem is land ownership and independence. Many farmers work land held by their family for centuries. Others have been tenants to landlords, their relationship one of generations. The newcomers have bought their way into agriculture mostly with profits from urban industries. In each case there is normally a pride of ownership, one inspired by the mystique of continuity from father to son and the other by casting urban lives back into the land from which their forefathers came. From this inspiration has come the deep-rooted creed of independence. The red rag to this inspiration is one of land nationalisation. Land ownership is considered sacred, each acre a birthright. When pressed some may conceed that ownership is a trust, each farmer pledged to farm diligently to produce food for the population and pass a fertile land to his descendants. The concept that food production and the whole issue of land-use are matters of national concern and that the trustees could direct their stewards, the farmers, in the management of the land held in trust throws all farmers into a rage, generated by the fear of being dispossessed.

Dispossession by land nationalisation is unlikely, at least for another generation. It would in fact be foolish since the agrico-industrial-economic planners in land-use do not exist capable of organising and directing agriculture. But dispossession by the cruel, relentless process of private enterprise absorption into larger units and into industrial ownership is a real and immediate threat. The external pressures of marketing and the process of vertical integration were examined in the last chapter. Under these financial pressures the whole structure of farming is changing. By degrees, but with accelerating effectiveness, farmers are dispossessing themselves by their own free-will of independence, and even of their birthright, the ownership of land. With gathering momentum a revolution started to gather speed during the 1960s. It is impossible to know whence it will lead, but it is certain that the structure of farming will be vastly different by the end of the century from that at 1950.

By the summer of 1966 there were 275 agricultural trading societies in England. About an eighth of these had trading accounts in excess of £1m the previous year. Most of these societies are for requisites, being descendants of the Agricultural and Horticultural Association formed in 1867. The remarkable factors in the present position of trading societies are fourfold. Turnover has increased by 600 per cent within two decades and expansion is continuing rapidly. There is growing interest in marketing groups, based on the realisation that collective marketing strength has become essential to compete with the industrial giants beyond the farm gate. Thirdly, as new groups are formed, others merge to form larger co-operatives and there are indications that soon there will be mainly only a few mammoth societies handling the bulk of the agricultural trade. Finally, as the movement becomes more powerful and organised there is greater need for trained management personnel at all levels, especially at the top.

Co-operation in marketing, though it must become the norm, is not in itself the most important aspect of the revolution. Collective marketing, to seek the new mass retail outlets, does impose a discipline on group members, many of whom must soon be producing food by contract for their organisation. This is a basic and far-reaching change in attitude, independence giving way to inter-

344

dependence. Co-operation between farmers is extending into farm management and farm work as well as into trade beyond the farm gate. Contract sales, of course, organised by a group do mean that the members must plan production as a team, individual management policies becoming dovetailed into a master plan. More significant is the fact that group syndicates are rising for the sharing of management overheads, machines and men.

Business co-operation between farmers is essential for the future, particularly linking the structure of small and medium sized farms together as specialist units to one overall management policy. Such ventures as the Mallingdown Farming Syndicate show the way for the future. Though individual farmers still retain a legal ownership over land, to all intents and purposes independence is surrendered to group action. In many cases the only manner in which modernisation can be afforded, especially for expensive machinery unjustified for small acreages (which may include anything less than 250-350 acres for some machines) is by the formation of a machinery syndicate. Within the last decade collective ownership of machines has, from a small start in Hampshire, become a normal feature for many farmers. Moreover syndicates have been extended to include group ownership over buildings, particularly those for grain and feed. There is already growing interest in the idea of syndicate production buildings. Again independence and individual ownership is sacrificed for collective security and efficiency. The concept of sharing labour is also growing. In fact a collective pool of skilled men is probably the only way of preparing agriculture for modern working conditions, allowing each man to be off work for well over a third of the year.

It is ironic that in a country renowned for its John Bull attitude of staunch independence and private ownership that collective action and ownership is gaining such ground, especially within the most traditionally conservative sector of the community. As yet collective thinking, still less action, probably only really concerns a tenth of the farming population—with the possible exception of group purchasing of materials through requisite societies which has a wider appeal. Nevertheless the change in attitude within a decade has been remarkable, indicative of a profound social revolution. Within the coming decades, the centuries-old divisions between farm and farm, between Farmer Giles and Farmer Jones, will disappear. It will become harder and harder to identify the ownership of farmland in terms of personalities and individuals. Co-operation leads to company farming, and company farming can lead to an individual type organisation of inter-related firms in giant formation. The birthright is changing hands.

8b The co-operative movement

Co-operation among farmers is not unique to this decade. Man has survived the vagaries of nature through history only due to co-operative action in obtaining food. The feudal village was itself largely a corporate system. In spite of this the growth of modern agriculture during the last three centuries witnessed a creed for self-reliance and independence in the farming community. New industrial trading patterns, emerging in mid-Victorian times, had some influence on agriculture and, by degrees and contrary to the general desire for complete independence, gave birth to a system of co-operation among farmers. Co-operation today has become a vital issue.

Agricultural co-operation had its birth in 1867 when the Agricultural and Horticultural Association was formed to organise the purchase of requirements for members, similar to the general principles of other consumer co-operatives existing at that time. This association which survived as an independent organisation in this century, followed the creation of a Central Chamber of Agriculture two years earlier to act politically for the farming community as a whole. Other trading and marketing societies were formed during the next decades, many failing within a short period. Nevertheless, the growth of co-operative groups continued until the Central Chamber felt it necessary to examine the thirty existing societies in the 1890s to consider their potential for trading and for marketing.

At the turn of the century, due to growing belief in agricultural co-operatives, an Agricultural Organisation Society was formed 'to secure the co-operation of all connected with the land, whether as owners, occupiers, or labourers, and to promote the formation of Agricultural Co-operative Societies for the purchase of requisites, for the sale of produce, for Agricultural Credit, Banking and Insurance, and for all other forms of Co-operation for the benefit of Agriculture'. This statement of policy, even after another two-thirds of a century, is still pertinent. In fact since political and economic pressures on agriculture have increased, it has become a matter of vital concern for all farmers. In 1900 under 5,000 farmers were members of nineteen English co-operative societies[1]. Their annual turnover was a little over £⅛m. The societies included a dozen purely for the purchase of farm requirements, with the others being for dairy and general farming co-operation.

In the early years of the century the co-operative movement expanded rapidly. In 1905 the Agricultural Co-operative Federation was formed, and two years later there were 106 member societies with an annual turnover of nearly £⅔m. Though most were still formed for the purchase of requisites, some societies were already

346

acting as marketing groups for pigs, dairy products, vegetables and fruit. By degrees, political and organisational problems grew within the movement as its membership and financial power increased. The federation was replaced in 1912 by the Farmers Central Trading Board which, during the war years following its creation, helped to organise agricultural supplies until it, too, was replaced by the Agricultural Wholesale Society in 1918. At this time membership of societies in England and Wales had risen to nearly 170,000 with an annual turnover of almost £9m. Agricultural co-operation having passed through a period of experiment in its early years, had become an important feature of the farming industry. Moreover the principles of co-operation had become accepted and encouraged in governmental policies and the National Farmers' Union, itself founded in 1908, also gave some support to the movement. Enthusiasm for agricultural co-operation was high, partly due to the general state of expansion and prosperous income in farming generated by the war. The following years of depression quickly dispersed this expansion, damped the enthusiasm and exposed many weaknesses in co-operative action. In 1924 the Agricultural Organisation Society and the Agricultural Wholesale Society collapsed, with co-operatives losing members and turnover. The Linlithgow Report, published a year earlier, had shown that farmers tended to be unwilling to pay for skilled management in the co-operatives and fully co-ordinate their requirements.

The decline of the movement, largely due to the rapid fall in agricultural prices, and the collapse of the AOS has important lessons for farmers today. As Knapp stressed[1]:

> We can see that the AOS was weak in that it was primarily a promotional body. It had no research base for its educational efforts and it worked largely on a trial and error basis. Plans were often made upon faulty suppositions. Business research would have provided the organisers with more careful direction.

The Wholesale Society, collapsing due to lack of capital, brought the downfall of the Organisation Society so largely tied to it. Though economic times were against the movement in the early 1920s, the need for research, business training and co-ordination is equally vital today in all corporate as well as individual endeavour among farmers. Though generally not so acute a problem forty years later, since some farming organisations are based on good industrial management principles, the same faults can still be found in many farm activities.

The co-operative movement, after its collapse, was reborn largely due to government assistance, particularly to a system of loans started in 1924 to assist societies establish land, buildings, machinery and equipment for themselves and prepare and market produce. By

347

degrees the National Farmers Union also became more involved in the movement. Co-operatives came fully into national scrutiny with the publication in 1930 of the study of Agricultural Co-operation in England by the Horace Plunkett Foundation, which led to a Co-operative Conference and a revival of corporate action by the many individual societies which had survived the failure of their federation. The movement suffered another setback as it was again expanding due to the 1933 Agricultural Marketing Act which created official marketing boards for certain produce to the detriment of independent marketing societies. At this time, 220 societies had an annual turnover of over £9m, equal to the amount handled in 1918, fifteen years earlier. The movement regained its national status in 1936 with formation of the Agricultural Co-operative Managers' Association to co-ordinate policy and provide a liason with other agricultural concerns. By 1938 co-operative societies were expanding again and progressing towards a position of financial independence. At the outbreak of war turnover was over £13m, of which £10m was for requirements.

Just as lack of management research and skill has led to weaknesses within agricultural affairs concerning the co-operatives throughout their history, so also has there been a fundamental weakness in the preponderance of requirement rather than of marketing societies. In both cases these weaknesses are still of concern. The problem of co-operation in marketing produce has been twofold. In many cases co-operative marketing has been merely a loose cover for shared overheads, broken in many cases by sharp practice. Many farmers have been known to break a semi-formal agreement to sell via one organisation when prices have risen elsewhere. Group marketing, to be balanced and successful, must be based on known levels of production, preferably balancing production to contracted market outlets. It must be a formal arrangement, binding on its members in spite of tempting offers outside the group. Secondly, organised marketing is a skilled job, needing trained personnel. In most cases, grouping has been an informal extension of marketing by one member acting as an honorary secretary over the telephone. From 1939, though the movement expanded and matured, especially due to the formation of the Agricultural Co-operative Association at the end of the war, political and economic problems were still paramount, particularly restricting the growth of marketing groups.

The ACA gave attention to standardisation of farm produce by grade and package as early as its foundation in 1945. Close links were forged with the National Farmers Union in its early stages, but tension developed in the early 1950s. Finance, due to a period of growing expansion, became more critical. The next decade, as the political climate towards agriculture became more stable and as farming rapidly entered its agrico-industrial revolution, was a period

348

of continuous heart-searching in the movement and new patterns were clearly emerging by the 1960s. By 1964 the total membership of the co-operative movement had grown to include almost 400,000 in Great Britain with a turnover of £246m. In England alone, there were 300,000 members with a turnover of over £200m by 1967.[2] The Federation of Agricultural Co-operatives in the same year laid down a guide to help farmers retain the distributive margins in their own hands in the face of growing opposition and power generated by the absorption of dealers and merchants into national and international trading concerns. Attention was closely given to democratic and organised societies working to gain commercial advantages for their members, at the same time safeguarding their independence. The ACA has also commissioned a thorough investigation into the co-operative movement by an American expert on agricultural co-operation. Dr Joseph Knapp reported to the Association in 1965.

Dr Knapp appreciated that the emerging pattern in co-operation was in the formation of large regional associations. At the same time he realised that co-operative marketing was limited for some produce by statutory marketing boards—for milk, eggs, wool, hops and potatoes. The boards for the most part regulate marketing conditions rather than undertake it themselves. Farm co-operatives can therefore work within the sphere of the board's conditions. Within the pattern of giant co-operatives were many small groupings of farmers with localised and specialised interests, but not strictly acting as an organised federation. True economies are generally in relation to the size of the co-operative. It is the large federations which can provide the most efficient service to farmers and yield the highest discounts. Knapp rightly stressed the urgent need for market research and organisation research, plus the training of personnel, to make the movement satisfactory for future growth. In particular, he stressed that the co-operative federation should be its own master, financed by its own resources, though helped by the Government to strengthen its fabric for the welfare of British agriculture.

The future of the co-operatives in agriculture is unclear. It is certain that giant regional trading societies will exist, possibly with some smaller independent co-operatives among them. The latter may primarily serve specialist interests. Whether or not the co-operative movement will check the power of external industrial companies from controlling agriculture is doubtful. It would seem more likely, in the nature of present changes, that the interests of the giant co-operatives and the giant processors and retailers will be found to have a common base. The result is likely to be a fusion of interests with much food production being forward planned to suit a predicted market, organised and controlled within a contractual marketing system. Similarly many of the raw materials for agriculture must also be preplanned if the production contracts are to be fulfilled.

The true distinction between a system of horizontal or vertical integration may be purely academic as far as the individual farmer is concerned.

The future position of the co-operatives in the nation is also of concern. It would seem that the bulk of the food produced, worth at present nearly £2,000m, plus most of the raw materials worth round £1,000m, could pass through an organised and centralised federation. If farmers should co-operate together to pool their needs and produce within a federation—and there is a growing move in that direction though at present representing perhaps but a tenth of the potential—then the combined economic and political power of the federation would be out of proportion to the numbers engaged in agriculture. But co-operation as examined in the next sections, is already being extended far beyond the confines of trade alone. Moreover, a new boost was given to co-operation in England in 1967 by the government sponsored Council for Co-operation aimed directly to encourage production groups, in addition to those for commodities. In the same year, the formation of the Farmers Overseas Trading Ltd organisation to act as a major trade link with the well established European co-operatives was a further move towards international streamlined business, especially trading in cereals, feed, seed and potatoes, but to be directed later also at livestock, fruit and vegetables.

REFERENCE

1 Knapp, Dr J., *An analysis of agricultural co-operation in England.* 1965, Agricultural Co-operative Association
2 Perry, T. 'Co-ops 1867–1967'. *Farmers Weekly*, pp 82–97, 5 May, 1967

8c Contract farming and marketing groups

The agricultural co-operative movement, with its century old history of development as discussed in the last section, is a mixed organisation. Its main concern has been with the supply of raw materials and equipment to farmers and to a lesser extent with the marketing of produce on behalf of its members. In some co-operatives, it can contract farming by contract or marketing in groups. A distinction has to be made between the traditional co-operatives and group co-operation as now required.

Most existing co-operatives and producer groups are unselective with an open membership and, in the case of marketing, unspecific standards over produce handled. Co-operation in the future must not be based on unselective trading societies but—whether for buying or selling—on large marketing units with close control over specified standards for the quantity, quality and timing of materials or of produce handled. Materials, purchased in bulk and passing through regional depots, should be handled primarily on the basis of forward planning and not as random requests. Produce, as supplied to processor or retailer, should be branded and dated as a surety of standard and an incentive to efficiency. Some groups of farmers are already working on this basis. Many see that selective group action is the antidote to the threat of vertical integration.

Contract farming, which is no more than a logical conclusion to any policy of forward planning—that is of producing food for a predicted or assured market—is a two-way process. It is at present a struggle for power. It is indeed a struggle for the control of agriculture including, as a corollary, the control or ownership of all farmland. Farming contracts can be made vertically or horizontally, though this is a fine distinction in the last analysis. Vertical integration, concentrating production, processing, distribution and retailing under one management, has already been discussed. In an integrated food industry each producer contracts himself to an urban master or, as already happens especially with animal feed compounders, the urban industries own their own farms or, as with animals, own the specialised buildings without much land. Ownership by contracts with the giant compounders, or the supermarket chains, or the prepackers—or an amalgam of all the various stages producing food for the consumer—can leave the small farmer in an invidious position since his independence is dominated by his economically stronger partner. Even the large farmer, with thousands of acres in production, has little economic strength within an integrated industry, bearing in mind that on average he gets but a third of the price of food charged to the customer.

A critical issue for farmers in vertical integration and vertical contracts, stressed in the 1965 annual report of the Agricultural Co-operative Association, is that compound mills owned by farmers will receive intense competition from the industrial compounders:

> It is not farmers who, by their co-operative activities in manufacturing feedingstuffs, are likely to be making the biggest inroads into this trade, but the mass producers of poultry, eggs and, maybe in due course, other forms of meat as well, who have already announced their intention of compounding their own supplies. Between the compound manufacturers vertically integrating their businesses to undertake livestock production, and the factory poultry and livestock producers vertically integrating theirs to undertake the production of feedingstuffs, there stands the ordinary farmer who, more than ever in future, will feel the need to have his own organisation behind him, both for selling and buying.

The last sentence summarises the situation. In the agribusiness world, the ordinary farmer, alone, is lost. He cannot compete with the compounders and, in other spheres, with the processors and pre-packers or the giant retailers. For this reason, the farmer's centuries-old independence has to be sacrificed for survival. For this reason also farmers are turning to the horizontal contract, or group farming within a co-operative. Geoffrey Sykes predicted the growth of contract farming in 1963[1].

I expect to see contract farming develop on a considerably wider scale, that is to say, the development of large companies specialising in various phases of animal production, operating really large dairy herds and chains of large dairy herds, chains of large beef-eating operations and of large pig production operations. These companies, in Britain, will not want to develop the heavy capitalisation necessary to purchase the large acreage of land needed for producing the feed for such large concentrations of ruminants. Hence we shall see the development of the large-scale contract growing of wilted silage, barn dried hay and wet barley. This will enable many medium-sized farms to streamline and reduce the cost per unit of their farming operation by specialisation in this type of work. Just as the contract growing of sugar beet is carried out under the supervision of the British Sugar Company's fieldsmen, so will the cropping and harvesting of these contract crops of roughages be carried out under the supervision of the fieldmen of the company owning and operating the large dairy herds and beef-feeding concentrations.

In milk production today, it is not difficult to organise a herring-bone milking parlour, in which two cowmen milk a herd of 250 cows, managed on a high milk yield basis. We shall see the development of chains of well managed dairy herds of this size of unit. The rearing of the replacement stock will be dealt with in a specialised manner with a similar meticulous approach to proper disease control, as is being developed by the modern poultryman in the new poultry industry.

This kind of livestock development—following in some ways the development we are seeing in the new poultry industry—this extension of contract farming in our arable farming, will accelerate the amalgamation of many smaller holdings into larger, more viable holdings, specialist holdings concentrating on a volume basis on the type of crops particularly suited to a particular area.

Many small and medium sized farms are seriously considering machinery syndicates, farm supply buying groups, group packing and merchandising of farm products together with the possibilities of amalgamation of holdings.

The facts of today's farming situation demand that such farmers should go even further and consider ways and means of developing and modernising their animal production and crop production by syndicate systems.

This would enable farmers to establish modern 200 cow herds, in beef rearing feed lots of 800 head minimum size plants, a five day week for the farmers doing the actual milking, the syndicate developing the crop conservation programmes.

It is doubtful if farmers individually can afford to do their own

352

ploughing in future now that larger capacity tractors are coming into England which in two ten hour shifts plough fifty acres a day. Obviously ploughing and cultivating is a job for the syndicates in future.

This philosophy, which is beginning to be put into practice, is preached by more and more agriculturalists. Many people now recognise that producers, especially small producers, must group together to market their produce from a position of strength. Sales by a group could be either direct to the industrial firms or via wholesalers acting as agents. In either case the farmers or their wholesaler agents would act under contract, marketing becoming a streamlined organisation within a rigid application of quality standards and uniformity.

During the last few years group activity and co-operation among farmers has been in ferment. This has fallen into three main classes. Bulk purchasing of materials and equipment to gain trade discounts has continued to expand. Secondly, and more important, there has been a ferment of co-operation in farms round specific enterprises. As discussed in the next sections, this has sometimes taken the form of syndicates for sharing management, machines or men. More frequently farming co-operation has taken the form of one farmer contracting to sell to a second farmer an unfinished product. For the most part this takes the form of a division between rearing and fattening livestock. Contracts direct between breeders and fatteners are becoming commonplace for pigs, cattle and sheep. Alternatively groups of breeders have a common organisation handling their youngstock to the fattening farms, usually not on contract but as a means of equating supply with demand through one channel—albeit rather crudely. Thirdly, groups of farmers have co-operated in marketing their wares as finished products to industry and retailers.

The cumulative effect of market co-operation between farmers and between farmers and the outlets beyond the farm gate began to be noticed in 1963. It was recognised as an explosion of group activity by farmers suddenly shedding their traditional beliefs in independence with far-reaching social and economic effects[2].

> Every week for the past year a group of farmers somewhere in Britain took the decision to market their produce collectively—not an easy decision to take. Their heritage was independence, they were their own bosses making their own decisions and mistakes in marketing. Now there is only the group. Overnight farmers stopped being individuals gambling on a market price that was often rigged against them and the taxpayer or depressed by gluts caused by their own ignorance of the supply position. But all this is changing rapidly. The group farmer is finding that far from losing anything by handing over his 'freedom' of action, he is gaining financially. . . .
> Almost every commodity produced on farms is now under the influence of the group movement—potatoes in Wester Ross and

N

Yorkshire, calves in Lancashire, bulbs in Lincolnshire, cauliflowers in Cornwall, lamb in Somerset, beef in Fife, bacon in Norfolk, Brussel sprouts in Bedfordshire, apples in Kent, weaners in Anglesey, reared calves in Cardigan, eggs in Shropshire. Many of the groups are small; some are too limited in their scope and may fail. Others are exciting and ambitious marketing concepts. Alone they are insignificant, but collectively they represent the biggest explosion of producer activity the industry has ever seen. And it is only starting. It is barely two years old, yet the group movement is creating a reformation in agricultural thinking. . . .

In the first six months of 1964 the *Farmers Weekly* recorded the formation of a score of new groups of significant size, in addition to other smaller co-operatives. Lewes Farmers Ltd, for example, linked twenty-six Sussex farmers averaging 800 acres each (within a range of thirty-five to 2,400 acres) and having a total purchasing turnover of £50,000 a year. The group planned to extend from bulk purchases to co-operative marketing of up to 10,000 lambs and 10,000 tons of cereals a year. Similarly the North Notts Farmers Ltd, an established co-operative, having increased turnover to well over £1m, formed plans to extend group trading to £5m a year and extend its co-operative farm secretarial services, its potato and produce packing, and the contract buying of barley, and enter a group marketing scheme for selling pigs, beef calves and other commodities. In the West Country two established farmer-owned egg co-operatives linked up to form a larger group owning a million birds and with an annual turnover of £3m. In the South-east, the Quality Veal Producers Group was formed by sixteen members to contract the sale of 2,000 calves a year to the City Meat Wholesalers Ltd. A more extensive scheme was formed by the West Cumberland Farmers' Trading Society in which they provided weaners and also prefabricated controlled-environment houses to farmers wanting to fatten pigs, backed by a bank offering credit facilities, and with the pork and bacon pigs produced under contract to the Yorkshire Farmers' Bacon Factory. This group operated in an area including Yorkshire, the northern counties and the south of Scotland. In Cheshire the North Western Farmers Ltd, operating within seventy-five miles of Nantwich with 9,500 members, were contracting 2,000 pigs a week to a bacon factory and handling among themselves half this number of weaners to the fattening farms, the other half being reared and fattened on individual farms. In the south Midlands the largest horticultural group, Pershore Growers Ltd, provided a full marketing service for its members, handling over £1m of produce a year, and was expanding into the West Country. In Devon, Avon Farmers Ltd, which started with eight members in 1960, had expanded to 500 farmers in 1964 with a total of 50,000 acres. Livestock sales had increased to justify the appointment of a full-time officer to cover

354

calves, beef, sheep and pigs and consider the possibility of contract selling. The Avon Group purchases at that time were round £⅔m a year and livestock marketing was aimed for the same figure.

By the summer of 1964, 300,000 farmers and growers in the United Kingdom were buying and selling through agricultural co-operative societies with total annual turnover in trade of round £175m—a remarkable expansion from the £25m of only two decades earlier. In 1961-2 the Minister of Agriculture set up the Agricultural Market Development Executive Committee to administer £1½m as grants to approved groups, improving their marketing techniques and efficiency. Grants were also made to help projects for market research and for promoting marketing of different products. Though only a small part of the fund was actually granted to help existing or found new producer groups—the climate in which AMDEC worked and the publicity made towards better marketing helped towards the group explosion among farmers. Since 1964, which was perhaps the main year of sudden upsurge and interest in grouping, co-operative trading and marketing has expanded and consolidated its position, though not as rapidly as at first indicated. Group organisation in marketing has been encouraged by the Government and the National Farmers Union.

During 1964, a spate of mergers among farm co-operatives began to make the headlines and set the pattern for the future. In the Midlands the Worcestershire and the Warwickshire Farmers Ltd, merged as a natural development between the two co-operatives, creating a joint annual turnover of nearly £6m. More dramatic was the £25m merger between the trading societies in West Cumberland and Yorkshire linking well over 20,000 farmers in one giant co-operative. By 1967 this group had 33,000 members in six English and eighteen Scotch counties, having an annual turnover of £28m. This merger marked the first real step towards a new concept for agricultural marketing. Sir Frederick Brundett, former chairman of ACA stated at that time that by 1970 there would be under eight giant co-operatives in England, a 100 smaller groups having merged into regional units handling vast quantities of materials to farms and produce from farms[3]. He believed that the Central Association in such circumstances might evolve into a co-ordinating organisation between the regions to create a marketing group on a national scale. It is obvious that such massive developments in marketing would be of considerable significance to the farmers themselves and the nation as a whole.

Research is still required into the facts of co-operation to understand and direct its growth for the benefit of the community as well as for the sake of the farmers themselves. In 1965 an agricultural economist suggested an authoritative enquiry was needed to study the group movement in order to provide informed guidance on the

355

organisation and finance of group action[4]. The growth of marketing boards, co-operatives, commodity commissions, production syndicates and buying/selling groups showed that farmers were willing to seek action on their behalf in new forms of marketing. Contract farming, which is growing out of this profusion of new co-operative action, has generated a 'proliferation of contracts calling for critical scrutiny and report'. Moreover—the trend in marketing farm products could alter the character of demand—as well as vice versa. Since processors and manufacturers were becoming important customers for farmers, contracts guaranteeing the constant supply of high quality products began to be formed. Professor Thomas has forecast that present agricultural policies would be increasingly integrated into an overall national economic plan with farming taken as a base in planning various sectors of industry, regulating output in the light of national needs. Later in 1965, AMDEC and the National Farmers Union started a study of trading patterns and organisation as well as of group marketing. Particular interest was growing in the financing of group activity. It became recognised by many that the expansion of the co-operative movement was perhaps the last chance for farmers to control their own destiny, before being engulfed by outside industries and organisations[5].

The co-operative movement is faced by the problem of how it should be financed and organised. Capital for group expansion can come from farmers themselves, from the Government under a process of grants or from the public. Farmers have proved reluctant to provide capital for the efficient staffing and equipping of high-powered co-operatives, though smaller groups have received considerable support. Even the large co-operatives, though they invest in their organisations, cannot hope to compete financially with the investments made by the external compounders and processors. The Government, without participating more directly in the formation of a new overall farm and market structure, are limited in the help they can give except by direct grant. Though the Government may wish to see a better organised marketing system, there is no reason why they should create opposition to the progressive power gained by external industries over agriculture. Such would be justified only if the Government directed a national food plan. Lastly there is the possibility of public finance. Farmers were disturbed when in 1963 the Kent egg co-operative, Stonegate Farmers Ltd, with 4,500 members, became a public company. Although this venture has proved successful—and it is a method for promoting public investment in the co-operative movement—it is a policy which is not attractive to most farmers since it renders them liable to take-over bids from external business interests. The latter would do just what farmers hope to prevent by group co-operation—let agriculture fall under the control of urban interests.

Farmers are in a dilemma. Too much public support, financial or otherwise, might create conditions leading to public or official control over their independence. Nevertheless farmers must be willing to create a trading flow which is preplanned and efficient from production to customer. Co-operation is essential in order to present a united front selling produce satisfactory to compounder, processor and prepacker, frequently under the influence of the supermarket retailers. Co-operation is a means of doing business and it must be organised and largely financed by the farmers themselves. Thus farmers must be prepared to surrender their independence to the interests of a farming group and finance that surrender. Once a group enters, as it must, into a contractual or highly organised relationship with the industries beyond the farmgate, then the group must become the master of the individual farmer. At the same time each group must become merged into vast, regional co-operatives, all being, to some extent under the direction of a national co-operative. The latter, being a national concern, may well cease to be strictly in the control of farmers or, it will at least have become big business in its own right, dealing with other big business interests at national level. Under the weight of this organisation, the individual farmer will be insignificant. It may well seem to him that there is little difference between horizontal or vertical integration—yet integrate one way or the other he must.

REFERENCES

1 Sykes, G., *Poultry: a modern agribusiness*, p225. 1963, Crosby Lockwood
2 MacDougall, A. 'The Group Explosion.' *Farmers Weekly*, p74. 23 August 1963
3 MacDougall, A. 'Five-year Co-op Shake-up.' *Farmers Weekly*, p41. 7 August 1964
4 Thomas, Professor E. Report. Askham Bryan Conference, 1965
5 MacDougall, A. 'Co-operation beyond the farm gate.' *The Times Agriculture Supplement*. 6 December 1965

8d Management co-operation

The old order of farming is passing. Nowhere is this change so revolutionary, yet becoming so apparent, as in basic attitudes to management. The traditional mentality of the self-reliant and independent farmer, determined to keep his policies secret from his neighbour and find his own salvation, is giving way to a new and acute awareness of inter-dependence with his neighbour. This is true not only of the recent growth of specialist agribusinessmen, but also of many within the hard core of family farmers. The idea of co-operation is being extended from trading into management itself, as well as into the sharing of machines and men as outlined in the next sections. Amalgamation of farms by purchase, can of course lead to reorganised management in larger and more viable units under one leader. More significant, since it shows a fundamental change in the approach to farm management, is the growing voluntary co-operation between farmers in order to co-ordinate policies and share overheads.

The traditional farmer, from his boundaries, watched his neighbour with suspicion. All too often he was prepared to imitate stocking, cropping and mechanisation techniques without making an analysis of his own basic requirements from first principles. Frequently such imitation might be made out of context. A rash of copy-cat buildings, have for example, often left their tell-tale legacy in a district. An allegiance to regional breeds of livestock, irrespective of their comparative performance with alien, but often more economic, stock also indicates the parochial farmer. The growth of county and multi-county shows in this century, as well as specialised farming societies, have helped to widen outlooks beyond the parish or district. Since the war the National Agricultural Advisory Service and the National Farmers' Union have done much to promote interest in comparative farm management. The extension of farm walks throughout the country, whereby farmers are conducted round each other's farms, examining and questioning policies and performance, has helped to break selfish attitudes among farmers. It has helped in fact to first promote interest and later practice in management co-operation.

It was—perhaps—the agricultural departments in universities which first developed the science of performance studies on a comparative farm basis. For some years—several of these departments have had groups of farms under their ken, extracting, analysing and synthesising records in confidence, from which comparative management studies have been published. These university reports have been invaluable. Both the NAAS and the National Farmers' Union have promoted schemes for farm recording, from which comparisons between policies and performance can be made. Similarly the growth of farm management consultants and the Farm Management Association in recent years is making cross-fertilisation of knowledge between farms accepted practice. Some agricultural journals, too, have bought farms for the purpose of planning them by open discussion, freely showing not only their failures and successes but also their expenditure and income to the last penny. Such frankness is admirable. All these factors are indicative of the changing climate of opinion towards national and public farm records. Few other industries have become so open in their management, yet this frankness is the antithesis of traditional agricultural thinking prevalent only a few years ago. Yet on the basis of this

358

frankness in management it may become possible to form a realistic national food plan which is an important and essential part of any plan for national land-use. This co-operation between farmers willing to exchange their management experience with each other is important in itself. It is, however, equally important since it makes other forms of farm co-operation possible and not only beyond the farm gate in trading groups.

Healthy and mutual co-operation depends on frankness and honesty in all matters. Suspicion and distrust make co-operation difficult, if not impossible. Shared records are an essential part of co-operation. The breakthrough towards co-operative farming has been since 1960. In fact to any real extent, it has been within the last three years. It has grown from co-operation in trading, which has had a long history, and from the machinery syndicates that have been promoted during the last decade. It has roots in partnership farming between landlord and tenant. The idea of landlord and tenant each drawing a salary, rather than the former taking a rent alone from his tenant, is not widespread. This system of tenancy is receiving considerable interest today and can lead to healthy co-operation in management between landlord and tenant. The Hilfield Estate, at Cerne Abbas in Dorset for example, has had a partnership of this kind since 1946, several tenants being individually in partnership with one landlord, but with machinery and experience shared collectively, and with seeds, feed, fertiliser and fuel purchased in bulk by the estate on behalf of each tenant[1]. The benefits of co-operative farming between individuals in one estate are real, depending as always in such ventures on personalities and on a mutual confidence in each other. Other forms of co-partnership on estates have previously been discussed (p225). Tenants willing to work together for the common good show principles that are significant for all farmers.

In the spring of 1962 management co-operation was forecast as an essential basis for future farming patterns[2]. Travers Legge suggested that business co-operation was essential between small specialist producers, working within one-man or two-men units, since an attempt to maintain freedom and independence was hopeless. Business technology might be shared either on an estate basis between tenants or organised within independent groups of individual farmers, perhaps under the guidance of the National Farmers' Union. Recognition that business co-operation must link small specialist producers, perhaps each responsible for one process in the production of any particular food, is essential for the future well-being of the nation. Luckily many farmers recognise that co-operation is their only salvation if they are to resist pressures by the merchants and processors, if not by the retail outlets, to absorb them within their vertically integrated empires. In the same year a farmer

359

at Ditchling in Sussex proposed a communal building to house a group herd of over 200 cows, managed by communal herdsmen but owned by seven farmers[3]. This kind of thinking, which is an extension of the principles in machinery syndicates having shared overheads, is vital in the move towards co-operative farming. Although this scheme did not get under way, in the same year the Mallingdown Farming Syndicate, also based in Sussex, forged a management link between fifteen farms with advantages which have developed into a progressive partnership which have already been discussed (p227). Thus by degrees such radical ventures are acting as pace-setters for a changed attitude towards ownership and management of land which must transform agriculture in the coming decades.

In 1965, the Director of NAAS suggested four ways in which the 120,000 small farmers could be helped towards solvency in the changing agricultural pattern and pressures[4]:

1 Exploitation of existing resources, particularly intensification of grassland utilisation.

2 Expansion of grouping and co-operation.

3 Augmentation of income from outside sources by changing farm systems to allow some for the family to work in industry.

4 Realisation that small farms on poor land could expect no technical solution and were uneconomic.

Within this need for pooling resources, particularly in engaging expert advice on management, there must be complete discipline in the group before co-operation could be effective. The aim has to be to equate all the resources to form economic production units, not only including land but also manpower, machinery and money, as well as the capacity of management to deploy its own resources effectively. These new ventures into co-operation demand more from the farmers concerned than the limited forms of co-operation known in the past. At the same time the benefits gained by close co-operation are financially greater. During 1964 several other management co-operatives were started. In Suffolk the Mendlesham Potato Growers Ltd pooled the resources of a group of farmers to grow, harvest, store and market their potatoes on an integrated basis. In Notting-hamshire, in the same year, seventy-seven farmers formed a Farm Business Association with monthly meetings studying rotations, marketing, beef production and sugar beet growing. An aim to share experience and knowledge in special study groups of this kind is the springboard for closer co-operation. By 1966, the Farm Management Association, as a national organisation, was able to set up similar types of regional groups, promoting interest in common management problems. There is a close link between sharing management studies and actually sharing policies by pooling resources.

Active co-operation in management is still the exception to the rule. Whereas before 1960 such ideas would have been largely ridiculed, today co-operation is being preached by many experts as the only hope for farmers wishing to control their own destinies. In addition a number of farmers have actually, within several schemes for co-operation, pooled their resources and responsibilities. These could be the forerunner of a tide that will sweep through agriculture before the end of the century. Voluntary amalgamation is the only answer to the threat of external amalgamation brought about either by big business industries integrating their processes back into agriculture or by the nation itself, becoming desperate that vital land resources should not be dissapated by fragmentation. The issues are essentially economic. If a skilled man, with the right equipment, can manage 100 cows, and soon 150, then smaller units are wasteful of labour. Similarly if one combine can harvest 250 acres economically, then smaller corn acreages may be wasteful of mechanical power. Progressive management is continually attempting to find the correct balance for all resources and, where one item creates a bottleneck, to eradicate any factor limiting maximum production for every acre, every man, every machine—or every pound invested. In many cases it is land which is too limited for modern capabilities of men or of machines. Sometimes purchase of additional land becomes possible, making it practical to expand production to suit the capacity of the other resources. Occasionally reallocation of land within a farm itself, possibly by the elimination of one enterprise, can achieve the same results. However, in many cases, expansion or reallocation of land resources prove impractical. In such circumstances, co-operation with a neighbour in similar straits can be the only solution.

Management co-operation can take place at various levels. Contract farming, as previously discussed, means that one farmer may contract to produce for another farmer such items the latter may need, but does not wish to grow for himself. One may rear youngstock, for example, for another to fatten, or grow barley for another to feed to his animals. The farmers concerned have to plan their production to suit each other's needs. In other circumstances, groups of farmers may collectively own one machine or engage a man between them. Again their own farm policies must be planned to make such co-operation possible so that each may use the machine or man in turn. For any of these co-operative ventures to work effectively, close management liason is essential. From such liason many other factors peripheral to the basic item of co-operation may have to be co-ordinated. It is a small step, co-operation being extended by degrees, for management policies to become closely integrated. Integrated and co-operative farming, with management dovetailed to a greater or lesser extent, will become normal practice

N*

in the coming decades. The seeds of this change have already taken root. From the national viewpoint, it is a change to be encouraged.

REFERENCES

1 Williams, M. 'Partnership Farming.' *Farmers Weekly*, p58. 6 August 1965
2 Legge, T. Warwickshire NFU Conference, March 1962
3 Report. *Farmer & Stockbreeder*, p63. 4 September 1962
4 Jones, W. E. Yorkshire Conference, 1965

8e Machinery syndicates

Group activity among farmers has been a phenomenon of the last decade. Within such activity, group ownership of equipment has proved a remarkable development and has done much to change basic agricultural attitudes. In the mid-1950s, it would have seemed an unrealistic pipe-dream to suggest that within ten years age-old barriers of mutual suspicion between farmers would have begun to evaporate. It would have seemed impossible that neighbouring farmers should not only help each other on a regular basis but should be pooling resources to buy, own and work equipment as a group. The fact that hundreds of machinery syndicates are now working throughout the country is one of the success stories of modern agriculture. The syndicate movement, which has helped to reequip many small farms with good machinery, is more important for the basic change it represents towards farm co-operation. The ramifications extend throughout the farming industry and its value is far in excess of the actual machinery now in group ownership. The revolution to co-operative ownership of equipment is probably unique among other British industries.

The syndicate movement had its birth as long ago as 1940[1]. In that year a Hampshire farmer could not get his corn threshed when he wished. Three neighbours joined him in buying a threshing machine—an act which was unjustified by any of them individually. In spite of early difficulties in corporate ownership, the venture proved a success. The group approached the National Farmers' Union with the suggestion that syndicate ownership might get official backing within a sound legal and administrative framework. It was not until 1955 that the first articles of association were drawn up for Syndicates Credits Ltd, in Hampshire. This was the formal start of a new idea in group ownership. A second four-farmer Hampshire syndicate was then formed for the purchase of a combine harvester and a sprayer. Since cereal acreages varied between sixty and twenty-five a farm in the group, none of them could afford such equipment on their own. Each paid for the machinery in relation to

362

his acreage and used it according to an agreed rota in proportion to their financial stake in the venture. By these means the four farmers had the use of good equipment, superior to any that they could justify by themselves, and were freed from the need to get external contractors to harvest their corn.

Since their formation in 1955, the National Farmers' Union has worked through their subsidiary organisation, the Agricultural Central Co-operative Association (now known as the Agricultural Co-operative Association), in order to promote syndicates within sound principles of association. Moreover financial loans of up to eighty per cent of the cost of new equipment, usually repaid over some four years, has done much to encourage farmers to reequip on a co-operative basis. Not only have many small farmers in a syndicate been able to work with high calibre machinery having greater power than justified for their own acreages, but many medium-sized farms have also found it profitable to form or join syndicates with their neighbours. On this basis a much wider choice of machinery can be afforded, extending the scope of practical farmwork. The movement has been notable in its freedom from failure and in the manner in which so many farmers have overcome their natural suspicion of each other to agree to group ownership. Considering that so much farmwork has to be done at unpredictable times to suit weather conditions, co-operative ownership is remarkable.

After the first Hampshire syndicates were started during 1955 others were formed by degrees in other counties. Five years later, sixty-five syndicates were in operation within a total of sixteen counties. Altogether they owned thirty different types of machinery. More important, as experience within the movement grew, teething troubles were overcome and confidence in co-ownership improved —though the bulk of farmers remained sceptical or hostile to the idea of surrendering their independence. The most important early change in direction was a venture in 1958 when another Hampshire syndicate of fourteen farmers erected a communal grain drying and storage plant costing over £10,000. This was the first syndicate to own fixed equipment rather than field machinery. Since their example many grain plants have been erected in co-operative ownership, some with costs in excess of £30,000. The range of equipment owned on a group basis has expanded during the last years. One syndicate, starting with a communal grain drying and storage unit, later extended their co-operation to include the whole of the corn harvest operation, with combines and lorries owned by the syndicate. Another three-farm syndicate installed a reservoir and irrigation system to serve their farms, and in Radnorshire another three farmers bought complete silage-making equipment to serve their combined 227 acres, which would have been unjustified for any of them alone[2]. The latter syndicate also worked together for the purchase of materials and in the erection of buildings on their farms, including silos, a sheep handling unit and other work. In time, co-operation was also extended to include livestock purchases.

The real breakthrough in the syndicate movement came in 1963. Within a year the total number of syndicates doubled to over 600, when between them they owned more than £1ms worth of equipment[3]. A new group was being formed every working day and its success was so great that a Federation of Syndicate Credit Companies was set up to co-ordinate the growth of the movement throughout the country. Expansion has continued at a fairly steady rate until there were over 1,000 syndicates in operation by the summer of 1967. Together these syndicates now own perhaps up to £2ms worth of equipment, operating in forty-seven counties in England and Wales. This is remarkable as a record of change that has occurred in a span of just over a decade. The momentum of the syndicate movement seems to be continuing and represents a fertile basis in which co-operation among farmers may be extended in the future. The scale and complexity of modern farm machinery can be justified only when used for large acreages. As machinery becomes more sophisticated, so will the need for co-operation between small and medium sized farms become greater. Syndicates are likely to become larger and include a wider selection of equipment. It could be that groups of farmers will eventually run their syndicates on a regional basis within a special centre to house the equipment. Since the machinery must be maintained in good order, this too could become a group responsibility. As soon as a syndicate holds equipment capable of being used for somewhere around 500 to 750 acres, equal to a large medium-sized farm or a small estate, the organisation would have to change.

A regional, syndicated machinery centre, if established, might serve a district of 500 to 2,000 acres, possibly even serving a group of smaller syndicates working within a common centre. This kind of centre would be managed with a full-time mechanic, capable of servicing all equipment in proper workshops. This in turn would be of great assistance to syndicate members, being available for welding and other work of a general nature for their farms. It is probable it would also include a store for spare parts and, with only a small extension of its terms of reference, a store for other materials used on farms, especially for building materials. Already another off-shoot inspired by the National Farmers' Union, the Agricultural Central Trading Ltd runs a service for supplying materials and equipment to farmers on a bulk-discount basis. They have a number of regional offices and sub-regional depots. It would be feasible for regional machinery centres to work within the framework of ACT Ltd, acting as depots through which materials would become available at near wholesale prices, including such items as seeds, fertilisers and fuel. This would be a form of co-operation among farmers logically developing as an extension to the present machinery syndicates. By this means many small farms—even including those of up to 250 acres—could remain as specialist units operated by one or two men, but with all the mechanisation advantages of larger estates.

The Lindsey Smallholders Trading Society is an example of another form of development which could be relevant for the future of group co-ownership. In 1939 twenty Lincolnshire smallholders co-operated to mix their own feedstuffs by hand in a common centre, a converted cottage[4]. A quarter-century later the society had 500 members owning about 3,000 acres within a radius of twenty miles of their depot near Boston. In addition they own one of the most automated mill-mixing plants in the country, handling over 10,000 tons of grain and compounding 4,000 tons of feed a year. Syndicates, which at present dry and store grain, could extend activities in a similar manner to act as compounders provided their turnover justified the necessary equipment. This could be the antidote to the present threat to farmers that they may become either dominated by contracts to, or even owned by, the big feed compounders.

The syndicate principle can be extended in other directions, particularly in production. In this manner small and medium sized farms could be organised to compete in scale and efficiency with larger estates. Such a development was suggested by ACA in 1965[5]. Production syndicates could operate in groups of holdings run and managed by full-time farmers with a nucleus of common land held by the syndicate. The common land would have to be large enough to allow for continuity and justify the necessary investment in building and equipment, even if the group membership fluctuated. The same would have to be true of any regional machinery centre. Production building on a basis of common ownership could be suitable for rearing or fattening of stock, milking or storage of grain and potatoes, in the last case already happening. Syndicate members would be responsible, in cases of fattening group schemes, for providing young stock to the syndicate or feedstuffs. The ACA is continuing its investigation into the management, finance and organisation of production syndicates. It seems probable that this form of co-operative farming will develop and extend its foundation in the future.

REFERENCES

1 Goodland, N. L. 'Growth of machine syndicates.' *The Times*, 5 July 1960
2 Hope, H. 'Tackle and Silage in a Three-farm syndicate.' *Farmers Weekly*, p55, 30 April 1965
3 Perry, G. 'Five Tackle Syndicates Born every Week.' *Farmers Weekly*, p53, 11 September 1964

4 Report. *Farmers Weekly*, p45. 21 June 1966
5 Evans, A., *Production Syndicates*. 1965, Co-operative Association

8f Labour syndicates

New patterns are evolving in the organisation of farm labour due to the development of corporate farming within a group. As with machinery it is possible for a syndicate to employ labour on a group basis. This arrangement can make labour planning more flexible. A reserve force can be held for peak work periods, such as at harvest, without each farm carrying excess men during off-peak times. This becomes important as more farmers cease to have mixed-farming policies, concentrating their efforts on only one or two separate enterprises. Equally, it is possible for a syndicate to solve the problem of organising farmwork on a basis of a five-day week, plus up to four weeks annual holidays, for each man. This is essential when planning the future organisation of any farm. Individually, for small or medium sized farms, it is almost impossible to arrange for relief labour, especially for stock men, since the relief might have nothing to do in the interim periods. A syndicate, however, can hold labour to work on the different farms in the group by rota, relieving the permanent staff. In fact, syndicates may prove the only way to provide modern working conditions and hours for the bulk of British farms.

Following the success in group ownership of machinery, it is logical that labour, too, should be organised by syndicates. It is possible, in some circumstances, that a syndicate might hold both machinery and the men to work it within one group. In this manner a group of under 250-acre farms can have all the main advantages of the larger estates which, due to their size, can both spread their machinery costs over the optimum acreage for each piece of equipment and hold a reserve of labour to cover their own relief. Nevertheless, as with machinery, the idea of co-operation between farmers would have been ridiculed only a few years ago. Yet interest in labour syndicates is now beginning to be serious. In fact several farmers are now co-operating with men as well as with machines.

In some cases co-operation over farmwork is mainly based on an informal neighbours' arrangement. In the summer of 1963, for example, two Sussex farmers, owning 100 and 280 acres, began to share labour and equipment for silage making[1]. Their combined grassland of 100 acres as used for silage justified a forage harvester, two tipping trailers and three tractors working as a team. The harvester was a joint purchase and the team was made up from both farms. This proved possible without disorganising other work on each farm. Since it proved successful co-operation was extended into cereal harvesting and other farmwork. Mutual arrangements of

366

this kind can do much to make smaller farms economic without actual amalgamation. Informal co-operation for specific tasks, usually between two farmers, is becoming an accepted part of modern practice.

The founder of the first machinery syndicate, Mr Leslie Aylward, forecast in 1964 that as the labour shortage became more acute, with more powerful machines coming into use, so would the need for syndicates to pool their resources for equipment and men become desirable[2]. In Hampshire two farmers bought a potato harvester between them in 1964 and each supplied three men to work as a team during harvesting. A more ambitious scheme was started in 1965 in the East Riding when the Hayton Villa Syndicate was formed by eight farmers[3]. The syndicate was planned to employ six men, housed in a hostel owned by the group and run by a housekeeper. A long-term plan aimed to train the labour within the syndicate for specialised work on the farms, perhaps in some cases eventually leaving the syndicate to work full-time on one farm. Young men in the syndicate could move round the farms gaining a variety of experience. Although generally no senior man would work on more than two farms, the syndicate had a reserve which could act as relief at times of illness or accident. The flexibility of this scheme, since individual farms ranged in size from forty to 340 acres and included a wide range of arable and stock farming, is obvious. The advantages of owning a hostel, with full amenities, especially for younger workers, can prove a real benefit to a community of farms. Training men in a syndicate is a valuable exercise for all the farmers concerned as well as for the men themselves.

The Hayton Villa Syndicate is one of the larger schemes of this kind. The principles of corporate action could be accepted in many other cases where a nucleus of farms in a district are too small to have flexibility in labour as individuals, but as a group could afford to carry extra men. The alternative is for farmers to contract out their work, or anyway relief work, to independent contractors (p198). Contract labour is a growing practice. Whereas contracting work to outside firm divorces, to some extent, a farmer's control over his enterprises, a labour syndicate keeps the management and worker relationship in closer unity. It is probable that schemes for forming labour in syndicates will grow during the next decade, as have machinery syndicates during the last ten years.

Both the declining labour force working on farms and the growing work capacity of all agricultural equipment are together posing a major problem for all farmers and particularly for those with under 250 acres. Coupled to this problem is the problem for planning farmwork, even dairy work, to be within accepted industrial hours. It is certain that there must soon be a major revolution in the organisation of farmwork. The implication is that labour must

367

become both more technical and specialist and at the same time more flexible in its working systems. Whereas each man will tend to be limited to specific, specialised tasks, he will have to work within a system whereby he can be relieved from a common pool. It is possible that the specialised worker too will have allegiance to a common pool or possibly a syndicate of labour. In this manner, traditional barriers and boundaries forming farms as at present known will begin to disappear. As labour and machinery becomes more fluid, working within schemes dovetailed to an overall plan agreed by a syndicate, so must the management between groups of farms come within the terms of reference of each syndicate. It would seem that, in addition to physical amalgamation of farms by purchase, the immediate future will witness an upsurge of voluntary amalgamations, varying in degree from simple mutual working agreements to full, corporate farming.

REFERENCES

1 Report. *Farmers Weekly*, p43, 26 July 1963
2 Ibid, p69, 18 September 1964
3 Ibid, 10 September 1965

1 GEM supermarket near Nottingham, designed by Austin-Smith, Salmon, Lord Partnership. The modern supermarket requires a vast floor area, artificially lit and with few internal supports, in order to cater for the wide range of goods to satisfy most domestic needs from a one-stop shopping excursion, in this case at an out-of-town regional 'supercentre'.

2 Norwich Market Place. In contrast to the supermarket, the traditional open-stalled market set in central town squares has great attractions. The modern layout in Norwich on market days draws a crowd of shoppers. The economics of this kind of shopping are becoming strained, but many markets may well survive in competition with the supermarkets.

The first beeflot, now closed, for
10,000 head in Britain near
Stowmarket, Suffolk, in 1966 when
nearly half-built and before
complete reorganisation. Problems
of access, vehicular movement
and drainage are clear to see.

1 A feedlot for 500 beef animals erected in 1964 at Coneycroft Farm, Compton, Surrey. Two hermetically sealed towers hold high dry matter silage, and two undried barley. The unit has been sited with care in the landscape. The building is 150 feet by ninety feet clear span.

2 Feedlot interior, Coneycroft Farm, Compton, Surrey 1964. Beef held in ten pens of fifty on bedding at the side of feed strip. Barley and silage are augered from towers under a catwalk. The latter gives access for inspection. The unit fattens 900 head each year.

371

1

2

1 Broiler production on contract. Eight broiler houses at Bushmoor, Shropshire, erected for Craven Arms Poultry Producers Ltd in 1965. Each house holds 8,000 birds kept until nine weeks old.

2 Feedlot for about 600 beef animals at Crowland Farm, Ancaster, Lincs 1965. The cattle are housed in semi-open strawed yards and are fed with food stored in the tower silos, five for grass and two for whole-crop barley.

3 Intensive pig unit, Hurley, Berks. 1965. The start of a 1,000 sow breeding-to-bacon enterprise at the half-way stage, with ten controlled-environment farrowing/fattening houses, each with a nine ton bulk hopper for feed, producing 7,000 bacon pigs a year under a foreman and a staff of four plus two assistants.

4 A 'Bacon Bin', being a trade name for a two-storeyed forty-eight foot diam pig house with full environment control, holds 500 pigs which are fed automatically from an external feed hopper and auger. This is industrialised agriculture far removed from traditional farming.

4

Azienda Agraria Italim, Acona, Italy. Half-way stage at summer 1966 in the erection of an Italian cotel to hold 700 cows in a perimeter of sheds, with radial feed areas and mangers supplied auger from eight towers. At the centre of the layout is a Rotolactor, which is a revolving platform rotating once every ten minutes on which a succession of cows

Beef and dairy unit, Albareto,
North Italy, designed by
C. Pusinelli, 1961. This unit holds
1,000 cattle, 250 being dairy cows,
fed from 375 acres from which
maize, corn and hay are conserved
in six tower silos. At the hub is a
circular parlour for milking cows.
Food is blown underground to
terminal points of the covered
mangers, which radiate inwards
from the perimeter covered yards.
Rotary conveyors complete the
mechanised feeding from tower
to cow. Exercise paddocks
radiate out from the yards.

1

2

1 Dairy Farm, Madison, Wisconsin 1962. America gave the lead for milklots. Here 150 cows and 150 followers to the herd are held in these buildings with one eight-acre paddock. Ten tower silos for grass or maize silage, holding 2,500 tons, are filled from crops harvested on an adjoining 600 acres.

2 A Danish cotel for Count Brockenbus-Schack at Gram, Jutland, designed by Uldall-Ekman in 1962 for 300-330 cows housed in three barns, formed from laminated timber arches and fed from six tower silos under a curved roof with an auger to the mangers.

9 FACTORY FARMING

Introduction

The concept of factory farming has become an emotional issue for many people. To some it has become associated with cruelty to animals and to others, that is to the core of traditional farmers with limited capital, as a serious threat to their livelihood. The age of farms managed like factories which has dawned during the last decade—and which will dominate food production by 1980—does pose vast problems. These are economic and social, basic issues which will determine the way in which people live and are fed. But above all problems is that of land-use in a restricted country which has a rapidly expanding population and a declining capacity to import food.

Although Britain is an industrialised and urban country, agriculture and its associated industries are the largest business concern. Farming must be recognised to be an important and vital industry. Farming must practice and be judged by industrial standards. The fields of Britain—those that are to be retained for food production—must be considered as a factory floor. Work must be mechanised and where possible automated. Personnel must be skilled technicians. Management must be based on technical and business expertise worthy of an industry with, at present, an annual turnover of nearly £2,000m. This is an industry which must be prepared to expand by at least fifty per cent during the remaining years of the century. It must implement this expansion within a predicted reduction of twenty-five per cent in its basic raw material—land. Only by turning all farmland into factories and all produce, as far as possible, into conveyor-belt production will it be possible to expand to the limit required to feed 75m people. This expansion can be planned only if the food producers, the factory farmers, are backed to the hilt by the population. This does not mean endless and vast subsidies, though these will still be necessary for some years yet. It does mean, however, making it possible for farm industrialists, the agric-businessmen of the next decade, to plan and invest with confidence over the long term. The speed of industrial change in farming is such that ten years is the long term.

377

As in any modern industry the annual turnover from a factory farm in relation to money invested, raw materials, factory space and labour must be geared to the maximum, but balancing each of these factors in relation to the mechanisation considered economic. High capital investments, on a corporate or company basis, must be encouraged. The basic raw material must be used to its optimum advantage, each zone of land being exploited to yield its maximum potential for production. This requires, in many cases, amalgamation and reallocation of farms to create viable blocks of land for each enterprise. Factory farming is only realistic if land areas are related to machinery power used in their cultivation, both being planned in relation to crop and yield. Labour must be planned in relation to the mechanical aids available to promote high levels of production per man. Skilled men must handle hundreds of acres rather than a few dozen, or must manage thousands of fattening stock rather than a few score, or tend a hundred milkers rather than the national average of less than a score. Skilled labour, adequate mechanisation, detailed planning and expert management are the basis for future, highly productive agriculture.

An appraisal of the existing situation, a tour of British farms and an investigation of present-day farmers would make any forecast of mass produced food from intensive farming throughout the country seem ridiculous. It must be acknowledged that the average farm does not indicate that factory farming has started. The most traditional quarter of British farms even suggests the reverse, a semi-mechanised version of mediaevel cultivations and stockmanship. The top quarter of farmers suggests a progressive, dynamic industry, but even this segment of agriculture does not indicate that a new and revolutionary age in farm technology has started. Even among the top ten per cent of farmers—the acknowledged cream of the industry—there are many who farm efficiently but extensively. This is the antithesis of factory farming; their aim is not to attain maximum turnover from high capital investment, but smaller returns with a smaller turnover for every acre, though not necessarily a lower return for every pound invested. Even the intensive farmers, efficient though they may be, are not all in the class of factory producers normally envisaged by the term factory farmer. There are many who look to the future with caution and hesitation and suggest that factory farming will remain a minor eddy, perhaps even an abberation, within the main stream of British agriculture. This will not be the case. There are too many markers now to believe that the floodgate of factory farming will not burst open to engulf the agricultural landscape before the end of the century, perhaps long before 1980. Public revolt against factory farming might hold the flood now. Like many such revolts, this would lead to hunger, perhaps starvation, for the population as progress would not only be halted but,

378

as with the Luddites, anarchy would replace the benefits of mechanisation.

It is essential to appreciate that factory farming has many facets. The vast fields cultivated with giant machines, the long rows of crops stretching across the landscape and the harvesters working round the clock on contract to the processing factories are the basis of factory farming. In essence it is an arable revolution, embracing corn, roots, vegetables and grass. The forcing glasshouses, the millions of mushrooms in caverns and darkened huts, the regimented orchards, all these are on the fringe of modern factory farming which, to some extent, becomes more like horticulture with every passing year. Plastic igloos now appearing in a few fields could be the forerunner of a new, space-age landscape. Land, in this new revolution, is not for grazing. It is too precious a commodity to be misused. Livestock is an essential part of the modern, factory farm complex, the one part given much publicity, but which cannot be considered in isolation from the arable revolution. Traditional definitions of farm operations are no longer adequate for modern practice.

It is perhaps best to consider food production in four groups. Arable farming today basically includes the management of all farm land. Livestock farming, which soon will have only a limited contact with the land, except in the disposal of its waste products, is becoming a self-contained independent industry. Horticulture is closely related to glass-house cultivations, most vegetables having become part of the arable farm group. Orchards are at some intermediate point, their main distinction compared with arable farming being their long-term rather than annual planting programme. In fattening livestock to produce meat, man exploits a natural process to convert coarse foods, whether grass or grain, into flesh. Obviously, the food conversion rate, that is the amount of coarse food required to increase the weight of livestock by each pound, is critical. The time taken for conversion is also critical. The principles are the same whether the stock graze the fields or are fed indoors. In either case, their brief lives are conditioned to man's requirements, no animal living out its natural lifespan. Since labour and machinery are expensive, and both are necessary in managing stock, it is essential to spread these costs over as many animals as practical without bad stockmanship. As Ruth Harrison complained, animals are indeed machines[1].

In the first instance, the conversion of grain into chickenmeat started the trend to intensive livestock husbandry, which is one facet only of the factory farming complex. Before 1955 chickens were a luxury food, so limited that the average consumption spread over the population was less than one pound for every person each year. Fattening chickens in pastures or in yards with huts was expensive in labour and grain. The modern version of perhaps 30,000 broilers, managed by a single man, each fed with only eight pounds of food in as many weeks to provide a meal for two people has changed this situation. The broiler industry, within a decade, has taken chicken production out of traditional farm patterns. This has been followed, almost to the same extent, by egg production. Broilers and eggs have become relatively cheap foods in a world of rising prices. More important, the techniques used in the poultry revolution of the last decade have made leading agriculturalists pause and think again on the basic assumption in efficient but traditional farm practice.

In the following sections the main farm enterprises are considered in the context of the broiler industry technology, which only started in Britain a dozen years ago. It is clear that the world is moving towards factory farming. The United States lead the way, perhaps because America has pioneered business efficiency throughout industry and commerce that her agriculture, too, has been the first to apply management control and integration in the food production, processing and distribution complex. As far apart as Yugoslavia and Cuba, or France and Japan, factory farming is becoming evident. In Britain, intensive farming can be found in every sphere of agriculture, even if, as yet, this has not changed the shape or texture of the landscape to any marked degree. Yet, there are those who have noticed a subtle change during the last few years. Many hedges have disappeared. Fewer men are seen working larger fields. Poultry are seldom seen. In many parts, pigs have moved from the landscape. Cattle congregate in larger numbers, some never leave their buildings. Machines are bigger and more complex. Mechanical handling has eliminated the pitchfork to the history books. The trained eye sees many changes. The agricultural press records this change, singly, as each farm improves, becomes bigger and, for a moment, makes its mark in the process of change. Occasionally the agricultural press pauses and reflects on where the change will lead. The industrialists, moving into agriculture, and the food processors and distributors, beginning to control agriculture, are clear where the change will lead. Many farmers too recognise that it is essential to intensify their processes and that, eventually, intensification reaches the stage when they cross an invisible line and become factory farmers.

REFERENCE

1 Harrison, R., *Animal Machines*. 1964, Vincent Stuart Publishers

9b Poultry industry

In the expanding world of agribusiness, the chicken came before the egg. Cheap poultry, prepacked in the American supermarket trade, heralded a new age. Mass produced chicken, promoted with industrial techniques in production, processing and distribution, was soon followed by the mass produced egg. The far reaching implications of low-cost food production in specialised and integrated industries have become real in all branches of agriculture and throughout the world.

The poultry revolution was generated by the restriction of grain exports from North America to Europe during the 1939 war and during the decade after it ended. This created favourable conditions for new techniques to be evolved in which surplus grain could be cheaply converted into animal products. Knowledge of genetics, nutrition and environment was improved rapidly which, coupled with the application of advanced mechanical aids, made intensive poultry husbandry practical. Industrial processes and management techniques were introduced into farming. From small beginnings mass produced chicken meat expanded rapidly, trebling output per head of American population during the 1950s to equal 24 pounds each by 1960, when nearly 2,000m birds were slaughtered—even though red meat consumption also expanded in that decade. This expansion was due to tremendous advances in poultry technology and business farm management. Units holding 30,000 to 50,000 birds, managed by a single poultryman, became common with many producers contracted to the prepacked supermarket trade and integrated in a business net from compounder and hatchery to the supermarkets. Producers became single cogs in a large machine having many parts. Broiler production techniques were followed by a similar revolution in the American egg industry, by which units holding 10,000 laying birds could be managed by each man. In both cases low labour requirements and low feed consumption for each pound of broiler fattened or for each egg laid dominated the system. By degrees similar thinking on production methods was extended into other spheres of American agriculture.

British broiler production began around 1953 with the freeing of feed trade restrictions. During the next decade, chicken consumption in England estimated at one pound a head in 1953 increased tenfold largely due to the rapid strides made by the new industry. By 1966 production had leapt to 170m broilers a year, worth £86m, equal to 16·5lb a head. A basically unsubsidised commodity outstripped the value of lamb and mutton production of traditional British farming, even though the latter received considerable government support. Even by 1963, with factory poultry production dominated principally by non-farmers, the success of the broiler trade had made little impact on British agriculture. Few at that time were far-sighted enough to recognise that changes had started for agriculture which will transform both food production and also land-use in the coming decades. Geoffrey Sykes has been a prophet for the new agribusiness era which is, and must, develop from the broiler revolution. Writing in 1963, he forecast[1]:

> The modernisation and industrialisation of our poultry industry will impose entirely new disciplines on farmers: the development of vertical integration in our animal industry will result in new relationships between farmers and the other sections of agribusiness . . .
> Our broiler industry is undergoing a phase of amalgamation and take-over bids, when companies are preparing themselves for the competitive times ahead, covering production, processing and merchandising. Hitherto such a development has been almost unknown at the level of agricultural production, but, during the next twenty years, I forecast that this type of business development will become normal throughout the whole of our animal industry . . .
> The broiler segment of the industry is doing much to spread agribusiness thinking in Britain . . .
> It would obviously be of great benefit to Britain to develop her farming into a modern, competitive industry, applying today's technology as rapidly as does modern urban industry . . .
> I forecast a future of horizontal integration by agribusiness companies with a diversified production . . . If and when we achieve a measure of economic integration with Europe, many British farmers will become European agribusinessmen . . . Many countries want to develop their agribusiness as a big jump ahead, a jump of many decades in one decade. Clearly, the only efficient method of making this development is to foster sizeable agribusiness companies capable of the work.

The basic raw materials for broiler production are day-old chicks and compounded feed. Breeding poultry, for broilers and, to some extent, layers, is controlled by a few giant firms and is based on accurate stock evaluation procedures backed by vast research programmes into genetics and nutrition. Similarly compounded food is largely in the hands of giant organisations capable of balancing rations to suit a precise specification of nutritional requirements. It is not surprising that breeders and compounders take a critical interest in each other and in the producers themselves. The British market of 60m chicks a year is worth £12m, with small breeders rapidly becoming insignificant in this market. In 1964 international poultry-breeding organisations became deeply involved in the control of British hatcheries. At that time, all but three of the big breeders in Britain were linked with international companies. One of the largest poultry food compounders now owns a breeding organisation. Broiler production itself expanded during the late 1950s, many producers scrambling for quick profits. Overproduction and, in some cases, inefficient production, was followed by a period of agonizing reappraisal in the industry. As an outcome of a price-cutting war, most producers now work in large group organisations

382

dominated by one or two giant firms and on contract to feed compounders or established markets. Many of the outlets for poultry—the wholesale and retail provision firms—have also developed direct interests in the processing and the production of poultry. The producer has become caught between the supplier of his raw materials and the market outlet for his broilers.

The egg industry, as in America, has followed the broiler pattern of large, low-cost production units. Egg production is worth about a tenth of all farm output, yet is rapidly ceasing to be a normal farm business. Giant units or multi-unit co-operatives dominate the market. At the other end of the industry are a large number of producers mainly interested in pin-money, labour not being costed at proper rates on the basis of the work being a family matter. Units between these two extremes have now almost completely disappeared. In this change the egg industry has undergone a shattering revolution and the aftermath has not yet been fully resolved. Between 1961 and 1965, the change was dramatic[2].

Due to unsettled economics, though supported by £20-£25m each year by the taxpayer, the national flock fell in numbers from 59m to 52m between 1961 and 1965. Nevertheless in this period there was a dramatic swing to large units. Flocks with more than 5,000 birds were concentrated in only 260 units in 1961, totalling a mere twentieth of all laying hens. Four years later there were 1,500 units of this size, totalling a third of the national flock. More important than the growth of the 5,000-bird unit perhaps was the dramatic introduction of the million-bird factories. In California one of the first million-bird units known as Egg City was completed in 1963. At about the same time, Jack Eastwood was planning six 2m-bird units for Britain, capturing a fifth of the national egg market in addition to his broiler empire (p287). A year later the first of his units shook the foundations of traditional farming and the reverberations still cause consternation throughout agriculture as the Eastwood aim to market 2,500m eggs a year develops. Similarly other large units though not quite so vast in intention have thrown a spectre over egg production. The basis of these egg empires in multi-million bird units has to be battery caged birds and low cost methods have led to three to four birds being caged together without space to turn round. This is a matter which has caused considerable public concern, leading to the report of the Brambell Committee proposing space standards for battery systems.

By 1965, well over a half of all British layers were kept in battery cages. Two years earlier, well under a third were caged in this manner. Yet in 1965 the fifty-three per cent of battery birds were owned by a mere ten per cent of all producers. This concentration of batteries in limited ownership speaks for itself. At the other end of the scale only ten per cent of hens are now free range, though these are owned by as many as forty per cent of all producers. The remainder, of course, are kept in deep litter or other semi-intensive systems. The efficiency of battery techniques for reducing labour and feed cost is well known. Equally significant is the fact that battery hens lay more eggs, now averaging over four eggs a week. In contrast deep litter hens only lay less than three-and three-quarter eggs and those on free range less than three-and-a-half each. In such circumstances, battery production, with full control over the hen and all mechanical aids for reducing labour, seems essential rather than just desirable to the industrialist.

In opposition to the multi-million bird empires, other producers have been forced to co-operate in buying their raw materials and in marketing eggs. After 1960 many co-operative groups appeared. By the summer of 1965, a process of amalgamation and take-over had reduced these groups into two main co-operatives handling over forty per cent of all trade. It seems that Thames Valley Eggs in the South and Yorkshire Egg Producers in the North will soon control more than half the market, taking over and managing packing stations and linking hatchery and merchant with the markets in their two multi-million pound enterprises. The existing 500 packing stations are already being streamlined and reduced in numbers as producers themselves amalgamate. Although in 1965 150,000 producers were selling eggs via the packing stations, only a twelfth of this number controlled three-quarters of all eggs packed. Moreover as the power of producer/packer groups increase, so will they begin to dominate the Egg Marketing Board itself. A new contract system introduced in 1966, with a more streamlined industry, should stabilise the economics for egg production. Modern egg-drying techniques might also capture a vast potential export market, which could expand production beyond the present £180m industry (p105).

The broiler chicken and the battery egg industries now largely consist of a few highly competitive companies with strong links with the hatcheries and compounders and with the retail outlets via the processing and packing stations. Such integrated and vast companies can operate at unprofitable levels for the farmer, though the latter if co-operating to form their own economic units can prove competitive. In the process it is almost inevitable that the farmer is himself transformed into a different person from the one known in the industry in 1960. The new agribusinessman may come from either industrial or agricultural backgrounds but the techniques he has to learn and practice are as removed from traditional concepts of farming as the Santa Maria is from space age rockets. The basis of modern agribusiness is to produce a cheap, mass food of standard quality to a precise specification and without seasonal fluctuations. This first proved possible with broilers. Between 1951 and 1965, a standard three-and-a-quarter pound broiler took three weeks less to fatten and consumed five pounds less food. This improvement was estimated by Sykes to be worth £20m a year[1]. Broilers are slaughtered at about nine weeks of age. Each bird only needs three quarters of a square foot of house space and five birds pass through this space a year. By these methods, with feed, water and environment automatically controlled, chicken has become a non-luxury food within a decade, though consumption is still less than half than America. By 1965 more than 160m broilers, equal to over three birds a person, came from British factories. Each stage of the fattening process has to be within a budget working to fractions of a penny. A minute difference in the costings at any stage can prove the difference between success and failure. This is the basic challenge to producers created by the new food technology.

Poultry units can have urban sites. Some are multi-storied factories. One erected in West Berlin in 1967 is 120ft high. The ground floor is complete with a provender mill, a plant for handling and marketing byproducts, and an automatic sorting and packing plant handling 12,500 eggs an hour. Nine floors above the ground floor each have batteries holding a total of 126,000 layers. The unit belongs to the Guenther Goede Egg Producers and cost £$\frac{1}{2}$m.

The broiler and egg complexes have promoted other intensive poultry units, such as for turkeys, quail and duck—though the latter are less amenable than hens to intensive housing systems. Turkeys are becoming available throughout the year, instead of solely being for the Christmas trade, 8m now being produced a year. This is equal to roughly a pound a person. Table ducklings, at about 6m a year, lag behind turkey production. Both are growth industries, backed by strong promotion policies. The poultry revolution has ramifications for the red as well as the white meat trade, as well as for much arable production. These factors are considered in the following sections. Nevertheless, as agribusiness develops, with large intensive animal units held together within mass feeding groups or feedlots, the location of these factories will become a critical national problem. It is essential that the development of massive agricultural enterprises, the growing factory farmed units, are planned so that the future 75m of the population can be fed economically and efficiently from a restricted land area.

The economics of low-cost food production are so stringent that the location of the units is of vital concern to the whole of the specialised trade. In the case of broilers, a ten to fifteen mile zone from the packing station is best. Too concentrated a density can lead to disease control problems. Beyond twenty-five miles production is too dispersed for efficient handling and animal weight losses in transit can become excessive[1]. Coupled to the problem of relating producer to processor and packer, either for broilers or eggs, is that of handling vast quantities of grain to the poultry and prepacked produce to the conurbations. Processing and handling manure from the units and by-products from the processors is a practical and economic problem with wide social and industrial repercussions. Nationally there has been little or no interest expressed in the location of modern farm factories to suit the future needs of the growing population. This is a matter of fundamental concern to the whole concept of land-use and it is vital for the future well-being of the nation that massive food enterprises, now coming into existence, should solve their location problems in regional studies and under a national framework. Private interests alone cannot direct development towards a balanced, national use of land.

REFERENCES

1 Sykes, G. *Poultry: a modern agribusiness.* 1963, Crosby Lockwood
2 *Report on* UK *Egg Production* 1964–65. 1966, Egg Marketing Board

9c Feedlots

The revolution in the poultry industry during the last decade has demolished the foundations for all traditional methods of livestock husbandry. As with poultry, intensive housing can contribute to less grain or grass being required for fodder, lower labour costs and more efficient use of agricultural land. The concept of a feedlot, as mass feeding of animals permanently housed in specialist buildings is often termed, became established in the United States for beef fattening, but is now becoming common for all classes of fattening stock. Though the principles of feedlot husbandry can hold true for small batches of animals, the term is more appropriate for agribusiness techniques dealing with thousands of stock under one management, perhaps within a single layout.

In the mid-1950s, the American beef feedlot business began to expand. Today over a third of her beef comes from feedlots with a capacity of over 1,000 head[1]. Economic units are within 10,000 to 26,000 head turnover a year, with 7,000 considered to be the minimum for streamlined administration. During the last decade overall numbers fattened from feedlots have doubled, with output controlled by even fewer businesses. This trend will continue, creating a mass produced beef industry, specialised and automated, serving the American supermarket trade and relying on large turnovers and low profit margins as in the poultry trade. All the main feedlot concerns have their own grain mills since the cattle have an eighty per cent grain diet, with some bulk roughages plus protein, vitamins and minerals being added. The vast American grain prairies have made this method of fattening particularly successful, the cattle only

386

requiring their standings with simple canopy roofs against the sun and a run of mangers which can be filled quickly and simply from a self-unloading trailer or auger. Cheap production makes it possible for American diet to average over 100 pounds in beef consumption for each person a year—more than twice that in the United Kingdom.

Beef feedlot techniques are being adopted in many countries. Europe followed the American lead during the 1960s. Yugoslavia, for example, started a beef industry from scratch, since in 1955 her only sources for beef were from oxen and culled cows. Yet in 1962 her beef exports to Britain alone amounted to 50,000 tons, worth over £12m thus becoming the third largest beef supplier to Britain, though dropping to under 35,000 tons in 1964. The state planned this feedlot industry as a scientific operation with numerous units holding 5,000 to 10,000 head. One near Ljubljana for example houses 7,000 head in 270 foot long buildings, each with slatted floors, timber frames and wide, overhanging eaves[2]. By 1966, Cuba had started a £2m animal research centre under Dr Reg Preston, who formerly pioneered barley fed beef in Britain. Cuba aims to become a beef exporting nation, possibly capturing part of the British market—like Yugoslavia starting from scratch.

Britain is the world's largest beef importer, absorbing 350,000 tons in 1965. In the previous two years a world beef shortage had forced prices up by a third. In 1965 home production of beef, which had fallen since 1963 by more than ten per cent, represented 817,000 tons or over two-thirds of consumption. Nearly a fifth of this meat came from beef fattened in Britain only during their last few months, being imported for this purpose as store cattle from Ireland. This is equal to some ½m head. With world trade having sudden and unpredicable fluctuations, and prices rising sharply, Britain should not rely on heavy beef imports, especially considering the urgent need to slash the import bill for food. Secondly with Eire seeking her own fatstock market, the traditional arrangement of importing store cattle, which in any case is inefficient, may soon fall apart (p326). With consumption per head at under fifty pounds a year, which is considerably less than the main beef producing countries, the beef industry could be expanded if supplies were reasonably cheap. The 1965 National Plan has proposed an expanded home beef industry to increase production by 125,000 tons before 1970, which would need ½m extra cattle for fattening. There is no chance of promoting substantial increases in beef production along traditional lines, since as reported[3]:

> Beef production is a slow process with high capital costs. On good land at modern rents, it is virtually impossible to make it compete with corn growing. The most economic way of converting grain into meat is through pigs, poultry or sheep. Unless we can get a quick breakthrough on conversion rates by a national breeding programme,

beef would seem to have little chance to compete as anything more than a luxury food. The roast beef of old England will not disappear altogether. But it looks like becoming more and more an expensive delicacy which the ordinary Briton is not prepared to afford.

The answer to increased beef production, in order to reduce the cost of imports, is by a national breeding programme and promotion of feedlots. The latter could quickly increase the 2·7m head of beef cattle to the 3·2m necessary to fulfill the National Plan, drawing calves for fattening from present wasted resources. Extra calves could come from the ¾m now-slaughtered soon after birth and from the ½m which normally die during traditional rearing. Feed could come from better and intensive grass management and expanded barley acreage. The cattle could be housed in units of 10,000 to 30,000 head. The aim would be to substantially decrease the £70-£100m spent on beef imports, and ensure uniform supplies irrespective of world fluctuations. Large beef units, by British standards, have appeared in the last few years. These are mainly housing between 100 and 500 cattle. One of the first to reach the 500 mark was at Keyingham, Yorkshire, in 1962 where the cattle are fed by auger from a fully automatic tower silo for barley. Another unit of similar size opened at Queensferry, Flintshire, in 1963. The following year, British Beef Ltd began their unit for 10,000 head near Stowmarket, Suffolk. In 1965, Westdock Quality Beef Ltd expanded their Midlothian beef enterprise, aiming to market 6,000 head a year. Throughout Britain units are getting bigger, many now holding hundreds of cattle and a few, perhaps, thousands. Within a decade, particularly as breeding and diet suitable for quick fattening are developed, large beef units may dominate the mass market as in America. Whether grain or conserved grass or whole crop barley is fed, with the type of housing preferred and the method for returning the slurry or manure to the land, will be relatively unimportant though, perhaps, influencing the location of the units.

During 1964–66 British Beef Ltd was at the centre of beeflot developments in Britain. Their Suffolk unit, now disbanded was much admired by many agriculturists and intended as a forerunner of a half dozen feedlots of similar size throughout the country. It broke new ground in cattle husbandry and cheap beef production for Britain. At the same time it drew the wrath of traditional farmers who feared the low cost techniques of the system would destroy the profit in fattening a mere twenty to fifty beasts at a time. As previously outlined, the feedlot also raised anger among planners because of the erection of the fattening factory without permission (p73). Nevertheless—though British climate is not as favourable as the mid-west of America, mass fattening of cattle is essential in order to supply cheap, standard lean joints for the future 75m population of Britain. Traditional grazing cannot cope with the situation and increased beef imports would be an unnecessary drain on the nation's economy. Traditional grazing will have to be reserved for the production of prime, and expensive, steaks and joints.

Pigs, like poultry, are particularly susceptible for intensive housing systems and vertical integration from producer to supermarket. In recent years pig production has started to become an integrated national industry, though much of it is still fragmented, regional and traditional in practice. Knowledge of breeding and nutrition is not yet as advanced as with poultry, but is more developed than for beef requirements. A sound and expanding pig market has not been encouraged to develop due to political fluctuations and foreign trade agreements. Although almost all pork is home produced, not much over a third of bacon comes from British farms. Nevertheless many big production units have developed, with great efficiency in management and with much of the work mechanised or even automated. In modern units three or four thousand fattening pigs can be looked after by one man with only occasional additional help. Though units are run on factory lines in well managed intensive systems the pigs are warm, comfortable and, apparently content. The Kingsclere Estate, near Basingstoke, has 2,200 pigs in seven fattening houses, 600 hogs a week going to slaughter. Culham Farms Ltd, at Hurley, Berkshire, rears and markets over 10,000 bacon pigs a year. Many other bacon and pork units are within comparable sizes. The Southburn Estates in Yorkshire include their own provender mill for feeding pigs and cattle with 2,000 tons of meal a year, the 800 baconers alone needing fourteen tons a week. Their feed is automatically taken from the mill by overhead conveyor and is distributed to the pigs three times a day by a travelling hopper, dispensing meal on a time switch device. Similarly, their special dunging areas are automatically cleaned. The pigman's job is to observe, weigh and record his herd, together with any veterinary work required.

Though some large pig herds, especially in the South-west, are managed in semi-open conditions, even combining automatic feeding techniques, most major producers find that mass feeding and management supervision is only possible with the pigs in controlled environment houses. In such conditions, efficiency, as with all feedlots, is attained only with large numbers since the latter justify the provision of proper housing and mechanical aids to management. The mass pig feedlot is an essential part of modern pork and bacon production, essential if consumption is to be supplied primarily from home fattened pigs. More units are likely to become established holding at least 2,000 and, possibly, 10,000, pigs, with feeding completely automated from mill to trough, especially if sited near grain producing areas. As with poultry, small scale operators will almost disappear with the next two decades. Yugoslavia, as with beef, is planning state pig farms. One, near Zagreb, will hold 5,200 sows and from them fatten 100,000 pigs a year. Units of this scale are feasible and could be developed in Britain.

Intensive mutton and lamb production, as with beef, pork and bacon, is gathering momentum. The potential for intensive methods in the sheep industry, which has been largely unexploited for 150 years, has only been appreciated as an industrialist's dream during the last few years[4]. Until recently sheep husbandry has been one of the most traditional of farm enterprises. Today industrialists are moving into the industry with the intention of transforming the breeding and fattening of sheep with methods akin to those in the poultry trade. The *Farmers Weekly* in a leader at the end of 1965 summarised the present trends as[5]:

> A widespread awareness that the new development in breeding and management which are crowding in could transform the sheep flock from the cinderalla of our livestock enterprises into one of the most profitable and productive. Planned, synchronised breeding is just round the corner. Indoor housing and intensive cereal fattening are already here—revealing sheep as a better converter of meal into meat than most cattle beasts.

Sheep numbers are rapidly expanding, there being over 20m ewes and lambs in England and Wales in June 1965 increasing at a rate of almost $\frac{1}{2}$m a year. Nevertheless, though more than $\frac{1}{4}$m tons of mutton and lamb are home produced each year, this represents considerably less than half consumption. The potential for the sheep industry becoming a growth market, even allowing for continued imports from New Zealand, is enough to attract the interest of modern agribusinessmen.

Even within traditional flockmasters change is rampant. The number of flocks having more than 1,000 ewes, for example, has doubled in the last decade and about a fifth of all flocks are now in this class. At the same time flocks with less than 300 ewes are rapidly decreasing. Attention is beginning to focus on the fact that up to a quarter of the 4m hill lambs born each year die before weaning. Heavy snows and cold winters also account for tens of thousands of ewes, sometimes in epic-making winters for millions of them on the bleak hillsides. The national loss is considerable. Winter sheep housing, though uneconomic only a few years ago, is now becoming accepted as a necessity, albeit mainly within very cheap forms of building. Some lowland flockmasters have started to keep ewes permanently indoors. In 1964 a farmer at Whittington in Staffordshire built a house covering half an acre to keep his 500 ewes and lambs, that is 1,200 sheep, permanently on straw bedding. Other flockmasters are beginning to follow this pattern, finding that high stocking rates on lowland acres become impractical if sheep graze their paddocks. Not only does feed go further in buildings but lambs

390

fatten faster with lower mortality rates and wool crops are also improved. Shepherding methods have to become streamlined if one man is to manage more than 1,000 ewes, as is now becoming practical, against the couple of hundred considered the maximum only a few years ago. Slatted floors, rather than straw, are becoming accepted especially for winter housing. Feeding routines become partially mechanised, though push-button methods have not yet proved economic. Machine clipping in specialised sheds now replaces hand shearing in fenced layouts in the open. Group marketing of lambs is beginning to replace the herding of flocks through markets.

Though flockmasters streamline their methods, it could be that many lamb and mutton requirements will come from new intensive units managed by industrialists. The traditional trade in store lambs for fattening by different farmers, in a chain from breeder to abattoir, concentrated in the spring, will come to an end. Genetic control is producing a new, hybrid sheep, capable of producing more lambs from each litter and more litters, with the lambs capable of being fattened faster at a lower conversion rate (p379). One poultry firm, the Thornber/Colburn group, is well on the way to producing lambs all the year round, fattened in controlled environment housing on a high cereal diet and suitable for the prepack trade. It seems certain that within a few years most sheep will be in intensive units—a trend that would have been ridiculed in 1960, but which had become clear by 1965. Lowland sheep, even now, are hard to justify with land costing £200-£300 an acre except in permanent housing. Soon lowland grazing will be completely uneconomic. The future of hill grazing during summer months, combined with winter housing, is less certain. It seems likely that ranch farming, with flocks numbering thousands managed by a few shepherds working shifts, backed by aerial inspection, may survive in selected areas. Whether such ranch farming may be combined with multi-landuse, primarily for recreation, is less clear.

Livestock, other than cattle, sheep, pigs and poultry, can become commercialised within intensive units. The fur trade, with mink, chinchilla and other such stock, is well developed in battery units. In the last three or four years intensive rabbit production has been consolidated to replace the 100m wild rabbits sold each year prior to myxomatosis. The largest rabbit farm in the world, Hether Rabbits Ltd, has a herd of more than 3,000 breeding does and 1,000-doe units can easily be managed by one man. The demand for white fleshed rabbits exceeds supply. It is probable that other small type animals could become managed in intensive units since the potential of this kind of production has received little examination. Honey, of course, is often concentrated in production from large hive groups. Reference has already been made to new food forms (p209). Fish farming has already started to eliminate the vagaries of deep-sea

391

fishing. Trout ponds, of course, have existed for centuries, recently becoming more concentrated in technique. By 1965 experimental battery plaice and soles were being fed on a diet of crushed mussels by the White Fish Authority in tanks heated with warm water derived from power stations, at Carmarthen in Wales and at Hunterston nuclear station in Scotland. These fish fatten in half the time, and at times in the year when growth is unnatural, compared with sea fish. At a hatchery in the Isle of Man a million plaice a year can be bred. Turbot, prawns and oysters are all being hatched in laboratories. In Argyl, five acres of sea have been enclosed to form a fattening pond for plaice. Other sites have been surveyed, perhaps capable of holding 30m fish in plots totalling 2,000 acres. Enclosures in the future might be sealed by nets, ultrasonics or electrical impulses. Other warm water ponds or lakes near power stations might become intensive fish factories. With such methods it becomes practical to rear thousands of fish of standard size, weight and quality, suitable for rapid harvesting, processing and packaging as fish fingers or in frozen packs. Commercial fish farming on a vast scale should start soon after 1970. The importance of this revolution in fish technology lies in water as well as land being made fully productive and in the fact that an acre of water can yield more protein in fish than can be gained from cattle or sheep on an acre of good agricultural land. Fish farming in enclosed lagoons or lakes can restrict the natural predators that kill most fish before they grow to maturity. Fishlots, to coin a phrase, may transform the whole concept of human diet. Moreover fish harvested in tens of thousands from warmed lakes are unlikely to evoke the compassionate human sympathy for warm blooded animals held in controlled environment houses.

If man is to remain carnivorous and if the world population, exploding dramatically in numbers, is to be fed with a meat based diet, then mass feedlot techniques for all classes of stock are inevitable. In Britain, with poor international credit and little land, intensively feed animals housed together in thousands from birth to slaughter and managed by vast companies, will gather momentum until only prime quality and expensive meat will be fattened in a natural environment. The siting and design of future feedlot units should be based on national requirements, generally in regional development plans. Feedlots should not just appear in the countryside. The problem of their correct location is complex and must be co-ordinated.

REFERENCES

1 Spikings, B. 'Feedlot USA.' *Farmers Weekly*, p80, 10 December 1965
2 Hope, H. 'Beef on the large state farm.' *Farmers Weekly*, p100, 22 October 1965

3 MacGregor, A. 'What beef shortage?' *Farmers Weekly*, p57, 22 April 1966
4 Cadzow, B. Hampshire Farm Institute Conference, 1966
5 'Sheep Farming.' *Farmers Weekly* supplement, winter 1965

9d Milk for the masses

The average size dairy herd in England and Wales has only twenty-six cows. In such circumstances it is difficult to believe that intensive milk production may ever dominate the industry. It is true that a decade earlier, in 1955, the average herd only had seventeen cows. But an increase in average size of under a cow each year hardly reflects an industry in a ferment of change. The pastoral image of the traditional British countryside, with small herds grazing quietly in buttercup meadows, remains valid. Dairying is still small-time business, being the mainstay of many small family farms. Nevertheless evidence of dramatic changes in the structure of milk production shows clearly that intensive methods, as with other livestock, will soon predominate.

During recent years, an average of a dozen farmers have given up milk production each day. It is expected that the peak number of over 160,000 farmers engaged in dairying in 1950 will have been more than halved by 1970[1]. The dramatic trend to fewer dairy herds is shown clearly in Chart 46. By 1967 numbers of milk producers in England and Wales had fallen to 96,000 and in Britain to under 120,000—in the latter case equal to a fall of over 17,000 producers in thirty years. At the same time, though herds grow fewer, cow numbers and milk production increase. In 1953, for example, the total national dairy herd totalled 2·5m cows. A decade later there were 2·7 cows. Similarly annual milk production in the same period in England and Wales rose from about 1,650m gallons to over 2,000m gallons. Thus the average cow produces more milk. Within the decade after 1955 she increased production by 110 gallons a year to just over 800 gallons. Not only do fewer farmers keep more cows, but the cows themselves yield more milk. Within this pattern of increasing efficiency in milk production, other factors are equally important. Fewer workers are required to manage the herds and less land is needed to keep the cows.

In any discussion of dairying it is essential to appreciate the tremendous range of technique between the intensive milk producer and the numerous traditional dairy farmers, though it is many of the latter that contribute to the rapid decline in overall numbers. For example, the national average of twenty-six cows a herd itself makes wide regional differences. The average in Wales is but seventeen cows, but around forty are averaged in the South-east, South and

o   393 mid-West of England. The small herd is rapidly disappearing. In 1955 there were nearly 100,000 herds, each with under twenty cows, but a decade later this number had been more than halved. In the same period, herds of more than fifty cows have doubled to over 11,000, embracing nearly a third of all cows in the country. Big herds are becoming numerous and the accepted scale is continually extended. A few years ago herds of fifty cows were considered to be large. Today the 100 cow herd is not exceptional and in 1963 thirty-four herds had more than 300, and of these four had over 1,000 cows, though not necessarily managed as one unit. The increase in large herds shown by the following analysis giving the number of herds in England and Wales in two cow-number groups:

YEAR	HERD SIZE 100-200	COWS 7,200
1955	457	48
1960	673	61
1967	1,364	131

Though the size of herd is relevant, it is of relative importance only since size has to be equated with labour and land requirements. In traditional cowsheds one man may be needed for every ten to fifteen cows. Nationally in 1963 each dairy worker only milked nineteen cows. This is a little better than in the days before machine milking. The average in the larger herds is forty-seven cows a man. Even this today is not exceptional. In 1960 sixty cows a man was considered to be advanced management. Five years later, eighty cows a man had become the progressive target with over 100 cows a man being attained with top level management backed by good layouts and equipment. One Pembrokeshire farmer, Hugh Prettejohn, being untypical of Welsh dairying, had ten herds in 1965, four of them with over 100 cows, each managed by one man. A few farmers already attain 110 to 120 cows to each cowman, others are beginning to plan 150 cow one man units with relief help. As herd sizes of about 100 cows managed and milked by each skilled worker become common, so will the technique of management change.

In order to concentrate on the milking and management of large herds, cowmen have to be skilled specialists with all drudgery eliminated. Management of calves and followers to the herd tends to be the responsibility of other men, so that the cowman can concentrate full time on milk production. Similarly all field work for growing bulk or concentrated fodder for the herd is undertaken by others. But the cowman cannot milk his herd twice a day, seven days a week throughout the year. Each herd needs a relief milker almost as skilled as the cowman himself. There is a growing recognition that the future structure of dairying will include groups of three herds, each of 100 to 120 cows, managed by four skilled cowmen, one being off-duty in rotation. Each can work a five day week. Proper industrial working hours must be allowed for all further farm work. There is still a long way to go before this trend among top farms has become national. At present, over half the dairy farmers employ no outside labour, managing with their families single handed. The family can never be off duty together. In contrast there is a growing practice for farmers to contract their daily management and milking of herds to specialist firms. Contract milking by these firms is often undertaken to cover sickness and holidays, but in recent years some farmers have committed themselves completely to contract labour, paying the firms 6d a gallon of milk produced for freedom from employing their own labour. Contract farming is a modern and growing practice (p350).

Specialist buildings and fixed equipment for large herds, providing good facilities for the cowman, are relatively expensive. They become more economic as more cows use the equipment included. One American firm is considering designs for automated milking equipment whereby one man will milk 500 cows in four hours. A computer will automatically ensure a cow is washed, led to her milking stall, fed the correct amount, milked, with the milk recorded for yield and rejected if abnormal, and released to return to her yard. The cowman will only have to attach a machine to the cow. It is believed milking parlours of this kind may be used in America by 1975. Milk today, of course, is extracted by machine and is piped direct to refrigerated storage tanks, from which it can be piped to a bulk tanker calling once a day. Intensive milklots are being seriously considered whereby large herds are kept together and managed by small teams of skilled men. In 1962 one agricultural specialist recognised that 1,000-cow herds would be concentrated round the big population areas in Britain, with the cows permanently housed, equipment automated and skilled men working a forty-hour week[3]. In America, for example, round Phoenix, Arizona, 266 dairy farms with 40,000 cows supply 800,000 people daily with 130,000 gallons of milk. One herd has 800 cows with the cows milked round the clock by men working eight-hour shifts[4]. Another American dairy farm near New York, with 1,100 cows, produces nearly $1\frac{1}{2}$m gallons of milk a year[5]. Milking takes place sixteen hours a day with two shifts of four men. The milk is piped to a 5,000-gallon tank, ten times the largest size at present on British farms. Heat from the cooled milk in the tank is used to provide 800 gallons a day of instant hot water as well as for heating the farm offices. Feeding bulk foods is a push-button job from tower silos. Another two men look after 700 young stock, another six men work the 2,400 acres and two mechanics service the equipment. Investment for each worker represents about £16,000,

each man attaining an output of 50,000 gallons a year. More dramatic is the project for a 'milk city' in Mexico housing 1,000 specialist
milk farmers in a total population of 15,000, managing a 100,000-
cow herd divided into units of 150–250 cows each.

The situation in Britain is now at the point of change to intensive
milklots, or 'cotels' as they are sometimes called. Large units of this
kind have developed in recent years in Denmark, Germany and
France, where cattle are permanently housed and fed from conserved
grass and arable by-products producing premium grade milk[6]. A
Jutland farmer, for example, erected housing in 1962 for 330 cows
to be managed by a head stockman and three men. At the same time,
a 500-cow unit was erected near Fontainebleau in an eight-farmer
partnership, owning 5,000 acres, plus a vet and an advisor. A large
unit, with 1,000 cows planned in 1966 near Essen, is doubling its size
in 1967 and hopes eventually to have a partnership holding 8,000
cows in four units. Near Lyons 800 cows are housed in one layout.
Nothing on this scale yet exists in Britain, though 300-cow units are
now being planned. For example, Rex Patterson has about 800 cows
in Wales in smaller units and produces $\frac{1}{4}$m gallons of milk a year,
equal to a pint a day for every person in Wales[7]. Eventually the herd
will be divided into several 120-cow one man units. Though this is
progressive and efficient farming, it is not equal to intensive Continental practice. Emrys Jones, now adviser to the Minister of Agriculture on technical development, foresees 1,000-cow milklots in
Britain by 1970, some of them operated by producer groups. The
system of milklots could be adapted for 300-400-cow herds, with
only one or two owners, or for several thousand cow units owned by
groups. The Ministry of Agriculture is setting up a 300-cow herd at
their experimental farm in Hampshire to study big herd techniques,
especially related to feeding, housing and milking. This is the first
step to a rapid change in the structure of dairying in Britain.

Cows, following poultry, pigs and other livestock, are now beginning to leave the land. Traditional farming practice, much in evidence
even in 1960, was based on a belief that every dairy cow needed two
acres of grazing land. In addition, she needed concentrates, which
required corn from other land. During recent years, intensive grassland techniques have increased the stocking rates possible with good
management. In 1960, intensive dairy farmers managed with less
than $1\frac{1}{2}$ acres to each cow and, five years later, one acre for each cow
was regarded good management without significantly needing
additional concentrate rations. Others, relying on more corn,
increase their stocking rates to a cow for only half to three-quarters
acres. As the stocking rate drops to an acre or less for each cow so
does it become critical to get the maximum value from the land,
which means that the cows should not trample their own fodder by
grazing. As more cows are managed by each man, so is there less

time to fetch and return cows to their outlying pastures twice a day —an activity which can easily absorb one to two hours in non-productive labour. In any case, since most cows are housed four to six months every winter, except in the South-west, it does not cost much more in buildings to allow for permanent housing. From almost all points of view, pressure is increasing to make permanent housing plus brought-in foods without grazing the only solution for future intensive dairying.

For some years the pattern of dairying has been for milk production to be concentrated towards the South and West grasslands and away from the eastern arable belt of England. The centre and East of the country had under ten cows to each acre of crops and grass in 1963 whereas the South, West and North-west had up to twenty per acre with as many as thirty-one in Cheshire. Most people believe the future pattern will exaggerate this division. There are some factors which could alter the feeding policy for dairy cattle. New methods for storing grain, without drying it, straight from a wet harvest have made it more economic to grow corn in the wetter parts of Britain. This makes it less essential to grow grass just because of medium to high rainfall which, in turn, can change dairying techniques. Recent interest in feeding unripened whole drop barley to cattle or, alternatively, chopped straw with additives, could change the emphasis placed on grass and conserved grass for dairy cows. Whether future cattle will be fed on grass or corn products is at present keenly debated. What seems certain is that there will be a move from grazing grass, possibly to feeding conserved grass, possibly to grain or grain products. The advantages of having cattle in the wetter parts of England may become less clear. Since the South-east is a major milk consumption area, much milk has to be hauled from other parts for the home counties and London. This has led to the nation paying a premium to milk producers in these areas, representing slightly less than 1¼d a gallon. Alternatively producers in the West are penalised because of the cost of transporting milk to the conurbations. Efficient farming and marketing in the future may concentrate production round the public dairies close to the conurbations (p116). This will become more practical as milklots for 1,000 head or more are permanently housed.

The future of the dairy industry, worth £350m a year to farmers, is an open question. Although home production accounts for almost 100 per cent of liquid milk consumption, there is a real fear that milk, which is the only major food not yet touched by the supermarket revolution, may be imported in powder, 'instant milk' form and more cheaply than can be produced in Britain[8]. Milk which can be kept easily for months may make it uneconomic to produce milk during the expensive winter period for cattle. Daily deliveries of liquid milk to the customer will eventually disappear. It is probable

397

that by 1969 deliveries may be every other day—possibly saving 5d per gallon of milk delivered. It is possible that with the development of long-life milk, which by the spring of 1966 was being experimentally exported to thirty-four countries, Britain might become, with other European nations, a major milk exporting country to the Middle East and other tropical regions (p106). Trehane, Chairman of the Milk Marketing Board, speaking in New Zealand at the end of 1965, predicted that there would soon be a world milk shortage, presenting a great challenge to the British milk industry.

Liquid milk is only part of the problem. More than half the milk products consumed in Britain are at present imported, being equal to 2,750m gallons of milk—more than the total existing production of milk in Britain. Trehane has suggested that an expansion of the national herd to over $3\frac{1}{2}$m cows is technically possible by 1970, providing an additional 470m gallons of milk, worth £70m in saved imports[9]. With expanding milk consumption throughout the world, backed by new techniques in keeping and transporting milk, there seems to be markets in Asia that can absorb all milk product exports from New Zealand. Even if New Zealand wished to continue her present levels of exports to Britain, there seems no reason why British production should not be entering a major period of expansion to suit her own increased consumption but also aimed to capture an export market in tropical countries. A healthy milk industry in Britain cannot continue with a herd average of twenty-six cows. In another decade the average may be over 100 cows. The first milklots, which will appear in the next year or two, will pave the way to a completely different structure of milk production.

REFERENCES

1 Many statistics in this section are given in more detail in *The Structure of Dairy Farming in England and Wales*. 1965, Milk Marketing Board
2 'One man will milk 500 cow herd.' *Farmers Weekly*, p41, 18 February 1966
3 Leslie, J. Association of Agriculture Conference, Norfolk, 1962
4 Roddick, N. 'Milking round the clock for 800.' *Farmers Weekly*, 14 May 1965
5 Jones, P. '1½ Million Gallon Milklot.' *Farmers Weekly*, p90, 30 October 1964
6 'Dairy cows by the hundred.' *Farmers Weekly*, 10 June 1966
7 'Streamlined for summer milk.' *Farmer & Stockbreeder*, p57, 1 May 1966
8 'Shadow on the pinta.' *Farmers Weekly*, p41, 29 April 1966
9 'Milk Board bid for bigger market.' *Farmers Weekly*, p25, 31 December 1965

9e Genetic control of livestock

Increasing demands on world meat resources make it imperative that Britain should expand her own livestock numbers. Imported meat supplies, adequate for the expanding home market, cannot be guaranteed for much longer at a price which the nation can reasonably afford. It is essential to establish adequate breeding stock known to have progeny that can be fattened quickly and economically to yield meat acceptable to the housewife. Similarly other cattle or poultry must be selected in strains known to give good yields of milk or eggs of predetermined quality. All stock must be able to improve and perpetuate their best characteristics through successive generations of herds and flocks.

Animal breeding is in a period of rapid change. The time available for improving the quality and proficiency of stock is limited by the urgent need for increased home food production and the science of genetic control is yet in its infancy. There is growing conflict between the new livestock geneticists and the traditional pedigree breeders. The pedigree breed societies, particularly for cattle, became established in the nineteenth century and they still flourish today. They have been largely responsible for the renown of British stock throughout the world and have set rigorous standards to maintain this reputation. Pedigree stock is judged almost entirely by external, physical appearance so that skill in assessing livestock, though an inexact art, requires considerable experience to see an animal conforms to type. But the characteristics admired, which may be for such physical qualities as coat colour or ear shape, may be those which are neither strong as heritable qualities, being from recessive genes, nor of importance to the quality of meat, milk or eggs. As Leyburn stressed[1]:

> This emphasis on type ensured that virtually no genetic progress was made in production characteristics. Most of the apparent improvement in performance was due to importations and better management techniques.

Important factors relating to the performance of an animal, as reflected in its progeny or yield, were considered of little relevance and went unrecorded. A fine looking bull would be valuable in its own right irrespective of the fact that his progeny might have limited fattening or milking qualities. To some extent this approach holds true today, especially in the case of cattle. Recording of stock, which is the basis for genetic control, is still too limited to make it possible to predetermine the qualities which are most valuable in food production.

Livestock records began to be established in this country about fifty years ago. A milk recording society was formed in 1914, one for pigs in 1927 and the first small sheep recording group not until 1952, while a major sheep scheme, using a computer, did not start until 1965. In fact the significance of recording did not become recognised to be of national importance until after the Milk Marketing Board became responsible for AI cattle in England and Wales from 1945. Today their records have proved vital as a check against the type characteristics admired by the breed societies. Since 1945 population genetics for all stock have slowly become accepted. The example in the poultry breeding world has been noted by most farmers and agriculturalists, though some are still blind to its true significance for all stock. Poultry changes can be attained relatively quickly in a breeding flock. Blood grouping can prove important as an aid to breeding, since grouping is inherited and can give proof of parentage, especially in keeping trace of strains in rapidly multiplying flocks. A foundation stock of 1,330 birds, for example, may produce 23m descendants in four generations[2]. This makes it possible to isolate and perpetuate strains that show improved performance qualities in a short space of time.

Sykes suggested that between 1951 and 1965 poultry strains improved so that pullets increased their egg yield from 180 to 250 a year while consuming only ninety-five pounds of feed in 1965 against 120 pounds in 1951[3]. Similarly in the same period broiler standards improved from a four pounds liveweight gain in twelve weeks, with a feed conversion rate of four pounds of feed to each pound gain in liveweight, to one of three-and-a-half pounds live-weight gain in nine weeks, requiring only 2·3 pounds of feed to each pound gain in liveweight. These improvements, reflecting better housing and management plus better feeds and disease control, could not have been achieved without highly developed genetic control with complete recording of all stock characteristics through the many generations of poultry bred during these years. As Sykes stressed in 1963[4]:

It is the post-war decades that the new poultry industry has developed modern, accurate stock evaluation procedures which have been a major factor behind the great leap forward in technologies achieved by this industry. These procedures have been so successful that the fraternity of the new poultry industry are able, with justification, to regard today's breeders of the larger farm animals as backwoodsmen, operating in the wrong age.
In her animal industry, Britain has a vast investment which is largely vitiated as a result of our using stock of less than the best performance-capacity throughout most of our animal industry for our requirements for the 1960s. The position, however, is much worse than this; the hundreds of millions Britain has invested in her land, her crop husbandry, her feed-compounding industry, her farm machinery and equipment and her food processing industry is wastefully invested

Helicopter used for spraying against potato blight. Aerial work for spraying and top dressing is part of modern agriculture, especially in the eastern counties. Large fields are required and trees, pylons, and wires are a hazard.

1
2

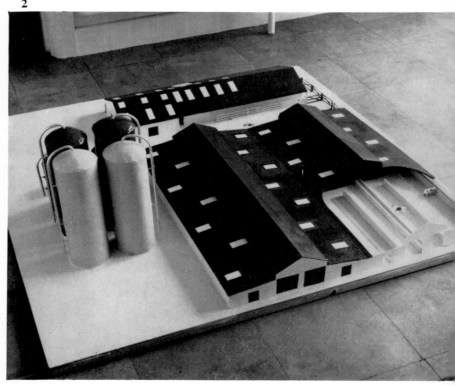

402

3

1 An airhouse, or bubble building, of plastic sheeting inflated by a small fan are still experimental for controlling horticultural crops. They provide a cheap method of control and many crops may receive this kind of protection during critical months of growth.

2 Model of cotel for the Bridgets Experimental Husbandry Farm, Hants, proposed by the Ministry of Agriculture for 140 cows, with an expansion planned to raise numbers eventually to 300 cows. This is the first time the Government has planned a large scale farm management/farm building research programme.

3 A farm a century hence. An algae pond with remote controlled suction harvesters and a central control station with raised tower, radar and meteorological plant and controls for field equipment.

Intensive harvesting. Combining for British Crop Driers Ltd in Lincs 1962. Teamwork is still required for harvesting. Fields must be large for operations of

purely and simply because the crops and the feed which result from this vast investment are fed to animals unsuitable for the nation's requirements in the 1960s.

The size of the animal agribusiness gross output at retail level is in excess of £2,000m a year. The loss to Britain in food production potential, through inadequate recording and through perpetuating poor stock performance, is as serious as the export trade gap.

In breeding future livestock strains, existing genetic material has to be selected and directed to give improved qualities since new genes cannot be created. Only in rare instances does a genetic mutation, which is an accidental change, assist modern needs. One instance has been the change from horned to polled cattle. This is a mutation estimated to occur once for every 20,000 reproductions and, being a dominant gene, has been used to perpetuate polled strains[5]. Selective inbreeding can concentrate desirable genes and crossing two inbreed strains each carrying desirable characteristics, can produce a new strain combining the best qualities of each. In any such breeding programme complete recording is obviously essential and to process detailed records the use of computers is a modern aid. Future breeding will be closely linked to computers which select from recorded statistics the stock most suitable for mating.

One result of the Breed Society policies has been to perpetuate too many breeds of each animal. Intensive poultry breeding, which needs a research programme backed by large financial resources, has reduced the main poultry breeders to a half-dozen giant firms and the numbers of breeds to a handful of proved hybrids. These firms, plus a few others, are moving into the market of pig and, more recently, sheep breeding where the scope for genetic improvement is vast. At present there are thirty accepted breeds in the country, and perhaps a score of pig breeds. In a few years, high pressure commercial breeding, backed by full recording, will have narrowed these animals into a handful of proven hybrid strains. In 1964 the Milk Marketing Board officially listed eighteen accepted dairy and beef cattle breeds, four used soley for milk and eight for meat production, the remaining six being dual-purpose breeds. It has been suggested that[6]:

> In the present state of our dairy and beef industry there is need for only four breeds. A big framed dairy cow producing a lot of milk of reasonable quality; a smaller dairy cow giving very high quality milk, though perhaps rather less of it; and two beef breeds whose progeny grow fast into good carcasses.

Changes in the strain of cattle breeds take much longer than poultry, since the generation interval is about three years. At present the Milk Board, with its associated AI centres, control the sire selection

405

of two thirds of the dairy cattle[1]. New developments in artificial insemination, using deep-freeze storage methods, could make it possible for 100 selected bulls to serve the national herd of $2\frac{1}{2}$m cows[7]. In a decade milk production could be transformed. Similarly beef production, which is the least advanced of all stock breeding, could be radically improved by 1980. Since it has been suggested that at least another million dairy cows are needed to boost beef yields in the next decade (p387), radical changes in breeding methods are essential. Sheep breeding has already entered a period of radical breed changes (p312). Sheep can now breed twice a year to give ten lambs against a more normal average of between one and two lambs.

Leyburn stressed that[1]:

> Recording is absolutely essential in an agricultural industry becoming more technical each day and placing even greater reliance on the scales and the butcher's hook. Grouping and co-operation, though more difficult to achieve, are equally essential. The terms animal breeding and population genetics are synonymous. And it is impossible to improve a population significantly unless it is big enough.

It is clear that breeding is too costly a problem for the small, or even large, farmer. It is a matter for big business concerns, though breeding stock may be contracted by these firms for individual farmers to house. Casual breeding, even for cattle, may continue for no more than another decade before farmers have to buy, for fattening or milking, from accredited and recorded hybrid stock produced by specification in agribusiness complexes. Traditional breeds, as fostered by the breed societies, will have historical interest, being perpetuated in a few reserves. There will soon be only a handful of super-breeds in each species, though new blood would occasionally be reintroduced into the hybrid strains from the special reserves of traditional stock. In recent years the need to introduce foreign stock into Britain to produce new and better strains has become apparent. Official opposition and procrastination, backed by pressure from the traditional breeders, has delayed importations. Charolais cattle imports were delayed five years after the first application in 1956 and Pietrain pigs seven years after 1958. It is clear that animal breeding is of international concern and, as it falls into big business operation, will become international in scope. It may well be, as predicted by Sykes, that soon fifty companies will control half of all the animals bred in Europe (p382). Moreover interest will not be confined to those animals traditionally associated with European agriculture. It is probable that experiment will be undertaken in the future to see whether other animals might not be more profitable for intensive food production. Similarly thought has been given to the possibility that goats or asses or other stock might be more useful as milk producers than the traditional cow[8].

It is certain that the animal kingdom has not yielded an iota of its potential for feeding mankind. Any change in the *status quo* of using animals is a matter of deep concern to many people, not only to those that are vegetarian. In 1965, Curry, then president of the North of England Veterinary Association, said that in twenty years' time incubated calves will be produced artificially in plastic bags, becoming standard practice. Test-tube breeding of livestock is almost practical and may well change future farming. It might prove that present interest in minimal-disease pigs, for example, using hysterectomy in producing the litter by destroying the sow, would become pointless since the sow would be by-passed. The effect of science in animal production is, indeed, frightening as the boundary between what is ethical and what is inhuman is a point of fine distinction. In 1962, at the World Poultry Congress at Sydney, the frightening developments in poultry breeding were made clear. Day-old chicks could have their characteristics changed completely by a process of irradiation, making it possible to produce any type of laying hen whatever its parentage. Quails and hens might be crossed to give better eggs. Hormone injections might be given in the future so that hens laid eggs every six hours to give 350 eggs in six months. Moreover, by developing reproduction by partogenesis, male birds might become unnecessary. Genetic control over livestock can enter, and is rapidly entering, a world far-removed from direct recording and selection in breeding.

Modern genetic techniques, among other factors, contribute to the reduction of disease. Livestock disease has been estimated to cost the agricultural industry as much as £150m a year, representing more than a tenth of the value of all farm animals at any time. This is an appalling national waste. In disease, which is sometimes entirely due to bad management, poor nutrition or inadequate housing, lies much suffering. These factors, with the chivying which sometimes occurs when animals are moved on the farm or through markets, contribute more directly to suffering than good forms of intensive housing. Mortality of up to one in every four animals born, especially with calves and piglets before they are weaned, is common. $2\frac{1}{2}$m piglets die each year and perhaps $\frac{3}{4}$m calves. Together this mortality represents a financial loss to farmers of up to £30m. In the statistics is hidden much suffering. Normal mortality before weaning, accepted by most farmers as satisfactory, will be one in every five or six born. Some deaths are inevitable, especially since litters are encouraged to be as large as possible, some weaklings have no chance of survival. Good management, with the right nutritional methods in good housing, especially in intensive units, cannot afford to allow mortality in young stock to exceed ten per cent and lower death rates, including those culled, should be achieved. Environment for farm animals on many traditional farms is far more conductive to physical hardship and suffering than in well managed factory units.

Some farmers have a parsimonious attitude to disease, being reluctant to spend money on precaution against disease or cure after its outbreak. A study of the agricultural press, in their answers to correspondents' questions, reveals that many farmers write for advice, outlining symptoms of dire diseases in their stock, rather than calling for a vet. Such attitudes are more serious, when considering cruelty, than the monotonous existence of livestock in most intensive units. The public indignation towards intensive livestock husbandry, leading to the report of the Brambell Committee at the end of 1965, is understandable, though often misdirected. It is not possible in this study to examine the welfare of farm animals. The problem is important and complex. The Brambell Committee were correct to stress the need for better education and training to promote good stockmanship[9]. They were equally right to insist on the need for a State Veterinary Service and for a Farm Animal Welfare Standing Advisory Committee. It is possible to extend these ideas for a State Veterinary Service in order that all farmers should contribute to a National Health Service for farm animals aimed at prevention as well as cure of disease. Prompt veterinary advice and attention could do much to reduce the heavy burden of disease and the suffering which disease creates.

Intensive farming, which encourages the essential need for good nutrition and housing, will eventually make squalid methods of stock keeping unprofitable. Bad management in livestock husbandry, which is the only real cause of bad welfare for farm animals, must be eliminated in both traditional and intensive units. The monotony of the brief and often sunless lives of modern food animals is a difficult moral problem. What has to be clear is that although certain extreme stock density levels might be prohibited, such as in veal crates, if the expanding population is to have better nutrition, including meat and dairy produce, from less land and with fewer imports, then almost all farm animals will have to be permanently housed. The relatively high capital cost of good housing and the need to reduce labour requirements to the minimum makes high stocking densities in the buildings inevitable. The standards of density and layouts, suggested by the Brambell Committee, since they were taken in the abstract apart from the overall environmental and nutritional policies, with the economic problems related to intensive husbandry, have not clarified the moral problem in depth but have tended to confuse the management and design criteria.

Some modern disease control is encouraging. In the last two decades, particularly the last few years, several severe diseases have been eliminated or brought under control[10]. Bovine tuberculosis,

408

due to a national eradication policy, is seldom known. Foot-and-mouth has been reduced to occasional outbreaks. Swine fever is near to eradication and fowl pest has been dramatically reduced. Some diseases, such as mastitis, still need a major breakthrough in research programmes into their prevention. British research in farm animal disease has had much success, winning international acclaim. Local veterinary study groups throughout Britain, formed since 1964, are doing much to encourage knowledge of stock health and encourage modern techniques of prevention, detection and cure. Geneticists help to promote healthy strains of stock in their research into breeding problems.

The conquest of disease in farm animals, with the promotion of better nutrition and housing and the genetic control of livestock breeding, with full recording of all stock at national level, is essential for the future of intensive agriculture and feeding the population. The time available for a major improvement in these subjects, dramatic though progress has been, is limited by the rapidly growing pressure for increased food production to reduce imports. The shape of future farm animals, due to improved breeding, is likely to be as different as those of today from those shown in Victorian paintings of farm stock.

REFERENCES

1 Leyburn, M. 'The changing world of animal breeding.' *Farmers Weekly*, February-March 1965
2 Dirom, M. 'Blood will tell.' *Farmers Weekly*, 8 March 1963
3 Sykes, G., *Poultry: a modern agribusiness*, p149. 1963, Crosby Lockwood
4 Ibid, p162
5 Henry, P. 'The science of animal breeding.' *Farmers Weekly*, January 1966
6 Henry, P. 'The case for fewer breeds.' *Farmers Weekly*, 22 October 1965
7 Perry, T. 'Deep freeze opens up new worlds for AI.' *Farmers Weekly*, 4 February 1966
8 Robinson, D. H. 'The cow is a dirty mistake.' *Farmers Weekly*, 25 February 1966
9 *Report of the Technical Committee to Enquire into the Welfare of Animals kept under Intensive Livestock Husbandry Systems*. 1965. HMSO
10 'Beating disease.' *Farmers Weekly*, p45, 10 September 1965

9f Arable factories

Arable land is defined as that which is fit for tillage. Historically this led to a distinction between grassland, normally being unploughed and used for livestock grazing and crops. The latter included, for the most part, corn and root vegetables. These due to policies for the rotation of crops and mixed farming tended to be interspersed by temporary grassland. Today such definitions are confused. Modern grassland, like any arable crop, is cultivated, requiring assiduous attention. Chemical rather than mechanical cultivations, coupled with seed drilling into unploughed land, contradicts the traditional concept of arable farming by tillage. Issues are further confused by much vegetable cropping becoming a farm operation in scale and technique. Arable farming today really includes the management of all farm land. Techniques are entering such a period of change that the term 'farm' itself has less meaning than 'factory'. Fieldwork and farm management are similar in technique to factory processes. Changes in the structure of farming make the concept of arable factories real when considering the future of agriculture.

Reference has already been made to certain modern changes in arable farming. Larger machines and new techniques have led to the removal of hedges. Field management requires large units under unified control. Intensive corn production for example is most economic with two large combines needing up to 1,000 acres. Future fields may range in size up to 2,000 acre units (p244). Irrigation has become a farming aid of considerable importance in many areas (p254). Field mechanisation has led to men working large areas alone, each man sowing, cultivating and harvesting up to 200-300 acres (p145). This section will consider some of the other changes turning arable farming into a factory process. It is partly a matter of increased yields, resulting from years of research into seeds and species of plants, since agricultural botany in Britain is highly developed and has international recognition, but also from improved field drainage, fertilising and cultivation. The *Farmers Weekly* recognised the significance of the present arable revolution[1]:

> Today's arable farmers are forced to be pioneers. Though the past twenty years have seen already more changes than the previous 200, there is good reason to think innovation will be happening at an even faster pace in the decade ahead . . . The development of remarkable new crop varieties, new ways with cultivations, new weed and disease control chemicals, new machinery and new approaches to marketing and—as important as anything else—new management techniques, are all a challenge to the judgment and technical competence of the individual farmer . . . Our present reading of the signs is that more of Britain's farmland will come under the plough—or at least be put into arable crops—in the period ahead.

Soil and terrain are naturally the basis of arable farming. It is believed that half the 28m farm acres are inadequately drained. There is no detailed information as to how much new drainage is needed, and a national survey now started will take several years to complete. Modern drainage, using mechanised trenching and plastic pipes, is easy and economic compared with methods available only a

410

few years ago. Modern machines can lay 500 chains a week against a normal rate of only 100 chains. As a further aid, radio controlled layers are being pioneered. Nevertheless new ditch and pipe work can cost £50-£80 an acre, depending on land conditions. Nationally £6m is spent each year on draining about 112,000 acres. This is a sound investment but at this rate another century will not have cleared the backlog of land restricted in cultivation by poor subsoil drainage. In addition much still needs to be known concerning the texture and structure of the soil itself (p35). The science of soil mechanics is still undeveloped compared with its potential for making food production easier and soil husbandry richer. Artificial fertilisers have made a mammoth contribution to modern increased yields for crops. Haughley has shown that organic farming can be better, but not necessarily more economic, than modern intensive agriculture which relies on artificial aids (p341). In any case animal manures or slurries are beneficial, when correctly applied to the land, and can reduce costs when easily available. Without the application of artificial fertilisers national food yields would be depressed and food costs increased. Fertiliser requirements are increasing at five per cent a year, being now worth £120m. Most applications range from three to ten cwt an acre, principally adding nitrogen, phosphorus and potassium. Modern developments include more concentrated nitrogen fertilisers and also liquid rather than granular applications. The latter in particular may be undertaken by contractors rather than the farmer with his own labour—as may many other cultivation processes (p198).

What artificial fertilisers did to improve arable farming in the last two decades, chemical cultivations may do during the next twenty years. Ploughing an ordinary acre of land means that nearly 1,000 tons of soil is lifted and moved and 'the immense amount of power, time and skill that this involves is nowadays largely unnecessary. Ninety per cent of the justification for mechanical cultivation is in its control of weeds. Control by chemical methods, which become better and cheaper with each month of research and development, may well replace cultivations altogether before long'[2]. Pests cause crop losses of some £80m a year in Britain—perhaps £10,000m in the world as a whole. Chemical pest control has broken the need for traditional crop rotations and has allowed narrower crop row spacings. Aphid control, for example, now allows seed potatoes to be grown in the South of England, upsetting former reliance on northern seed for southern main crops. More important with weeds chemically retarded or destroyed, drilling can take place in unploughed land, requiring only a third of the time needed to establish a crop with conventional methods. This in turn makes the process not only quicker but allows large areas to be sown at exactly the right time. Thus chemical farming is transforming the technique of food crop production, giving greater flexibility in management, lower labour requirements and higher yields. Moreover it makes it possible, in suitable soil and weather conditions, for rotations to be omitted and continous crops to be grown on the same land. With minimum soil disturbance weed seeds diminish, having less chance for growth. This in turn may limit the reliance on chemicals. In any case minimal cultivation technique can mean that less powerful farm machinery is required, a factor which will cause less soil damage and make field work physically easier.

Continuous wheat cropping of the same acreage has proved successful, though reservations are still placed on the ultimate and universal application of this technique even in good conditions. Selective herbicides are also making it possible to look critically at the 14m acres of permanent grassland which is capable of better production. Only a small area of grassland is devoted to the more productive species; but control of undesirable grasses, possible with chemical spraying, opens up new possibilities[3]. In recent years attempts have been made to find and successfully import herbage with winter growth, as opposed to native grasses limited to spring and summer. If this proved successful, it too would transform the traditional approach to grassland. Grass husbandry and grass conservation, with the exception of the top ten per cent of grassland farmers, is abysmal. Grass as a feedstuff, perhaps because of this factor, is being replaced to an ever greater extent for cattle by cheap cereals and straw plus additives. But minimal cultivation techniques with old pastures being sprayed by bipyridial herbicides, which kill green tissue but become inactive on contact with soil, followed by rotations to give a tilth before direct drilling, makes it possible to gain new pastures where ploughing would have been difficult. At the same time, new techniques and improved efficiency in conserving grass, whether barn dried, or stored in towers or in vacuum packs, or possibly turned into compressed wafers as in America, can mean that the revolution in grass technology is only just getting under way.

The *Farmers Weekly*, in a leader in the autumn of 1965 foresaw the effect of chemical farming as[1]:

There is every promise that it will soon be possible for previous crop wastes to be mulched, seed and fertilisers to be injected, and pre-emergence weed sprays to be applied in a single pass by one machine, so that a 'blitz' sowing job can be done whenever conditions are right. This, in its turn, will lead to demands for new 'blitz' harvesting methods to match—and for the breeding of new crop varieties which can use optimum soil and weather conditions. Hard on the heels of such developments will come demands for systems of crop transport which will allow unheard of yields and acreages to be snatched from field to steading at rates impossible now. Other industries have not hesitated to tackle the transport congestions which new production techniques have brought. Shall we soon be sending fertiliser and

412

seed out to our fields by pipeline—and later in the season send grain back by the same route?

Modern arable technology is assisted by aerial spraying, fertilising and even seeding. It is estimated that by 1965 18,000 aircraft treated about 875m acres throughout the world using helicopters, small monoplanes and even jet aircraft. Soon electronics and computers will be used to mark land to be treated. New low volume concentrated insecticides are being used, with heavy droplets to counteract drift, which has been one of the main problems in aerial spraying. In America alone there are 5,000 agricultural aircraft. In Britain aerial work has been more limited, mainly concentrated in the eastern arable areas. It is estimated that in 1965 250,000 application acres, allowing for some crops receiving more than one application, and 50,000 top dressing acres received aerial treatment[4]. Aerial work permits fast work when ground conditions restrict tractors. In particular eighty per cent of the pea and bean acreage suitable for aerial spraying is treated and of the potato crop, only two-thirds of which is suitable, thirty-five per cent of this amount is already being sprayed from the air. Top dressing nitrogen on winter wheat and fertilising rough grassland or grassland for early grazing is equally suitable for aerial work. Nevertheless climatic conditions, pylons, hedges and trees all make Britain less satisfactory for aerial farming than more open parts of the world. But this technique will remain a valuable extension to normal farming methods. As a further aid to agriculture, aerial photography is a sophisticated method for tracing the source and spread of crop diseases, especially blight. Furthermore aircraft have become a popular form of transport for farmers, many having their own landing strips. Aircraft, though mainly used for travel, can be used for inspecting farms quickly, a method particularly suitable for ranch farming, whether with sheep or cattle.

Chemical farming, though an exciting technical development changing the whole concept and pattern of food production, is a matter of concern, Rachel Carson in *Silent Spring*, published in 1962, intensified a natural and public fear that chemical aids to farming are dangerous. Herbicides, fungicides, and particularly insecticides, having become a necessary part of intensive farming, contain chemicals with various properties, some relying on poisons or hormones potentially harmful for humans in certain doseages and situations. There is no final answer to this problem, as with nuclear power, except through future history. A mistake could have serious or final repercussions for human life. In the meantime, vigilance, observation and research are vital factors to keep control on the situation. Without chemical farming, there is no hope of feeding the populations of the world.

Chemistry is only part of the science fiction world of arable

P

413

farming now developing that will change the concept of rural Britain. Vegetable production is perhaps a pointer to future factory methods on arable land. Four-fifths of the coarse vegetables and over a half of the salad crops and herbs are grown by farmers on field techniques and scale, totalling over a ½m acres with thirty per cent of this acreage within forty miles of Spalding. Mechanised production for the processors and prepackers, much of the vegetables being grown under contract, dominates the situation. To aid crops, plastic igloos are appearing in the fields of Britain. A Hertfordshire farmer near Ware covered 10,000 square feet of lettuces in 1962, as well as strawberries, sprouts and beans under plastic domes supported by low powered fans. Airhouses, cheap in this form, can act as cloches and are a valuable aid of controlling crops. Another farmer in 1966 had an acre of strawberries under polythene over wire loops, though his method is more like a real cloche than the airhouse. The future of plastic on frames or supported by air pressure from fans is far from clear, though plastic protection seems valuable for many crops during winter and early spring. It seems probable that more land, anyway during these months, will disappear under large plastic domes, transforming parts of the countryside into a fantastic, space-age landscape of inanimate matter. An alternative aid, pioneered by one farmer in 1967 near Southampton, is to have underground electric cables for crops such as strawberries. At the same time, more specialist crops are disappearing from natural sunlight into artificial factories. Much rhubarb, for example, is now artificially produced in electrically lit environments. Mushrooms have long since ceased to be a crop of the natural meadows, 20,000 tons a year coming from artificial cultivation. One producer alone grows one-and-a-half tons a day in limestone caves behind Bradford-on-Avon, workers looking like miners with lamps on the heads harvesting the mushrooms from compost filled boxes.

Robot farming, whether in factories or fields, is beginning. In glasshouses, as with livestock, heating, ventilating, watering, feeding and other tasks can be automated. In 1962 the Dutch produced an experimental plough, capable of working a field on a preset course. By 1966, robot tractors were so advanced that it has been suggested they would be on the market in five years, capable of ploughing, harrowing, discing, rolling and drilling. One man could supervise several tractors from a central control office, the tractors working round the clock in different fields, information being fed to the office by close-circuit television[4]. It seems probable that in the coming space age, robot arable farming will change the present concept of agriculture. Hovercraft too, experimentally developed for agriculture in 1962 for crossing wet land unpassable for tractors, could have a place in future farming. The first farm hovercraft was made in 1967 in Leicestershire, capable of carrying three-and-a-half

414

tons, spraying through a sixty foot boom, spreading fertiliser, and both cultivating or towing hovertrailers behind it. In 1963, a hydraulic seeder was imported from America. This machine can spray three acres of hillside an hour with seed, fertiliser and protective mulch of wood and cellulose pulp, making it possible to cultivate steep, sloping land. Mechanical aids to cultivation, like those of chemistry, are on the threshold of a new age.

Reference has already been made to possible new foods (p209). Protein extraction from leaves and grasses, as well as from methane gas, could well change the present emphasis placed on arable farming. Moreover it seems certain that water farming is also on the threshold of a new era in two different spheres. Algae could be an invaluable source of new foods, perhaps with robot harvesters farming the world's oceans. Algae too could be farmed in special ponds. A phantasy projection has been put forward for a farm a century from now[5]. Such farms would include an algae pond to grow high-protein plants, automatically fed with plant-food chemicals in a controlled environment, with the crops harvested by a suction fan passing over the pond, dispatching the algae to a centralised processing plant. The central station would also, (perhaps powered by solar energy) include a controlled research factory within which crops with fast growth cycles, developed from genetic mutations, would be cultivated in artificial environments. The station, also embracing its own meterological recording plant, would control all crops in the surrounding fields, with any cultivation and harvesting equipment required. There seems little doubt, though any projection of this kind is suspect in detail, that a change is starting in arable farming which will render present fieldwork with men on tractors, tending ten, thirty or even fifty acre fields, as in most of Britain in the 1960s, as old-fashioned as horse-drawn wooden ploughs seem today.

REFERENCES

1 'Arable farming.' *Farmers Weekly* supplement, October 1965
2 'The challenge of chemistry.' *Farmers Weekly*, p37, 12 November 1965
3 'Fourteen million acres in our hands.' *British Farmer*, p42, 6 July 1963
4 'Robot tractor is only five years away.' *Farmers Weekly*, 22 April 1966
5 'Down on the farm 100 years from now.' Autumn 1965, Bury Free Press Supplement

APPENDICES

Appendix A Land Classification

	England Wales and Isle of Man		Scotland		Great Britain	
	Acres	%	Acres	%	Acres	%
I Good Quality Land not elevated, level or gentle slopes: good aspect deed soil, good texture, favourable water	17,845,900	47·9	3,963,300	20·8	21,809,200	38·7
II Medium Quality Land high elevation, steep poor aspect, shallow, defective water conditions	11,933,800	32·0	2,877,400	15·1	14,811,200	26·3
III Poor Quality Land heavy, wet, extreme elevation, or shallow soil	6,350,900	17·0	12,113,800	63·5	18,464,700	32·8
I						
1 First class capable of intensive cultivation, especially of prime foodstuffs	1,963,100	5·3	396,800	2·1	2,359,900	4·2
2 Good general farmland for ploughing	7,065,600	18·9	1,735,900	9·1	8,801,500	15·6
Good general farmland for grass or crops	2,636,900	7·1	192,900	1·0	2,829,800	5·0
3 First class water conditions favouring grass, some might be drained	1,234,800	3·3	8,700	0·0	1,243,500	2·1
4 Good, but heavy restricting range of crops	4,945,500	13·3	1,629,000	8·6	6,574,500	11·7
II						
5 Medium light land usually shallow depth, suitable for ploughing	2,402,100	6·4	77 400	0·4	2,479,500	4·4
Medium light land usually shallow depth unsuitable for ploughing due to rock	220,300	0·6	300	0·0	220,600	0·4
6 Medium light land but varied quality due to relief, aspect, watertable	9,311,400	25·0	2,779,700	14·7	12,111,100	21·5
III						
7 Heavy land intractable clay or lowlying areas needing drainage	825,900	2·2	54,100	0·3	880,000	1·6
8 Mountain and moorland varied character and vegetation	4,516,800	12·1	12,001,700	62·9	16,518,500	29·3
9 Light land overdrained, sandy and heathland	811,800	2·2	57,900	0·3	869,700	1·5
10 Poorest land agriculturally useless, but some might be reclaimed	196,400	0·5	100	0·0	196,500	0·4
IV Closely built over	1,142,700	3·1	114,200	—	1,256,900	2·2
TOTAL	37,273,300		19,068,700		56,342,000	—

England alone (32m acres at 1951 census)

*Ministry of Town and Country Planning, National Planning Series, 1944. Stamp, L. D., *Man and the Land*, pp242–48, 1955, Collins

1 Agricultural Research Council
2 Agricultural Workers, National Union of
3 Agriculture, Fisheries and Food, Ministry of
4 Atomic Energy Authority, United Kingdom
5 Automobile Association, The
6 Botanical Society of the British Isles
7 British Broadcasting Corporation
8 British Field Sports Society
9 British Industrial Biological Research Association, The
10 British Industries, Federation of
11 British Manufacture of Agricultural Chemicals, Association of
12 British Mountaineering Council, The
13 British Museum (natural history) The
14 British Railways Board
15 British Travel and Holidays Association, The
16 British Waterways Board
17 British Waterworks Association, The
18 Camping Club of Great Britain and Ireland, The
19 Caravan Club, The
20 Chemical Industry, Society of
21 Civil Engineers, The Institution of
22 Common, Open Spaces and Footpaths Preservation Society
23 Country Landowners' Association, The
24 County Councils Association
25 County Councils in Scotland, Association of
26 Crown Estate Commissioners
27 Defence, Ministry of
28 Development Commission
29 Duchy of Cornwall Office
30 Electrical Engineers, Institution of
31 Electricity Board, South of Scotland
32 Electricity Council, The
33 Electricity Generating Board, Central
34 Farmers' Union, The National
35 Farmers' Union of Scotland, National
36 Field Studies Council
37 Fishmongers' Company
38 Forestry Commission
39 Game Research Association, The
40 Gas Council, The
41 Geological Conservation Council, The
42 Housing and Local Government, Ministry of
43 Hydro-electric Board, North of Scotland

*These organisations attended the 'Countryside in 1970' Conference in 1963

44 Land Agents' Society, The Chartered
45 Landowners' Federation, The Scottish
46 Landscape Architects, Institute of
47 National Coal Board
48 National Parks Commission
49 National Trust for Places of Historic Interest or Natural Beauty, The
50 National Trust for Scotland for Places of Historic Interest or Natural Beauty, The
51 Nature Conservancy, The
52 Nature, Council for
53 Nature Reserves, Society for the Promotion of
54 Physical Recreation, The Central Council of
55 Physical Recreation, The Scottish Council of
56 Pilgrim Trust, The
57 Post Office, General
58 Power, Ministry of
59 Public Building and Works, Ministry of
60 Ramblers' Association, The
61 Red Deer Commission
62 Royal Automobile Club, The
63 Royal Fine Art Commission
64 Royal Forestry Society of England, Wales and Northern Ireland, The
65 Royal Geographical Society
66 Royal Institute of British Architects
67 Royal Institute of Chartered Surveyors, The
68 Royal Society of Arts
69 Royal Society for the Protection of Birds, The
70 Rural England, The Council for the Preservation of
73 Rural Wales, Council for the Protection of
71 Rural Industries Bureau
72 Rural Scotland Association for the Preservation of
74 Science, Office of the Minister for
75 Scientific and Industrial Research, Department of
76 Scottish Office
77 Timber Growers' Organisation Ltd
78 Tourist Board, The Scottish
79 Town and Country Planning Association
80 Town Planning Institute, The
81 Trade Board of
82 Transport, Ministry of
83 Treasury, HM
84 Water Engineers, The Institution of
85 Wildfowlers' Association of Great Britain and Ireland, The
86 Wildfowl Trust, The

87 Women's Institutes, National Federation of
88 Youth Hostels Association (England and Wales)
89 Youth Hostels Association, Scottish

*Appendix C Chart of Human Impacts on the Countryside**

1 LAND RECLAMATION, DRAINAGE AND IMPROVEMENT

1.1 Sea defence works
1.2 Winning new land
1.3 Drainage of fresh water marshes
1.4 Making of new drainage channels
1.5 Straightening and deepening of existing channels and main rivers
1.6 Improvement of mountain and hill land
1.7 Peat extraction
1.8 Rehabilitation of derelict land

2 FORESTRY AND SILVICULTURE

2.1 Planting of timber
2.2 Exploitation of natural or semi-natural stands
2.3 Establishment and maintenance of: amenity woodland, shelter belts and windbreaks, Roadside and hedgerow trees etc

3 AGRICULTURE

3.1 General
3.2 Cultivation
3.3 Livestock and animal rearing

4 FISHERIES

4.1 Offshore fishing
4.2 Inshore fishing (incl. Shellfish)
4.3 Salmon netting
4.4 Fish hatcheries

5 WATER

5.1 Supply undertakings and similar developments
5.2 Abstraction
5.3 Reservoir construction
5.4 Recharging of ground water supplies
5.5 Industrial reuse of water
5.5 Recharging of ground water supplies

*Prepared for the 'Countryside in 1970' Conference, 1963

6 EXTRACTION OF MINERALS OTHER THAN COAL

6.1 Sand and gravel
6.2 Clay extraction
6.3 Opencast iron working
6.4 Road metal quarrying
6.5 Quarrying for Masonry and building materials, eg slate
6.6 Limestone quarrying and cement making
6.7 Underground mining and salt
6.8 Underground mining for lead

7 COAL EXTRACTION

7.1 Opencast coal mining
7.2 Underground coalmining
7.3 Subsidence
7.4 Coal pithead installations
7.5 Spoil disposal, bings, tips etc
7.6 Other processing plant, depots and stocks

8 OIL INDUSTRY

8.1 Oil drilling
8.2 Shale working
8.3 Oil shipping
8.4 Oil refining
8.5 Waste disposal and pollution
8.6 Installation and maintenance of pipelines
8.7 Distribution depots and roadside filling stations

9 ELECTRICITY SUPPLY

9.1 Generation, nuclear
9.2 Generation, coal
9.3 Generation, oil
9.4 (1) Generation, hydro A
9.4 (2) Generation, hydro B
9.5 Transmission and general distribution
9.6 Switchgear and substations

10 GAS

10.1 Manufacture and storage
10.2 Installation and maintenance of pipelines
10.3 Underground storage

11 MANUFACTURING INDUSTRY

11.1 Factories and sites

12 DISTRIBUTION

12.1 Depots, bulky dangerous or nuisance items
12.2 Wharfage
12.3 Packing and packaging
12.4 Mobile selling points, eg Ice cream cars, refreshment vans etc

13 BUILDING AND HOUSING

13.1 Housing estates and other grouped housing
13.2 Individual dwellings
13.3 Institutions and other large buildings in the countryside, eg educational institutions, prisons, hospitals

14 SEWAGE AND RUBBISH DISPOSAL

14.1 Piped transport and underground sewers
14.2 Open sewers
14.3 Industrial and sewage effluents
14.4 Sewage farms
14.5 Incinerators etc
14.6 Rubbish dumps
14.7 Waste metals iron etc

15 TRANSPORT

15.1 New roads, eg Motorways
15.2 Road widening or straightening
15.3 Road maintenance, highway verges
15.4 Use of road vehicles
15.5 Railway modernisation, reconstruction and maintenance
15.6 Abandonment of lines, stations etc
15.7 Canals and waterways
15.8 Ports and harbours

16 DEFENCE

16.1 Permanent training areas
16.2 Temporary or occasional training areas
16.3 Artillery, vehicle and missile testing areas
16.4 Former training and testing areas
16.5 Former defence installations
16.6 Sites for secret or dangerous installations
16.7 Ancillary facilities, eg housing

17 TELECOMMUNICATIONS

17.1 Masts for telecommunications TV radar towers etc

18 AVIATION

18.1 Military airfield operations
18.2 Commercial and passenger and freight airline services
18.3 Private flying
18.4 Helicopters
18.5 Hovercraft
18.6 Gliding

19 TOURISM

19.1 Motoring and sight-seeing from vehicles or stopping places
19.3 Sightseeing on horseback
19.2 Sightseeing on foot
19.4 Chair lifts, viewing towers observation posts etc
19.5 Information and education services for visitors
19.6 Fixed accommodation for tourists, eg motels, caravans, youth hostels, climbing huts etc

20 CAMPING AND CARAVANNING

20.1 Private unorganised (temporary) sites
20.2 Commercially organised (permanent sites)
20.3 Gypsy encampments (tinkers in Scotland)

21 EDUCATION AND FIELD STUDIES

21.1 Organised youth activities out of doors, eg School games, field studies, 'Outward Bound', voluntary conservation and re-habilitation schemes, Combined Cadet Forces
21.3 Field scientific work
21.2 Field natural history
21.4 Archaeology
21.5 Bird watching and bird photography

22 RECREATION

22.1 Aquatic sports
22.2 Land sports
22.3 Picnicking

Appendix D Selected bibliography *

Barber, E. H., *Win back the acres—ash and agriculture*. 1963, Central Electricity Generating Board.
Best, R. H., *Major land uses of Great Britain*. 1959, Wye College

*Annual reports of statistics and pamphlets are excluded

Best, R. H., and Coppock, J. T., *Changing use of land in Britain*. 1962, Faber & Faber

Bracey, H. E., *Industry and the Countryside*. 1963, Faber & Faber

Brambell, F. W. R., *Report of the technical committee to enquire into the welfare of animals kept under intensive livestock husbandry systems*. 1965, HMSO

Bramley, M., *Farming and food supplies*. 1965, George Allen & Unwin

Brett, L., *Landscape in Distress*. 1965, Architectural Press

Burton, T. L., and Wibberley, G. P., *Outdoor recreation in the British countryside*. 1965, Wye College

Caborn, J. M., *Shelter belts and windbreaks*. 1965, Faber & Faber

Christian, G., *Tomorrow's Countryside*. 1966, John Murray

Crowe, S., *Forestry in the landscape*. 1966, HMSO

Crowe, S., *Tomorrow's Landscape*. 1963, Architectural Press

Cullingworth, J. B., *Town and country planning in England and Wales*. 1964, George Allen & Unwin

Culpin, C., *Farm mechanisation management*. 1959, Crosby Lockwood

Davis, J., and Goldberg, R., *A concept of agribusiness*. 1957, Harvard Business School

Denman, D. R., Roberts, R. A., Smith, H. S. F., *Commons and village greens*. 1967, Leonard Hill Books

Dexter, K., and Barber, D., *Farming for profits*. 1961, Penguin Books

Edlin, R., *Forestry in Great Britain*. 1967, Royal Forestry Commission

Gasson, R., *Influence of urbanisation on farm ownership and practice*. 1967, Department of Economics, Wye College.

Giles, A. K., and Cowie, S. J. G., *The farm worker, his training, pay and status*. 1964, Department of Agricultural Economics, Reading University

Goss, A., *British industry and town planning*. 1962, Fountain Press

Harrison, R., *Animal machines*. 1964, Stuart

Hayes, G., *Farm organisation and management*. 1960, Crosby Lockwood, 1960

Highbee, E., *The squeeze*. 1961, Cassell

Green belts. 1962, HMSO

New towns of Britain. 1964, HMSO

The New Towns. 1967, HMSO

Britain: an official handbook. Annual, HMSO

Agriculture in Britain. 1964, HMSO

Countryside in 1970. Proceedings of the Study Conference held in 1963. 1964, HMSO

Hoskins, W. G. *Making of the English landscape*. 1955, Hodder & Stoughton

Hoskins, W. G., and Stamp, L. D., *Common lands of England and Wales*. 1963, Collins

426

Hunt, K. E., and Clarke, K. R., *The state of British agriculture.* 1966, Agriculture and Economic Research Institute, University of Oxford.

Knapp, J. G., *Analysis of agricultural co-operation in England.* 1965, Agricultural Co-operation Association

McCrone, G., *Economics of subsidising agriculture.* 1962, George Allen & Unwin

Mortimer, R., *Mechanical livestock farming.* 1964, Farming Press

British Agriculture looks ahead. 1964, National Farmers' Union

Shape of things to come. Report of Nineteenth Oxford Farming Conference. 1965, The Conference

Rowland, F. E., *Electricity in modern farming.* 1963, Land Books

Scott, P. C., *Report of the committee on land utilisation in rural areas.* 1942, HMSO

Senior, D., *Derelict land.* 1964, Civic Trust

Stamp, L. D., *Man and the land.* 1955, Collins

Stamp, L. D., *Land of Britain, its use and misuse.* 1962, Longmans

Sykes, G., *Poultry, a modern agribusiness.* 1963, Crosby Lockwood

Tracy, M., *Agriculture in Western Europe.* 1964, Jonathan Cape

Weller, J. B., *Farm buildings, techniques, design, profit.* 1965, Crosby Lockwood

Wibberley, G. P., *Agriculture and urban growth.* 1959, Michael Joseph

Williams-Ellis, C., *Britain and the Beast.* 1937, Dent

Williams, H. T., *Principles for British agriculture.* 1960, Nuffield Foundation

Contract farming and vertical integration. United States Department of Agriculture Bulletin 198. 1958, the Department

INDEX

431

441

70/-